W9-ACI-056

There She Is

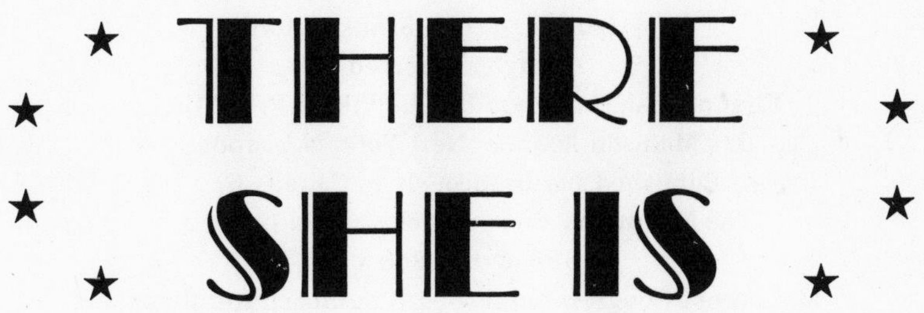

THERE SHE IS

The Life and Times of

MISS AMERICA

Frank Deford

★ ★ ★

NEW YORK ★ THE VIKING PRESS

First published in 1971 by The Viking Press, Inc.
625 Madison Avenue, New York, N.Y. 10022
Published simultaneously in Canada by
The Macmillan Company of Canada Limited
SBN 670-69858-x
Library of Congress catalog card number: 70-156755
Printed in U.S.A.

ACKNOWLEDGMENTS

Bud Burtson: "So What" by Bud Burtson. Copyright 1945.

Edward B. Marks Music Corp.: "Miss America" by Bernie Wayne.
©—Command, E. B. Marks, 1954.

Rheingold Corp.: "Miss Rheingold" (1959).

For Louise McAdams Deford

Author's Note

Beginning in 1950, the Miss America title was postdated. There was no Miss America 1950. Miss America 1949 was crowned in September 1949 just as Miss America 1921 was crowned in September 1921. However, Miss America 1951 was crowned in September 1950, and the postdating procedure continues until today. As a rule of thumb, everything is titled by the calendar year in progress *except* Miss America herself. Thus, the 1969 *Miss America* Pageant was held in September 1969, with the fifty 1969 state queens competing. Miss Michigan 1969 was elected Miss America 1970.

Acknowledgments

I should like to acknowledge my appreciation to the *Miss America* Pageant for cooperating with me so willingly in this project. The largest measure of my gratitude must be reserved for Albert A. Marks, Jr., the chairman of the Pageant executive committee, whose views on an inquiring, even prying press, are nonetheless remarkably similar to those noted under the First Amendment to the United States Constitution. Among his associates, for their help, I would also particularly thank George Cavalier, Mrs. Kathleen Ryan, Miss Ruth McCandliss, and Mrs. Doris Kelly in Atlantic City, and Mrs. Lenora Slaughter Frapart in Scottsdale, Arizona.

A special appreciation must also be awarded to Swayn Hamlet and the Wilson (North Carolina) Jaycees, and to Bill Ruth and the Raleigh Jaycees, and, of course, to all those Miss Americas, who were so very gracious and helpful. Except in rare instances, I have, throughout the book, referred to the Miss Americas, and to various other distinguished ladies, by their first names or their maiden names. I hope they will forgive me this familiarity, which is employed only in the service of clarity.

—F.D.

Contents

Illustrations follow pages 82 and 274

There She Is

★ 1 ★

Buying a Piece of the Dream

Maligned by one segment of America, adored by another, misunderstood by about all of it, Miss America still flows like the Mississippi, drifts like amber waves of grain, sounds like the crack of a bat on a baseball, tastes like Mom's apple pie, and smells like dollar bills. Miss Liberty, looking out, away from the land, has never been quite the same since the McCarran Act, and Grace Kelly no longer calls Philadelphia home. But good old Miss America still talks like Huckleberry Finn, looks like Patti, LaVerne, and Maxine, and towers over the land like the Ozarks. She really is the body of state, and the country is in her eyes.

Miss Americas have been selected at Atlantic City for a half-century now, the first one having been chosen in 1921, just after women had gained the right to vote and young Bert Parks's permanent teeth had come in. If not spectacular, these first fifty years have certainly been lively and spangled, and the Pageant and its queens have become a substantial part of the Americana trust. This much we do know: one Miss America inspirationally out-talked Billy Graham, another flatly turned down an offer from Howard Hughes, and another was held a prisoner in a small room in the Waldorf-Astoria. Various Miss Americas have danced in the Rockettes, earned Phi Beta Kappa keys, and ridden across the country accompanied by an entire All-American football team. Miss Americas have graduated from Ivy League colleges and played opposite Fatty Arbuckle as well as Elvis

Presley. One Miss America borrowed flat shoes, so she would not embarrass little Eddie Fisher when he took her out. Several were fat as children, and one used to recite the Lord's Prayer regularly in the bathtub.

In Atlantic City, Miss Americas have run away and hidden after they were crowned, been searched for falsies, been tape-measured, been nearly disrobed backstage by the producer, played *Clair de Lune* on the vibraharp, exhibited a bustline smaller than Twiggy's, refused ever to pose in a bathing suit, played "Ol' Man Mose" on bass, and Betsy Ross in a parade.

Miss Americas have married childhood sweethearts, Phil Silvers, the first man on campus who talked to her, professional athletes, doctors, a professional athlete who became a doctor, a movie monster, a man who knocked a polo ball into her lap at a game, and an unemployed friend on his way *to* Oklahoma during the Depression. Roberto Rossellini threw one Miss America over for Ingrid Bergman. Another, with her mother, was accused of getting her two-year-old daughter intoxicated regularly. One Miss America has been cast as both Betty Coed and Jack Armstrong's sweetheart.

Or, none of the above.

There are always two Miss Americas. The one is the queen herself and the other is the nonprofit organization, *Miss America* Pageant, and while neither one of them makes a great deal of sense, both manage quite well in spite of themselves. Yolande Betbeze, who was Miss America 1951, says, "Miss America is the kind of girl who would go into a bar and order orange juice in a loud voice." Harry L. Godshall, the only surviving founder of *Miss America*, says, "It never changes. The Pageant today is run exactly as it was in the beginning. Exactly, except for the talent, it's never changed at all—and that's the whole trouble with the thing."

Possibly, however, there is a charm in, even a hidden demand for, changelessness, as well as one for nervy, sober women. More than one billion people have seen *Miss America* since it went on television in 1954. Every year, about half the population of the United States reserves the second Saturday night in September to watch a new Miss America being crowned. That it reserves the rest of the year to forget about her is nearly as well-documented. But it comes back, every year on schedule, perhaps a hundred million strong, drawn to watch the strange event in Atlantic City. Scientists, meanwhile, speculate on what makes the swallows come back to Capistrano on time. Who knows the why about a phenomenon?

This much we do know. There are two kinds of people who are most deceived by *Miss America*, and they are: 1) those who criticize it the most, and 2) those who praise it the most. Part of the problem for both these groups is that *Miss America* is confusing—and it is either purposely confusing or congenitally so. Surely, no U.S. institution could be riddled with so many contradictions by accident.

Miss America is, for instance, a bathing beauty show embarrassed to death about sex, bathing suits, and possibly even girls. It manages to become more Victorian as the country grows more permissive and tolerant. *Miss America* is flat broke, but it is, surely, the only successful enterprise in the State of New Jersey (and, as a matter of fact, including the State of New Jersey) outside of the Princeton University annual giving campaign that is not controlled by the Mafia. And this much we do know. Contestants are advertised clamorously as being upright and wholesome, but the Pageant's confidence in their behavior is expressed by its rule which forbids the girls even to talk to their fathers alone in public.

The Pageant brings Atlantic City untold amounts of publicity and considerable revenue, but the resort, although maintaining a viselike grip on the attraction, has no feel for the Pageant and does not support the show. *Miss America,* always based in New Jersey, is strongest in the South and the western United States, and increasingly in the small towns and cities—as the country becomes more metropolitan. "They don't give a damn about her in the big cities any more," says Margaret Gorman, the first Miss America. "The girl only goes over in the podunk towns." Yet perennially, only Bob Hope earns better ratings on TV than *Miss America.* The one program that then Vice President and Mrs. Nixon used to let little Tricia and Julie stay up late to watch every year was *Miss America.* Annually, the Pageant estimates that 200,000 citizens across the land volunteer more than 6,000,000 man-hours of service to produce 3000 state and local preliminaries in which 70,000 girls compete and millions more watch.

Miss America, dependent on good will, is surely the only organization of its size without a public-relations man or any expertise in the area. It has tried desperately to rid itself of its theme song, "There She Is," that is instantly identifiable to tens of millions of Americans, to whom it immediately conjures up images of *Miss America,* Bert Parks, and Atlantic City. The Pageant provides more scholarship assistance for college girls than any other private agency in the world, and yet it is women who have always led the most virulent attacks on Miss America and all that she stands for.

Presented as representative of American youth, Miss America is, instead, no more than the choice of a group of inexperienced middle-aged judges, who are required to arrive at their decision with an eccentric system that is intentionally constructed so that the most important factors in determining a queen are never officially considered.

The queens themselves, and other *Miss America* contestants as well, are surrounded by the most misconceptions. To many, Miss America is an ideal, nearly of wonderment, held in such esteem that her mere appearance on a runway occasions them to rise dutifully, out of respect. In the more sophisticated national mind, Miss Americas are dolls, playing little people. They are dismissed as professional jingoes, military cheerleaders, and dumb and vapid repetitions of each other. In fact, Miss America has recently become nothing more or less than the girl who won the *Miss America* Pageant competition over 70,000 other hopefuls. Miss America may be the best of the best, or she may be—as in Senator Hruska's encomium of Judge Carswell—the chosen representative of the mediocre. Somehow, it really does not matter.

Miss Americas look alike and act alike because that is, apparently, the most convenient way one gets to be Miss America. Actually, the queens are much more varied than the public supposes, but that doesn't matter either, because they program themselves or permit themselves to be programed to fit the same recognizable type. Evelyn Ay, Miss America 1954—a queen from the pre-TV era, when girls could be themselves and Miss Americas too, both at once—recalls overhearing a conversation between two recent Miss Americas that illustrates to what lengths contenders for the crown will now go to subjugate themselves to the role. One of the young queens inquired of the other how she felt at the moment she realized that she had won. The second replied that she felt no emotion whatsoever, neither elation, gratitude, nor surprise, because she was completely preoccupied with trying to remember exactly what motions her predecessor had made at this point the year before—that is, how she cocked her head to receive the crown, how she reached for the roses, and to what extent she smiled and nodded thanks.

The contestants at Atlantic City are girls as pretty, smart, and sweet as could be rounded up by any other method, but the race does not go to the fairest, or the most talented, or the sweetest. Great dancers or singers do not show up at *Miss America* any more than great bodies do. If she is that good at something or has that good a figure, a girl does not have to depend on a beauty pageant for approbation and reward. Miss Americas are not even necessarily very versatile, although they may dabble in a lot of things. They are inner-directed, well-ordered, and oriented toward accomplishment.

Not so long ago that striving for personal achievement was the ideal for young Americans. Now, of course, the celebrated modern youth is supposed to be contemplative rather than competitive, and, if active, outer-directed and involved in social or political therapy. On these terms, anyway, Miss Americas are behind the times with their image. In the broader sense, however, they are not the agents from the past that critics accuse them of being —and that some Pageant functionaries would like to make them over into. Miss America has evolved today into one sure thing only: she is the best at winning beauty pageants. That much we do know.

While the basic types of Miss Americas change, the appeal seems to remain constant. Miss America provides, first of all, a coveted touch of royalty for a republic's citizenry, but it is only a benign tease of monarchy. The fact that *Miss* America is *crowned* is, after all, such a deceptively magnificent compromise that it must have been hammered out by the Founding Fathers themselves, on the same day they hit on the idea of giving the small states the Senate and the populous ones the House. Obviously, if it made any sense, it should be Queen America or, at the least, Lady America. But then, of course, it wouldn't be America.

In the same clever style, the Pageant manages to mix up its sex with respectable community boosterism. You get to examine all the girls, but always end up cheering for the one who comes from home. Miss America may be the only institution in the world that succeeds in getting the most out of both Freud's sexual drives and the baboon's territorial imperative. The best 100 breasts in the nation with the purest 50 hearts in the land beating beneath them would not be enough to sustain the phenomenon were not those banners, MISS ALABAMA to MISS WYOMING, there as well.

At last, though, beyond the aristocracy and the geography and the sex there lies the fantasy kingdom where the Pageant and its people really reside. The critics who attack *Miss America* for being irresponsible and escapist miss the whole point. Of course it is. *Miss America* is escapist, and so are Disneyland and the Baltimore Colts, so is a skinny dip and so is Johnny Carson, and so is a ski lodge and so is visiting the koala bears in the San Diego Zoo, and so are the Indianapolis 500 and a dirty movie from Sweden and so is Don Ho, and so is a brook that runs through a park in Denton, Texas, with shade trees and flowers and small dogs barking at a clear blue sky. So, too, was *The Saturday Evening Post* before it became topical and tough and unpopular. "I think if I had to do it all over again, I would keep Norman Rockwell on the cover," Clay Blair, the editor who changed the magazine, has written. "I would try to find the things in America that are beautiful and good. In other words, the positive aspects of our society. . . . I think the people are damn sick and tired of trouble, trouble, trouble."

Bert Parks, *Miss America* emcee since 1955, the one person, male or female, who is most identified with the Pageant, says, "It's corny. Let's face it. It's corny and it's basic and it's American. But in this sick, sad world a little fairyland is welcome and refreshing. Apparently, from the figures, we are right. About the only thing I agree with Mr. Nixon on is that, yes, there are a lot of nice people out there beyond the big, slick areas—and these are good, straight people for the most part. Perhaps they are narrow, but they have a great longing for normalcy, as so many of us do, and *Miss America* buys them a piece of that dream. For two marvelous hours, you have it all. For two hours out of 365 days."

That much we do know. The rest is somewhat incidental.

★★ 2 ★★

Beauty and Everlasting Faith at the Local Level

DORIS: "Miss America stands for the good part of today's youth—not the drug-taking element. She stands for the clean-cut, not the shaggy-haired, and she stands, above all, for intelligence and beauty."

JUDI: "I think Miss America represents the best in the female. I met one once, I forget which one she was, at the Azalea Festival one year, and I have always looked up to Miss America. I think she is a serious person."

I

In America, every year, at least a quarter of a million girls enter formal beauty pageants, and that figure does not take into account the hundreds of thousands more who volunteer for the more casual competitions sponsored by schools, sororities, neighborhoods, clubs, businesses, and other institutions. Beyond that, more than a million people donate their services to produce pageants, and several million others attend the shows. All those figures have been steadily swelling for more than a generation so that a huge segment of the population has grown up expecting beauty pageants as a natural part of the calendar, like Thanksgiving and back-to-school sales.

Except where an authoritarian church or state bans them,

beauty pageants are in evidence practically everywhere in the world, and in such disparate places as Thailand or Brazil they are often a modern passion. Nowhere, though, does the phenomenon extend with such broad scope as it does in the United States. The wide acceptance of beauty pageants here is curious, for in one sense they are quite un-American: that is, they are not profitable ventures. A pageant utterly depends on volunteer labor, and, even then, the profit margin tends to be thin and hardly commensurate with the amount of energy applied.

It may be, of course, that at the grass roots this is the salvation of the institution. If some promoter could come into town and make a quick profit on a beauty show, it would be all too obvious in most communities that there was a high correlation between sex and remuneration—and also, ultimately, surely, municipal depravity. Under such a light, pageants could not long survive, for respectable girls would not enter them, and respectable citizens would not support them.

The basic, and base, pageant appeal is, and always has been, girl-watching—and the fewer clothes the better. Nobody, of course, even dares suggest this any more, so pageant people have quite convinced themselves that everybody is there for all sorts of different, more uplifting reasons. Just to be sure, though, pageants keep introducing diversionary distractions. So, we have talent and evening gowns and scholarships and interviews and taste and poise and production numbers and certified ladies and gentlemen as judges. It took the Women's Liberation Movement to point out the really rather obvious truth that if beauty pageants were substantially more than girl-watching exercises, why, there would be pageants for men too.

Pageants are, of course, perfectly harmless. Very few sex maniacs start out their careers hanging around them. Still, in much of America, the ingredient of sex must be played down. This has been effectively managed by euphemistically calling pageants "projects." Usually the word "community" or "civic" is prefixed. It is all for a good cause, run by good people. The fact that few pageants make great sums of money lends more respectability to the enterprise, since that fact attests to the inherent purity. Everybody knows that dirty stuff makes lots of money; the inverse should also hold true.

This philosophy is widespread and supports the existence of most pageants. In fact, in many places a pageant is such a respectable and popular project for the community that the service or civic organization that sponsors it—usually the Jaycees—is soon stuck with the show, for better or for worse. In the town of Wilson, North Carolina, the Jaycees readily admit that running the Miss Wilson Pageant, a franchised *Miss America* local, requires an inordinate amount of effort over a long period each year, but that even if they wanted to abandon the project—which they do not—they would suffer such disapproval in town that their effectiveness and initiative would be blunted on other fronts.

The Miss Wilson Pageant is a typical endeavor of that sort in a typical American town. The 1970 Pageant was put on by 78 of the Jaycees, who were subdivided into 19 committees. They donated 1295 man hours, with specialized help coming from the rest of the community, as well as donations of prizes, equipment, talent, and moral support. Over-all, the Pageant grossed $4913.13, but expenses amounted to $4686.71, so that the Jaycees netted only $226.42. If everybody who had worked on the project had just contributed 17¢ for each hour he worked, they could have made as much that way. In contrast, in just a couple of nights of selling brooms door-to-door, the Wilson Jaycees make $800. Picking up old newspapers and magazines four days a year will bring in $500. The Kiddie Karnival at the Parkwood Shopping Center will net $2000 in a week, and all that it demands is hiring a guy to bring in some rides and then sending a few Jaycees out to Parkwood to take tickets every night. A beauty pageant is strictly deficit-volunteering.

Yet, while this is a common example, beauty contests are ingrained into the American consciousness. *Miss America* alone has 3500 locals and 70,000 contestants annually and there would be many more except for the logistical problem of how to handle more entries at the state level. Though never with much financial success, the Wilson Jaycees have been presenting their local pageant every year since 1958. It was started as far back as 1944, when their first Miss Wilson went on to become first runner-up for Miss North Carolina.

In 1946, Miss Wilson was Trudy Riley, who went on to become Miss North Carolina, but since then the local queens have been eliminated at state competitions. This string of losers would seem to be disappointing to a town, and a few do give up after a long succession of defeats, but many towns and counties never really expect to get a winner. It is not an overriding concern anyway. Their boldest aim is just to "make ten"—get their girl in the state semifinals—or, glory be, "make five." All Wilson really wants is a nice, sweet, reasonably pretty local girl, who lives in town, whom everybody knows, and who will make a fine representative of the white community wherever she goes. If the Wilson Jaycees can catch lightning in a bottle and come up with a genuine state contender that will be so much the better, but it is by no means a high priority.

For this reason, the Jaycees' rules are even more restrictive than the national rules for *Miss America* locals, and they will not accept entries from some of the good-looking girls from out of town who are living at Atlantic Christian College. The Jaycees figure that if they did that, the way they used to, they might just end up with another strange girl from Virginia winning it, which is what happened one year. A girl from Virginia, or from Rocky Mount, for that matter, is simply not their idea of Miss Wilson. As a result, the Wilson Pageant always ends up with a high percentage of local high-school girls, which reduces the level of competition from the start. High-school girls have no chance at all at *Miss America*.

In 1970, three of the eight Wilson contestants were high-school seniors, and all of them were rated as top contenders. They could sweep the finals. In most pageants, there are five finalists, but with only eight girls, the Jaycees did not want to have a situation at the end where only three girls would be left sitting on stage as also-rans. So at Miss Wilson it was decided that there would be only three finalists. It was a very considerate thought—and would have been an even better idea if the judges and accountants had also been advised of the arrangement. The Jaycees are invariably tactful, though. While personally they were not above discussing the merits of a large, fetching mole that one of the contestants featured in her cleavage, they did not require that the girls make public their measurements.

The winner will have to disclose this information when she goes on to the State Pageant, though. The Jaycees will escort her there, and provide her with a chaperone who is usually a member's wife. They also will help finance the trip. They paid for three gowns for Miss Wilson 1969, Alice Beasley. Moreover, before the State Pageant, they sent Alice off to a charm school in Goldsboro for a three-day crash course in which she was, at one point, even taken out to a restaurant dinner to make sure that she knew which were the proper table utensils. Alice also attended Jaycee meetings, an opening of the First Union National Bank, a Battle of the Bands, various other local pageants, and races at the Wilson County Speedway before she proceeded on to the State Pageant. Her reign did not end there. The Jaycees paid an $80 entrance fee to allow her to compete in the Apple Blossom Festival, and at Richmond, for another festival, Alice personally met a television star named Peter Graves.

Most local winners have a longer incubation period before they compete at the state level. Miss Wilson is selected in February, but many local pageants are held in the fall, or even late in the summer—more than a full calendar year before the girl would advance to Atlantic City, were she to survive the competition till the end. This long interval is important to many towns, because it provides the local organization with more time to drill their queen, to teach her pageant tricks, and to smooth her out in all the right places—even redo her completely if that is possible. Wilson continues to hold its Pageant in midwinter, though, because it is traditional and fits into the Jaycee schedule, and because it is also more agreeable to sell ads for the Pageant program in December. That is a good month for this particular activity, as the Christmas spirit is in the air.

It is also important to line up prizes for the future winner then. The 1970 Miss Wilson was assured a $500 college scholarship from the Jaycees; but also, from other local sources: a TV set, a bathing suit, shoes, sunglasses, perfume, a pearl necklace, gloves, a steak dinner, a shampoo and set, a camera, evening bags, a billfold (lady's), earrings, an alarm clock, movie passes, a cleaning certificate, a blouse, a slip, a travel iron, and many other items and services. The top runners-up benefit accordingly. Nearly everybody in town, it seems, pitches in for Miss

Wilson. It appears to be imperative to make a contribution if you are a merchant who believes in the town and the project.

Jimmy Dempsey, for instance, of Jimmy Dempsey Cleaners, can invariably be counted upon to buy an ad or to give a $20 gift certificate, or perhaps even both, if it has been a good year, and the Jaycees hit him with their sales pitch right after the University of North Carolina Tarheels have won a big early-season game. Now Jimmy stands by the window of his laundry and watches the cars go by. Almost every second or third one honks at him, and he waves in recognition. Wilson, 45 miles east of Raleigh, has a population of 30,000, and is the largest bright-leaf tobacco market in the world after Salisbury, Southern Rhodesia, but it is still a tight community. "It's just getting now, I suppose, that you don't know everybody in town," Jimmy Dempsey says. "And not long ago, it was more than that, too. You knew everybody your age, anyway, over at Rocky Mount or Tarboro or Greenville or Goldsboro."

Family, as in so many towns of this size, is still very important in Wilson and exerts another pressure not to have some stranger elected as the local queen. Dick Ellis, who served as master of ceremonies for the pageant, says: "I'm on TV in Raleigh, and it comes in here, so it's a pretty big deal. I know the Governor and all that. Down here, though, I'm still Dicky Ellis, and all they remember is that my mother was a bookkeeper."

It was not until the 1950s that any substantial industry came to Wilson. The economy before that time was based on tobacco, and there are still great fortunes made that way in town. Up to a decade ago, merchants carried as much as a third of their customers on the cuff for a whole year, waiting for the tobacco crop to be sold before settling accounts. The average wage in town is $2.10 an hour now, though, and the meat cutters at Swift are even unionized. There are also other changes. Once, when the magnificent azaleas came to bloom in March, Nash Street was transformed into as beautiful a residential thoroughfare as there was in the country, but today many of the gorgeous brick mansions stand vacant or house college fraternities. The prestige addresses are in the suburbs now, and the shopping centers make it hard on the downtown merchants. Wilson is like a lot of places.

The town is split, too, in textbook style, with the black section on the other side of the railroad tracks. Blacks comprise about 40 per cent of the population, a figure hardly changed from the spring day in 1865, near Appomattox, when the Wilson men of Company F of the 4th North Carolina Regiment, CSA, fired the last volley of the Civil War. A third of Fike High School is black now, and the 1969 football team charged to new glory, led by a black fullback named Carlester Crumpler. Bussing is the pressing concern, however, and as the Miss Wilson Pageant approaches, it becomes the dominant subject in town. A new private school's tuition at the elementary level is set at $790; "Mr. HEW" is the town villain.

But after race, basketball is the leading topic of conversation. There are 81 physicians in town, 62 churches, 24 bowling lanes, 3 radio stations, and a stock car track. Besides the Jaycees, there are Masons and Shriners and Elks and Moose. Real-estate taxes are higher all the time, but kids are driving to school in Rivieras and GTOs, with $104 tires. In attitude, and in style, Wilson is a fairly representative small city, coincidentally Southern, the kind that is backbone for *Miss America.* Somewhere, in a town like Wilson, in a Pageant run by Jaycees, a local winner is moving up the ladder, and, by September, she will be Miss America. That she will not come from Wilson, North Carolina, is only incidental. In a place like this, this is how she begins, every year.

II

The Wilson Jaycees are a real gung-ho group, which is the way all Jaycee chapters are supposed to be. They're into everything in town. Running a local *Miss America* Pageant is a year-round proposition in itself for the chairman and some of his top committeemen. To make Norwood Barnes, an antique dealer, take the job for the 1970 production in Wilson, Swayn Hamlet, an optician, who was then the president of the Jaycees, rounded up some other members and they kept Norwood up past midnight for a couple of nights in a row, alternately praising and berating him, until he finally agreed to take the job.

Norwood won some compensating assurances, though. Swayn, who has the reputation in town of being among Wilson's most promising young men, agreed to handle the entries committee, and Barry Lamm, the architect, said he would write the script again. Since the date for the Pageant happened to fall on Valentine's Day, that made the idea of a theme a natural, although it was also decided to bring back all the former Miss Wilsons as well, right back to Jean Fritz, 1944.

Then the rest started falling into line for Norwood. Tom Campbell, who manages radio station WGTM, agreed to take charge of sound. Squire Watson, the local Texaco oil distributor, would handle the lighting. Pinkie Jefferson, who runs a chain of washerettes, said he would handle the props again. Pinkie seldom even shows his face at Jaycee meetings, but he can always be counted on to handle the props at Miss Wilson. For concessions, Bill Hill, a banker, was the man, and Dr. Vincent Thomas, an optometrist, agreed to run the judges' committee. Dave Orcutt, a lawyer, would be the head usher, and Littlejohn Faulkner, an insurance broker, would handle the curtain. At rehearsal this gave him the opportunity to leer at the girls and pretend that he was peering down their fronts. Husky Alan Bass, who has the local Ford tractor dealership, was named to head the committee that was responsible for assembling the runway, and Mrs. Bass headed up the wives of the Jaycees (who are called Jaycettes, of course), who would serve as chaperones for the contestants. Miss Pattie Ruffin, who works in the Wilson recreation department, and who is, it is said, the only honorary female Jaycee in the land, agreed to pitch in again as the resident Girl Friday.

Wayne Garris, who sells Cadillacs—and sales were doing fine despite the economy—was put in charge of trophies and crowns. Local pageants may buy their awards at any jeweler's, but trophies with the official *Miss America* figure and seal on them can be obtained only from the Pageant's recognized Atlantic City jeweler, and the Jaycees grumbled that he charged too much. Gene Deans, a salesman for engineering equipment, not only volunteered to work with Gordon Wilson in set construction, but he also advanced the idea of designing a genuine Miss Wilson coat of arms. He painted it himself. It was blue and white, Jaycee colors, with the motto, *color fidesque perennis* (beauty and everlasting faith). A crown was in the middle of the shield, and around it, in the four quarters, were a torch for inspiration, a lion for courage, a four-leaf clover for luck, and a star for destiny. Conceivably, it was the only beauty-pageant coat of arms in the country.

Some changes did have to be made. Mrs. Gay Butner, of nearby Rocky Mount, was brought in to direct the show. A onetime Miss Kinston who made five at the State Pageant, Mrs. Butner had also gone on to become runner-up for Miss VFW, and to marry her Jaycee manager. Widowed and left with four sons when her husband was killed in an airplane crash in 1968, Gay had moved to Rocky Mount, where she opened up the Gay School of Charm and tutored beauty-pageant contestants. A positively beautiful woman, tall and dark, and always impeccably dressed, she was as much an ideal for the girls as she was their trainer.

To help her with the pageant, Gay brought in two other professionals. Gene Barnes was put in charge of the opening production number. Gene runs what amounts to the closest thing in Wilson to a night club. He lived in New York for nine years, wears alligator shoes and wide lapels, and has a very difficult job, it develops, because two of the contestants are nearly incapable of dancing, such as the art is known. In the end, he does teach the eight girls to do two basic little steps in time to "Peg o' My Heart," which is in keeping with Valentine's Day. Gay also brings in her sister, Elizabeth Katherine (Betty Kay) Herring, to assist the girls with their make-up and hairdos. "In an area like Wilson," Gay says, "the girls just know so little about make-up. Everything is just so much more cosmopolitan about those things in larger towns." In some North Carolina counties, as late as 1969, the girls who won local pageants wore skirts that reached to their knees.

Finally, the Jaycees signed up Dick Ellis, their native son, now the Raleigh TV newsman, to be the emcee. At most local pageants, a former state or national winner is brought in for the job. Atlantic City shills shamelessly in behalf of that sort of family casting, and in the past, Wilson had gone for that, too. For the previous two Pageants, the Jaycees had hired Jeanne Swanner, who had been Miss North Carolina 1963 and Miss Congeniality at Atlantic City. Jeanne is over 6 feet tall and extremely popular in North Carolina, but for both the 1968 and 1969 Wilson Pageants, she told exactly the same jokes and stories. Not only that, but in the fall of 1968, she came to Wilson with George Wallace, and on that occasion she employed the same routine all over again. The people of Wilson love Jeanne Swanner dearly, and, for that matter, the town voted for George Wallace, but even Jeanne Swanner's best stuff had worn too thin the third time around. That was why they went for Dick Ellis.

He said he planned to keep most of his jokes to a local level, since he was a home-town boy. For instance, he said he would lead off by asking Mr. Woodard, the principal of Fike High, if he were in the audience, " 'I'm sure you remember me, Mr. Woodard,' " Dick would say, " 'because I was in your office more than you.' Then I'm going to tell the one about how I got injured playing football. You know, I fell off the bench."

Friday night after rehearsal, the night before the Pageant, Dick went out for some eggs and bacon and grits at the Essofleet truck stop on Route 301, between Wilson and Rocky Mount. Gay Butner and her sister Betty Kay; John Winstead, the Jaycee president; Bill Hill and Littlejohn Faulkner came along. Littlejohn told about the time he hit an 8–5 quinella for $200 on the first occasion that he ever went to the dog races in Miami, and then Dick started into some jokes, which became increasingly risqué. It was good that he had a chance to go over his repertoire, though. He did not know it at the time, of course, but the next evening, at the Pageant, things were going to take such a surprising shift that Dick, desperate, would again have to tell the one about the Catholic priest and the commode to the audience.

III

Doris Smith attends Fike High School, where she is a senior and head majorette, a member of the Booster Club, Modern Dance Club, and the Concert Band. She lives, with her mother, in a tidy house at 514 Gold Street, which is not in the best section of town. Her father, a milkman, died when she was seven, and her only brother has grown up and moved downstate to Fayetteville. This will also be Doris's last year at home. Next fall she hopes to attend the University of North Carolina at

Chapel Hill and study to become a dental hygienist. "A dental hygienist makes $850 a month," Doris says, "and I could help Momma for a while, and then go into modeling or something glamorous like that. I still wouldn't be too old then." Right now she is eighteen.

In the mail one day, November 12, 1969, there is a letter for her, and she tears it open and reads it with excitement, and then rushes to the phone by the front door to call her mother, who is at work as an insurance clerk. Doris has been invited to make an application for the Miss Wilson Pageant if she is interested. She definitely is. Though quiet and nearly shy, Doris is popular, mature for her age, a young woman of strong will who knows what she wants.

At the time her father died, she had been taking dancing lessons for several years, ever since she was three and one-half years old, and she loved the exercise. She recognized, though, that it was a luxury that her mother could suddenly no longer afford. "I knew that my momma would have done everything in her power to let me keep going, and we couldn't afford it, so I waited a while, and then one day I just told her that I really didn't like dancing, and there was no need for me to keep going." The lessons were suspended.

The $500 Miss Wilson scholarship appeals particularly to Doris and her mother; they are delighted at the opportunity to enter the Pageant. That is not the majority response, however. In fact, 121 other girls around Wilson are opening invitations about that same day, but only 20 of them will show up with their mothers a couple of weeks later at a tea, when the Jaycees explain the Pageant further and distribute application blanks.

The lucky 122 girls originally approached come from all over Wilson County, which surrounds the town. These girls have been selected by what the Jaycees call a "Board of Governors," a group of distinguished Wilsonians, mostly educators, who carefully screen the qualifications of almost every white girl in the county. At last, the Board ranks the girls by separating them into three categories. The "A" list, composed of those who appear most qualified, is then issued invitations. Depending on the response of the "A" girls, the Board will then proceed to invite the "Bs," or even, in a disastrous year, the "Cs."

The Jaycees start compiling dossiers on potential candidates more than a year in advance of the Pageant. Even before the year's Pageant is presented, they already have a long list of younger girls who are prime contenders for the following year. If a girl is a really promising type, tight research is done on her, and as many as 15 of her friends might also get invitations, even though none of them may actually be given any chance for success in the Pageant.

This procedure is followed, however, because peer-group opinion is a major factor in influencing a girl's decision to enter. Parents or boy friends, particularly those who are uptight about their girl getting ogled in a bathing suit, are other prime reasons girls do not enter; but most of those who do turn down the invitation do so because they decide themselves that their figures or their talents are not sharp enough to go on display. Thus, it is often crucial for the Board to invite a whole group of girls simply so that they can all strengthen each other's resolve—and preserve the interest of the one top girl that is desired.

The major misconception about *Miss America* is, after all, that it is an open competition. Technically, of course, it is, but girls must first enter at the local level—where Atlantic City neither possesses nor seeks any real authority short of making sure that its jeweler gets all the crown business—and there the sponsoring organization usually turns it into a *de facto* invitational. The procedures followed at Wilson may be more complete than those at most local pageants, but they are approximately the same everywhere. Girls who might enter *Miss America* are thus first screened, then invited to apply, then prejudged, then at last invited to enter. Entry blanks are never left around town like so many BankAmericards.

In Wilson, so far as anyone in the Jaycees knows, no girl who has not been invited has ever applied on her own. This means, obviously, that no black girl has ever had a chance to be Miss Wilson. That is the situation at many *Miss America* locals, in and out of the South. "No, I'll be honest," Swayn Hamlet says. "We've never invited a Negro girl. But then, the subject has just never come up. We've never had a Negro apply for the Jaycees either." These facts are not mutually exclusive. A few months before, a girl named Pauletta Pearson, Miss Newton-Conover, had become the first black ever to qualify for the North Carolina State Pageant, and she had come to the attention of the local Pageant only because the Jaycees in her community had accepted their first black member. It was he who nominated her and another black girl.

Five months from now, at the state Pageant, Pauletta will win her talent division over Miss Wilson. Now, though, it is still only February, and the Wilson Jaycees are not sure how to evaluate this new situation. Swayn says, "I just don't know what we would do if one applied. If it did happen, I guess we would go to the girls first and see how they felt about it."

The girls would almost certainly take it in stride. They are, after all, exactly the same sort who will mob Pauletta Pearson with shrieks and tears of joy the night she wins her talent division, and the same girls who will also elect her Miss Congeniality. "I feel one way so strongly," Doris says. "I just can't stand it when someone says something like 'niggers.' I was brought up down here, and I've heard a lot of things, but I just can't stand things like that."

Naturally, the black people in Wilson, who comprise nearly half the population, have no interest in the Pageant because it does not involve them. At Fike, only the white kids seem to know that Doris is in the running. One day, shortly after it was announced that she had been accepted as an entrant, one white kid—"one of those real stupid guys," according to Doris—screamed, "Hey, Miss Wilson" at her all the way down a hall. Another time, another fresh classmate started giving her a hard time about it while a bunch of them were standing around before a class.

Suddenly, the wise guy found himself yanked back hard, and, shaking, he dared to look up. The fellow holding him was the football star, Carlester Crumpler, who is 6 feet 3½ inches, 225 pounds, and black. "Hey, you can't talk to her that way," he said to the pest, shooing him off.

"Thank you, Crump," Doris said.

Until now, Ava Gardner, who was brought up at Rock Ridge, retains the distinction of being the most famous native of Wilson County. Soon, Carlester Crumpler may succeed to that honor; at this time he was considered by some college coaches to be the best high school prospect in the United States. Since he integrated the Fike High School team in 1967 as a sophomore, it had gone on to win three state championships in a row, which is a rare feat in any state. It was decided early in his career in Wilson that Carlester had a tendency to get whiter as he came closer to the goal line. He was so good that even in his first season of varsity play, Judi Brewer and the other cheerleaders created a special cheer, just for him: "Car*les*ter, Car*les*ter, Car*les*ter, let's go!"

Judi was a senior that year at Fike High, and is now a sophomore at Atlantic Christian College, where she is preparing for a career as an elementary-school teacher. It is now Friday night, February 13, 1970, though, so Judi is back at her old school. It is the dress rehearsal for Miss Wilson in the auditorium. Judi is one of the favorites. Carlester is performing across a common lobby in the gymnasium, playing center on the Fike basketball team. Two other of the Fike starters are black, as are all of the opponents, one of the referees, and many of the spectators. In contrast, the Miss Wilson rehearsal next door seems curiously anachronistic in its whiteness.

At least Judi herself is one throbbing contemporary element, for she is a classic example of the modern Southern belle, the type that invariably is favored at Atlantic City. At this time, in another Southern town of a similar size to Wilson, there is another unknown girl named Phyllis George. She is a year ahead of Judi in school, is more mature, prettier, and more talented, and will go on in a few months to become Miss America 1971. Essentially, though, Phyllis and Judi share the same fundamental Southern-belle personality. Judi, like Phyllis, is vivacious, sparkle-eyed, full of fun, capable of laughing at herself, and incapable of speaking either a) briefly, or b) without using the hands to illustrate all points. Judges cannot resist this prototype, so Judi is clearly stern competition for Doris. So is Rita Deans, who has a good singing voice, is stacked, and has attended Sunday School for fourteen straight years without a miss. Sharon Shackleford, another high-school senior from way out in the county, and Wendy Formo, a tall, self-assured college girl, are considered the dark horses. Connie Whisenant, Rose Thorne, and Peggy Murphy are rated the outsiders.

Only a few of the girls knew each other in advance of the first meeting of all the contestants, when Gay Butner assembled them all at the Moose Club. There, a few weeks before the Pageant, Gay began to teach them the mysteries of walking in a swimsuit on high heels. It costs only $15 a year to join the Moose in Wilson, so there are always a lot of members around the hall. There were more when the word got around about the beautiful widow Butner, and they embarrassed some of the girls.

Gay steered them about. She was paid $10 a girl, which could hardly pay for her time, but she worked them hard. "Glide," she would say, walking out herself to set the example. "Glide. Look up and out. Don't hold your shoulders back. Relax them. Chin level to the floor. Let your body go long. Go long. Don't slouch. Tuck your derrière under." In the beauty-pageant world, people really do say derrière.

Judi Brewer, exasperated, laughed at her own efforts. "For nineteen years I've been walking the way I wanted to, you know. Now I can't do anything right," she said, talking with her hands, doing something else wrong. Still, she was better than most of the other novices—although not nearly as impressive as one of them. Gay Butner was shocked at first and would not believe it for some time, but, obviously, the one girl who was completely in control, the one girl who possessed *poise*, was Doris Smith, the quiet little high-school senior. At last Gay knew she was not being deceived. "You can bluff personality up there," she explained. "You can bluff talent. You can't bluff poise. If you can fake poise, you have it."

Talent, of course, is something else again; it is the rule to fake it. Doris does have a real talent, baton-twirling. She has been to the Tarheel Twirling Camp for three summers and has become the head majorette at Fike. Unfortunately, unbeknownst to Doris, beauty-pageant judges have placed baton-twirling at the bottom of their talent pecking order.

Doris, of course, is not aware of this widespread bias. She picks out a record by an instrumental group named the Ventures and begins polishing her routine. At that, she is better off than Judi, who admits that she is at a loss for any talent at all. She has sung in a choir, though, so Judi figures she will sing for her talent. Borrowing the music to "Kids," a song from the musical *Bye-Bye Birdie*, Judi decides to compose her own words. The song will be called "Boys," and it deals with her ambivalent feelings on that subject. For instance, boys, she declares in a preliminary discourse to the song, are "Bullies-Oafs-Yokels-Stinkers." But, on second thought, they are "Bright-Optimistic-Youthful-Swingers." Then, acronyms out of the way, Judi moves on into the new lyrics themselves:

> Boys keep us girls all torn up in parts,
> Then they bind up the pieces and give us their hearts.
>
> My poor mind is shattered with grief,
> With honest and complete disbelief
>
> That the male of the species is blind
> And I think that I shall never find
>
> What's the matter with boys.

Judi finds a pianist to work up a background arrangement, and Chip Raines, her boy friend, and his mother construct a dummy of a boy "out of old hose and pillowcases" that helps brighten up the act. Although she discovers that she has a hard time hitting high notes if she is nervous, Judi is soon pretty confident about her talent, not long after she invents it. "What scares me most," she says, "is, you know, grace and charm. I keep talking with my hands." Her father also keeps telling her that she says "you know" all the time, but Judi is particularly concerned about any time that she might come into proximity with the judges, because she has it on the best authority that they count the exact number of times that a contestant raises her hands while speaking and then mark points off accordingly. Doris has been told an even better story, that the judges fix the rug in the interview room, so that when the contestant comes in, gliding, looking up and out, derrière tucked under, she will trip on the rug. This way, Doris explains, a contestant's composure will be put to a good test. She is reluctant to be talked out of this old wives' tale.

IV

As the Pageant approaches, Judi and Doris, closer than ever as new friends, begin to realize that they are almost certainly each other's stiffest competition. All of the girls have become friendly competitors, though. Connie and Wendy are away at college, but the others always make an effort to include them in their activities when they come home to Wilson. Doris gets Connie a date with her older brother, and Wendy turns out to be a real lifesaver because she finds "sheer hose" for everyone in a Greensboro store. Sheer hose may be worn in the swimsuit competition.

While Judi knew only Peggy Murphy, a classmate, before work on the Pageant began, and Doris knew none of the other girls, they both soon stand close to all the others. "It's weird," Doris says. "On TV, I always thought that stuff must be phony, the way girls all talked about how nice all the others were and how they liked everybody in the Pageant. But now I know it's true. There's not a single girl I wouldn't mind seeing win."

On Wednesday, three days before the Pageant, Doris, Sharon, Rita, and Peggy, who had caught the flu, went over to Judi's house, so they could all work on their hair together. Judi lives at 1000 Vance Street. It is a better section of town than where Doris lives—a large, homey white frame house, with the paint just beginning to peel in some places. Mr. Brewer works as a mechanical supervisor at the Wilson *Times*, the local daily, while Mrs. Brewer works part time as a secretary. The Brewers are in a much better position to afford to have Judi be a contestant than is Mrs. Smith. Doris and her mother shop carefully for her Pageant wardrobe, making sure to buy items that will not become obsolete after their use in the Pageant. They spend about $185, which is absolutely the minimum cost for getting into a local Pageant.

The Brewers laid out a little more than that for Judi, but they too were judicious shoppers. The various required items build up, though: evening gown, swimsuit, cocktail dress for the opening number, luncheon suit, photographs, piano arrangements, shoes, extra make-up, sheer hose. Judi, like most of the girls, is able to get her swimsuit at cost price from a girl who had worn it in the Miss Rocky Mount Pageant and was trying to unload it. This is especially helpful to both girls since, on the one hand, the suits demanded for *Miss America* are seldom available for purchase in America or anywhere else; and, on the other, girls dislike them so that they would never appear in them at the beach, and it is thus found money if you can stick some other poor contestant with it.

Unfortunately, Judi suffered something of a disaster when adjustments were made in her new $60 luncheon suit. "It made me, you know, all flat," Judi explained, gesticulating in detail, "and tight across, you know, here." That is her bottom, which, she says, contains three extra pounds that she always intended to lose before the Pageant but never did. Luckily, though, she was able to borrow a suit from an aunt that displayed both her top and bottom to best advantage. Right after that crisis was averted, on Sunday, six days before the pageant, Judi went over to Chip Raines' house to give her first public performance of "Boys." It was received enthusiastically by Chip, his parents, and an aunt and uncle, who were lured over to fill up the house. Judi was growing more sure of herself all the time.

Gay Butner's instincts about Doris were proving correct, too. Each day she seemed to be more self-possessed. "I'm confident now, because I've really gotten into it," she said a couple of days before the show. "I think if I can just fool the judges and make them think, 'I'm not scared of you,' then I got it knocked."

That day at school she dropped over to the auditorium in the afternoon, found it empty, and went in with her baton. Alan Bass and his crew had constructed the ramp by now, but the place was dark and lonely. Without music, Doris began practicing her routine. She was working so diligently that she did not notice when a couple of her schoolmates came in and stood at the back of the hall and watched. She was trying to work on two things simultaneously. The one was baton-twirling; the other was smiling. She is not vibrant and open like Judi, nor as striking either. Doris's is a tender prettiness, with soft green eyes and honey-brown hair. Her smile does not sparkle at a distance; at the Pageant she had to put Vaseline on her lips, to make them slide more easily over the teeth and form the broad smile that an audience likes to see.

"You really have to try to win them over," she explained. "No matter who she is, people naturally are just waiting for the girl to drop a baton." Now, in the dark auditorium her own baton slipped from her fingers and flew out into the house, clattering against the seats. Someone came down and retrieved it for her, and for the first time she realized that she was being watched. A few of the kids moved closer to watch her, and one of them, a boy named Vernon Wells, said, "Hey, Doris, what'll happen if you do that Saturday night, lose hold and have that baton go flying right out into the crowd?"

Doris replied, "Oh, I guess someone will be good enough to throw it back to me."

V

The judging formally begins with the Saturday luncheon at the Heart of Wilson Motel. Dr. Vincent Thomas, the head of the judges' committee, welcomes all the judges, and is himself thereafter always introduced as "Dr. Vincent," by Jerry Ball, the well-known "dean of beauty-pageant judges." Jerry has sent two state queens on to become Miss America, and judged in states as far away as Alaska. Jerry is joined on the jury by Mrs. Judy Cross, who was Most Photogenic at Miss North Carolina a few years ago, and by Mrs. Marilyn Hull, a former Miss New Jersey. She is married, as so many beauty queens are, to an athlete. Her husband is Bill Hull, a former Kansas City Chief. The other two judges are Jim Church, chairman of the board of the North Carolina Jaycees, and Bob Logan, Charlotte sales manager for Fabergé, the beauty products concern. It is a hot-shot panel for any local Pageant.

The eight contestants keep a wary eye out as they sit down to lunch and make sure to reach for the correct implements. The judges, however, show no interest whatsoever in what eating tools are being utilized. They are genial and pleasant; the girls could be dispensing peas with a knife for all they seem to care about such formalities.

Doris's hat tumbles off. She does not realize it has gone, which is not surprising, since hats are as foreign to these girls as bustles or U.S.-Army fatigues would be. Judi has a hat on for exactly the second time in her life. The first time was when she was in another beauty pageant. There are speeches and everyone in attendance is introduced. Then the room is cleared, and a table set up for the judges at the far end. It is time for the serious interviewing. Officially, the girls in any *Miss America* Pageant are not graded on their interviews. Actually, it is the underside of the iceberg that determines the winner.

The girls are directed to another room where, one by one, they will be funneled toward the judges. Following an interview, the contestant will proceed on to another room for a sort of debriefing. The judges arrange themselves and pour coffee. The men must concentrate to do their best, for the South Carolina–Duke basketball game is just starting on TV, and their hearts all lie there. Jerry Ball presides in the middle, like a Chief Justice, a leader among equals, and everyone agrees that there will be no set order to the questioning, just "catch as catch can."

Dr. Thomas sits at the other end of the room with a stop watch. Jerry says, "All right, Dr. Vincent, bring in the first young lady." The girls have been assigned an order in which they will present their talents in the show; they visit the judges in the same order. Rita Deans is first. Like all the others, she has her little hat on and carries a handbag, and she walks, as she has been taught, in the proper manner. This is an unfamiliar gait for all the girls and makes them resemble the little dogs on the Ed Sullivan Show, who have outfits on, are balanced precariously on their hind feet, and take desperate little steps to keep from pitching forward.

Rita, seated, is straightforward and demure. She assures the panel that her fourteen-year Sunday-School record is not in any danger of being jeopardized by a victory tonight. The judges spring what is considered as a controversial question: what does Rita think of coed college dormitories? Rita thinks awhile. "Well, I haven't formed an opinion about that," she finally says. Mrs. Butner has instructed the girls to answer that way whenever they feel that they are unsure of an answer. The judges nod and agree that Rita would be unwise, indeed, to venture into unknown philosophical territory.

Sharon Shackleford is next. Talkative anyway, she seems especially garrulous when juxtaposed to Rita. "You've got to pull the plug on her," a judge says upon her departure. Wendy Formo, the third contestant, makes the best approach of all. Over six feet tall, she cannot help walking like a normal person. Also, she shuffles a question about Vice President Agnew beautifully, and the panel is obviously impressed. "It reminds you," Jim Church says. "I always liked that Jeanne Swanner."

Bob Logan asks, "What time is it?"

Jerry answers, "About the end of the first quarter."

Peggy Murphy, recovered from the flu, is next, and for her, the judges reach back for a classic old standard of a question: what kind of person do you think you are yourself? There is one stock answer to this question, which every girl ever in a beauty pageant has always provided. In so many words, it is: that I am naturally a shy, thoughtful person, but I love a good time on occasion. Also, I am nuts about people. Peggy is close enough.

The interviewing is now halfway through, so the judges stand and reach for some coffee. Doris comes in. She is in yellow, with a matching handbag that she sets on the rug by the side of her chair. She banters back the usual polite preliminaries, and then one of the judges asks her if she believes there is a generation gap. "Yes, I definitely believe there is one," Doris replies firmly. All the judges sit up and cock their heads. The regular answer to this question is that there certainly isn't one around my house, where everyone works to understand each other better. Doris proceeds. "Ours is the first generation brought up with the threat of the hydrogen and atom bombs, and the first generation to have grown up with television as a major force in our lives. I really don't even believe it is surprising that there is a gap. Maybe we should only be surprised that there is not more of one."

The judges nod sagely, and to test her further, pull another old chestnut out of the fire. All right, what about coed dorms? Doris backs down here; she comes out with the company line. "It may be fine for other people," she says, "but I can certainly see enough of the opposite sex on dates and other things." Doris has inserted a proper amount of righteous indignation in her voice by the end of her speech. The judges draw a breath, relieved not to have a genuine revolutionary on their hands. They are spent, though, so they ask her if she has any questions for them.

Gay Butner has informed the girls that they may be faced with this request, and to have a question on stand-by. "Yes," Doris says, "I'd like to know why you're still interested in judging. Does it keep you closer to our generation and help close the gap for you?" Yes, the judges agree, yes, it certainly works that way for them.

Time is up; the panel smiles and thanks her; and Doris is hardly out of the door when Jerry slams his hand down. "She came through like 'Gangbusters,'" he exclaims. "She took everything we threw at her and came right back."

"A live cookie," Jim Church says.

Vince Thomas goes to fetch Judi. She comes in, smiling broadly, wearing her aunt's bright orange sleeveless dress. She talks enthusiastically, almost conversationally, from the moment she deposits herself in the chair before the judges. It is as if she has been doing this all her life. Judi is restrained only by what she keeps reminding herself, to keep her hands anchored in her lap and not to say "you know." She is bright and cheery and carries the judges along with her. "Learn to gain control over the interview," Gay has told all the girls. "Give a brief answer, then lead into another area that you particularly like to talk about."

That advice was like giving Judi a license to steal. She and all the other modern Southern belles are born and bred in this briar patch. In Atlantic City a few months later, Phyllis George, Judi's temperamental and verbal kin, babbled on with such dazzle about her pet crab and her dog that the most serious thing that the judges found time to ask her was whether or not she liked beer—and Phyllis even side-stepped that one, and went rambling right on, absolutely stunning the judges from start to finish of the interview. Judi's footwork is proportionately as good at the Heart of Wilson Motel, but she slows down and twice permits the judges time to reach into their portfolio of controversial questions.

First, they want to know if Judi endorses drugs. Well, she doesn't. Then Marilyn Hull remembers Doris. "Do you think there is a generation gap?" she asks. Judi pauses but for a second, then replies: "I don't think there's any more gap now than there's ever been." The judges nod, and then they want to know if she might have a question for them.

Judi has come loaded for that bear. "What is your idea of a Miss Wilson?" she rips back at them.

A girl with poise, the judges solemnly agree.

"Now, do you have any other question you would like to ask us?" Jerry asks. This is a formality, like drop-over-some-time-and-see-us, but Judi tears into it at face value. "Do you think there is a generation gap?" she asks. Marilyn fields the answer, uneasily, and this time Jerry does not ask Judi if she has another question to ask. "I'm afraid Dr. Vincent is signaling that our time is up," he informs her. Judi thanks everyone and leaves. As soon as she is out of the room, the judges start marveling about her performance. "Imagine," one says, "we asked if she had another question, and she did." There is a first time for everything.

They are still chuckling at Judi's effervescence as Rose Thorne comes in. She expresses a solid opposition to coed dorms, and then Connie Whisenant finishes up by voicing displeasure at those college students who had participated in the Vietnam Moratorium.

Outside the room Doris and Judi are already comparing notes. It is immediately obvious to each that her rival was not disappointed; at the least, neither felt she had done poorly. Judi is stunned to learn, though, that Doris has actually said that there is a generation gap. Was she right? Was that the correct answer that the judges were fishing for? Anyway, it only reinforces Judi's growing opinion. By the time she goes home to put her hair up in curlers, and to affix false eyelashes for the first time in her life, Judi Brewer is absolutely convinced that Doris Smith is the only thing that stands between her and Miss Wilson 1970.

VI

A local Pageant is a festive occasion, a teddy bear's picnic for everybody there. It ranks well ahead of the church fair and high-school graduation and all civic functions and most football games. Some of the Jaycees are in tuxedos. For those who have worked on the project, there is a country-club dance afterward, and following that, a breakfast party back at the house of Norwood Barnes, the pageant chairman. Norwood even wears his false mustache for the occasion. The scene is much like a high-school prom. There are blue lights and corsages and the band, the Semanons (which is Nonames spelled backward) has been buttressed with a couple of smooth saxes, so it can play some creamy dance music. The place is packed, all 1040 seats. Like pugs before a prize fight, visiting queens are introduced: Miss Goldsboro, Miss Dunn, Miss Rocky Mount, the Blueberry Queen. They all have their crowns on.

But the judges are more magnificent. They are the real stars of the show. The contestants are, after all, just girls down somebody's street in the neighborhood. Most of the people in the audience can remember them as scraggly little kids with runny noses, wearing T-shirts. It is the judges who bring celebrity and glitter to the scene. They are distant dignitaries, all fashionable and up-to-date and nearly as impressive as people from network television.

Dick Ellis, in a wild red shirt for the first act, introduces them. Jerry Ball, the "dean," comes out on stage, carrying a ladies' pocketbook and moving with a mincing pace. This brings the house down. It is a tough act to follow, but Judy Cross appears next in a gorgeous sequined pants suit, which has certainly never before seen the light of day in Wilson or a lot of other places. The laughs for Jerry turn to ohs and ahs, but Jim Church, next, is no slouch in a four-button double-breasted powder-blue suit, and Marilyn Hull is out of this world in a stylish short evening gown ensemble. Bob Logan completes the stunning scene, revealing himself in a red-and-black paisley tuxedo. After the judges, the Wilson girls-from-next-door are going to be hard-pressed to make any dent in the audience.

The Semanons strike up "A Pretty Girl Is like a Melody," and the curtains part, and then, more up-tempo, it is "Peg o' My Heart," and here come all eight contestants, doing Gene Barnes' two-step in a chorus line. The people are pleased and applaud generously at this presentation. But enough of the frivolity; now the real contest begins. There are three competitions in a *Miss America* Pageant that the judges grade: swimsuit, evening gown, and talent, the latter counting double the other two.

Rita opens the talent portion of the show, singing "It's a Most Unusual Day." She employs a hand mike, and effectively, although all the literature from Atlantic City cautions against its use. Sharon Shackleford is next, with a scene from *A Streetcar Named Desire*. There is some problem at first. Some of the little flashlights that the judges have do not work, so the judges have to move their seats to get some light. This necessitates Pinkie Jefferson coming out with his prop crew to move the table Sharon is using so that she will have the best placement *vis-à-vis* the new judges' location. After this delay, though, Sharon performs admirably, and is even able to sneak some pepper into her eyes so that she draws tears. The judges appear impressed at this finale. Wendy Formo's interpretative dance follows, and goes off without a hitch, and after some initial spotlight trouble, Peggy Murphy's organ rendition of "The Shadow of Your Smile" is without mishap. Squire Watson, barking into a two-way radio, gets the spotlight snafu corrected.

Doris is next. She does not lose the baton at all, but in fact, moves flawlessly, and receives one shrill whistle as well as a good hand all around. Judi, in a bright green and pink outfit, is very well received with "Boys." She messes up a few lines, which troubles her, but no one else appears aware of the omission. Rose follows with her version of "The Spider and the Fly," the poem Evelyn Ay recited on her way to becoming Miss America 1954. Connie concludes the talent by doing a little dance in an outfit she has designed herself. The fans retire to the concession stands. The judges mark their ballots.

For the second act, Dick Ellis changes into a turtleneck; the Semanons welcome the show back with "My Funny Valentine." The stage, of course, offers a Valentine motif too. Everything is hearts, in red and white. Backstage, the girls, each with her own Jaycette in attendance, are changing into their swimsuits. Each first reaches for the sheer hose that Wendy has brought from Greensboro. Until recently, of course, no such item was permitted. Now, though, clear stockings are *de rigueur* for the swimsuit competition.

Judi begins to get into her suit, but somehow she catches the sheer hose on her identifying number—six—that is affixed, with a pin, to the left side of her swimsuit. She gasps as she sees that the sheer hose has not only come out of this encounter with a run, but that a huge hole is beginning to eat its way into the stocking at the thigh. Judi moans in anguish. Even if she wanted to buy some, she would not be able to, for there is not another pair of sheer hose in all of Wilson County.

Judi has only one extra pair of stockings with her. She just threw them in her traveling bag as she left the house. "I don't know why," she explained. "They were so dark, they were like colored people's." But Gay Butner, who has been summoned to the emergency, tells Judi to go ahead and put the stand-by pair on. Judi protests that her legs will look different standing next to all the sheer-hose legs, but Gay will not back down. Reluctantly, Judi gives in and starts to put on the dark stockings.

The Semanons strike up "You Were Meant for Me," and the swimsuit parade is on. Finished with their individual turns, the girls form a row. All eight of them stand, as they are supposed to, their feet at the traditional right angle, heel to ankle. Rita, bursting nicely in a shocking pink swimsuit, is particularly well received. Doris, convinced all along that she is too skinny, is, on the contrary, greeted with deserving whistles, and Judi gets a large, enthusiastic round of applause, too.

It is hard indeed to believe this, but not one keen-eyed judge in the place realizes that Judi is not wearing sheer hose!

Dick, offering a description that Atlantic City would surely find too sexy, asks the crowd to cheer for "our eight bathing beauties." There is a final enthusiastic response, as the judges mark their ballots.

While the girls return to their dressing cubicles to change for the evening-gown finale, Dick introduces the former Miss Wilsons. In another quick change he is now in black tie, and he troops the line of the past winners, chatting pleasantly with each of them, repeatedly praising the durability of their looks.

Backstage, Wendy decides at the last minute that she wants her hair up, and Betty Kay Herring rushes over to oblige. Then she moves to Doris, and asks if it is all right with her if Betty Kay takes her hair and shifts it around to the side. "Anything you want," Doris says, but Betty Kay draws back in shock. Doris' voice is hardly above a whisper. Her eyes peer out vacantly. She had been up early that morning, the first one to see Betty Kay at the motel to have her hair fixed. At the judges' luncheon, Doris had played with her food. What supper she had, she threw up. The show, under bright lights, has been going on for almost two hours. She is spent.

Doris struggles to get into her evening gown, and as she starts to put an arm into her sleeve, she suddenly begins to sway. Betty Kay grabs at her. "Doris, are you all right?" she cries.

"I feel so light-headed," Doris says. There is no color left in her face except for the make-up. She is weak. Onstage, Dick is now up to the queens in the late 1950s. It is not long before the contestants will be required back onstage.

Betty Kay and a Jaycette help Doris to a seat, and Betty Kay fans her with a book. She begins to come around a little. Another Jaycette rushes in with an ammonia ball, and gives it to Doris. They instruct her to carry it in her right hand, to remember it, and to thrust it to her face if she feels faint again. It seems to have revived her some, although she nods without expression.

Dick finishes speaking with the former Miss Wilsons, and they file back to their seats. Doris manages to get back on her feet. There is some blood back in her face. Before going onstage, she moves over and stands next to Judi. Betty Kay looks at them. "I just want to say," she says, "that I'm sure that one of you two is going to win, and I want to wish you both the best of luck."

Judi and Doris turn from her and look at each other. With her left hand, because the ammonia ball is clenched in the right, Doris reaches out and grabs Judi's hand. They murmur good-lucks. They would have clasped one another except for what it would have done to their make-up and everything.

The music for the finale is "Satin Doll," and the refrains go on and on, over and over, until all of the girls have walked the runway, done their turns, and come back to their seats. Backstage, everyone is staring at Doris. Just this last exertion seems to have drained her again. Once more, her face has lost its color.

She is seated, number five, immediately to the left of the empty throne, which holds stage center. Judi, number six, is the next girl over to Doris's left. Judi herself is slumping in her seat from fatigue. At least she had a ham sandwich for dinner. "Sit up, Judi," Betty Kay calls. "Back up. It's only a few more moments." Judi responds, mechanically, and restores a pasted smile to her face. "Put the ammonia to your nose now," Betty Kay whispers offstage to Doris, but she does not seem to hear and only stares ahead.

Killing time, as the judges mark their evening gown ballots, Dick begins to delve into his joke repertoire. At last, he is reprieved. He is presented the envelope with the judges' choices. He explains to the audience that as soon as he reads off the names of the three finalists, two will be taken backstage, where they cannot hear, while the third will remain behind to answer a question. Then, in turn, the other two will be brought back onstage and presented with the same question. Then the judges will vote for the winner and the two runners-up. Right now, Dick explains, the three finalists will simply be named in numerical order.

With all that straight, Dick takes the envelope, and with appropriate dramatic gestures opens it. He studies the contents, turns it over, and looks at it again. A puzzled frown crosses his face, and he says, "Wait, I'm not sure how this . . ." It is a personal reflex, but then he realizes he is still onstage, in charge, so he stops, straightens up, and proceeds boldly. "All right, here we go," Dick says. "The first finalist is . . . number one, Rita Deans."

Rita smiles happily, and the other seven girls have no trouble continuing their poses. Number one eliminates no one. Rita gets up and walks over to take her place in one of the three chairs by the side of the stage that are reserved for the finalists. Judi sighs. It is all going the way it figured. Next will be Doris, number five; then herself, number six.

Dick Ellis says, "The second finalist is . . . number two. . . ." Judi is staggered. "Wait," she thinks. "It has to be five. I don't even know who two is." ". . . Sharon Shackleford," Dick says. She rises and takes a seat next to Rita. Doris shows no reaction. Judi stiffens. She will not let her disappointment show. She knows they must call Doris's name next. She has lost. She mixed up the words to her song, and she tore her sheer hose. She permits only one small thought of consolation to cross her mind: at least now she won't have to stand up on the stage and answer some hard question.

Dick Ellis says, "And the third and last finalist is number five . . . Doris Smith." Some strength ebbing back by now, Doris rises and moves to join the other two finalists. Judi and the other losers all smile bravely. At his place on the aisle, Jerry Ball turns to confer briefly with Judy Cross, two seats away; then he bolts from his chair and dashes to the back of the auditorium.

Dick begins to explain the rules again. Swayn Hamlet comes out with the envelope that contains the question that the Jaycees have thought up. The question is: "In your opinion, what are some of life's greatest treasures?" Dick takes the envelope, still unopened, from Swayn, and turns to Sharon and Doris. Before he asks the question, to Rita first, they must leave the stage. Suddenly, down below in the front of the auditorium, there is noise, then, unmistakably, shouting. At first Dick ignores the distraction, hoping it will pass. But it does not, and at last Dick realizes that the voices sound official and are calling him.

"What?" he says, moving to the edge of the stage. "What? You're kidding. There's been a mistake? Oh, no! Everybody, hold on. There's been some kind of a mistake."

Judi and the other four leftovers cannot believe this good fortune. They all break into broad smiles. By contrast, Rita, Sharon, and Doris look puzzled, nearly indignant. Everyone else is bewildered, including Dick, who has no idea what is going on. He just knows he's stuck holding the stage. He starts telling jokes, the clean ones he had started off with the night before at the Essofleet truck stop. Nobody is paying much attention to him. There are murmurs everywhere. In the back of the hall, judges, Jaycees, and accountants are huddling together.

Time drags on. Dick starts introducing everybody he has not yet introduced who had anything to do with the show. That done, he tries another Essofleet joke. He is getting a little desperate until someone mercifully remembers that they haven't announced Miss Congeniality yet. Swayn brings the envelope out to Dick. He draws out the announcement, killing time. Doris has been voted Miss Congeniality by the other girls. She accepts the trophy happily, but, still bewildered, returns to her seat. She still is pale; at least, all this is giving her time to rest.

The cheers for Doris die down, and Dick is still stuck. Back to the Essofleet repertoire—and a little of the blue material. What would Jeanne Swanner do in a spot like this? The crowd is growing restless, more murmurs all the time. "So," Dick says, "the hillbilly says to him, 'How did you break your arm?' " Nobody is listening. Even Judi has stopped smiling. Dick says, "And he says, 'I fell off a commode.'" There are not even any titters. Gamely, Dick keeps on. "So he says, 'All I want to know is, what's a commode?'" A few people chuckle to be polite. The Semanons look around for a cue to strike up; perhaps "The Star-Spangled Banner"? The crowd is really getting a little annoyed now.

At last, Dick sees movement in the rear of the hall. He nearly runs to the front of the stage, and indeed, his valiant effort is done. Doris squeezes her ammonia ball; Judi tenses. Dick gets the explanation: the judges and accountants thought there would be five finalists, but Dick knew there were only supposed to be three. So when he got the envelope listing five, he had just assumed that the first three on the list were the top three. Actually, they were just the first three in numerical order. Now, to be fair, it was decided to forget a top three and work with a top five. "There will be two more finalists," Dick announces to the crowd. "They are, number six . . . Judi Brewer, and number eight . . . Connie Whisenant." Judi bursts forward at her name. Chairs are found for the two new finalists. Just what the Jaycees had vowed to avoid has happened—only three girls, forlorn and alone, have to sit by themselves as also-rans.

Now it runs quickly, though. Rita stays onstage, while the others depart, to come back and ponder, one by one, what might be some of life's greatest treasures. Rita says they are education, a wonderful man, and a houseful of children. Sharon suggests happiness, helping humanity everywhere, and making it possible for someone else to be happy too. Doris opts for being happy in what you are doing, being peaceful within yourself, and feeling that you are contributing to someone else. Judi, worn down by her cliffhanger, suggests only that you should be yourself and you can never go wrong. Connie thinks people to love is the answer.

Under the circumstances, there are no bad responses, only one inane question, and the judges wisely, sympathetically, disregard the whole exercise. As they make their final vote, though, poor Dick Ellis is left in the middle of the stage again.

This time, however, everyone is making sure that there will be no mistakes in tabulation. In a local *Miss America* Pageant once, it seems, the wrong girl was announced as the winner. When the sponsors came around to her the next day and asked her to relinquish the crown to the rightful winner, she just told them to buzz off, and slammed the door in their faces. In 1965, a re-check of the ballots for Miss Tan America showed that the wrong girl had been declared the winner. The officials let the result stand and quickly concocted the title of Miss Tan International for the true winner. Obviously, Wilson could afford no such luxury as Miss Wilson International. The votes are checked and rechecked, before, at last, the list of three winners is presented to Ellis.

He wastes no time with dramatics now, but reads out the names with dispatch. The second runner-up, he declares, is Rita Deans. Judi and Doris look straight ahead, smiling. After everything, it has come down to them, just as they always figured. Dick reads the name of the first runner-up. She rises proudly, almost sprightly it seems, despite her disappointment, to accept her trophy. Her tears do not come until a few minutes later, after the winner is named and they all have finished posing, and the balloons that the Jaycees put in a big net above have cascaded down to the stage on top of them all.

By late that night, the winner's trophy and the Miss Wilson coat of arms, the shield of blue and white, the motto of "beauty and everlasting faith," sit proudly on the mantel at the home of Miss Wilson 1970 at 1000 Vance Street.

★ 3 ★

Looking for Fanny Overhang

Of everything about Miss America, nothing becomes her quite so much as the system that commissions her, one that is so incredibly arbitrary, imperfect, and inconsistent that it fairly revels in its own whimsy. Judging a Miss America is the work of committee at its worst and individuals at their weakest. Quite appropriately, all of this is genially acknowledged by the people who work in pageants. Indeed, it is standard procedure for contestants in every Pageant to be briefed at the commencement of the competition that winning does not reflect any genuine verdict since "with a different group of judges a different girl would win every time."

By this bald-faced, shameless admission, or by any other measure, judging good-looking women is such a subjective discipline that any serious effort to obtain consensus is folly. Sympathetically, it may be said that a Miss America is selected every year only because the apparatus built to select her has no alternative. That is, legs are just long enough to reach the ground. As if the whole process were not nearly impossible to start with, the Pageant has also managed to insert artificial complications along the way.

For instance, different types of judges are usually found at the various different levels. Generally, this is upside-down, too, with the most inexperienced judges at Atlantic City, and the most seasoned ones at the lowest level. Not only that, but the formula for picking a winner remains the same through every vote until the penultimate one—when the 70,000 entries have been reduced to 10. Then, and only then, a whole new evaluation is introduced, which is exactly like running all Olympic 100-meter-trial races at 100 meters, taking all the final qualifiers on that basis, and then determining the 100-meter champion with a 150-meter race.

Personality, deemed to be the most important factor of all, is never officially judged. Instead, like a flask, it is passed around covertly to other areas, where the judges nip at it as they are so inclined. Thus, a girl who gets high points in the evening gown competition, or even swimsuit or talent, may really be gaining marks for her personality. One remembers Alice: "I can't explain *myself*, I'm afraid, because I'm not myself, you see." "I don't see," said the Caterpillar.

Nearly everybody accepts these failures and misrepresentations cheerfully, if only because no one has yet devised a better way—if indeed there can be an agreeable method in such a volatile field. Each Pageant is, in fact, marvelously cathartic. Once a queen is chosen, she is immediately accepted without complaint, as if she had been ordained in heaven. There is only a small amount of Monday-morning quarterbacking in pageantry, even if the judges have been blasphemed as biased or incompetent all week. A Miss America, or any beauty queen, is welcomed like a grandchild who arrives six months after the marriage. Everyone is mad at the process and the people responsible for her presence, but once she arrives, she is joyously acclaimed, and all the foregoing recrimination is promptly forgotten.

There is a truism among Pageant people that incompetent judges, of which there are seldom any other kind, it seems, will invariably botch up any Pageant, and select eight or nine semifinalists who are undeserving—but they will be touched by divine inspiration and always choose the one right girl. If she does not appear to be the right girl at this moment, she will eventually be revealed as such. Faith in this belief is somewhat self-serving, since most Pageant officials serve as judges themselves, but, more important, since everyone realizes that the whole system is tacitly capricious, even corrupt at its worst, the faith is required to justify devotion to the whole concept.

Miss America is selected by, formally, a very simple process. Judges usually vote for the top five in each division, thus crediting 5–4–3–2–1 in swimsuit and evening gown, and 10–8–6–4–2 for the top five in talent. During this preliminary period, the judges also meet with each girl for the one five-minute interview. When all the contestants have competed in all areas, the votes for them are tabulated. In a large field, such as the fifty at Atlantic City, the top ten vote-getters move on to the semifinals.

The judges—there are usually nine at Atlantic City, five elsewhere—never know, officially, how their co-Solomons are voting. (Neither does anybody else know except the CPAs who tabulate the ballots.) Anyway, all the primary votes are scrapped at this point, and everybody left starts out even again, with the ten girls competing strictly against each other in the same three categories—swimsuit, evening gown, and talent.

At the conclusion of these semifinal presentations, the judges are once again polled for their top fives. At the local and state levels the point distribution is identical to that in the preliminary, with talent marks counting double. In Atlantic City, however, a sudden arbitrary change in the scoring is made, and talent value is halved, counting the same as evening gown and swimsuit. The reason is pragmatic, if unfair to the girls who have been playing by another set of rules all along. It is more important for a Miss America to have looks and charm than talent. With talent weighted double in the scoring to the end, Atlantic City could end up with a winner who is a hot-shot performer but short on commercial charm. So, it hedges its bet at this point.

The semifinal ballots are counted, and a final five emerges. These girls neither perform nor model again. They are merely presented on stage for their last task, when, singly, they move forward and answer a few casual questions that the emcee asks them. During 1970 the procedure was modified so that the emcee is now merely required to chat pleasantly with the girl about herself, family, studies, hobbies, career. Previously, as at Wilson, each girl was asked The Question. This was a formal, stilted query either about love, God, country, or responsibility that never failed to leave every stomach in the house queasy. What are you looking for in a husband? If you were President of the United States, how would you help bring peace to the world? Who do you think is the greatest man in the world today, and why? One way or another, the answers had to be uniformly wretched.

Also, the procedure was unfair, since some of the questions were much easier to field than others. Many, for instance, required little more than a forthright approbation of peace or brotherhood. Religious girls who got ethics questions could deliver reflex stump speeches. Two of the last three winners, when the system was in force, were asked giveaway questions as to what advice they would give a younger sister. In the pre-TV era, the finalists were taken offstage and brought back, one by one, as they were at Wilson, whereupon they were all asked the same series of questions. That was both fair and instructive, but would have been bad TV.

The present arrangement is an improvement, especially since the whole purpose of the exercise is merely to find out whether a girl can think fast and talk well while on her feet. In 1970, for instance, Miss Mississippi answered only "yes" to a simple conversational question, and thereupon immediately destroyed any chance she had for victory. By this point in the proceedings, though, the judges have almost certainly made up their minds. Particularly as the system is now, a finalist cannot improve herself much; her answers can only be used against her. In any event, when all five girls have finished chatting with the emcee, the judges cast their final ballot, ranking the survivors. They base their decision strictly on the whole girl; how she fared in the individual categories is immaterial. Obviously, when it is down to the last five, how the girls impressed the judges in the personal interviews becomes the most important factor of all. The highest total vote wins, even if no one judge places the eventual winner first on his ballot.

Obviously, this formal process is unique and bizarre enough, simply by definition. But it is just a skeletal structure with so many loopholes that the actual procedures dictating the choice of a queen bear little or no relationship to those that are spelled out. There is even no agreement among judges as to the rather elementary question of whether they should be honest or not. One veteran Midwestern official declares, "You've got to manipulate. If you don't, you might lose your best girl on a fluke. Judges should talk things over all along, and if they're any good at all they should have it narrowed down to two or three girls after the first day or so. Then you can concentrate just on making sure. No Pageant can afford the luxury of a bunch of judges thinking by themselves. They're not out there to fall in love with a different girl each. They're out there to pick a winner."

A judge who has served on the Atlantic City panel disputes this view completely. "The one thing you shouldn't do is talk among yourselves. You do that, you turn it into a political convention. One judge can sway a whole panel—particularly if some of the people are inexperienced. Everyone is looking for guidance on a *Miss America* panel. You cannot let yourself be led. The only fair way is for each one to depend on his own instincts."

Ideally, a beauty panel should be of like mind in its manner of selecting a winner, but it should be composed of many different types of people, so that a full, rounded judgment is offered. In fact, however, at Atlantic City, judges who work in the arts predominate. A majority coalition at *Miss America* is virtually always formed by the producers, actors, singers, and dancers. There are few educators, and virtually no peers of the contestants. In the last decade only two out of one hundred one judges have been in their twenties. On the contrary, judges tend to be grandfatherly and grandmotherly types, which helps account for the fact that Miss America always seems to bear such a close resemblance to Wayne Newton.

Miss Americas always succumb to the vanity of babbling about how they "represent" youth. That is so much absurdity. Miss Congeniality, who is chosen by the other girls, could lay some claim to that contention, but Miss America represents no more than what the older generation thinks youth should represent. Through no fault of her own, she is a puppet of middle-aged values. Even the big-name judges at Atlantic City—up to three of the usual nine panelists each year are celebrities of some note—are typically outdated, with a fame that means something to the adults who run the show, but not to the kids who are putting themselves on the line: Ted Mack, the late Mimi Benzell, Fran Allison, Vincent Price, Norton Mockridge. The best-known male musicians to serve on the Pageant in the 1960s were two old men—Arthur Fiedler and Donald Voorhees—who are least identified with youth and its music. The leading actresses chosen were Joan Crawford (when Pepsi-Cola was a sponsor), June Allyson, and Arlene Dahl. The *most* contemporary celebrities invited to appear in the course of the last decade would probably be: Hal David, Jim Aubrey, Ed McMahon, and David Merrick, and they are all, significantly, younger in spirit than in actual age.*

The state *Miss America* organizations are generally opposed to the national judges—not so much because they are old fogies, but because they are so often inexperienced. The really dedicated judges, like Jerry Ball, those who officiate at dozens of local and state pageants every year, are never invited to Atlantic City. The argument runs that a judge who participated in, say, the selection of Miss West Virginia, would be prejudiced for her if he had to consider her candidacy again at Atlantic City. There is also another attitude that militates against the choice of these qualified old pros. They have too much expertise for their own good. Judges at the lower levels tend to be more technical. They are authorities on all sorts of body details—neck posture, hand placement, clavicle extension—that the novices at Atlantic City know nothing about, much less how to judge them. The national Pageant doesn't want to get hung up on this kind of minutiae. It wants a queen who can get in and out of an Oldsmobile gracefully.

Says the official of one small state pageant: "Atlantic City really uses the states. They make us count talent all along at a double rate, so they have a better chance of coming up with some good acts for their TV show. Then, as soon as they have that, they knock down talent and try to fix it so they'll end up with a sweet little thing that is just right for the sponsors." Several states have secretly begun going against the rules that Atlantic City requires they follow, and running the state pageants just as Atlantic City runs the national one—with talent counting only one-third in the semifinal tabulations. They figure that a girl has a better chance at *Miss America* if she has already won under *Miss America* rules and qualifications.

The change in the weighting of point values is something of a

* See Appendix 1, p. 297.

manipulation. There is, however, no evidence that *Miss America* has ever been fixed in any traditional way. Nor is there any evidence that the judges have ever used the power of their votes to extract favors from the girls; nor that the girls have used the powers of their favors to extract votes. At *Miss America* there is not even the breath of a fix anywhere in the past. One Pageant official does recall that several years ago he had a straight-out inquiry from a man who wanted to know how much it would cost to fix the title for Miss Florida. He laughed at the man. There is no way conceivable to fix *Miss America* from the outside and no motive for the Pageant to be crooked on the inside.

Nowadays, not unlike a jury that is locked up at night, the judges are isolated in one hotel and kept apart from all Pageant proceedings except those that directly involve them. This removes them from even subtle, informal pressures, which they sometimes received during the more than thirty years that Lenora S. Slaughter ran the Pageant. A strong and outspoken lady, Miss Slaughter ruled through 1967, and she occasionally made it plain to the judges with which girl her sentiments rested. Especially when the Pageant was basically a one-woman operation, Miss Slaughter could wield a large, sympathetic influence, telling the judges things like: "It's easy for you to vote for Miss X, but you're not going to have to work with her all year, or travel with her."

Whether Miss Slaughter's bruising hints had any effect on the judges is open to question. Certainly, she suffered many setbacks, most notably when Colleen Hutchins became Miss America 1952. Lenora favored a beautiful North Carolinian, Lu Long Ogburn, and at first appeared only bemused by Colleen, Miss Utah, who stood nearly six feet tall, and well over that in heels. She said things like: "I know you can't pick that big Mormon. She's even taller than I am." Later, as Miss Slaughter realized Colleen had genuine support, she grew even more expressive, an overt lobbying that may well have backfired against Lu Long. She finished third, and when Colleen was announced as the winner Lenora nearly broke into tears backstage.

Judges themselves are spared individual criticism because their votes are never disclosed. Nevertheless, even though they do not have to explain themselves and they receive no compensation beyond reimbursement of expenses and stout and gracious hospitality, they take the assignment seriously. In the modern era, no judge has ever been disqualified, although once, back in the 1950s, a beloved TV personality handled the job with such disdain and indolence that the other judges almost requested that all his ballots be voided. One night, he sat reading *The New Yorker* during the whole show. The one judge to have suffered some attack was Bennett Cerf, in 1958. Within earshot of a *Time* magazine reporter he made the mistake of idly inquiring at a judges' luncheon one day, "Do you think they're all certified virgins?"

The next week, when the remark was printed, it drew the ire of the whole State of Mississippi, whose queen, Mary Ann Mobley, had been named Miss America 1959. For reasons that are not clear, the Magnolia State took Cerf's general remark as a specific indictment of Mary Ann, though certainly her credentials of virtue were beyond dispute. She had not been allowed to date until she was sixteen and had used the occasion of her first trip to New York to go hear Norman Vincent Peale preach. Cerf was a bit hard for Mississippi to get at, but for being a party to his slander, Time Inc. suffered the cancellation of some Mississippi advertising that had already been placed.

In years such as Mary Ann's, when one girl is an overwhelming choice, and there is no real dispute, judges usually let on afterward that they personally voted for the winner. As a general practice, judges do not reveal their selections, nor is it considered proper etiquette to ask them how they voted. The votes are audited, the whole panel's choices are announced, and then the ballots and score sheets are sealed up in a bank vault, where they are forever beyond the sight of all but God. Apparently, the only time that the ballots were ever exhumed for re-examination came in 1956, when a girl named Carol Morris was voted Miss Universe in Long Beach, California. Carol Morris had been Miss Iowa at Atlantic City two years previously. Although *Miss America* absolutely never divulges the order of finish of the also-rans from eleventh place on, in this instance the special check of the 1954 ballots was made, so that a vengeful declaration could be issued that Miss Universe had been only fourteenth in *Miss America*.

Because judges are immune to disclosure, they have a license to contrive ballots that not only work for the girl of their honest choice, but against the girl considered to be her main competition. Apparently, this pushmepullyou voting is an old and widespread swindle. It works this way. Say there is a ballerina among the judges, and another judge assumes she will give first place to a dancer. The other judge is for a classical singer, so, even though he believes the dancer is a second best, he rates her fifth. The ballerina is doing the same thing with the classical singer. Then everybody always wonders how the innocuous little sweetie who played "Lady of Spain" on the accordion won.

The system works harshly against the girl with strong character and encourages the celebration of mediocrity. In the finals, a girl with three first-place votes (15 points) and two fifth-place votes (2 points) totals 17 and can be beaten by a girl who gets no first-place votes at all, but is a simple compromise choice with three seconds (12 points) and two thirds (6 points) for an 18 total. This sort of thing happens fairly regularly. In fact, it is said that one of the recent Miss Americas was a strict compromise choice. The girl who finished second was strong in every category, including confidence. When the competition had been narrowed down to the two girls and they sat there awaiting the announcement, the little compromise turned to the strong girl and offered her congratulations. "Thank you," she replied without doubt. Then the announcement was made that the judges had played it safe and voted for the bland compromise. It would be fairer, as well as reduce some of the abuses built into the system, if only first-place votes were used to select a Pageant winner.

Ballot balancing is no new ploy, though, being a nearly acceptable form of skulduggery that dates back to the mid-1930s. Until then, the judges' panels were homogeneous gatherings that were composed almost exclusively of male artists. When other men, and even women, were invited to judge, the artists viewed the newcomers as intruders to their domain. "Sure," says Russell Patterson, the creator of the Flapper look, who judged nine times at Atlantic City before he and all artists fell out of Miss Slaughter's graces for good after World War II, "sure, if we thought the others were pushing another girl, we'd all compensate and mark her low. That's where all that started. When we knew the others were grouping up on the artists, we fought like hell against them. Anyway, it was all over as soon as Lenora brought the women judges in. They'll kill anything sexy. They all like the mousy type."

Women judges—particularly pretty women judges—are pickier than their male counterparts as a rule. They are more likely to seek defects and mark off in swimsuit and evening gown, whereas men tend to look for positive factors. "I look at the parts of the body," one female judge says; "most men look at a body." Whereas almost all judges would prefer to meet the contestants in interview first, so that they can assess them as individuals right away, some women judges would ideally rather see the girls in swimsuit first. "You might as well know the truth right away," one says. "If she's got bad legs or a scar on her knee, then you can cross her off. If evening gown comes first you might have wasted points on her. It also can affect your talent consideration, especially at the state level where you have some choice. Say she plays the piano. Well, at Atlantic City there's going to be girls who play the piano who don't have bad legs or a scar, so there's no sense sending somebody like that on just to get beat. Talented ugly girls finish runner-up."

Experienced judges look for proportion first of all. A big bust is more of a detriment than an advantage in beauty pageantry. Till recently, a 10-inch hourglass, 34–24–34 or 35–25–35, was considered perfect, but now, 12-inch is the usual model: 36–24–36, for instance. Technical judges look for firm bosoms, shoulders that do not slope to one side (which is natural in most people) and which are not too wide. Necks should not be stiff, nor too long or short—especially they should not be too short. Wing-bones, or any kind of bony back, count off heavily. A girl should glide, not walk, with her arms moving attuned to her movement. When she stands for inspection, her thighs should touch, just so, but there should be a space visible between her knees and her calves, and again between her calves and her ankles—shorter girls may be excused the knee-calf opening.

The most critical area of all, though, is the bottom, including the suburban thighs. A broad beam or meaty thighs count off heavily, and even if a girl works hard to rid herself of these infirmities she can still be penalized harshly for retaining the dreaded Fanny Overhang. The emphasis that knowledgeable judges place on the derrière is obvious; they reserve their most brutal and cryptic comments for this area. "If someone asked her to haul ass, it would take two trips," is a typical expression of the argot. A judge who notes "BFCB" on his pad next to a girl's name is using judges' shorthand for "Built for Child Birth." More simple designations include P (Plowhorse), T (Turkey), and FB (Fullback, from football). A complete over-all loser merits YGTBK (You got to be kidding).

The women, for the most part, judge swimsuit by the book, granting some personal expressions of natural vanity. A short, busty judge is indeed likely to look with favor upon a short, busty contestant. What fantasies may enter the men's heads is another thing altogether. Talent is alleged to be the keystone of the modern pageant—and, remember, it is weighted double in value—but despite this fact and all the accompanying propaganda, the winners are still the bathing beauties. Since all Atlantic City panels and most others possess a male majority, it is certainly possible to postulate that there is some correlation between these points. The last three Miss Americas—1969, 1970, 1971—all won swimsuit preliminaries. For the last two years, the one-two finishers both won preliminary swimsuit trophies.* Women regulars at the 1970 Pageant were stunned when, on separate nights, Miss Texas and Miss South Carolina won swimsuit despite technically unacceptable heavy upper legs. Miss South Carolina had not even won swimsuit in her state pageant.

Why the girls won became quite obvious Saturday night, when they finished one-two in the whole competition. Transparently, the male judges were voting their taste in women, with no regard for swimsuit minutiae. "The whole trouble with male judges," a female judge says, "is that they can look right at a fanny and not even see the fanny overhang." Sex is a very ambivalent feature of *Miss America.* Discredited, and supposedly an insignificant ingredient, in fact, it rears its ugly head and often decides matters.

Of course, no man, or woman either, will admit that he is

* See Appendix 2, p. 297.

less than expert in the matter of judging a female body. There may be divergent viewpoints about what determines a quality body, but at least all profess competence and confidence in their judgment. Talent, however, is a baffling and humbling exercise. To compare singers, pianists, actresses, dancers, artists, and other miscellaneous performers is fairly impossible. Besides, few judges have any critical expertise in any more than one or two talent areas, and unbalanced knowledge can be an unfair thing. For instance, a judge who is a pianist may be inclined to vote for a contestant who plays the piano. On the other hand, he is also capable of being more critical, and will be excessively harsh on a piano performance while giving high marks, say, to a flashy dancer whose presentation is just as flawed, but which he has no background to evaluate.

Because judges are so unsure of themselves, they tend to smorgasbord ballots—one dancer, one piano player, one popular singer, one classical singer, one drama performer. In the preliminaries their selections of an earlier evening can intimidate later choices. If a violinist wins talent on the first night, the chance of another violinist winning on a later program is sharply reduced, even though she may be more competent. Judges do not want to be tagged as "violin judges" or "dancer judges." The issue is slanted further because a great many judges, despite themselves, are prejudiced against certain talents. Baton-twirlers, for instance, are usually dismissed as second-class citizens. One or two usually make it to Atlantic City every year, but none has ever won. Some old-line judges have little more stomach for artists or athletes. There was an undercurrent of discontent in 1968 when Judi Ford, a trampolinist, was elected Miss America. To many Pageant conservatives it seemed that the judges had gone slumming.

"I simply can't stand any of that," a lovely lady judge from the South admits. "I can't even bring myself to vote for the little things who bring their paintings or clothes they've made. Artists have their own competitions and sewing is a hobby or a business. It is not a talent for the stage. Now this one time, I won't tell you where, because I think they're still looking for me, I came into this little town and as soon as I got there, I knew there was trouble because the Jaycees already had their winner picked out. We judges were merely there to confirm it, you see.

"They were already discussing how she'd do at State. I said, 'Well, what does this little angel do for her talent?' And now, if you can believe this, they told me that she fly casted. I said, 'Do you mean to tell me . . . fish?' They said yes indeed, she fly casted, and Lord, they said, if she ever got to Atlantic City fly casting on that huge stage where she didn't have to concern herself with hooking anything—that alone was enough for me. And let me tell you honestly, she was the prettiest girl there, she was darlin' in swimsuit, she was easily the smartest, and to tell you the truth she fascinated me to death flickin' that big ole pole around once I was assured that there was no hook on it.

"But I don't mind tellin' you that if it's the Virgin Mary herself that I'm judgin', if she is a fly caster, honey, I just can't bring myself to vote for her in any *Miss America* Pageant. Luckily, I found a couple of the other judges felt as I did, and we stuck together and voted for a little singer, bless her heart, and gave the fly caster, poor thing, first runner-up. Well, there was such a hue and cry after that that the Jaycees said we judges had better not go to the after-party. In fact, they took us out to some deserted railroad station and held us there for a few hours till the heat was off. They told us, honest to goodness, that the fly caster's father and his friends were irate. But I just can't vote for any fly caster. I'm sorry, but I just can't, lovely as she was."

A contestant who fills out a bathing suit well enough and who also performs with an acceptable talent would appear to be a serious contender. She has, however, only passed the ritual phase of the competition. Winners are determined by considerations that are nearly subliminal. A new judge once asked Lenora what he should look for in a Miss America. "Honey," she replied, "just pick me a lady." In more modern terminology, that would be *a girl with poise.* As every judge in beauty pageantry maintains, poise is the key that unlocks the title. That is fine and dandy so far as it goes; unfortunately while every judge swears that he is seeking *a girl with poise,* there is not the least agreement as to what constitutes poise.

By different judges, in no particular order, poise is defined as: the evidence of good breeding; the way a girl takes care of herself and her appearance; femininity, with character; you can see it when you look in her eyes; the ability to handle any situation in good taste; carriage, that's all, really; style and grace, with just the right amount of confidence; something you are born with that can't be described, but you can see it; etc.

While most judges think that the best place to see poise is in the eyes, others uncover it in the way a girl walks or sits and talks. Poise reveals itself in many mysterious ways. A veteran female judges reports, "You must look at the feet first, because that is going to determine the bone structure, and if you don't have good bone structure, you cannot walk well, and if you cannot walk well, you cannot possess poise."

Anyway, whatever the poise bone is connected to, it is the singular ingredient that every *Miss America* judge at every level is searching for. Swimsuit counts 25 per cent, evening gown counts 25 per cent, talent counts 50 per cent, and poise counts approximately 800 per cent. Luckily, since poise is strictly in the eye of the beholder, there is usually plenty to go around. Poise is a marvelous catchall. Whatever a judge likes in a girl, he calls it poise and satisfies himself and everyone else. Determining poise is a very private thing. Nobody ever argues about whether a contestant possesses it, because when a judge says that he has found *a girl with poise* all the others realize that is a code. It means: "I love you," or, "You have my vote."

The trouble is, there is no ballot for poise, just as there is none for personality, charm, intelligence, or any of the other vital characteristics that are revealed in the five-minute interview. The trick, then, is how to distribute nonexistent Poise and Personality (P and P) points into areas where real points are given. The situation is somewhat akin to attaching riders to congressional bills that have nothing whatsoever to do with the bill, although in the case of *Miss America* the P and P riders often overwhelm the stated bill.

The easiest place to dispatch P and P Points is in the evening-gown competition, an arrangement Atlantic City encourages by scheduling a group's interviews on the afternoon before they perform in evening gown. Except for the experienced judges, who check necks, wingbones, and glide styles, evening gown is devilishly difficult to judge in itself since almost every girl looks lovely when she is so attired. If other considerations were not permitted, it would be almost impossible to settle on one winner. As it is, the evening-gown winner is not even revealed, which gives the judges all the more informal authorization to make determinations on any basis they choose. This means that the evening-gown competition produces a winner who is not disclosed, voted on by judges who do not have to disclose their votes, and with reasons that are not disclosed, except that they have very little to do with evening gowns.

Few of the contestants themselves are deceived by the processes that determine their lot. Particularly they appreciate that the interview, tucked away in a hotel conference room, private and quick, means as much, or more, than all the hoopla that goes on stage and television. Of all the girls ever to appear in *Miss America,* one of the most distinctive was Jeanne Swanner, the famous Miss North Carolina 1963. She was by far the tallest and largest contestant ever to appear in Atlantic City, standing 6 feet, 2 inches, weighing 160, and measuring 39–25–39. She is intelligent, articulate, and blessed with great wit, if with no particular standard stage ability. For her talent Jeanne sang, accompanying herself on the ukulele—either that or she played the ukulele, accompanying herself by singing. She was from the little country town of Graham, and she went to the North Carolina Pageant with no illusions.

"I had no inkling of winning," Jeanne says. "I went there to have fun because I figured that there was just no way for the judges to vote for girls who were as different as I am. I was halfway through the week before it even occurred to me that I had a chance. It was simply that I met the judges and they liked me. That's all there is to it. I told them they could call me Highpockets, and they laughed, and we joked together, and I left that room and I knew that they liked me. That was all in the world. They liked me. I left and I thought, 'Hey Jeanne, they really like you. You can win this thing as well as anybody else.'

"Well, I went to Atlantic City in the same frame of mind. I gave myself no chance. . . ."

(An experienced North Carolina judge says, "She didn't have a prayer. The state judges knew that when they chose her. Usually, you send what you think Atlantic City wants. We're like everybody else. We're scared to do anything else. So we send a pretty, talented girl up there and she wins a talent award. That one year, the judges had guts. They said to hell with it, we'll send the best ambassadress we can find, and that's what Jeanne was. If those judges up there had been willing to take the same chance, they'd had the best Miss America ever. But the state judges knew when they sent her they'd never even consider her.")

Jeanne continues, ". . . But by now I knew how it worked. Who knows. Maybe the judges there would like me too. It's all straight luck. If there had been just one little man on the state panel, I wouldn't have won. One little bully man who was threatened by a tall girl, and I had no chance. I never had a chance to be deceived at Atlantic City, though. My group had swimsuit the first night. Fourteen of the eighteen of us had won swimsuit at our states, but the judges picked one of the four girls who hadn't. They had found what they wanted. The rest of us could have gone home at that point. They voted that girl right along into the finals.

"But at least until I had my interview the next day I thought I might have some hope. I was in that room for thirty seconds when I knew I was going nowhere. They just didn't like me. I don't know if my being tall had anything to do with it. That doesn't matter. All that counts is they didn't like me. They don't need any reasons. No wonder men find pageants so dull now. It's all decided in a little room, and then everybody wonders why the good-looking girls on the stage don't get anywhere."

At the time Jeanne was interviewed, girls were seen by the judges in Atlantic City in trios. (That system began in 1961 and ended in 1969.) Now that the girls are confronted individually, the interview is more pointed, if no more scientific. A friendly Coke party for the judges and girls follows the afternoon's conversations, but often the formal interview itself is not much more than cocktail chatter. After her interview in 1970, Miss California searched for the ultimate put-down, at last sputtering, "Why, I've even had more serious discussions with newspapermen. They can't possibly know anything about me."

Most of the contestants enjoy the interview, though, if only because they receive much easier treatment from the judges than they anticipated. The judges themselves think that the little conversational workout is sufficient to gain a fair evaluation of the girls. "Sure it's short," says one experienced Atlantic City judge, "but you can see what you have to in five minutes. Look, if you're a baseball scout, it only takes five minutes to decide how well a guy can pick up ground balls at shortstop."

The judges usually do make an effort to insert at least one controversial question if the colloquy becomes too fluffy. The stockpile of controversial questions includes such old stand-bys as Vietnam, the generation gap, or interracial dating, or fresher conundrums, such as Vice President Agnew, drugs, or Women's Lib. In the time allotted, there can be no effort made to probe a girl's views. The judges are only seeking to discover if she speaks clearly, forthrightly, if she can construct good arguments and defenses, and if she is reasonably well informed. It is said that at the height of the Korean War one gorgeous Southern girl had Miss America locked up until she expressed total ignorance of the 38th parallel. At least with the new system, whereby each girl is interviewed head-on, judges have a more reasonable chance of divining a contestant's awareness. The last queen to be selected from group interview was Pam Eldred, 1970. The day following her coronation, she met with the press and replied, "I really couldn't voice an opinion—I don't know enough about that," in response to questions about the following diverse topics: drugs, U.S. priorities, nudity in the theater, student unrest, unisex fashions, and the vote for eighteen-year-olds.

Judges try hard now to select the most mature queens. Girls who have not yet reached college have little chance at victory on the local levels, and virtually none at Atlantic City. Actually, it is hardly an issue there any more, because the local and state judges are simply refusing to vote mere high-school graduates on into the national Pageant. Since 1965, no more than six of the fifty contestants in any one year came without college credentials. It has been a full decade since a noncollege girl won. Nancy Fleming, Miss America 1961, had graduated from high school only three months before she was elected, while her successor, Maria Fletcher, 1962, had graduated a year previous to her crowning but had then spent a year in Manhattan as a Rockette. That would just never do nowadays. If Dorothy Parker and Madame Curie came back together, reincarnated in the lean, supple body of Ali MacGraw, with the voice of Joan Baez, and the magic feet of Dame Margot Fonteyn, in the form of a girl who had just graduated from high school, the judges at State would advise her to try again after a couple of years of maturing at college.

As a rule, the judges at Atlantic City are more gentle with the girls in interview than many of the cagey old pros at the lower levels. Vincent Price, among recent national judges, had the worst reputation among the contestants; he was known as mean and tricky. A celebrity, merely by his presence, can fluster the girls. A former Miss New Jersey recalls, "It was all very sweet, and then they asked so nicely, 'Now, would you like to ask us a question?' and here I am looking straight at Joan Crawford, and I know damn well that there is no question in the world that Joan Crawford could possibly be interested in hearing from me."

Never at Atlantic City, and only rarely at the lower levels, do the judges resort to bluffs and deceits to catch the girls off guard. Most judges are too nice and enjoy the girls too much ever to get tough or original in the interviews. Some judges have, however, feigned rudeness or contentiousness to see how a girl reacted. One judge liked to call a girl by a wrong name to see if the contestant had courage enough to correct her. At Atlantic City in 1970, several of the girls reported that one judge would mention how much she was looking forward to hearing them perform—when she already had. Whether she was being devious or ignorant is unknown. Other gimmicks are to ask a girl to say goodby in three different moods, or, quickly, "Who are you? What are you?" The oldest chestnut of all is to ask a girl to describe what kind of person she is. Mostly, however, and particularly at Atlantic City, it is just a few ground balls hit toward shortstop that really decide who Miss America will be.

Nevertheless, there is no evidence that the present quixotic, free-form method is not the best. At various times, for instance, *Miss America* has instituted strict point systems for the judges, but they have proved to be hopelessly confining. As early as

1923, when the seventeen artist judges included Norman Rockwell, James Montgomery Flagg, and Howard Chandler Christy, this severe 100-point body breakdown was utilized:

construction of head:	15 points
eyes:	10
hair:	5
nose:	5
mouth:	5
facial expression:	10
torso:	10
legs:	10
arms:	10
hands:	10
grace of bearing:	10

Careful dedication to all this mumbo-jumbo—including "grace of bearing," which is almost surely a forerunner of poise—produced exactly the same Miss America as the year before, when less precise meters were employed. Still, as late as 1935, judges were required to provide explicit body and personality marks. The present grading system began in 1938, when talent was introduced as a competitive factor, on equal terms with swimsuit and evening gown. Not until 1941, however, were judges even required to attend all the preliminaries, and it was in 1960, as the demands of television grew, that talent was doubled in value.

The interviews have been part of the proceedings from the first. Mary Katherine Campbell, the second Miss America, in both 1922 and 1932, has said, "The strange part is that the only thing different now is the talent part. We had to do all the other things—have people judge our personalities and so forth—that they do now." In those early days, the judges were permitted to talk with the girls on a more informal basis, usually at meals, but as early as 1936 the finalists were required to meet individually with the judges before the latter could vote on a queen.

That same year, to help break up the judges' cliques, a ruling was established, wistfully, that judges could not confer about their choices. The judges have never been required to divulge their personal selections, although in the earlier years the total vote was sometimes disclosed, occasionally with a spectacular if maladroit flourish. In 1925, for instance, the finalists met with the judges at Atlantic City High School on the morning of the last day of competition. They were carefully examined, and then their number was reduced to two secret titlists.

Each of the fifteen judges then voted for one of the two girls, placing his ballot in a large golden apple, made out of an unidentified substance. The apple was held under guard all day, then escorted to the Million-Dollar Pier on the Boardwalk, where the plan was to open it, draw out the ballots one by one, and tabulate them on a blackboard as the suspense built. The reigning Miss America normally would have been accorded the apple-breaking honor, but, in a dispute, she had refused to return to the World's Playground, so the esteemed duty fell to the local queen, Miss Atlantic City.

Alas, she was a frail lass; or it was a hard apple. Miss Atlantic City thumped it four times, straining inelegantly at the end, but without success. At last, one of the heftier judges came to her aid, and smashed the apple to smithereens with one solid blow. The result was anticlimactic. The two finalists turned out to be Miss California and Miss Los Angeles, who had already competed against each other for the state title. Once again Miss California won with ease, 12–3, and after this landslide vote, apples were retired from the proceedings. Judges, however, remain as necessary evils.

4

How to Be 36-24-36 in a Swimsuit

While no major changes are anticipated in the judging system, a strange alliance has been formed to remove swimsuit from the Pageant. This would not only drastically affect the whole judging process, but it would alter every aspect of the Pageant and threaten to drain it of its life blood. The abolishment of the bathing suit can logically be expected, however, for it would be the natural conclusion of the whole modest drift of *Miss America*. It began as a stated revue of bathing beauties on the beach fifty years ago. After a quarter century, the word "bathing" was literally banished from the Pageant vocabulary as a shameful, misleading word. For the bathing suit itself to be cast out after another quarter century is a nearly predictable extension—despite whatever diversionary concessions the Pageant might make to bare midriffs and skirt lengths, and despite the fact that society at large displays a greater tolerance to near-nudity, even to total nudity.

Actually, the Pageant has never been very earthy. In sexual matters, it has settled for a pale imitation of the reality around it. For instance, in the first year, 1921, there was a city ordinance that prohibited any display of nude limbs, but, joining in the spirit of the promotion, the Atlantic City constables just made sure that nobody was watching them as they watched whenever any of the more daring beauties rolled down their stockings on the beach to reveal dimpled knees to the sun. Later, all in the name of art, of course, and in glorification of the perfect female form, quick-fingered judges found it imperative that they measure the contestants themselves.

Two-piece bathing suits were not at all uncommon on contestants in the 1940s, and the official poses that the girls took, for Pageant publicity, were revealing, if not downright provocative. Learning from Hollywood pin-ups, *Miss America* contestants were often pictured in the classic breasts up-and-out, head back, hands-back-of-the-neck-come-on shot. Others looked from sultry quarter-turns, with hands on hips. The Pageant countenanced others appearing in head-on poses, standing or kneeling with hands on knees so that the camera was invited to peer anxiously down into the cleavage. A few even encouraged more enticing views by drawing their elbows up and forcing their breasts out in an old stripper's stance.

The Pageant itself participated in the tease by giving its queens tantalizing marquee titles. Jo-Carroll Dennison, 1942, became "The Texas Tornado," Jean Bartel, 1943, was christened "The California Coed," Venus Ramey, 1944, was tabbed, of course, "The Modern Venus." It all helps to lend a certain amount of credence to this glib contention made by Dr. David Reuben in his best seller, *Everything You Always Wanted to Know about Sex and Were Afraid to Ask:* "Predictably, strippers don't get much other sexual satisfaction. They usually have trouble attaining orgasm and never find much real pleasure in genital sex. The same holds true in general for beauty queens. Their activities have more social approval, but the game is the same. They show off their breasts, hips, bottoms and a discreet outline of the vulva (through a bathing suit) to admiring men. Miss Artichoke . . . has a lot in common with Bubbles La Tour and her Magic Balloons."

Bess Myerson, in 1945, held the first Miss America scholarship, presumably because she was so talented musically, but Miss Myerson has often credited a tight bathing suit with playing a large part in her victory. She wanted to wear a size 34 white suit, which she felt did the most for both her figure and her tan, but her hostess was a bit put off by the tight fit and suggested Bess wear a lime-colored size 36. She appeared in this suit at an impromptu veterans' hospital show that was staged the day before the Pageant officially began. "They hooted and hollered at the other girls," Bess said. "When I passed they politely flipped their hands together."

Back at her hotel that night, Bess conferred with her two sisters, and it was decided that Sylvia, who was a size 36, would sleep in the white 34 to stretch it just a bit. This Sylvia did, but the next morning they still couldn't get the straps to fit Bess, so her sisters sewed the straps shut. Bess had to wear the suit under her evening gown and other performing clothes when she was sewn back into it for the competition. She was a smashing victor.

As late as 1953, a contestant's official photograph for the Pageant showed her in a bathing suit, and even a few years past this time it was not considered untoward for girls to pose before the judges, hands on hips, and then throw a come-hither glance over the shoulder at them. By contrast, many contestants today are frightened by having to walk down a runway in a swimsuit. Many perspire heavily, shake, gag, or even throw up. A state Pageant that is televised is not permitted to show the girls on TV in their bathing suits without special sanction from Atlantic City. As it is, to spare the poor girls embarrassment, hardly more than half the state pageants even request such authorization. Albert A. Marks, Jr., a stockbroker who as chairman of the executive committee is the top Pageant official, is firmly on record forecasting the demise of the swimsuit competition at *Miss America*, and since Miss Slaughter departed, whatever Marks has first hinted has ultimately been transformed into fact in almost every instance.

The Pageant first started on the warpath against the bathing suit after World War II. The first serious blow in behalf of modesty came in retaliation to the artists, who made their last strong stand for sex in 1946, according to Russell Patterson. "We had sort of a revolt against talent that year," he says. "This was when the rubber bathing suit came out, and we picked the girl with the best of everything showing." That was Marilyn Buferd, Miss California, who went on to enjoy a limited film career. Subsequently, though, Miss Slaughter began packing the judges' panel with more genteel types. "I always had trouble with those artists," she says. "All they ever saw was legs, and I was a Baptist and my board was Quakers."

Nineteen forty-six was also the year when Lenora heard E.B. Stewart, the president of Catalina, the bathing suit firm that was one of *Miss America*'s sponsors, roar on one occasion, "It's not a bathing suit, dammit. You bathe in a tub. You swim in a swimsuit." Lenora liked this definition and promptly decreed that thereafter there would be no such thing as bathing suits at *Miss America.* There is not, to this day. Girls wear swimsuits in the swimsuit competition.

But live by the sword, die by the sword. E.B. Stewart should have known that once you banish one word from the vocabulary, it is not hard to banish another. Five years later, the missing word was Catalina. When Yolande Betbeze, Miss America 1951, refused to pose in a bathing suit, Lenora supported her, and Catalina abandoned *Miss America* and started Miss Universe.

In the interim, Miss Slaughter had greased the skids for this ultimate detachment by taking away the swimsuit's most important publicity gimmick. She decided to have Miss America crowned in, of all things, an evening gown. (Evening *dress,* by the way, is considered just as improper terminology as bathing suit.) In point of fact, Miss America 1933, Marian Bergeron, had been crowned in a gown, but the Pageant that one year was run under a management that was subsequently discredited and the precedent had been forgotten when Lenora approached the Convention Hall photographers in 1947 and informed them of her plan. They balked at the proposition and bluffed her out of it, telling her no self-respecting newspaper would run such a ridiculous picture. In tears, when the photographers even threatened to take down their lights, Miss Slaughter withdrew her edict.

The next year, however, she made up her mind that America was ready for a well-draped queen, and stood her ground when the photographers began their charade of taking down their lighting apparatus. They were there in their usual force later that evening when BeBe Shopp was crowned Miss America 1948 in a decorous long dress. Of course, it also happened that she was surrounded by her four runners-up, who were all garbed in gauche zebra-striped bathing suits. And it remains one of the psalms of the Pageant that late that night, as the lights dimmed in Convention Hall, members of the photography corps, heads bowed, feet shuffling, approached Lenora, and, each in his own apologetic way, mumbled, "You were right. *Now*, this is the kind of Pageant where I would be proud to let my own daughter compete."

Miss America's increased embarrassment with the bathing suit has been accompanied by a parallel decline in the enforcement of what is permitted underneath the suit. Put another way: at first the pageant did not care what kind of suit you wore as long as it was all you wore; but now, the Pageant polices only the kind of suit you wear, without regard for what kind of contraband may be required to hold it up. Once the demand was for bold honesty, now for modest deceit. Morals to the story are optional.

At first, padding or more complicated construction was banned absolutely. Many of the contestants were unaware of the existence of sophisticated accessories, while others assumed that no girl with any pride in her figure would stoop to such subterfuge. Certainly, if there was any conniving taking place in the early years, few were very adept at it, as these measurements indicate: 30–25–32, 32–26½–37½, 32–26–36. (The figures cited all belong to Miss Americas.) It was 1939 before a queen's bust was larger around than were her hips and before a Miss America could boast of a bust measurement of more than 35 inches.

Miss America 1927, Lois Delander, says that contestants were physically tape-measured by the judges her year, and it is possible that this sort of shenanigans also took place in 1925 and 1926—though there is no evidence that the technique was applied either before or after this period. Ruth Malcolmson, Miss America 1924, vows that there were no tapes deployed her year.

No girl has ever been exiled from *Miss America* for excessively doctoring up her figure, but the threat of exposure long served as a sufficient deterrent. Claire James, Miss California, runner-up to Miss America 1938, was supposed to have been denied the crown because she used too much make-up for the satisfaction of the judges. Bleached hair was not even legal in those days; ironically, blonds probably fare worse in any beauty competition because lighter hair shows up poorly under bright lights. Rosemary

LaPlanche, Miss America 1941, was hauled out of line during rehearsal and informed that two other contestants had accused her of wearing falsies. Rosemary denied the allegation, but her word was not sufficient, so serious was that particular indictment in those times. She was taken backstage to an empty room, where two matrons frisked her top. She passed inspection.

Today the situation is completely reversed. "We won't permit anything obviously engineered," Albert Marks says, "but we certainly don't investigate." The swimsuits that the Pageant itself endorsed for the contestants in 1970—and that most of them chose to wear—were such marvels of construction that they appeared more armament than beach attire.

Among themselves, the girls make no effort to conceal their dependency on store-bought paraphernalia. Contestants estimate that up to three-quarters of the girls pad themselves. Jerry Ball, one of the most experienced judges in the country, says it has all suddenly come about in just the last few years. "Now," he says, "some of them are wearing so much padding that you can see the stuff falling out the sides as they walk down the runway." The number of girls wearing hairpieces is increasing apace and it is almost a universal practice to wear them, even in some states where such equipment is technically still against the rules.

While the widespread employment of padding for gown or swimsuit is relatively new, padding the biographical figures is an old game. Almost half of the early queens added blithely to their ages—as late as 1950, Miss America, aged eighteen, posed as being twenty-one—but the girls did not start falsifying their statistics in abundance until after the war. Since there are no checks run on the figures, many of the girls write down almost anything that comes into their heads. Almost every girl under 5 feet 6 inches adds a half-inch to her height listing, and many of the really short contestants boost themselves a whole inch, or more. For weight, it would spare the Pageant time if it just put down "ideal" for every girl instead of bothering to record the three-digit fiction that most of the girls dream up.

The bust game is more subtle, since big bosoms are really not approved of at Atlantic City. One poor innocent state queen wrote on her *Miss America* entry blank that she was 38–24–34. Miss Slaughter says she took one look at that and decided that it was out of the question. She arbitrarily recorded the girl at a more tasteful 34–24–34. Needless to say, the young lady came in, very definitely, 38–24–34. Apparently, no girl has ever won the title with anything more than a 37-inch bust.*

The Pageant dutifully lists Venus Ramey, Miss America 1944, as 37½–25–36½, but on the biography sheet that Miss Ramey herself filled out when she won as Miss Washington, D.C., she very clearly wrote 36½ next to BUST, 37½ next to HIPS. The figures were transposed sometime later. This suggests that the true bustiest Miss America was Evelyn Ay, 1954. She and Bebe Shopp, 1948, both measured 37 inches, but Miss Ay's waist was three inches smaller, giving her the clear edge on perspective.

Assuming that there is some truth manifest in the figures that the girls provide on their own behalf, there is no doubt that they fill out bathing suits better all the time. Every year until 1948, and as late as 1954, most girls had 34-inch busts. Thirty-fives reigned for the next decade, but first in 1958, and for every year but one since 1966, 36 inches has been the most common measurement. The Pageant began keeping statistics in 1937. In the first seven years that records were kept, ending in 1943, 278 girls competed and only one of them listed a bust greater than 36 inches. That's less than 0.4 per cent. In the last seven years, from 1964 on, 63 of the 350 girls (18 per cent) have boasted of a bust measurement greater than 36 inches. So much for the good old days.

However, while girls have unquestionably grown bustier, their imaginations have only grown more artistic. God may be making bustier women, but it is hard to believe that He is producing symmetrical ones at such a prodigious rate. For years, women appeared to have accepted the fate that they must be bigger round in the hips than the top. The first 11 Miss Americas and 14 of the first 15 boasted hips larger than busts. Acceptance of that verity died violently, it seems, in midwar, which happens to have been, coincidentally, the heyday of the sweater girl.

To that point, the average *Miss America* contestant measured

* A full analysis and summary of all contestant statistics available, as well as biographical information, can be found in Your Miss America Scorecard, beginning on page 313.

about 34–25½–36, and it was the rare girl who matched bust and hip figures with precision. In 1943 only 3 of the 33 contestants had matching hips and bust. The next year 6 of the 33 claimed that distinction, and the figures have soared since then. By 1970, 37 of the 50 contestants solemnly decreed that their hips were exactly the same size as their busts. When filling out a sheet these days, the only important decision a girl must make is whether she will list herself as 36–24–36 or 35–23–35. It is no wonder that the judges pay no regard to the dreamy figures on the biography sheets.

The flight from reality was certainly encouraged by the Pageant itself, which began to thrive on its own fantasies in the 1960s. Miss Slaughter did not like miniskirts. Of course, many people did not like them, but Lenora's operative mistake was that she absolutely refused to believe they would last. "All right, I was wrong," she admits today, but she adds suddenly, purposefully, fervently, "But I still think they're awful. They're—they're—why, they're ungodly!" Miss Slaughter barely managed to acknowledge associate evils such as new styles in hair, heels, and bathing suits, so that by her last year, 1967, *Miss America* had begun to resemble the ghost of Christmas Past. In deference to Lenora, even for a year or so after she retired the Pageant still refused to change and nearly became a complete laughingstock. It was not funny to the girls who were entered and had to dress to Atlantic City specifications, however. They quickly discovered that they were not buying a wardrobe for a Pageant; they were buying one for a week-long costume party.

Miss New York 1969 recalls the experience: "We spent days shopping. Almost every weekend during the summer, from noon to dinnertime, and sometimes evenings during the week too. We had to find the right things. There weren't many of the one-piece swimsuits around—I mean, you had no choice—and the shoes with the three-inch spiked heels, they were virtually impossible to find. The clothing styles had to reach within two inches of the knee, and they just weren't selling any dresses like that. We knew that all we could do was lengthen dresses that we bought, but the problem was that *we couldn't even find dresses long enough so that when we let them down they were long enough for the Pageant.*" *Miss America* had reached the point where it was demanding that its contestants wear clothes that literally did not exist. No wonder the girls felt no compunctions about writing down measurements that did not exist either.

The nonexistent bathing suit for this passé Pageant ensemble was called, in the trade, a high-cut panel. It had been the overwhelming choice at Atlantic City since the 1930s. Since the late 1940s, when the two-piece went out of fashion, it had been the only style. The panel is certainly a curious style. It is, on the one hand, not flattering. On the other, since it is constructed at the bottom with sort of an attached underpants effect, it has the very disconcerting property of riveting attention right to the crotch. Albert Marks himself muses that he doubts whether the most revealing two-piece bikinis in the land produce, per capita, the random lascivious thoughts occasioned by panels. Apparently, Marks did not ever let on to Miss Slaughter about this spectacular additional property of the panel. It was always officially considered the very height of propriety.

The Pageant clung to the panel as its security blanket right up until 1970. Then, a committee from *Miss America*'s middle-aged hostess group began making trips to New York to examine the new bathing-suit styles, which are first shown in the spring of each year. Ironically, following Marks's modern counsel, Atlantic City was suddenly prepared to permit two-piece suits, but *Miss America* was so far behind to start with that by the time it caught up with two-piecers they had already been phased out of prime fashion.

Actually, the possibility that any contestant would select an offensive or daring suit is so remote as to make the whole project a waste of time. The contestants are permitted, provisionally, to wear suits of their own selection, but the fact that Atlantic City endorsed two models (out of eighty-four examined from four major manufacturers) placed silent pressure on the girls to play it safe and go with the house brand. In the first year the new system was in effect, well over half wore one of the Pageant-approved swimsuits—"conservative, in good taste, and potentially the most flattering." Aside from the shell-like frontal construction that robbed the body of any spontaneity, the chosen swimsuits were otherwise attractive, with a V front and no back. Of course, the contestants said they wouldn't be caught wearing the thing on a beach. You parade down the runway in a swimsuit; you swim in a bathing suit.

By all odds, however, the present arrangement is merely a holding action, until the Pageant can find a tactful way to eliminate swimsuit for good. Marks terms it a "sooner or later" proposition, and he has strong backing from the contestants themselves, who feel at ease on a beach in a bikini, but uncomfortable walking down a one-hundred-forty-foot runway in a more modest coverall, as fully dressed spectators gape at them. The anti-swimsuit coalition is further joined, at least in spirit, by Marks's sworn enemy, the Women's Liberation Movement, which claims that *Miss America* demeans the female race by parading girls around as sex objects. Teen-age pageants have drawn good TV ratings without swimsuit competition.

Curiously—but then, everything about *Miss America* is upside down—those left to defend the swimsuit display are the conservative old-liners who otherwise preach scholarship and the Pageant's community involvement. A very responsible lady, a western state Pageant official, says, "What do they want in Atlantic City? They've already almost killed the thing by turning it into nothing more than a singing contest for TV. They take away swimsuit, then all you have is an amateur hour. Ted Mack doesn't come on my set any more, and he was the original amateur hour. How are we going to last as an imitation amateur hour? Atlantic City just talks about the scholarships. That's fine. How many people do they think want to *see* a scholarship? People want to see pretty girls. Men and women want to see pretty girls."

A shrewd compromise solution is offered by a middle-of-the-roader named Ken Gaughran, who runs the Miss Westchester County Pageant in suburban New York. Gaughran, an astute promoter, does not want to see the swimsuit go, but he also sympathizes with the girls' embarrassment. In his small local pageants leading up to Miss Westchester, the shows are semi-private, with only judges and parents allowed to watch the girls in swimsuit. "All you have to do," Gaughran says, "is stop calling it 'swimsuit.' You call it 'Physical Fitness.' It's the same thing as always, but all of a sudden, it's health, not sex. Nobody can be against physical fitness."

Off the Assembly Line, onto the Runway

Since a Miss America gets a $10,000 scholarship and makes anywhere from $55,000 on up in her year, there is too much at stake to permit any girl to advance on Atlantic City by herself. Nowadays, it is not uncommon for a contestant to be subjected to professional advice and coaching from experts for months, even before she enters a local pageant. Sadly, those who endure the most training are often the losers; the same poor affluent things who note on their biography sheets that they have studied dance for eight years and piano for twelve—and then read Kipling poems for their talent instead. Still, even the most outstanding girl requires some training in the intricate mysteries of pageantry—walking, standing, sitting, for instance. Girls can no longer just walk off the street, slip into bathing suits, and win—especially since the judges at the lower levels are keener at spotting detail.

Girls receive instruction from a variety of sources. In most cases, the local Pageant provides a tutor, a woman who specializes in instructing these sciences. As a girl wins, at local or state level, she is provided with more attention by the sponsors, so that by the time she has qualified to move on to Atlantic City, she has received consummate training in every phase of the competition. In some places, frightening big-brother efforts to remodel her have been applied.

This detailed shaping process dates back in earnest at least to

1949, when Jacque Mercer of Arizona became Miss America by carefully developing and marketing a product, herself, that the judges would buy. Her book, *How to Win a Beauty Contest* (Curran Publishing, Phoenix, 1960), still provides the most complete study of the subject, and shows to what lengths modern contestants must go in order for them to have a serious chance at victory. Even then, a girl usually has to make two or three runs at the crown before she gains enough Pageant knowhow to become Miss America.

Miss Mercer devotes whole chapters to subjects such as How to Wash Your Face, Perspiration Problems, Smiling When You Don't Want to, Talent Competition Selections, Learning to Laugh, How to Sound Pretty, How to Accept Applause, and on and on, so that no part of the psyche or body is left on its own. Miss Mercer explains what words are not to be used in conversation with the judges, and in what shapes your jewelry should be; she advises contestants how to apply baby oil to the body and reminds them always to make last-minute checks for wayward pubic hairs that may be visible in swimsuit. She lists what clothes to wear at all times, what to think when on the runway, and forty-one items—including vibrator, Jell-O, candy bars, laxatives, and a girl's own pillow—that any well-appointed contestant should bring along to a Pageant.

Lest there be confusion about the right way for everything, Miss Mercer explains, in the best Army-manual style, how to put on a bathing suit: ". . . first, roll it as you would a girdle. Pull the suit over the hips to the waist, then, holding the top away from your body, bend over from the waist. Ease the suit up to the bustline and with one hand, lift one breast up and in and ease the suit bra over it. Repeat on the other side. Stand up and fasten the straps."

"Every move I had, every one, was planned," says Vonda Kay Van Dyke, Miss America 1965. For weeks before the Pageant, she gave twelve ventriloquist shows a day, six days a week, at an amusement park, where she kept notebooks cataloguing the timed response to each gag in her act so that she could build a three-minute bit for the Pageant that perfectly appropriated every second. Most queens are not permitted such independent options, however. The girls settle on their talent presentations only after long consultations with their advisers and outside experts. Ideally, a number should be easy, flashy, and popular, but appear to be quite difficult.

Once the talent selection is agreed upon, appearance becomes the main consideration. Attention to the hair borders on the fanatical. What style? What length? What kind of fall? The trainers get rid of the bangs on the girl with the low forehead, or smooth out the curls on the girl with a curved profile. A contestant is started on a regular program of rinsing her hair in beer, or even in detergent, to give it more protein and body; fine hair will need it in Atlantic City, where the heavy, humid air leaves it limp. A girl must go on an exercise program to tone herself up, and possibly diet as well. There might still be just enough time, with dumbbells and calisthenics, to pump up the bust an inch or so and to melt off some fanny overhang. Rehearsal of the fundamentals drags on. Up and down a girl walks, hearing her own drill sergeant in the background. "Roll your hips, don't stride. Lift your shoulder. Don't carry your feet, glide with them. Toes touch first, then the heel. Don't forget the three Bs: Bust Out, Belly In, Butt Under."

The candidate will meet with former queens for briefing sessions, so that nothing will seem unfamiliar when she arrives in Atlantic City. Travel plans are perfectly plotted. Arrive early and pick up a little extra publicity and some time to get settled? Or wait till the last minute, saving every ounce of energy for a blitz? Mall Dodson, the Pageant's part-time publicity chief, remembers when, in 1965, he was dispatched to the airport to meet the last arriving contestant, Miss Kansas, Debbie Bryant. "It's just as well you're meeting me now," she said, "because you're going to have to get to know me anyway after I win this thing." And, of course, she did.

Experts will show the girl make-up tricks, and groups of state Pageant authorities help her in selecting a wardrobe. The queen is usually permitted to pick out her own clothing, but veto power is often held by some state official or her personal trainer. Each year, Atlantic City pays out about $55,000 in scholarship money to the fifty contestants, but in competing for this prize, they spend an aggregate in excess of $150,000 retail in clothes. Atlantic City beseeches the girls to come to rehearsals in casual clothes, but most of the contestants will be married in less elegant finery than what they choose to practice in.

Official photographs are taken. They must be just so. Too good, and the judges are let down when she appears before them in person. Too bad, and they are reminded unfavorably of her whenever they flip through their contestant notebooks. Biographies offer a greater latitude in imagination. Besides subtly distorting statistical facts, girls also are encouraged to puff up and enliven their historical summaries. Texas officials point with pride to how much improved Phyllis George's biography was in 1970, as opposed to the year before, when she finished as a runner-up at Miss Texas. Under OTHER FACTS Phyllis set off an entire paragraph to mention her pet crab and singing dog, and both in her judges' interview and again, on stage as a finalist with Bert Parks, these were virtually the only subjects she was asked to comment on to determine her aptitude for becoming Miss America.

Under SCHOLASTIC HONORS girls list everything but their social security number and certification of birth. Here are samples from just the last couple of years: Top Ten Twirler at Indy 500, All-State Cheerleader, Chairman of Pledge Skit Night, Sang at YMCA State Banquet, Drum Major, Betty Crocker's Homemakers of America Award, Class Play Committee Fashion Board, West Shore District Volleyball Championship, Attended American Cheerleader's Academy, Department Store Teen Board, Miss Kiwanian.

A girl who is well trained will receive mock interviews and be quizzed on current events. Some chaperones work up background reports on the judges as soon as their identities are learned and brief the girls on their interests and views, suggesting what controversial topics to skirt and what opinions should find the most appreciative response. "I don't think that's conniving at all," says one state queen indignantly. "I think that's intelligent." Diligent coaches know that it is well to take nothing for granted. At the North Carolina Pageant in 1970, for instance, the judges were collectively of a liberal bent—which is unusual, particularly in the South. One of the judges said: "It was obvious that many of the girls had been told to expect conservative judges. You could tell, with some of them, that they were searching to cover up their own liberal views and to give answers that they thought we wanted to hear."

Miss Winston-Salem remembers being the last girl to be interviewed in her group. "They asked me what I thought of Agnew," she says, "and I said: 'Can I tell you that I think he puts his foot in his mouth?' And one of the judges said: 'You're the first girl to answer that question truthfully all day.' "

Too often now, girls are not coached, they are manipulated. In the General Chairman's Guide, one of several detailed instruction booklets that Atlantic City sends out to all preliminary pageants, there is an entreaty: "It is not your desire to change her [your new queen], but to help her gain in poise. . . ." However, many states still try to make her over into a carbon of the girl who became Miss America the year before. Because brown-haired girls won ten years in a row, from 1958 up to 1967, the states assumed that nothing else mattered. After Judi Ford won as Miss Illinois, the state officials tried to force her to dye her blond hair brown. She refused and became a blond Miss America. But many girls cannot resist such state pressures, and a generally diverse group comes out looking like fifty plastic ukuleles in a row at Atlantic City. Evelyn Ay, Miss America 1954, says, "They're so overtrained and overcoached now. They're told over and over what the one right way is, so that they become frightened that they're going to forget and do something different. You can't be human under those circumstances. Everybody says the girls are different today from us. They're not. It's the veneer that's placed over them that makes them seen different."

The states maintain, naturally, that training seeks only to improve a girl, not change her, but the whole system encourages the promotion of girls who are malleable. At the lower levels an unconscious conspiracy neatly sorts out the rebels and independents. Pageant people interchange jobs. Pageant directors judge other pageants and help train girls. Judges get invited back by being agreeable. It serves everyone to place a high premium on whether or not a girl "will be easy to work with," which means a girl who will not dispute adult advice. In that sense it is a biased sample that reaches Atlantic City.

The pattern across the states is not consistent, of course. In some states, Pageant organization is sloppy, the officials are indolent; queens are lucky to get even basic training. In other states, there is new, progressive management. Black girls are being sought as contestants in many places, including the host state of New Jersey. In Alaska, an ample, energetic woman named Mrs. Kay Linton, who wears a folded five-dollar bill on a finger as a ring, carries the *Miss America* message into Eskimo villages where girls have never worn—even seen—high heels or bathing suits. Her 1970 candidate came from north of the Arctic Circle. Some state directors are encouraging the operation of more state pageants on college campuses, which helps them get the city girls, who have no pageants to turn to where they live. There is also some effort being made in various states to move beyond the usual incestuous judging circles to seek new, young opinions on the panels.

In many states, though, the queen is subject to the whims of the entrenched Pageant organization. State queens can make up to $15,000 a year, plus scholarship and commercial considerations, so they are somewhat at the mercy of the people who are managing and booking them. Queens are ordered, more or less, to transfer to a college of the organization's choosing in or near the town where the state pageant is held. Miss America 1971, for instance, was required to transfer from North Texas State to Texas Christian University in Fort Worth, after she was crowned Miss Texas. After it was disclosed that Miss Iowa 1968 had been a go-go dancer some time previous to her participation in the Pageant, her title was frozen until the state Pageant officials could run a check on her past. She was cleared, the Jaycees declared unctuously, only because "we decided that she was a very nice girl with good parents." In fact, despite the embarrassing shadow cast upon her, she was a nice enough girl for the judges at Atlantic City to declare her second runner-up.

These confrontations are rare, but they are bound to happen occasionally as long as the major contradiction exists: that a girl is celebrated as a state queen, but permitted to be no more than a pawn in the hands of the state organization. The most shameful recent episode of this stripe took place in the summer of 1970, when the Billings (Montana) Jaycees forced their Miss Montana to resign.

Miss Montana 1970 was a girl from Helena named Kathy Huppe. She was eighteen, a gymnast, supposed to be more proficient in the art than the gymnast who finished fifth place at Atlantic City, later in 1970. Kathy was also bright; she was going into her freshman year at the University of Montana in a special program in the humanities and social science. On her entry blank she carefully noted that she had participated in the Vietnam Moratorium and had contributed work to an antiwar underground newspaper. The judges were aware of these views of hers when they voted for her, but Doug Feller, a Billings banker, who had served as business manager for Miss Montana for two years, says that the Jaycees were caught off guard when this presumably intemperate behavior was revealed.

Following her election, Feller asked Kathy to take charm-school courses to prep for Atlantic City. Kathy refused. The Billings Jaycees also wanted her to transfer to Eastern Montana University in Billings, where she was handier for bookings. Kathy turned that request down flat, too. Suddenly, the Jaycees decided that they had a subversive on their hands. Miss Montana was not easy to work with.

"My brother goes to Stanford," Kathy says, "and he wears long hair. To the Jaycees, that means he uses drugs, and because he does, I must. That's the kind of logic they employed. They even got mad at my mother, because she refused to be a real gung-ho pageant mother. She was a little uncertain about it all along."

"Her mother was against her being Miss Montana," Feller says. "I felt if we could get Kathy to stay in Billings for a few weeks, her mother could get more used to the idea. Kathy said she didn't want to. Nothing was ever said straight out, but she gave me the impression that she thought I was trying to separate her from her mother. You've got to understand what kind of family she was brought up in. Her father was a lawyer, and she is naturally inclined to think that way."

"The Jaycees didn't want me to hold the views I did," Kathy says. "For that matter, they didn't want me to hold any political views. They just wanted me to be a china doll. I tried to explain to them that my beliefs made me, and that if they would not let me express those beliefs, they would not have the girl that won Miss Montana."

"I'm not against her views," Feller says. "Listen, we need people like that in the United States. I just told her, 'At least try not to get most of the people in the state up against Miss Montana.' We've had Miss Montana several years now, the Billings Jaycees, and we normally keep her kind of busy. Finally, I asked her if, in certain situations, if she was really behind something, in California or somewhere, would she go to that instead of fulfilling some commitment we had made for her. She said, well, if she was really behind it, she would have to go to that and break the commitment for Miss Montana."

The matter came to the breaking point when, Feller says, he tried for a whole weekend to telephone her to inform her that she was supposed to make an appearance at the Miss Colorado Pageant. Kathy says that he could not have called her house, because her mother, a registered nurse, was required to be at home on call all that time in question, and Feller had never called when he says he did. At last, though she did make the Miss Colorado Pageant, she was—depending on the version—either informed that the rules required her to resign or she volunteered to resign. She lost her $1000 Miss Montana scholarship and a guarantee of the $500 minimum scholarship that all contestants receive at Atlantic City. "They really did screw me," Kathy says.

Kathy's view was also supported, if only intramurally, by the United States Jaycees. "In a matter of words," says Feller, "they just did not back us. They said it was our fault, we shouldn't have let her resign." The Jaycees have been closely identified with *Miss America,* at least on a local option basis, since 1944, but the relationship has become increasingly strained in Tulsa, where national Jaycee headquarters are located. Says Tom Donnelly, recent executive vice-president of the Jaycees, "*Miss America* is no longer consistent with our ideals that focus on the needs and priorities of the community." Privately, Jaycee officials admit that they would prefer all its chapters to disassociate themselves from *Miss America,* that the money made is worth neither the aggravation nor the dubious affiliation.

Obviously, the bumbling Billings Jaycees embarrassed the national organization, but the episode was even more damaging to *Miss America.* Miss Huppe drew a full-page picture in *Life* magazine—devilishly saved to run the week of the Pageant at Atlantic City—and a national television appearance on *To Tell the Truth,* as well as other sympathetic publicity that rivaled that which Miss America herself received. Nevertheless, while the politics of the Huppe affair make it spectacular, there are, every year, smaller, sadder tales of manipulation that are more representative and damning of the *Miss America* process.

Most troubles are, unintentionally, caused by trainers, which is the preferred word used to define the women who coach contestants. Trainers are usually required to double as chaperones to earn their fees, but they are a breed apart from the predominant chaperone type. Trainers bear some resemblance to boxing managers for, like them, they use the first person plural to describe victories but opt for the third personal singular in the event of defeat: we won at State; she lost at Atlantic City.

Trainers range in age from the thirties on up. Most of them are attractive, many so beautiful and so well appointed that they seem to rival their own young charges. They are totally devoted to the concept of the beauty pageant and to the ideal of femininity that it celebrates. Indeed, most of the abuses that these women commit can be attributed to their zeal and fervor rather than to any conscious malevolence. They are evangelic, convinced not only that pageants are right, but that they alone are right for pageants. The more fanatic trainers make it clear that they believe that pageants are really run for them, the permanent cadre, and that contestants are merely utilitarian transients whose presence must be tolerated.

Most trainers participate altruistically, as a labor of love. Only a few have their motives called to question: they are searching for daughter substitutes, vicariously reliving their own belle days, or worse, in a few cases, actually suspected of enjoying the Fagin-like manipulation they can exert, or of being latent Lesbians. Anyway, there is not enough money in the field for any trainer to make a living wage by training alone. Most use the extra cash they do earn to indulge themselves in expensive clothes. A fairly large percentage of them take an additional profit out of the publicity they receive, if their girls win or place high. These women make the bulk of their income in related beauty fields, as cosmetologists, beauticians, hairdressers, or charm-school headmistresses.

Beauty pageants are aligned with all other elements of the beauty culture, particularly in the small towns. Lip service to scholarships aside, in rural areas the main justification for pageants is that winners and losers alike are taught the proper moves, rules, and adult etiquette, while gaining confidence and, of course, poise. It would seem that there must be a cheaper and more expedient way for young ladies to be instructed in how not to scratch or wear pink plastic curlers in public, but a pageant makes the learning process more fun and authoritative, as well as potentially rewarding.

Commitment to protocol is still high in small-town America. That world turns on the faith that the most beautiful, smart, talented girl can be brought crashing down to a just defeat for failure to employ the proper fork, hat, or salutation. This confirms the suspicion held in many quarters that those who live in better suburbs, with richer husbands and large Pontiacs, are so situated mostly because they were fortunate enough to have fallen privy to the secrets of correct etiquette at a right age. Obviously, if a woman is secure in this belief, she is anxious to see her daughter increase her chances for success by participating in pageants. She may also feel that late rewards are also possible, and enroll herself in a charm school. Both pageants and charm schools turn on the same axis, which helps explain why so many women are involved in both enterprises.

Gay Butner of Rocky Mount, North Carolina, could never be described as typical, being much too conscientious and beautiful, but she is at least representative of the type of woman that runs a charm school, while, on the side, dedicating herself to training girls, and directing or judging pageants. Her association with *Miss America* definitely helps her charm business. At the school, just as though she were preparing for a pageant, a woman is provided instruction to cover every contingency, so that she will know how to react correctly whatever the circumstance.

"The matter of gloves," Gay explains as an example. "A thing that causes so much anguish to so many women. When exactly are you required to take them off? We point out to them that there is never any reason for concern, because there are specifically only four times when a woman is ever required to remove her gloves: 1) when meeting head of state, 2) when meeting head of church, 3) when taking communion, and 4) when eating. When women who have never known these facts all their lives learn them, you would be surprised at how so many of them are given a great peace of mind."

Notwithstanding that King Hussein and the Archbishop of Canterbury only irregularly come through Rocky Mount shaking hands, the fact is that insecure women in the small towns are comforted by such revelations. Trainers are also accorded a higher appreciation in rural areas. In the more up-to-date metropolises, a girl accepts a trainer as some harmless specialist who has been assigned to teach her the silly embroidered bagatelles of beauty pageantry. In small towns, the contestants view a trainer as a sage who will reveal the very secrets of the happy life. Generally, the more rural a town, the greater is the justification of a pageant as socially educational for the participants.

Unquestionably, too, *Miss America* remains a small-town, middle-class attraction. There are local pageants offered in few of the nation's largest cities, from New York on down (although there is a Miss Staten Island). Even the state pageants are increasingly held in the small cities: Sandusky, Ohio; Santa Cruz, California; Mexico, Missouri; Oshkosh, Wisconsin; Monroe, Louisiana; Olean, New York. Ken Gaughran, the Westchester County Pageant promoter, an ABC editor who lives in New York City, explains: "Miss Westchester has folded seven times. It isn't just cities, but even some suburban areas are becoming too sophisticated for *Miss America.* A beauty pageant must be a community-oriented project and in larger areas, people just do not care enough. Olean is a perfect spot for Miss New York. Everyone up there is so happy we are in town, because the Pageant helps Olean—it is something for Olean—and Olean is glad to help the Pageant in return. Who would care, much less be happy, if it were in New York or some other big city? We'd be just another thing." In Jackson, Tennessee, Pageant week is second only to Christmas for retail sales in town. Stuckey's, out on the Interstate, has its best week of the year when the Pageant is held.

A Southern Miss America admits, "The South likes to believe we have prettier girls because we do so well in *Miss America.* We do well in *Miss America* for one reason: we don't have many metropolitan areas. We have all those little towns and cities and Jaycees that don't have anything better to do than run beauty pageants. It's not the Southern girls, it's the country girls. The chances of a girl winning from Atlanta or New Orleans are just about as good as from Boston or Chicago." Most big city Northern contestants are shanghaied into local pageants, drugged with giddy scholarship promises. By contrast, James Rucker, a Vicksburg mail carrier, who was executive director of Miss Mississippi, the only state ever to produce back-to-back queens at Atlantic City, says, "In Mississippi, it's tradition for the best girls to come out for the Pageant. In Mississippi, the best girls just *want* to be Miss Mississippi."

Miss Americas of the past decade have almost exclusively married doctors and lawyers, the traditional pillars of small-town America. Contestants' fathers are professional men and white-collar workers. Hardly more than a half-dozen of the fifty 1970 state queens had fathers who were blue-collar workers. Instead, they were daughters of doctors and insurance men and engineers, small company presidents and contractors and ranchers, a banker, architect, lawyer, journalist, accountant, photographer, and minister.

The Pageant is structured by state, like the Senate, and also like the Senate it is weighted toward small towns. In 1970, only 8 of the 50 contestants came from the nation's 25 largest Standard Metropolitan Areas, where 70 million Americans live. The demography of the country is changing rapidly, while a roll call of home towns from the previous census year, 1960, nearly perfectly resembles the 1970 distribution pattern. In both cases, 16 girls came from metropolitan areas—large cities and their suburbs—and in both cases 15 of the girls come from small cities, places like Pocatello, Sioux Falls, Davenport, Owensboro, Roanoke. The plurality—19 in 1970, 22 in 1960—are strictly rural America.

1. 1921 Margaret Gorman, Miss Washington, D. C.

2. 1922–23 Mary Katherine Campbell, Miss Columbus, Ohio

3. 1924 Ruth Malcolmson, Miss Philadelphia

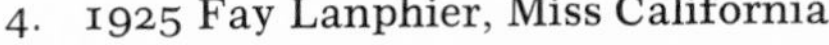

4. 1925 Fay Lanphier, Miss California

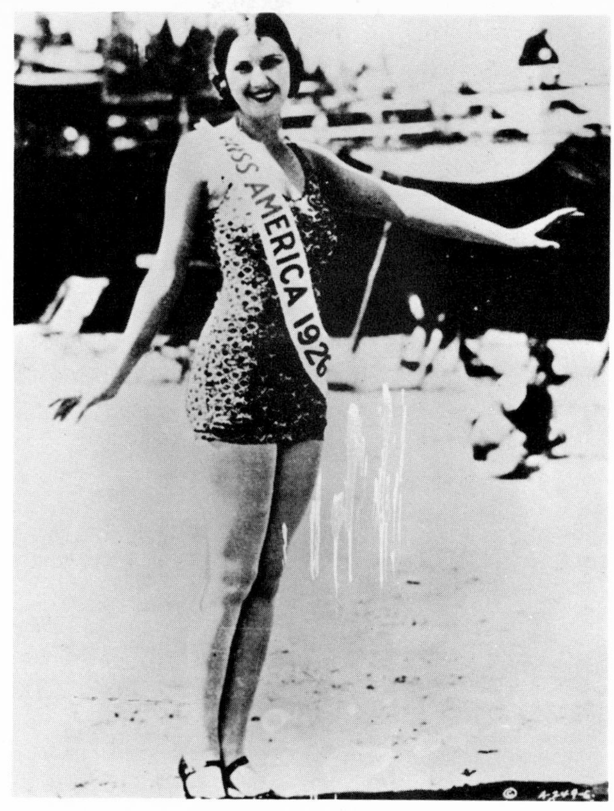

5. 1926 Norma Smallwood, Miss Tulsa

6. 1927 Lois Delander, Miss Illinois

7. 1933 Marian Bergeron, Miss Connecticut

8. 1935 Henrietta Leaver, Miss Pittsburgh

9. 1936 Rose Coyle, Miss Philadelphia

10. 1937 Bette Cooper, Miss Bertrand Island

11. 1938 Marilyn Meseke, Miss Ohio

12. 1939 Patricia Donnelly, Miss Michigan

13. 1940 Frances Burke, Miss Philadelphia

14. 1941 Rosemary LaPlanche,
Miss California

15. 1942 Jo-Carroll Dennison, Miss Texas

16. 1943 Jean Bartel, Miss California

17. 1944 Venus Ramey,
Miss Washington, D.C.

18. 1945 Bess Myerson, Miss New York City

19. 1946 Marilyn Buferd, Miss California

20. 1947 Barbara Jo Walker, Miss Memphis

21. 1948 BeBe Shopp, Miss Minnesota

22. 1949 Jacque Mercer, Miss Arizona

23. 1951 Yolande Betbeze, Miss Alabama

24. 1952 Colleen Hutchins, Miss Utah

25. 1953 Neva Jane Langley,
Miss Georgia

26. 1954 Evelyn Ay, Miss Pennsylvania

27. 1955 Lee Meriwether,
Miss California

28. 1956 Sharon Kay Ritchie, Miss Colorado

29. 1957 Marian McKnight, Miss South Carolina

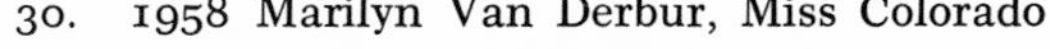

30. 1958 Marilyn Van Derbur, Miss Colorado

31. 1959 Mary Ann Mobley, Miss Mississippi (standing), with 1960 Lynda Lee Mead, Miss Mississippi

32. 1961 Nancy Fleming, Miss Michigan

33. 1962 Maria Fletcher, Miss North Carolina

34. 1963 Jacquelyn Mayer, Miss Ohio

35. 1964 Donna Axum, Miss Arkansas

36. 1965 Vonda Kay Van Dyke, Miss Arizona

37. 1966 Deborah Bryant, Miss Kansas

38. 1967 Jane Jayroe, Miss Oklahoma

39. 1968 Debra Dene Barnes, Miss Kansas

40. 1969 Judith Ford, Miss Illinois

41. 1970 Pamela Eldred, Miss Michigan

42. 1971 Phyllis George, Miss Texas

Reaching Atlantic City from any town requires a contestant to pass herself along a Virginia Reel of escorts, tutors, and guides. These will include personal trainers (some supplied by local and state officials), business managers, and chaperones. The really professional trainers wield their greatest influence at the state level, where perhaps 20 per cent of the contestants put themselves under the aegis of an experienced pro. By the time a girl gets to Atlantic City the tree is bent, and there is seldom enough time left, as the expression goes "to train a girl out of" any defect.

Jo Ann Frank of Hendersonville, North Carolina, is the prototype of the successful trainer. Striking, impeccably groomed, she believes that pageants are "the ultimate" for girls. While even Miss Frank is unable to support herself exclusively from pageant work, however, she has such a prized reputation that she can be selective in the girls that she agrees to work with, and demanding in what she requires of them. Those who oppose her methods and successes accuse her of being a martinet, and a profiteer as well. It is said she moves in and snaps up a contender just before a pageant, just in time for her to take the credit someone else deserves.

"That's ridiculous," Jo Ann says. "I had Anita for nine months before she won at State. I would rather have a girl for a long time. I'm not a miracle worker. I practice no deception. I make no guarantees; except that if I do have the time and the cooperation, I can lead someone from being a girl to being a woman, and make it self-rewarding for her. If anything, I will often hold a girl out for an extra year, just enter her in small pageants so she can gain some confidence, and then we can come into something big like *Miss America* later.

"The only reward in this work is the satisfaction you can get out of it. There is just not enough money in it, so you must look for something else—the development of the girl. Before and after—you would not know they are the same girls. Girls that do win without a trainer, well, they're just lucky. Unfortunately, not every girl does have someone like us."

The reigning Blueberry Queen, one of Jo Ann's girls, says, "We are like apples on a tree, but Jo Ann knows how to polish us, while anybody can rush out and pick us before we're ready."

Jo Ann goes on: "But a girl must have a spark to begin with, a desire to want to do what we want her to do, what she must do to win. Girls are all different, and their personality is already molded when I start with them. You can't change them. You just teach them grooming and self-improvement and try to improve their poise. Poise? Well, it's very difficult to define. It's definitely an acquired thing. It's how a girl handles herself, how she speaks, how she reflects her best. And I want my girls to have a healthy mind in all things, whether sex or life in general.

"I never have any problems with my girls. You ask them. If they don't like my methods, if they don't agree with them, it is a waste of time for both of us. There's no sense in me trying to force anything. For instance, I demand the final say in what clothes my girls will wear, but what good is it for me to put them in something they really don't want? It will show. I don't let my girls date for the whole month before a Pageant. Otherwise, I take the chance that I'm out six-eight-nine months' work because of some little boy. But believe me, if a girl wants to do well at Pageant, she does not want to bother with the petty details of courtship."

All trainers have this nearly mortal fear of boys—though not so much of sex, but of old-fashioned love. Sex is a diversion for a would-be beauty queen, but love is a distraction that lingers. When trainers assemble, much like old army buddies, they begin, one after the other, topping each other with warlike stories about love, each more gruesome than the one before: the girl who fell in love a month before the Pageant, then the girl who took a ring two weeks before the Pageant, then the girl who wrote love letters all during the Pageant, then the girl who ran off with him after winning swimsuit. "One of the best girls I ever had," says Liz Cole, a sweet, low-keyed trainer, who is a district manager for the World Book, "had a real chance at state. She didn't just get a ring; she got married about three weeks before Pageant. Well, you see, she didn't want to let on. She didn't want to let the Jaycees or anybody in her town down by pulling out, but she certainly couldn't win either, because then there would be even more of a fuss when she would have to give up the title and admit she was married. The trouble was, she was a very proud little girl. She wasn't going to look bad on stage. She had to make sure she lost in the interview. And she did.

"I asked her later what she had done. In the South, there is a horrible expression we try to train girls out of. It's: 'ridin' on cars.' It's used frequently, and means 'riding *in a* car.' This girl used to use that awful expression all the time, and I kept stressing to her how it could ruin her chances. So, in the interview, she said that was practically the very first thing she said. She could see all the judges scrunch up their noses right away, so she used it a couple more times. 'Oh, we were just ridin' on cars.' She did very well all through the Pageant, but the judges stopped wasting points on her as soon as they heard that."

However much trainers' methods and motives differ, on one issue they all stand together in a strident phalanx. Hair. Not the least bit coincidentally, hair is where Atlantic City stands to face the real world now. The battle of the hemlines is over, the battle of the panel bathing suits is over; even gloves and hats are succumbing by attrition. There is nothing else left to defend in the last stand of the 1940s. Hair is as much an issue with the girls of *Miss America* as it is with the boys everywhere else in the world.

Most trainers have a hair fetish that is not quite obscene; the affection is much too genuine for that. Hair is a plaything, rather like live Silly Putty. You can help a girl choose a new talent number, you can tell her what exercise to use to rid herself of fanny overhang, you can help her buy the right clothes and the right amount of padding, and advise her never to say "fantastic, gorgeous, marvelous, and you know" when in the company of judges—but hair is better than all these things. While, on the one hand, hair has an air of authority—trainers always talk about *building* and *constructing* styles—hair is also something you can monkey around with every day. Each time a girl leaves her room you can have her leave with different hair. Hair has even more unlimited possibilities than clothes.

Also, hair you can do yourself, or, even better, you can bring in a hairdresser and have her do the job exactly to your specifications. You can shape hair, tease it, curl it, cut it, dye it, put things in it and on it. You can brush hair, comb it, rinse it, dry it, tie it, and try things with it all the time.

Of course, having fun with hair is nothing new. Trainers have always enjoyed playing with hair. The trouble is that all of a sudden virtually every white girl in the United States wants to wear her hair straight and down. Straight-hanging hair is the style. Trainers are poleaxed by this fashion, because there is nothing they can do with it. It just hangs there.

"Well, I don't like it at all in the swimsuit, although I suppose I can tolerate it there," Jo Ann Frank says, wrinkling her nose at the very thought. "I hate it in the evening gown. I hate it. It gives a hot smothered look and girls look wilted. For real sophistication, a real queen must have her hair up."

Miss Williamsburg, Virginia, a blonde, dressed to Barbie-Doll precision, stands next to Jo Ann as they visit another Pageant and explains what sacrifices she was required to make in pursuit of a crown. "Well, first I had to give up all my little-girl ways," she explains, in the manner of a sinner just having found the truth. Little-girl ways, like what? "First would be starting to wear my hair up," Miss Williamsburg replies stoutly. "Why, before I met Jo Ann, I just never wore my hair up."

Though *Miss America* is invariably called to task for its antediluvian views, in this one regard it is far out in advance of the states and locals. The national Pageant officials have been delighted that the traditionalist hair-up stalwarts have begun to suffer a few defections in their ranks. The fact that Phyllis George made Miss America 1971 with soft, long brown hair cascading easily down over her shoulders is not sufficient by itself, however, to put old-time beehivers to rout. Indeed, because hairpieces are permitted now, trainers can offer even more alternatives for hair and that many more reasons why it should stay teased up. Trainers have, anyway, always intimated that God meant *Miss America* contestants to keep their hair stacked like so much cord wood, because, after all, He makes Atlantic City humid in Pageant week, a climate that can leave hanging hair droopy and stringy. The powerful bouffant lobby has cited this meteorological argument so persuasively that it has long claimed a comprehensive control of the Pageant coiffure. Jacquelyn Mayer, Miss America 1963, even wore her magnificent 52-inch locks piled upon the top of her head.

The issue is more sharply joined today only because of the

disturbing contrast. The bouffant creatures that walk the runway are synthetic impostors, bearing no resemblance to the fresh and pretty young girls who volunteer to begin the trek up the Pageant ladder. Their hair is maimed. Miss Michigan 1970, for instance, who has beautiful glimmering chestnut hair that falls down below her shoulders, had had it taken and drawn up and back in tiers of French twists. It did not appear that this arrangement could have been constructed; surely it could only have been poured out of a spigot from down at the Dairy Creme. Yet for the many Pageant functionaries who still delight in antique beauty, such a beehive is a work of art, and the demands to salvage it, to bring it out of mothballs every September and parade it before a baffled Pageant audience remain strong.

State pageants and Atlantic City have no real disagreements about what constitutes a Miss America, but the national Pageant is increasingly displeased about the assembly-line beauties, who come in fixed up to look like each other, and like 1961. In celebration of the 1960s, *Life* ran mug shots, side-by-side, across two pages, of the ten Miss Americas of the decade. The lay out shocked some Pageant bigwigs because it forced them to see what they had denied all along: that Miss Americas really were being made to look alike.

To the traditionalists, though, the spread only offered more comfort. Miss Slaughter was so pleased that, in retirement in Arizona, she was moved to write Albert Marks. "Frankly, I took those *Life* pictures as a great compliment," she says. "I immediately wrote Al Marks and said, 'In this decade of confusion, the *Miss America* Pageant can be proud that it is one thing that has stayed the same.' "

★ 6 ★

Big Momma and Her Gang Go to State

Big Momma and her gang arrived in Raleigh for the North Carolina State Pageant on Monday. They were in from Elizabethtown, in the White Lake area of Bladen County. At Big Momma's flank was her side-kick, Margaret Herring, who is a pocket-sized edition of Big Momma, and her partner at El-Mar Textiles, which specializes in the sale of fringed, accent area-rugs. The rest of the entourage was dominated by Marie Nobles, a beautician with a huge, heaving bosom (which has occasioned Margaret to observe: "If Marie ever gets a chest cold, we're all in trouble"). The junior members of the group included Judy Cross —one of the Wilson judges, she is Big Momma's daughter—and Carol Ann Bass, the Rhododendron Queen, formerly the Blueberry Queen. Big Momma chaperones her.

Big Momma makes a lot of noise as she enters the hotel lobby, for she recognizes a good many people there for the Pageant. One man standing by the check-in desk says, "Look, there's Big Momma. She's known all over the State of North Carolina."

His companion replies with disdain. "Are you kidding?" he says. "Big Momma is known from Atlantic City to the Lawrence Welk Show in Hollywood." Moments later, Big Momma wrapped this man in her folds and kissed him. "Doll," she said.

It is possible to reach her by mail merely by addressing the letter to Big Momma, North Carolina, and many long-distance operators are also capable of reaching her when provided with no more information. Big Momma's square name is Eleanor Andrews, but except for her old buddy Margaret, no one, herself included, refers to her any more by her Christian name. Certainly, she comes easy by Big Momma, being a huge, tall woman in her forties, of indeterminate girth and poundage. Her eyes are narrowed, peering out above puffed cheeks. Aside from the obvious recognition of her obesity, it is almost as immediately apparent that a beautiful face is masked by the layers of fat.

The trouble with Big Momma is, simply, that she eats too much, each day. She starts slowly, but accumulating meal momentum as time wears on, she is, by late evening, consuming nearly everything in her path. Upon awakening, Big Momma often skips breakfast, beginning her business day with a moderate lunch and incidental afternoon snacks. Dinner is more representative, and then, following the evening's activity, hamburgers or pizza are called for. Normally, a day might conclude at this point, but at State Pageant, the social life of the Big Momma Gang is only beginning to thrive about this time. Big Momma seldom drinks, so, while others imbibe, she turns to Carolina peanuts or Hostess Twinkies to tide her over until a late breakfast, with bacon and eggs and grits and toast. By now, the machine is really in high gear, so Big Momma is liable to go crosstown to the twenty-four-hour doughnut shop, where a constitutional supply of Krispy Kremes may be obtained for consumption on the way back to the hotel. It is going on four or five o'clock by now. One of the reasons that Big Momma doesn't eat a whole lot in the morning is that, during Pageant week, she seldom stirs before afternoon, when she goes down to the auditorium to watch the contestants practice their talent.

"Sometimes," said Margaret, who is petite and round herself, "it takes something really dramatic to shape a woman up. You ever notice how much better widows look? Now if Eleanor was to be a widow, if Junius was to die . . ."

"Well, hush, don't be nasty," said Big Momma.

". . . you'd see the lard just melt off her," Margaret went on.

"I'll tell you what, my husband even thinks I'm pretty now," Big Momma said. "Isn't that right, Margaret? He doesn't even know I'm fat. Love is blind. He still gets things for me. He buys things for me. Junius and Margaret's husband, they've known each other, I don't know how long. Margaret, you and me got two wonderful husbands, don't we?"

"They threw away the mold after they made those two," Margaret said.

Big Momma, Margaret, Marie, Judy, and Carol Ann were stationed in the lobby of the Sir Walter, the headquarters hotel for the Pageant. Even a state pageant such as North Carolina, which has more contestants than Atlantic City, is a more intimate affair than the national proceedings. Except for the judges, all the participants and officials are quartered in one hotel, so that it is easy for Big Momma and her gang to operate out of the nerve center. The whole show takes on the air of a large sorority picnic, a fact sadly and most particularly noted by the hotel barkeep, who impatiently awaited the arrival of a more convivial businessmen's convention after all the girls were gone.

The contestants and chaperones all eat in their own special dining room, and are carted to the auditorium and other events, such as the opening night luau (featuring a flame-eater for entertainment) in buses. Unlike Atlantic City contestants, everybody is reasonably close to home, so that well-wishers are always in evidence. When a girl from a small town wins a preliminary, it is not uncommon for hordes of her neighbors to descend upon the proceedings. Parents and siblings, taking a family vacation, throng the lobby to be with Sis, and boy friends are also often in attendance. The same stiff parietal rules as at Atlantic City are in effect, however, and, indeed, there is even more of a Puritan air. It is considered indecent for a girl to parade in bathing suit without incongruous references being made to her less sensuous assets. Thus, as a well-turned little bundle struts down the runway, in high heels and bathing suit, the emcee intones, deadpan, "She was a member of the choir and the school newspaper," or "She placed second in a golf tournament in 1967," or "She says her most rewarding experience was the tutoring of underprivileged children." In 1961, striding along, listening to her praises, a contestant tumbled right off the runway.

So clubby is the whole scene that it is traditional, although by no means obligatory, for a contestant to leave small gifts, one for each of her competitors, on a large table in the hotel lobby. Some of these items are geographical tokens—seashells from an ocean county contestant, peanuts from an area where they are grown, peaches (which Big Momma availed herself of) from a peach county. The other gifts are only insignificant items—pens and pencils, needles and thread, work gloves, and other curiosities. One contestant, transparently lobbying for Miss Congeniality, appends a note to her gift display: "A small token to our friendship. But it is given with a warm heart. Good luck to *all*."

Big Momma keeps a careful eye on these goings-ons from the comfortable chair that she has appropriated in the Sir Walter lobby. Hers is the most strategic vantage point, not only for examining the seventy contestants close up, but also for corralling other Pageant regulars. There is an underground of trainers, chaperones, judges, promoters, Jaycees, and other ancillary beauty personnel who surface regularly at State Pageant time. It is there in the lobby, for instance, that Big Momma and her gang discover an old buddy, Ward Sutton, the undertaker from Rocky Mount.

Ward, spare and angular, is glad to find friends. He is in Raleigh with his wife, but she is the chaperone with Miss Rocky Mount, so he is looking for company. "I reached back to scratch my butt," Big Momma tells her gang, "and look what I found."

Ward blushed and kissed Margaret on the neck. "Don't stop, don't stop," she panted.

"Hush," Big Momma said, "I'm surrounded by tackiness."

"Who do you like, Ward?" Judy said.

"Well, I haven't seen 'em all yet," he said, "but I think we've got a chance to make ten. Then there's Asheville, Winston-Salem, Ahoskie. . . ."

"That's Jo Ann Frank's girl," Big Momma revealed.

"Wilmington will make ten, Ward," Judy said.

"And, doll, that Newton-Conover will be there," Big Momma said. Newton-Conover was Pauletta Pearson, the first black girl ever to make a Southern state pageant. "I've heard that she's got the voice to get the job done."

"Ward, do you know anything about these judges?" Judy asked. The panel was a curiosity to many Pageant regulars, because two of the five judges were working their first pageant, and there was no firm track record for the other three in this area.

"I'll tell you what," Big Momma said. "With some judges you just can't figure. The year Judy was in this, the press photographers voted her Miss Photogenic, and in swimsuit she was just outstanding. There was no way she couldn't get the job done in swimsuit. Everybody was coming up and telling me she was bound to win. But I had been watching those old judges we had that year. Every time a girl would come out with big boobs, they'd look down. Judy never had a chance. That's what got me interested in this. Things I can't understand bug me, and I'll tell you what, I can't rest till I figure out what makes something tick."

While it is nearly statutory for every Miss America to claim, wherever she might be, that her hosts have made her a second home, only North Carolina can truly claim the honor. Almost every year, Miss America spends more time there than in any other state. For a long time, too, the Tarheels offered the largest state pageant in the United States, with up to 100 entries, although by 1970 the number had been reduced to 70, just short of Minnesota's 72.

Still, even with that large a field, the contest remains nearly unmanageable, since it is easy to miss a true contender. In years past, the judges would often go through the file of pictures of the contestants the night before the show began, and flip them into three piles—yes, possible, and no chance. A girl with a bad picture or some surprise good ingredient could rise from the "no" pile to make ten, but it was rare. The judges were not just being cruelly expedient bookkeepers, because they had to make some effort to pare away the outsiders early on, so that they could more fairly and competently judge the few real contenders.

Avoiding North Carolina's plight, many states restrict the number of entries, and many critics within the state contend that one of the major reasons why North Carolina has not had so much as a semifinalist since Maria Fletcher won in 1961 at Atlantic City is that the Pageant is so quaint and unwieldy. They maintain that the best prospects get lost in the hordes, and the judges are forced at last to base their decision mainly on talent. By contrast, and to Atlantic City's continuing embarrassment, the one state in the union that operates differently from all the others has recently been the most consistently successful state at

Miss America. That is Alabama, which strikes at the very heart of the *Miss America* strength by avoiding the grass roots.

There are no locals certified in Alabama. Instead, all would-be queens come to the State Fair Building in Birmingham in June, where they compete in a series of private judging sessions over a week or so. Many of the approximately one hundred seventy-five contestants do not even compete in swimsuit, seeking only special grants that are distributed from a scholarship pot that reaches nearly $40,000—second in the land only to Atlantic City's. Only the ten finalists do perform publicly, before a live and television audience. The system is carefully structured, obviously the fairest and most efficient at producing a national contender. Of course, it is also so antiseptic and analytical that the whole pageant concept is robbed of its special flair and charm.

Effective as the Alabama system is, to North Carolina and most other big *Miss America* states, their queen is too important to be robbed of her local subjects and the attendant pizzazz. She is acknowledged as a nearly official state envoy, and her obligations are such that, as does a Miss America, she must give up school for the year and devote herself to appearances that can net her well in excess of $10,000. Everybody takes Miss North Carolina seriously. It did not seem offensive to anyone, obviously, least of all herself, that every night of the 1970 Pageant, the retiring Miss North Carolina, Patsy Johnson, made a little speech that referred specifically, every time, to "the wonderful qualities that go to make up a Miss North Carolina."

Nevertheless, despite the embarrassment of riches that she nonchalantly claimed to possess for herself, Miss North Carolina still was required to play second banana, because Miss America herself, Pam Eldred, was also on hand. The Jaycees had leased her for the week for $1700, a small investment in a spectacle that can gross up to $50,000, make as much as $7500 for the Jaycees, and stir up an estimated $325,000 for the host city. The State Pageant can be such a profitable prestige item that in states such as North Carolina, various Jaycee groups scuffle for the rights. It had come to Raleigh only because a diligent Jaycee named Bill Ruth, a department-store executive, spent six hard months of political infighting to secure it. Then for nine months, one hundred of the Raleigh Jaycees devoted themselves to the project. As everywhere else, the Carolina State Pageant could not succeed without volunteer labor.

The Carolina Pageant was so large that it required four nights of preliminaries, with seventeen or eighteen talent presentations each evening, an oppressive number under any circumstances, more so since nearly everybody sang. On top of this, the auditorium was waterlogged by additional entertainment every night. Miss America danced. Miss North Carolina sang. Four young male dancers did two numbers. The emcee sang, and another singer, identified as "the most promising young male vocalist in North Carolina," performed an original lyric entitled "It Won't End on Saturday Night." Moreover, clutching telephones, all seventy girls appeared on stage together at the start of the show in a production number celebrating the theme of the Pageant, "a salute to the miracle of communications."

As it turned out, a more substantial accolade was paid to the specific miracle of television. Because the North Carolina National Bank had paid $10,000 for the privilege of televising the Saturday finals (to an estimated four hundred thousand tuned-in homes), the whole operation was soon given over to TV. By Friday, light stanchions and camera platforms were erected amid the paying customers, occasioning some cryptic comment from Big Momma, whose view of the stage was not improved by these devices. Other spectators bowed obsequiously to the intruders, enduring, without visible protest, a full hour-long intermission Saturday night, between the first part of the show and that which was televised. "Watch me for the applause cues and I'm sure everything will turn out all right," the emcee informed the customers, who then cheered loudly for commercials and station breaks. Such tyranny by television seems complete, all over the land. Should any despot come down the street and say, "Hand over your property and your liberty," the residents would fight him to the death. Should the same man come down the same street and say, "Now this is going to be for television; hand over your property and your liberty," the same people would not only fumble to produce their house keys on the spot, but they would also inquire as to what other ways they might accommodate the demands—as, for instance, applauding on cue.

Except on this final night, when a capacity crowd of about twenty-seven hundred filled the Memorial Auditorium, the crowds were sparse, as they usually are everywhere on preliminary evenings. About the only people who attend preliminaries are families and friends, who show up on the night their girl performs her talent. As each girl comes on, a certain little section of the hall will suddenly cheer, then grow silent thereafter, as the applause takes hold again in some other area.

Certain types of performers, notably dancers and baton-twirlers, have a distinct edge in this department, because their acts usually have some high spots where it seems appropriate to interrupt with applause. Unless a singer manages something really gimmicky, it is difficult for even her family to interrupt with "spontaneous" applause.

A veteran Pageant promoter named Alan Bull, from Winston-Salem, gathered his girl's rooters about him in the lobby shortly before she went on. Her name was Amelita Facchiano, she owned a superb voice and the best stage presence of any girl, but, unfortunately, she had chosen to sing "Show Me" from *My Fair Lady,* and unless she stood on her head and juggled flaming bowling pins as she sang, there was simply no legitimate point in the number where applause from the galleries could be introduced in an effort to stampede the judges to vote for Amelita. Amelita's accompanist and chaperone both tried to explain this to Bull—much to his dismay. "We're not down here to be entertained," he protested. "That's all very nice, but you've got to make the judges realize that there's people here who like her."

When Amelita did not, in fact, win her preliminary, Bull was outraged and beseeched her, if she should make the finals, to select a new song that would be more receptive to intermittent applause. An observer stifled an impulse to suggest "The Mexican Hat Dance." Cooler, Big Momma only declared that her worst suspicions about the judges had been confirmed. "Sometimes you can't tell what's going on," she said. "One November I had twins, and another baby next September. Three children in less than a year. For a while there, I thought it must be the water I was drinking. We just don't know what these judges are into."

Nevertheless, she and her gang gathered for the nightly post-mortem, which requires everybody to start making out projections of their ten semifinalists. This is *pro forma* among beauty regulars. Ward, the undertaker, began reading off his list. Settled comfortably in her lobby chair, awaiting a pizza delivery, Big Momma critiqued his choices. "Ward, hush, she could use plastic surgery on her behind cheeks," she replied to his first selection. Ward read another. "You could drive a truck through her legs," Big Momma said. Provisionally, she approved his next two choices, awaiting their talent presentation on later evenings.

Buoyed by this approbation, Ward reached for a long shot. Big Momma just laughed. "Her departure from the beauty-pageant world is imminent," Margaret said.

Then Judy offered a selection of her own. "No," Big Momma decided after some thought, "she was all right but then she went and done all that jitterbug talk before she started to sing."

Ward tried again. "Well, by golly, she can talk," Big Momma said. "She's an English major."

Judy proposed another girl. "Now Judy," Big Momma told her, "you know she is just eat up. She ought to get a medal for guts."

"Ahh, Big Momma," Carol Ann said.

"Well, Momma," Judy protested, "somebody's got to make ten. There's no one left."

Margaret came to her confrere's aid. "No, I believe Eleanor's right," she said. "This is just a bad year. The ugly stick has been beating a regular path through here."

"Hush, don't be so tacky, Margaret," Big Momma said, though her eyes were nearly jiggled shut in her chubby face, she was snickering so hard. The truth was, she had her candidate, even if she wasn't in the running. Carol Ann, her Rhododendron Queen, had been disenfranchised, and Big Momma was still annoyed at her plight. Carol Ann had been such a formidable candidate that despite all Big Momma's efforts, she was unable to get the minimum number of girls to run against Carol Ann in her home county so that she could qualify as a local winner at State. It was only after Carol Ann was securely shut out of *Miss America* that

Big Momma entered her for Rhododendron Queen, which she won easily. Big Momma just couldn't stand to be away from the beauty-pageant action.

Starting with her daughter Judy, she has made an avocation of taking care of beauty queens. Margaret usually accompanies her in this pursuit. Both maintain that it is a more interesting diversion than dalliance might be. Big Momma had taken charge of Carol Ann the year before, when she became the Blueberry Queen. On that occasion, she had advised her to switch from the piano to singing. "She sings Vikki Carr stuff," Big Momma explains. "Sad stuff. I won't let Carol Ann sing any jivy stuff. The audience feels sorry for her. And doll, I'll tell you what, it gets the job done."

With her husband, Junius, offering sporadic protest at her absence, Big Momma took off with Carol Ann in tow. "We started off hitting festivals, pageants, Rotary Clubs, Lions Clubs," she says. "Carol Ann was the best thing Blueberry's ever had. In Raleigh, Governor Scott just plain fell in love with her. He gave her a Tarheel button. The whole state department fell for her. They said, 'Big Momma, you can bring her back any time you want.' Everybody loves Carol Ann. It's a sin she couldn't get into State. She'd go into Winn-Dixie and places like that promoting blueberries, but she'd go to hospitals too. There's nothing that little girl wouldn't do.

"So then we took off for Hollywood. Me and Margaret and Carol Ann. We had $1000 and two credit cards. We were complimentary at every Holiday Inn, coast to coast. Every place we'd stay, they'd say, 'Big Momma, you're the only one I know who is complimentary, except Billy Graham himself.' They Holidexed ahead everywhere to let them know we were coming and to have blueberry pies waiting for us. Holidexed ahead. I don't even know if they ever even Holidexed for Billy Graham. I don't know how many states it was we went through, but I'll tell you what, it was a pile of miles.

"We got to Hollywood, and it was the same thing. I mean every place we went they put us in those roped-off areas like we were somebody. I don't go no place that I don't get to know people. We made 'The Dating Game.' They let us make our own questions up. We met Robert Wagner, and we had cocktails at

George Gobel's house. He said, 'Big Momma, you can come back any time, so long as you bring Carol Ann.' They all loved her. Then we went on 'The Donald O'Connor Show.' We were just supposed to make an appearance, but I'll tell you what, they liked her so much they started writing her into the show just before she went on. It burned up that Buddy Hackett, because it cut down on the time he was supposed to be on.

"Another time we saw Jimmy Dean. I know him. He calls me The Warden. I was with Carol Ann and another beauty queen, and I set them down on the one side of me and Jimmy Dean on the other, and he didn't like that one bit. He said, 'Big Momma, I'm not going to attack them.' I said, 'Maybe, but if you get a mind to, doll, you're going to have to go through me, and I may just like it and not let you go any further.' "

Carol Ann is a certain beauty type, a careerist, if not indeed a professional. She is pretty, quiet, modest, and by now even stands naturally, at all times, with her feet set in Pageant style, at right angles to each other. There were girls in the North Carolina Pageant, too, with the same dedication to the genre; they are always Miss Somebody. But the only three girls marked on virtually everyone's list were all new to this world. Moreover, to indicate that a Pageant can attract diverse types, even in a rather homogeneous Southern State such as North Carolina, the three favorites were Jewish, black, and Italian.

The girl to beat was obviously Miss Asheville, Connie Lerner, the daughter of concentration-camp refugees, a dark, commanding young lady whose forbidding reserve masked a gentleness that was not visible on the surface. Her sweetness was only evident when her frankness found a confluence with it. Speaking of her family once, she suddenly stopped and said, in a disarmingly even tone, "Everything, everything, in my life is adorable." She was tall and sexy enough, an able classical pianist, smart, and in clever hands, under the tutelage of Mrs. Murph Gudger, who had trained another Miss Asheville, Maria Fletcher, all the way to Miss America 1962. Connie had certainly been weaker in Pageant ritual than in talent, so she had gone to charm school, lost seventeen pounds, scoured the East Coast for the right swimsuit, and "gotten to know my hair better."

Miss Newton-Conover, Pauletta Pearson, the first black girl, was another solid favorite, and strictly on merit. Appealing and friendly, bright and a leader in any company, she was also a stunning vocalist. Pauletta was named for Paulette Goddard, but changed her own named in the fifth grade to be distinctive. She was to win Miss Congeniality in a breeze. The affection that the other girls showed her was nearly matched by that they accorded Amelita, Miss Winston-Salem, who was nearly as distant from the pageant norm as Pauletta. Amelita was scorned as a "hippie" by uncompromising Pageant hard-hats. She had been named for Amelita Galli-Curci by her parents, both of whom were eye doctors in Chicago. Amelita was attending school in Winston-Salem at a unique institution named the School of the Arts. Peering out from raccoon eyes, "with a fat can, and I'm not stacked either," she could be nearly abusive about the whole beauty-pageant concept. "The amount of scholarship is not large enough to make it worth while," Amelita said. "We're up there for nothing, doing a show for a whole week for the Jaycees. It's a form of prostitution." However, among the other girls, so many of them unsophisticated country types, Amelita was gracious and winning. Many of them still wore Bermuda shorts, and a few were in a hotel for the first time in their lives. In the ladies' room at the luau, one girl had to fight back tears as she declared earnestly, "This will always be the most wonderful evening of my life." When an industrious young local newspaper reporter tried to poll all the contestants with a brief questionnaire, her forms were confiscated by a Pageant official, who informed her that that was out of the question. "There are some girls who may not know or could not make an intelligent answer," he explained. Indeed there were. One assured the judges that she kept up on current events with *The Saturday Evening Post*. Yet it was many of these same country Southern girls who voted Pauletta Miss Congeniality and requested, when Amelita sang, that they might come up to stage level and stand and watch her in quiet respect from the wings.

Each night, when not performing, the girls would gather together in the dressing room, and with Joan Mills, Miss Apex, on the piano and Amelita leading the chorus, they would pass the evening in a chummy campfire sing-along. Trite though it may sound, beauty-pageant contestants are drawn together in a bond and do come to care for each other quite as much as they always swear they do. In a fashion not unlike soldiers, they are determined, if necessary, to create a common enemy which can join them all the more closely. At this Pageant, it was easy. The villains were the judges, whom the girls found cold and erratic; they all booed them joyously in the dressing rooms Saturday night as they watched them being introduced on TV. However, were the judges not vulnerable, something else must be found: the Pageant officials, the schedule, the accommodations, the orchestra, the town, the weather. There is a real need to create this devil without, for were the girls to direct all their animosity toward one another, everything is so close that the whole Pageant would shatter.

It is to their credit, too, that so many girls can contain their disappointment. For instance, Wilson's representative, Judi Brewer, was dispirited from the moment she arrived and realized the level and sophistication of her competition. Gay Butner, who had directed Miss Wilson, was also on hand, as Miss Dunn's trainer and chaperone. Her girl, Beth Wellons, also happened to be in the same group as Judi, and also that of Pauletta Pearson. Like Pauletta, Beth was a ballad singer, although without her range or authority. Gay plotted a course for Beth that, she felt, offered her her only chance for victory.

First, Beth went to work on her figure and posture. She took off 19 pounds, going from 129 to 110 and from size 11 to 7. She won *Miss Dunn* at 32–24–39. By Raleigh, she measured 34–23–35½. Next Gay went to work on her wardrobe. Since Beth was a mature young lady, and a fashion major in college as well, Gay permitted her to choose all her own clothes and accepted her more as an associate in the venture than as a pupil. They also settled on a number of hair styles to match outfits, and a song medley that was both dangerous and tricky in its delicate and rapid changes.

"She must catch that audience, and carry it with her," Gay explained. "We want her clothes to create different airs and moods—all-American in the day, sophistication at night, so that each day of the Pageant Beth stands out more, and develops a poise and a presence that she can feel herself." The strategy went into effect the moment Beth arrived in an unusual tam o'shanter and pigtails. Thereafter, she was never the same twice, clothes or hair. Gay had brought her sister, Betty Kay, along specifically to handle the latter. Beth appreciated that most of the time she was dressing for the other girls, and not for the judges, but the whole scheme was based on momemtum. If Beth dressed the queen and played the queen all week until she felt the queen and others about her began to too, this feeling could surely be transmitted to the judges, if she made the finals. On Wednesday, she met with the judges, and everything was going so smoothly that she was able to laugh and joke with them. "I would recommend to any girl to enter a pageant," she told them. She had talent Thursday and swimsuit Friday ahead of her.

Big Momma would have been delighted to see Beth win, for Gay Butner was another one of her cronies. Gay had been on the panel that had voted for Carol Ann as the Rhododendron Queen. Everything is very close in Pageant. But Big Momma didn't give Beth much chance, and no one else had come forward either to offer a real challenge to Miss Asheville. Big Momma had to find herself a dark horse to make this interesting.

Midweek, she said: "What about this McDowell County?"

"She's real pretty, Momma," Judy said, and Carol Ann nodded assent.

"She's only high school and real country," someone else said.

"I know she don't know what she's doing up there," Big Momma said. "You see her in swimsuit last night when Asheville beat her? She's the prettiest thing up there, but I'll tell you what, in that swimsuit, it's hard to tell. And she don't have no idea at all even how to stand."

"She didn't even have her knees together when she was standing before the judges," Margaret said.

"Is that so?" Judy said nearly incredulously, and Marie heaved a huge sigh at the thought.

"Poor thing," Big Momma said. "If she got some help, she might have a chance if she can just make ten. There's no tellin' how these judges will vote. You never know. I was judgin' one time with this man, and he said, 'Big Momma, tell me, how do you judge a winner?' And while I was startin' to answer, he said, 'Well, I'll tell you how I judge a winner. I just pick the one I'd like to sleep with the best.' "

"What'd you say to him, Big Momma?"

"I said, 'You dirty dog.' And then I said, 'Well, I don't judge that way.' "

"You know, Momma," one of the gang informed her, "McDowell County was taught dancing by Maria Fletcher herself and Maria's father helped choreograph her talent here."

"Hush now," Big Momma said, very impressed at that. "McDowell County might just be the one to get the job done if we're not too late." She solicited some more information from her spies on the young lady.

McDowell County was a tall eighteen-year-old with the rhythmic name of Aletha Ballew. She was from the little town of Marion in western Carolina, but although she was backwoods—answering "Mercy" whenever she was complimented or flustered—there was a style about her, too. Her mother, who had come with a hairdresser for the whole Pageant, was a courtly woman, and her father was not only the Buick dealer back home but he also headed the school board. Big Momma was even more impressed to learn that if Aletha did not become Miss North Carolina, her father was going to take her to Europe. Aletha was obviously a girl you could work with. Besides her own hairdresser, she had brought the following to Raleigh: seventeen pairs of shoes, three evening gowns, five pants suits, six dressier dresses, seven casual ones, six boxes of make-up, and the one unfortunate swimsuit. Big Momma decided she should offer help to McDowell County.

Aside from her natural disposition to want to be in the middle of things, and also to want to seek out stray cats and provide them with her comfort and counsel, Big Momma is obliged on her own behalf to look for fun. She and her gang turn to pageants for this release. They eat when they please, sleep when they please, gossip, throw their clothes and hair accessories about their rooms like schoolgirls, and generally behave as mischievously as they can.

They also make it a point to keep up with everything that is going on all around. At Charlotte one year, they even took it upon themselves to harass a young man they only vaguely knew, but who had succeeded in securing a lady friend in his room. Big Momma and Margaret stood at his door whispering, "Hey doll, hey doll," and making panting noises and such, when, to their utter surprise, he came out of another door and confronted them in the act of tormenting him.

Big Momma and Margaret turned heel and started galloping down the hall, a full quarter-ton on the hoof, with the man, loping and laughing, in a friendly pursuit. "These were some antics," Margaret says. Every time she would try to duck by Big Momma and get into the lead, Big Momma would throw out her arms, virtually filling the whole corridor with her extended bulk, and blocking Margaret's advance. Finally, they rounded a corner, and ducked into one of the anterooms where the soda pop and ice machines were kept. There disaster struck. "Eleanor was breathing so hard and laughing so hard," Margaret says, "that when she sat down on the drink boxes, she just wet her pants."

"Hush," Big Momma says, laughing. "Oh, I was so tacky, so tacky."

This was, however, only a temporary setback for the devilish duo. When Big Momma spotted the man the next afternoon, she was down by the pool, while he was up on the motel balcony, in the company of yet another woman. "Well, I see you've finally got someone to say yes to you," Big Momma bellowed out.

"That's right, Big Momma," the guy yelled right back, as everybody around the pool sat up and listened intently to the exchange, "and she has better kidney control than you, too." For once, Big Momma was silenced.

What always intrigued Big Momma was the possibility of going to Atlantic City again for *Miss America* itself. A few years ago, the parents of the reigning Miss North Carolina had invited Big Momma and some of her gang to come along in a well-appointed bus that they had acquired to help carry Tarheel rooters to Atlantic City. Nothing has appealed to Big Momma more since then than the thought that the state judges might have the sense to select a queen whose parents would have the inclination and the wherewithal to provide another private bus to Atlantic City.

Among other things, the time there was a bus, the men aboard soon drifted to the back, where a bar was installed, and struck up a friendly card game. After a decent interval, to let the gentlemen get a couple of drinks under their belts, and confidence, Big

Momma, at her most demure, went to the game and inquired if she might enter. She professed a passing knowledge of the procedures, and was welcomed to the table. She made a quick $38, and might have wiped out the whole gathering before the bus reached the New Jersey line, had not Margaret smelled too much of a good thing herself and come back and said, "Well, Eleanor, how're things doing tonight in Big Momma's Casino?"

"Hush, doll," Big Momma said, but it was too late. The men had been alerted. Thereafter she and Margaret were able to take only modest amounts of cash from the men players.

With the idea that she might be returning to the World's Playground, should Miss McDowell County win, Big Momma approached Mrs. Ballew with some suggestions. She agreed immediately to buy a new, racier swimsuit. Aletha was instructed in the fundamentals of walking and standing with her knees together.

Mrs. Ballew said, "Oh, if someone could give me just one word of encouragement, I believe I'd make sure they got a new Buick."

Big Momma said, "Well, I think she can win, and you can make that an Electra."

Margaret said, "I'll *assure* you she'll win, and I'll settle for any new model at all."

Big Momma then informed her gang of Aletha's progress. "I told Mrs. Ballew that there will be no difficulty about anyone missing out on a trip to Paris if she should win. If McDowell wins and can't go, I told her, 'Don't worry, I'll go with your husband.' "

"Have you ever seen him, Eleanor?" Margaret asked.

"Doll, for Paris," Big Momma replied, "I'll take pot luck."

Judi, Miss Wilson, knew she never had a chance as soon as she arrived, so as the week went on her spirits even revived and the defeat did not jar her. A few weeks later, in the large competition at Hendersonville, she was named the North Carolina Apple Queen. By contrast, Beth, Miss Dunn, went downhill. She blew her chances at making ten Thursday, when her talent song medley, which had to be perfect, was a disaster instead. She was developing laryngitis, she couldn't hear the orchestra well, and she moved tentatively down the ramp at the back of the stage and caught a frog in her throat halfway through. Beth left the stage with her head down and her teeth gritted. The next night she looked fine in swimsuit, but the judges had lost interest. "I have only one regret," she said. "I'd just like the chance to meet with the judges again. I just want to tell them that I take back what I told them about recommending a beauty pageant for any girl. Never again."

Aletha did not make ten either, although it was difficult to understand how she failed. The judges voted her the most talented nonfinalist, and the press photographers voted her most photogenic, so she was acclaimed the prettiest girl of the seventy and one of the most talented, but was still shut out. She asked a judge afterward what she should have done differently to improve her chances, and he said there was nothing he could think of. Pam Eldred, Miss America, made a point to come across the stage afterward specifically to see her. "I lost once at State," Pam said. "I know how you feel. I really think you ought to try again. I wish you would." Aletha thanked her for the encouragement, but she didn't know. These things didn't seem to make any sense.

Amelita went out next. She lasted to the semifinals, but did not make the top five. Anyway, she got to sing on television, which was the most important thing to her. "I'm just not a pageant person," she said. "I knew that I must be gracious because this was my new city that I was representing, and I was grateful for what they have done for me. But I'll never enter another. I'm not used to this sort of crap, being treated like cattle. They wouldn't even let me talk to my friends from school, friends I see every day, because they're boys. What childishness. I don't feel sad now, because I just want to get away and be with real people again." Afterward, a friendly judge took her aside and said that he was glad she did not win, because he and his wife had discussed it and had decided that she was not a pageant type and should not waste any further time in the environment.

Pauletta won not only Miss Congeniality, but finished second runner-up, which is much better than any white representative of Newton-Conover had ever managed. She was pleased with her performance and grateful for the experience. "Miss America stands for all the talented young ladies of America," she said. "All her poise, grace, and dignity are unbelievable." As expected, Connie, Miss Asheville, won, and she was composed, almost sure in victory, it seemed. Her parents—Mr. Lerner is a successful self-made textile executive—and a younger brother were always more excited and nervous than Connie. "If there's anything I can do, I want to do it, if I can help," Connie said. "I feel very fortunate to represent two worlds, the one my parents had to leave, and this one, that we all love."

Big Momma and her gang offered their observations. Most everybody thought that the judges had probably made the right choice, despite themselves, but that almost every other decision that they made was wrong. The lobby was thronged with families and boy friends, and blind dates that some of the contestants had arranged for their new friends. Refreshments were served in the dining room, and the little queen who lost forty-five pounds after she had won her local was polishing off most of them. "She started with two pieces of pie last night," her trainer said. "I screamed at the judges back home when they gave her to me. They said State would be an incentive for her to lose weight—that's why they voted for her. I said, since when is a beauty pageant some kind of rehabilitation? All it will do is break her heart. Now she'll put seventy-five pounds back on faster than she took the forty-five off."

Big Momma bade her farewells and offered her congratulations and consolations before she headed off to a final all-night party. "I'm sorry for so many of them," she said. "That's why I won't judge myself any more. I've got too much compassion for young people. I'll go to any pageant, I love them all, but I won't judge. I can't do it to the young people. I can sit on the side and judge them when it doesn't count, but I can't be the one that really decides.

"Of course, a lot of people think none of it's any good, it's all silly. My husband for one. And it is so shallow. Oh my God, some of them are so surface. But it gets in your blood, and then it's worth it all to find the ones that are sincere. Doll, for the money, I could have gone to the Bahamas instead of coming here to State. Now you know how I must feel about pageants. Margaret and me are just lucky we got husbands who let us do these crazy things. I'll tell you what, you should see our antics when we go to the carpet show in Atlanta in the winter."

"Yeah," Margaret said, "but pageants are always better for us, because they're the one place anywhere where all the good-looking girls have to go to bed, and that leaves all the escorts for Eleanor and me."

"Hush," Big Momma said, "don't be tacky."

★ 7 ★

King Neptune and the Venuses of the World's Playground

While it is sometimes coyly suggested that the whole beauty-pageant concept is founded grandly in antiquity, with Paris and his golden apple, the formal pageant appears to be a modern creation with no obvious antecedents. In the years immediately preceding *Miss America,* casual bathing revues were held on many beaches, particularly on the West Coast, it seems, but the idea of actually selecting the fairest of the fair is apparently original with Atlantic City. Harry Godshall, the only surviving member of the original Pageant committee, cannot recall specifically who suggested the idea for a beauty pageant. Nor do contemporary accounts credit the source. Probably, it was something that evolved out of discussions, and, anyway, at the time it did not seem to be particularly important. The contest was only a small part of a big September show.

Nevertheless, while *Miss America* is the truly seminal beauty contest, inspiring all that followed, it cannot claim the distinction of being technically first. So far as is known that honor must belong to Rehoboth Beach, Delaware, which, forty-one years before, held a "Miss United States" competition in 1880. Until new evidence is presented to refute the claim, the Rehoboth credentials must be accepted. The resort itself, a quiet family retreat, makes no fuss about the fact, boasting instead of being "The Nation's Summer Capital," since a large part of its tourist population comes from Washington and the diplomatic community. Richard Nixon vacationed there immediately after winning the vice-presidential nomination in 1952, and Lynda Johnson and Chuck Robb were the sweethearts of its beaches the summer before they were married. Rehoboth is easily the largest resort on the Atlantic coast of Delaware, and, appropriately, it does host the Miss Delaware Pageant every summer. Still, it is not the town but an organization called the Pennsylvania Folklore Society that has been responsible for establishing Rehoboth as the site of the first beauty contest.

This is because it was a Pennsylvania girl who won the title that year. Her name was Myrtle Meriwether; she possessed, coincidentally, the same rather uncommon surname as the lady who won the first televised *Miss America* seventy-four years later. Myrtle came from the town of Shinglehouse, Pennsylvania, in the Oswayo Valley, only four miles from the New York state line. She was corresponding secretary for a women's business league, when a young public relations man in Buffalo convinced the girls to hold their convention at Rehoboth Beach. The PR man was none other than Elbert Hubbard, who was to become famous later for writing *A Message to Garcia* and editing the inspirational *Philistine* magazine.

According to Colonel Henry W. Shoemaker, the former president of the Folklore Society, who is responsible for salvaging this piece of history, Myrtle was strolling on the boardwalk one day when she noticed posters announcing the contest. She inquired further of a Joseph H. Dodge, one of the local officials who were sponsoring the contest in an effort to attract publicity for the resort. They had, among other things, signed on some real celebrities as judges. According to Colonel Shoemaker, "Dodge sized her up admiringly and called her attention to the specifications: single, not more than 25, minimum height 5 foot 4 inches, maximum weight 130 pounds. He praised Myrtle's evident qualifications and assured her she would win the Pennsylvania position, if not for the whole nation, should she stay over. Having another week's vacation from her gift shop remaining, she decided to stay."

Myrtle was obviously attracted by the potential rewards. The winner was assured a gilded plaque and a complete bridal trousseau worth $300, as well as the distinction of being entitled

"Miss United States—the most beautiful unmarried woman in our nation." It was an arduous competition, though. The judging lasted all week, and girls were examined on the basis of face, figure, hands, feet, and hair. Grace was also evaluated, and, of all things, so was poise. Besides all this, however, "costume" rated a full 50 per cent of the total judging, and this last factor meant that Myrtle had to go out and buy a new gown. As a consequence, she soon began to question her decision. The cost of the dress and other additional expenses would mean that she would barely have enough money left to pay her railway expenses home to Shinglehouse. She is reported to have slept fitfully that first night after she entered the contest.

By the time of the finals, the event had caught the full attention of sleepy old Rehoboth. Colonel Shoemaker reports, "The grounds were packed as far back as one could see when the parade of vestals (as it was called) began—the girls, with proud appeal, marching first in a group, then singly, around the open-air stage." The judges deliberated thoughtfully, we can be certain, since they composed, surely, the most distinguished beauty jury of all time. The three men who guaranteed themselves a place in history with this assignment were Judge Harrington of the Delaware Supreme Court; Monsieur Banwart, the French envoy to Washington; and a tinkerer by the name of Thomas Alva Edison.

When their decision was rendered to "a deeply impressed multitude, Myrtle almost fainted from shock and trembled like an aspen when she was led forward." Alas, she had to sell her brocade costume at half-price the next day, in order to get up enough scratch to return to Shinglehouse. The contest was not very successful either. Myrtle only settled back into her "quiet old routine," despite the fact that she was the most beautiful unmarried woman in our nation, and Rehoboth did not consider the event enough of a tourist attraction to repeat it. At least Edison does not appear to have been affected by his participation. He is still the most famous man ever to have judged a beauty pageant. It was not his fault that there was no more work in the line for another forty years.

The proceedings that eventually led to *Miss America* began in 1920 in Atlantic City with an idea from a gentleman named H.

Conrad Eckholm, who was the owner of the Monticello Hotel. He convinced the Business Men's League to sponsor a so-called Fall Frolic in an effort to keep tourists at the beach after Labor Day. Along the East Coast, the loveliest weather of the year comes in September, but tradition and the beginning of school have always dictated an end to the season precisely on Labor Day.

The Business Men's League, always searching for an attraction that could extend the season, bought Eckholm's idea. The Fall Frolic scheme seemed too frivolous to some of the men, and it was agreed to tie the event in with the paving of Atlantic Avenue (a main road, some blocks inland, which parallels the Boardwalk). So it was that that first year the Frolic—featuring an International Rolling Chair Pageant—was held on September 25, well after Labor Day, and on Atlantic Avenue, not on the Boardwalk. The parade of these wheeled wicker chairs—an Atlantic City institution today still, although now they are mechanized—lasted an hour, heading from the Inlet section to Chelsea. Appropriately, the procession was headed by a beautiful woman.

She was Miss Ernestine Cremora, who may be classified as a precursor of Miss America. Ironically, in light of the fact that Miss America is sometimes criticized today for being hawkish, and a veiled adjunct of the military, it is interesting to discover that this original pre-historical Miss America was attired in flowing white robes and identified clearly as "Peace." Later that evening she joined the others at a masked ball on the Steel Pier.

Harry Godshall, still active as an insurance man, calls himself "the last of the Mohicans" for being the final survivor of the Pageant founding fathers. Alert and precise, he is a dapper old gentleman, favoring bow ties. He recalls that this whole Frolic was far short of a success. Chamber of Commerce estimates were that the Rolling Chair Pageant drew one hundred twenty-five thousand spectators, but all such figures are suspect, since crowd estimates at Atlantic City are always provided by self-serving tourist officials, who are almost duty-bound to exaggerate. Maybe fifty thousand came to watch.

If the Frolic was not immediately successful, though, it unquestionably offered potential. Mayor Edward L. Bader termed it "a pleasant surprise," and a few of the more euphoric city officials dared venture the opinion that someday it could be the equal of the baby parade up the coast at Asbury Park. The president of the Chamber of Commerce was sufficiently impressed to appoint a committee to examine the possibility of repeating such a program the next September, 1921.

Thomas P. Endicott, who ran a dry-cleaning establishment ("When you see a spot, call Endicott"), was named Director General of the committee. Harry Latz, of the family that ran the Almac Hotel, was appointed vice-director general and chairman of the bathers' revue. Young Godshall was one of eight others named to the committee.* This was, by now, around February 1921, and the idea of a beauty contest was obviously settled on at least by this time, since Godshall was made chairman of that one aspect of the event. Godshall could count on some assistance from Herb Test, a reporter for the Atlantic City *Press*, who had been hired to handle publicity.

It was decided in committee that newspapers in the Atlantic City trading area would be approached with the suggestion that they use the beauty contest at Atlantic City as a gimmick to increase circulation. The papers would run a contest, urging readers to submit pictures of beautiful girls. The sponsoring newspaper would pick a winner and then buy her wardrobe. Atlantic City would pay for her transportation and the week at the seashore. Various other details were ironed out among the group, and then came the classic moment. There is no doubt who christened it all. Godshall says, "We were finishing up, and everyone was enthusiastic about what we were deciding, and it was then that Herb Test said, '*And we'll call her Miss America.*' "

Godshall himself chose, strictly off the top of his head, the cities that were invited to send their queens. He says that the first newspapers he selected at random quickly accepted the offer. Pittsburgh, the most distant from Atlantic City, was the farthest west; Washington was next farthest away, and the southernmost.

Little Margaret Gorman was fifteen that summer. She remembers no details of the time except that she was "madly in love" for the first time in her life. She cannot recall who sent her picture in to the paper or when she learned that she had won. In

* See Appendix 3, p. 301.

those years, her family would spend most of the summer in Lanham, Maryland, where her grandfather had a farm. Her father would commute to work at the Department of Agriculture. The Gormans were a respected Washington family. They lived at 3515 Cambridge Place, in Georgetown, which had been in the family since before the turn of the century.

John Boucher, who was then a reporter on the Washington *Herald,* says that it was a slow Saturday late in the summer when the word came down to the city room that the *Herald* judges had sifted through the pictures and decided on a winner. It was a Miss Margaret Gorman, 3515 Cambridge Place.

Boucher says that he and another reporter were dispatched to her house to give her the good news. It was a viciously hot day, and at 3515 the two reporters were advised that Margaret could be found in a nearby park, where it was cooler. Continuing their search, the two delegates were directed by other children to where they might find the first Miss Washington. Boucher says when they discovered her—the woman who, next month, would be declared "the most beautiful Bathing Girl in America"—she was shooting marbles in the dirt.

Margaret did turn sixteen about a week before she went off to Atlantic City with her mother and a chaperone, but even by her own judgment, "I was just a little schoolgirl." She measured 30–25–32, counting less at the bust than Twiggy, and at 5 foot 1 inch, 108 pounds, she was much the smallest of the contestants—in fact to this day she is still the tiniest of all winners, although Jacque Mercer, Miss America 1949, maintained after her coronation that she contained "less cubic inches." Anyway, little Margaret was cute, with an engaging smile. "She was very attractive for a kid," Mr. Godshall says.

Margaret and the other "beauty maids" arrived in town the day after Labor Day, Tuesday, September 6. For weeks, posters had dotted the East, featuring pictures of alluring bathing beauties; publicity releases promised: "Thousands of the most beautiful girls in the land, including stage stars and movie queens, will march in bathing review before judges in the Atlantic City Fall Pageant." In fact, while there was great variety, there were hardly thousands of beauties who paraded Wednesday morning on the beach, struggling in hot, loose sand. In an area roped off and decked out with flags, the girls sashayed a distance of about 1300 feet between the Garden and Steel Piers.

Aside from the girls, though, there were also competitions between children, men, organizations, and those in comic bathing attire. The "section for beauty" was subdivided. One class, containing the newspaper choices, specifically declared that "*no* actresses, motion picture players, or professional swimmers" were permitted. Margaret, who had maintained her amateur status in marble-shooting, competed in this field against half-a-dozen others.* They were usually referred to as the "Civic Beauties." Even though Herb Test had coined the perfect name, it actually found little currency at first and was seldom used for many years. The complete bulky preliminary title, "Inter-City Beauty Contest Winner," seemed, for some reason, to be the most favored identifying championship reference.

All the judging took place in one day, Wednesday. It began at noon in the Keith Theatre on the Garden Pier, where the civic beauties competed for a "beauty urn." Margaret won it, with Kathryn M. Gearon, Miss Camden, named first runner-up. The complicated rules of the time then required Margaret to compete in a play-off against the winner of the other major beauty division. That was Virginia Lee of New York City, who had been awarded the Endicott Trophy as "the most charming professional." The action moved to the Steel Pier, where the five judges—headed by Howard Chandler Christy, the artist, and John Drew, the matinee idol—looked the choices over.

Virginia Lee, flashier, more mature, certainly older, was the favorite, but sweet little Margaret was the judges' choice. Perhaps that set a pattern. In a showdown—whether two, three, five, or ten finalists—the judges will almost never vote for the one girl who exhibits the most brazen femininity. Why they picked Margaret in this case will never be known, but certainly the fact that they did established an original bias that has obviously influenced many decisions since then. For her victory, Margaret won the grand trophy, a Golden Mermaid statue that was 36 inches long and 10 inches high. It was valued at $5000, and actually worth about $50.

Within a couple of days, the first Miss America was on her

* See Appendix 4, p. 301.

way back to Washington. She received some recognition. "There were a bunch of people in the station to meet me, and all that foolishness," she says, but it faded away quickly, and for the rest of the year at Western High School hardly anyone even bothered to mention her feat to her. Widowed in 1957, Margaret has lived in Washington all her life, and now, in fact, resides in a town house not far from her childhood home on Cambridge Place. Her Golden Mermaid, which is probably the most valuable and memorable Pageant artifact, is no longer with Miss Gorman (whose married name is Mrs. Victor Cahill), nor is it in Atlantic City, which should be its natural home. For a long time, Mrs. Cahill's brother kept it at his swimming pool at Miami Springs, near the Hialeah race track. He sold the house there recently, though, and Mrs. Cahill believes that the original Mermaid has been moved to another house in Boca Raton, Florida. "It's right pretty for an old thing," she says.

That first show was such an instant hit that hardly was it finished before Harry Godshall sat down and wrote a letter to a prominent newspaper in every large city in the United States. The Pennsylvania Railroad, which catered to passenger traffic in those days, declared that "as an advertising campaign, the Pageant was, and is, a masterpiece, and it couldn't be bought for half-a-million dollars." In 1921, the city had tentatively chipped in $1000; in 1922 it upped its appropriation to $12,500, and the whole budget almost doubled, from $27,000 to $51,000.

The production became more sophisticated. In fact, the Pageant today is nearly a copy of the 1922 plan, with slight modifications. Only the United States Senate and Jimmy Durante have changed less than the Pageant since 1922. That year, the program was lengthened, with girls arriving on Wednesday for a dance and presentation at the Garden Pier. Thursday was devoted to the Rolling Chair Parade, which lasted two hours and offered one hundred prizes, and in many ways received more ballyhoo than the contest. That night, at the Music Hall on Steel Pier, the contestants were judged in "evening costume." It was not until Friday, the last day of the competition, that the girls were revealed in their sexy swimming garb, and then the Inter-City Beauties were only one of seven bathing divisions offered for inspection. It was more like a family cook-out than any skin show. City commissioners, police, firemen, members of the bands, and the whole pageant committee were among those dressed in bathing suits. That night, back at the Garden Pier, semifinal judging was held, and then, a couple of hours later at the Million Dollar Pier, Miss America was named.

Besides providing a neat model for the modern Pageant, that second year of competition also inspired local preliminaries for the first time. Fifty-seven girls, from as far away as Los Angeles, San Francisco, Seattle, and Toronto, qualified for the Inter-City competition, "beating thousands of the fair daughters of Uncle Sam" in the preliminaries. In Baltimore alone, a record seventy-five hopefuls competed, and Irma Knabe, admitting that her sights were set on Hollywood, was the winner. Sixty girls were entered in Miss Philadelphia. There was even a Miss Greater Camden. Four of the Ohio winners detoured on their way to the beach and invited President Harding to attend. Considering his keen eye for a good leg, it is surprising that he did not accept the invitation. He did send word that he would try to make it next year, but unfortunately he was dead by then, and no President has ever showed up. Two seaplanes from New York carried beauties from the big city, and Mayor Bader himself went up to wave greetings from a Curtiss seaplane. Daily reports detailed the progress of a train speeding in from the west, with a carload full of beauties.

From Columbus, Ohio, in the company of her mother, came Mary Katherine Campbell, the fifteen-year-old daughter of a CPA. She was a straight-A high-school student, who was later to attend Ohio State and Ohio Wesleyan. Her hair was nearly red and she wore a size three shoe. "I was pretty naïve when I was starting," she has recalled. "Mercy, after all I was only fifteen. You were supposed to be sixteen, so I was sixteen, but I was really only fifteen in May. I came home and told my mother, 'I was chosen Miss Columbus, and they said it's because of my figure. Mother, what's a figure?'

" 'My mother said: 'It's none of your business.' "

Obviously, Mary Katherine was a fitting successor to Margaret, and she was a favorite as soon as she arrived for the official greeting. This took place on Wednesday, along with supporting events such as golf, tennis, and kite tournaments, soccer, boat races, ocean swimming, and an automobile run clear to Camden. The big attraction, however, was King Neptune, who was the male star of the show for years, until someone at last had the sense to invent Bert Parks. This first big year, King Neptune was played—robes, beard, pitchfork, and all—by Hudson Maxim, who was sixty-nine then, with a real beard, and contacts to local hotelmen, who had bestowed this honor on him. Hudson Maxim was the inventor of smokeless gunpowder, and thus a celebrity of sorts. He was absolutely humorless. This may be partly accounted for by the fact that he had inhaled so many vapors while experimenting with smokeless powder that he had become terribly sensitive to almost all smells of the powder family. Just a strange whiff of talcum, for instance, would drive him up the wall. As a consequence, he was surrounded at all times by a court of honor composed of eighteen powderless beauties whose sole job it was to keep King Neptune clear of all potentially offensive odors (and any people who might be possessing them). This staff was actually known as The Scent Guard.

The pretentious accounts of the Pageant in those early days gloriously overdid King Neptune. He was invariably referred to as His Oceanic Majesty or The Marine Monarch of the Sea, and he was given full credit for dealing with the weather, either O. Sol or Jupiter Pluvius. Usually, he ruled from a throne on stage that was placed in front of a large facsimile of a sea shell, with his court and all the contestants about him. The girls were always known as Venuses—Venuses of the great West, a Venus of the Sunshine State, a dimpled Venus. The year an observing queen from Australia showed up, she became, predictably, Venus of the bush country.

For a party, there was the Frolique of Neptune, and it was often deemed most appropriate to first bring him to Atlantic City via a sea route. Saluted by an aerial display, Hudson Maxim and his Scent Guard, in the lead boat of a whole fleet, landed at the Inlet Yachtsmen's wharf, where, according to the local newspaper, this scene greeted him:

> Miss Margaret Gorman, who, as Miss Washington last year was crowned "Queen of the Pageant" because of her Pickford-like beauty, tripped blithely from behind the scenes to the water's edge.

> Wearing a silver crown studded with pearls and a gown of silver and sea green, giving the appearance of seaweed mottled with sand, the captivating capital beauty turned, and with outstretched arms, released a large American flag that rippled out from her shapely shoulders as she bowed in acknowledgement of the cheers that volleyed from the beholders jammed about the clubhouse and adjacent bulkheads.

As His Oceanic Majesty marveled at this, Atlantic City's Safety Director, William Cuthbert, who was obviously just as taken, stepped ashore, lost his footing, and tumbled into the water, where he was nearly crushed to death between the boat and the dock. Others leaped in to help and "the throngs cheered them on for their presence of mind." Then, on the heels of this mishap, everyone proceeded to the country club, where many of the contestants were bade to stand up on chairs for a group picture. The chairs collapsed, "putting a thrill into the occasion." Miss Philadelphia was knocked cold on the veranda floor, but revived for the competition.

Thelma Blossom, Miss Indianapolis, was the early leader. She won the Pageant's first evening-gown competition, and was also a big hit in the parade, since she was wheeled along in a rolling chair that was shaped like an ear of corn. Mary Katherine had the staying power, though, and won the Inter-City, whereupon she moved into the finals against three other championship contenders—the professional division winner, the amateur winner, and the defending champ, Margaret Gorman. The rules permitted repeat performances then. Mary Katherine won the votes of six of the eight judges, however, and was proclaimed the new Miss America. She reacted by reaching to her throat with a gasp, while Margaret set a precedent by crying for joy for her victorious rival.

Mary Katherine returned the following year "in Aphrodite-like form" to defend her title, and Margaret came back for another shot at it too. By now, at the advanced age of eighteen, Margaret was no longer the shy lass of 1921; she shocked some of her fans by eschewing the more modest skirt-type bathing suit and appearing in a clinging adhesive style. She and Mary Katherine were waived to the finals, where they faced off against fifteen preliminary winners.

By now, there were seventy-five contestants from thirty-six states, even though most of the girls still represented cities or regions instead of whole states. In only its third year of operation, though, *Miss America* had grown so fast that Mississippi was the only state east of the Mississippi River without representation, and the eleven Western states not present were almost all the least-populated states in the union. It was truly a national event, which had, the Atlantic City *Press* rhapsodized, "outgrown our fondest dreams . . . outreached our most ambitious plans." Norman Rockwell and James Montgomery Flagg were among the six artists who served on the judges' panel. The Associated Press sent out two hundred words a day, and *The New York Times,* which now devotes about two paragraphs to the event, turned over a whole two-page spread in its rotogravure section to the Pageant. News of the proceedings was wired to Philadelphia, and then broadcast on radio to a waiting world. The Chamber of Commerce president called it, simply, "priceless propaganda," and there were only a few complaints from grouchy municipal gadflies that the city had agreed to double appropriations to $25,000—despite a 1922 deficit of $9231.87. The Chamber dismissed these critics—who had taken to calling the event "the Pay-geant"—by explaining that the loss was due only to "paying carfare and entertaining the beauties."

Everyone raved about the high quality of the girls. Several had been to college, or, on closer examination, had at least considered the possibility. Miss Syracuse was advertised as fresh from a convent. Miss Hammonton, New Jersey, had been chosen in absentia that summer while making the grand tour of Europe. Miss Chicago had been selected over 4300 entries. Miss Gloucester, New Jersey, had been elected rather like Miss Rheingold in the years ahead. She won with 182,678 votes cast at the local Lions Club. But Mary Katherine was still "the fairest daughter of Venus."

She beat Miss Brooklyn, Ethelda Bernice Kenvin, in the finals at the Million Dollar Pier. Though Miss Columbus was startled at her second straight win because she thought Ethelda to be "the most beautiful thing I had ever seen," her victory saved the Pageant some embarrassment in that it turned out that Miss Kenvin was actually Mrs. Everette Duane Barnes, whose husband had just been called up from Peoria to play first base for the Pittsburgh Pirates. Nevertheless, Mary Katherine's back-to-back wins occasioned some local anxiety, the fear that one popular girl could grow bigger than the whole Pageant. It was decreed that anyone who could win three times in a row would take home a permanent Golden Mermaid and be retired from the competition.

When Mary Katherine came back the next fall in that quest, she had to face the largest field in history. There were eighty-three contestants, and it seemed as if every town in America wanted in. The Newspaper Publishers Association issued a bulletin advising its members not to associate themselves with the Pageant and sponsor its local contests because it was providing Atlantic City with "the most flagrant use of free publicity" in history. But not a paper backed out.

The Pageant was extended to five full days—Tuesday through Saturday—and there was plenty of activity. While the talent competition had not yet been conceived, the girls were put through a heavy schedule at a fast pace. Miss Chicago sighed, "This business of being a beauty is getting to be as strenuous as being the Prince of Wales." Since pure looks counted so heavily, it was important to catch the judges' eye. Miss Austin was immediately distinguished by her hair, 54 inches long, still the unofficial record. Miss Brooklyn "was conspicuous because of a vividly-colored butterfly which had been painted on her right shoulder."

"They just paraded around," says Adrian Phillips, a past president of the Pageant. "In those days, you could have a pretty good batting average picking the winners just by looking at the pictures when they came in."

Even at that early date, though, the girls had to undergo informal interviews with the judges. "It was not nearly as pointed as it has become," says Ruth Malcolmson, who was Miss Philadelphia that year. "We would sit at lunch with the judges and carry on a friendly conversation. It was a great deal more casual. For instance, Jack Dempsey was a friend of one of the judges, so he just sat down at the table and chatted too."

Ruth was, like Mary Katherine, a returning champion. The year before, 1923, she had won a silver sea shell as best in the amateur division. This year she returned, but as Miss Philadelphia in the Inter-City. She was the people's choice, too. Atlantic City has always depended upon Philadelphia to supply the bulk of its tourist population; even today, Miss Pennsylvania draws applause in Convention Hall equal to Miss New Jersey. To that point, the fourth year, to the dismay of the promoters, no Philly girl had ever fared very well.

Ruth was cut in the classic mold, though. Her mother was her chaperone. She sang in the choir in her Lutheran Church back home. She had never been to a hairdresser's in her life, and used no make-up except lipstick. Her bathing suit was a demure little number that she says was "much like a mini dress." Certainly, it did not cling. Nevertheless, it seemed to her that she was beaten before she got started. The Rolling Chair Parade was still the main feature of the week. It showed off the whole Boardwalk, which was vital in obtaining the support of the merchants. That year, the Parade featured fifty bands and floats that were valued at $250,000. In this company, you had to be spectacular to gain attention. Ruth took one look at the float she was supposed to ride on. It was so spare she broke into tears and cried to the point where a doctor had to be summoned.

She pulled herself together, though, and went back out to mount her float. It was a bare flat-bed truck, with only a fake fireplace, spinning wheel, and a throw rug. Ruth was assigned a black taffeta dress, and given a court of honor dressed as Quaker maids. She was supposed to be Betsy Ross. Naturally, she won the parade award, but, for the first time, there were rumbles that a Philadelphia bias was showing.

On Friday night, though, Ruth also won the bathing revue in the stifling heat of the large hall on Steel Pier. There was no place there for spectators to sit down and watch, but the hall was so packed that people could not fall down when they fainted. Then, on Saturday, Ruth and fourteen other regional semifinalists were taken to Atlantic City High School for closer inspection. The girls were dressed in knitted skirts, with stockings. Besides the judges, only chaperones and mothers were permitted to watch. First the group was pared to ten; then to a final five, who would compete that night at the Million Dollar Pier against the unbeatable Mary Katherine.

The Pier featured an electric American flag that waved over the proceedings. Spectators watched in rocking chairs, but there were precious few of these and most fans had to stand. In the heat, four women fainted, while the judges deliberated endlessly. At last, the Mayor of Philadelphia left and went across the Boardwalk to a theater, leaving word that he be notified should Ruth win. She was sitting in a balcony box with her parents. It took the judges four hours to make up their minds. "Finally," Ruth says, "someone just came up to me and said, 'You're wanted down on stage.' "

The crowd began to stir with anticipation even before the crimson curtains parted. In the confusion, Mary Katherine was told to step forward, and there was a gasp from the floor. Then Ruth was informed that she was the winner, and she moved out ahead of Mary Katherine. No one was quite sure what was happening until a big voice boomed out from the middle of the crowd: "Philadelphia win the prize." Somebody ran for the Mayor. Mary Katherine rushed to kiss her successor. "You have been my choice," she said, and Ruth cried, "I am so happy." The band broke into the national anthem; the electric flag waved.

Philadelphia rushed to honor its queen, the first home town to really put on the dog for a native Miss America. A reception was scheduled at City Hall, with the Mayor himself as the host, and on the way back from Atlantic City to this celebration, Ruth was met by a police escort while she was still almost forty miles from town. A special ferry boat was used to carry her over the Delaware River. In Philadelphia, crowds twice broke ranks and pressed up against her car. At City Hall, she was presented with her own Rickenbacker automobile. As much as seven years later, when she married Carl Schaubel—whom she had met at a polo game, when he knocked a ball into her lap—she remained enough of a local celebrity so that the crowd around the church held her up and almost forced her to be late to her own wedding.

Ruth was eighteen when she won *Miss America,* and a high-school graduate, so that she was the first winner in a position to exploit the title. Margaret had gone back to Western High practically unnoticed. After each of her wins, Mary Katherine had received some offers: all told, from three movies, two musical comedies, a circus, and vaudeville. The second year, her mother rejected a Ziegfeld proposal with horror, but did permit Mary Katherine to go out for a few weeks on the Keith Circuit and make a stab at singing. "You couldn't hear me past the third row," Miss Campbell explained later. Then she went back to school again, too.

Ruth had no objection to show business, but she also had no interest. Out of curiosity more than anything else, she did agree to go watch some Ziegfeld rehearsals, but she quickly turned him down. "It just didn't appeal to me," she says. Instead, she limited herself almost entirely to making appearances at hospitals, institutions, and church bazaars around Philadelphia. She made one substantial trip, traveling as far as Minneapolis, where she was made an honorary princess of an Indian tribe. In the end, she refused to come back to Atlantic City and defend her title, charging that professionals had infiltrated the Inter-City competition. The Pageant promoters promptly changed the rules, on this cue, and declared that any former Miss America was ineligible to enter the lists again. The rules in this regard were firmed up even more after the 1941 Pageant, when Rosemary LaPlanche, the 1940 first runner-up, returned to take the crown. Since then, no contestant has been permitted to compete at Atlantic City more than once, although of course, there is no limit placed on the number of locals that she can win or state pageants that she can enter.

Although certain different types of Miss Americas appear, often in groups over a short period of time, the first three queens were the prototypes of the dominant strain that invariably exerts itself and comes to the fore again at regular intervals. This model Miss America is generally a shy woman, with no sustaining interest in pageants or any other form of publicity; but for this one incidental burst of fame, she is never again in the public eye. This type almost always has a happy and successful marriage—so long as she does not make the mistake of marrying in haste too quickly after her reign. It is the rare girl who has her wits about her sufficiently to make such an important decision after a year of such concentrated adulation. The type marries a successful, level-headed man, and not infrequently lives happily ever after. Margaret married a real-estate agent. Mary Katherine married

Frederick Townley, a Du Pont executive. Twice, for long periods, she has managed to escape into anonymity; the Pageant has lost track of her again. Ruth married a military man, who subsequently became a college administrator. They still live quietly in Philadelphia, speaking softly in the recognizable accents of that city. The Golden Mermaid is kept down in the cellar, in the recreation room, along with some polo mallets and other memorabilia of their lives that are regarded as equally important.

By contrast, the fourth Miss America was the original of the other main stock of Atlantic City queen—the Hollywood dreamer. While she soon ended up as an unknown housewife, just like her predecessors, Fay Lanphier, Miss America 1925, started out by breaking much new ground. She was the first winner from the West. As Miss California, she was the first winner to represent a whole state, not just a city. She was the first Miss America to profit from the title, the first to make a movie, the first to get a divorce, and, at last, the first to die. She succumbed to virus pneumonia at the age of fifty-three in Oakland in 1959, survived by two daughters and a second husband, her high-school sweetheart, who had married her in 1931. They lived in the East Bay suburb of Orinda, where, at her death, Fay was a member of local Athens Chapter No. 277 of the Order of the Eastern Star. After all those years, only the obituaries brought her out of obscurity.

Thirty-four years before, upon her victory, Fay seemed assured of a lifetime of celebrity. She already was signed to a movie contract, and her victory guaranteed her the title role in a film entitled *The American Venus.* Three hundred thousand people were supposed to have watched the Rolling Chair Parade; anyway, it was the largest crowd ever. The Pageant itself had live national radio coverage. Stars surrounded Fay. De Wolf Hopper was emcee; Ernest Torrence, a well-known character actor, was His Oceanic Majesty; and his son, Triton, appeared for the first and only time with sixteen-year-old Douglas Fairbanks, Jr., in the part.

The year before, as Miss Santa Cruz, Fay had finished third, trailing only Ruth and Mary Katherine, and she returned as the obvious choice. In the final balloting, she won twelve of the fifteen votes. Besides, her runner-up, Miss Los Angeles, had already lost once to Fay in Miss California. She attended local Episcopalian church services the morning after her coronation, and was then whisked to New York for a special salute that was apparently arranged by her new film employers. Will Rogers and Rudolph Valentino were among those to toast her. It is estimated that she took $50,000 out of a sixteen-week personal appearance tour that followed.

Fay then hied to Hollywood, where she made *Venus*, and, somewhat later, a Laurel and Hardy film. Those who were privileged to see her in these vehicles are reluctant to term her the worst actress in film history only because no one person has ever seen all the actresses in all the films. Her option was dropped. She promptly ran through a six-month marriage with a "furniture manufacture," and by 1930 had returned to Paramount Studios as a typist. "I'll make a success on the screen this time," she vowed. Luckily, her childhood sweetheart returned the next year and took her away from all that.

Fay was succeeded in 1926 by Norma Smallwood, Miss Tulsa, who topped some seventy-two other girls, including Miss Dallas, Rosebud Blondell. She grew up to be Joan Blondell, the actress, and was the first of several also-rans in the contest who went on, eventually, to more fame and success than any winner. Miss Blondell had, at the time, been appearing with her father's vaudeville troupe, Ed Blondell & Co., when it began to run short of funds in Texas. In those days, when the local pageants were newspaper gimmicks, some locals offered bigger money than Atlantic City. Miss Dallas carried a $2000 first prize, which was calculated to be enough to get Ed Blondell & Co. back to New York.

"I was just fifteen and already had a good, big chest, the kind garbagemen whistle at," Miss Blondell has reminisced. With the Dallas banner decorating that attraction, Rosebud made the semifinals, but her mere participation is more interesting as a commentary on the rule enforcement at the time. Two good, big breasts notwithstanding, Rosebud was still only fifteen and a professional entertainer in a contest which specifically prohibited girls younger than sixteen and professional entertainers of any age.

Norma Smallwood, the winner, was a petite brunette, with

an acute financial sense. It is said that she milked $100,000 out of the title, and while that figure may be somewhat inflated, she almost certainly made more money that year than President Coolidge or Babe Ruth. And she had staying power; she married not one, but two oilmen. In being severed from the first of these gentlemen, she also achieved the distinction of enduring the messiest divorce among Miss Americas, although Bess Myerson must be credited with the most spectacular separation since first her first husband accused her of kidnaping their daughter, and later Bess had him arrested for entering her apartment, ripping off her pajamas, and grabbing her by the throat.

Anyway, Norma first married oilman Thomas Gilcrease, who later became quite famous as a collector of Indian art. The product of this union was a daughter who was named Des Cygnes L'Amour Gilcrease. This means "Of the Swans the Love" Gilcrease. Sadly, love was otherwise soon missing from the Gilcrease household, and when he left on a trip, Norma moved her mother in and they proceeded to set up what was described as "a beauty business" in the house. Gilcrease should have been forewarned. When Norma was named Miss America, her first words were: "I am too happy to talk now. Does Mother know it yet?"

According to the 1934 divorce proceedings, after Gilcrease left, Norma and Mother also started giving little Des Cygnes L'Amour, then aged two, sips of highballs. On one occasion, according to the testimony, the tyke even passed out from this family exercise. Also it was alleged that Norma entertained men on numerous occasions while Gilcrease was away, a revelation that later occasioned many references to her as "Mistress America." The husband's complaint included these charges: "Plaintiff further states that in the spring of 1933, the defendants, Norma [Smallwood] Gilcrease and Mahala Dickerson [Miss America's mother], fitted up what they called a studio in a building about two hundred yards from the plaintiff's residence house and said studio was equipped with an electric refrigerator, a piano, a radio, a lounge or day-bed, various cushions, rugs and other paraphernalia, and the windows, in said studio, were curtained so that the curtains could be drawn to shut off the view from the outside. . . . That the said defendant, Norma Gilcrease, permitted married men and others to come to plaintiff's residence house in his absence and to fondle her person and to hug and kiss her, sometimes in the presence of servants; that one man commonly called Napoleon . . . came frequently to plaintiff's residence house during his absence within the last year and on several occasions fondled, hugged and kissed plaintiff's wife and she did not protest, but apparently participated in the performance . . . and at a later period and early in the year 1933, to wit, about the month of May, the said defendant, Norma Gilcrease, became infatuated with [a certain gentleman] . . . and during plaintiff's absence, the said [gentleman] came to plaintiff's residence house and took up his residence for a week or more, slept in plaintiff's bed and brought with him changes of clothing and hung them in plaintiff's closet; that he entered plaintiff's house without knocking and had free access to all of the rooms in the house and for his night-wear, used a part of plaintiff's night-clothing." Gilcrease got the divorce and, as well, custody of Of the Swans, etc. Norma married another oilman. Besides Fay Lanphier, she is the only Miss America to have died.

Norma had not returned to Atlantic City in September 1927 to pass her title on. She had demanded $600 for the appearance, and when it was not forthcoming she took the best available offer and went to North Carolina, where she crowned some county fair queen. By now the Pageant was under fire from a growing number of hotelmen who felt that it invested the town with a tawdry and libertine image, and Norma's action was a painful blow to the defense. Nevertheless, this growing critical attitude was not reflected into the precincts, and sixty-nine girls made up another large field. Almost a third of them boasted of some college affiliation, and two contestants sought careers as "aviators." Norma's successor as Miss Tulsa had brought her identical twin sister along; they planned to assault the New York stage next, as a team.

The winner, though, was cut from the original sweet mold. Lois Delander, Miss Illinois, was sixteen years old, the daughter of a county clerk from Joliet. A high-school junior, she was an honor student excelling in Latin, and she had won both a music-memory course and a medal for knowing Biblical verses. Her lips had never touched coffee or tea. Also, she looked very good in a red and blue bathing suit. Lois entertained no real thoughts of victory, though. She had entered a local contest only because her ballet teacher had encouraged her too, and in Atlantic City, she gave herself so little chance that she packed her bags for departure the night she won. Upon victory, she spoke mostly about losing valuable time in school, and her parents took her almost directly home.

Lois, a grandmother of seven now, still living in suburban Chicago, says that she won a scepter, four trophies, a Bulova watch, an Oldsmobile, and a screen test that she never took. Though she had a subdued role as Miss America, she says she did have the privilege of meeting President Coolidge, Red Grange, Charles Lindbergh, Fred Waring, and Amelita Galli-Curci. Also, in a sense, Lois had the longest reign of any Miss America, since the Pageant was put in mothballs after her victory, and was not held again until 1933. Lois went on to college, and then, like so many other Miss Americas, was happily married and never heard from again.

Bette, What Are You Going to Do if You Win This Thing Tonight?

For some mysterious reason, the Pageant has always taken pains to promulgate the fiction that it closed down for several years because of the Depression. This was not at all the case, especially considering the fact that the contest folded early in 1928, almost two years in advance of the Crash. Prescience has never been a strong suit of *Miss America,* nor is there any evidence to suggest that the Pageant suffered a flash of it then. The Pageant was a promotion. It was abandoned because the key persons in the resort, the hotel operators, who had once championed it, soured on it.

They became convinced that the Pageant, for all its notice, gave Atlantic City a bad name, and cost the hotels respectable cash-and-carry patrons. Once this view prevailed, the venture was lost. The last Pageant of the early era, in 1927, actually made a profit of $7000 on a gross of $130,000, and attracted the largest crowds to that point, but the hotelmen had made up their minds that it was "worn out and useless" and "a cheap exploitation of physical beauty." Many also disapproved of growing political encroachment; there was some dark talk of graft.

For support, dubious sweeping charges were trumped up. Hotel Men's Association President Julian Hillman declared: "There has been an epidemic recently of women who seek personal aggrandizement and publicity by participating in various stunts throughout the world, and the hotelmen feel that in recent years that type of women has been attracted to the Pageant in ever-increasing numbers." An associate added, "Many of the girls who come here turn out bad later and though it may happen in other cities, it reflects on Atlantic City."

Many were not deceived. "There is no moral question involved," the Atlantic City *Press* assured its readers, and Dr. I.N. Griscom, the president of the Realty Board, reminded the hotels of their heritage. "It was not the wealthy, but the masses that made Atlantic City," he said. "Atlantic City was made by the hot dog stands and the 5¢ beer gardens, and our present Boardwalk hotels are the result. You hotelmen have said that our Pageant is vile and obscene, yet bathing costumes worn by [your] patrons on the beach every day are worse than any that are worn in the Pageant."

The hotelmen were moved, least of all, by such painful reminders of their plebeian past. They voted their pocketbooks, 27–3, at a March 1928 meeting. The decision to cancel the Pageant was tempered only by a tacit agreement to examine the possibility of reinstituting the enterprise again in 1929 or 1930, when the magnificent new $10,000,000 Convention Hall would supposedly be ready for occupancy.

Of course, it must be said in the defense of the hotelmen that there was more than fancy to the claims that *Miss America* engendered notoriety. Predictably, there was some sort of hassling every year, and much of it was of a spectacular nature. In fact, virtually until 1951, hardly a year went past when the Pageant or Miss America herself was not attended by controversy or even threats of scandal. In this respect, it is worth noting that in modern times the single beauty pageant that attracted the most attention was Miss Universe of 1957, when the newly crowned Miss United States, one Leona Gage of Maryland, was stripped of her title after helpful neighbors back home volunteered the information that she was in fact a wife and mother, on her second marriage at age eighteen. That contest drew 20,000,000 breathless newspaper lines, and catapulted the erstwhile Miss Gage onto the Ed Sullivan Show, a Las Vegas revue, and beyond. It is the best recent reminder of all the controversial surprises that used to happen regularly at *Miss America.*

In 1923, for instance, when Miss St. Louis, Charlotte Nash,

was eliminated from the evening-gown competition at the Garden Pier, there was nearly a riot. Charlotte had won the Rolling Chair event, and was a huge local favorite, known thereafter as "the lovely and unspoiled daughter of the great American West." Though suffering this defeat, she had her dimples insured for $100,000, and had her face printed on advertising fans that Yellow Cab distributed, where she was identified as "Popular Favorite," as if she were some up-and-coming welterweight contender. Miss Nash went on to marry theater magnate Fred G. Nixon-Nordlinger a year later. The marriage was terminated in a Paris hotel on March 11, 1931, when he was shot dead. Charlotte was tried but acquitted, whereas at Atlantic City, the 1923 jury had put her fourth.

That same year, Miss Alaska had showed up from Juneau to hosannas since "her startling beauty was untouched by the rigors of over 5000 miles that required dog-sled, aeroplane, train and motor car." Unfortunately, Harry Godshall fell privy to some contradictory information. "She had never seen Alaska," he says. "She was the wife of a fellow by the name of Earl Liederman, who was a physical culture expert looking for publicity. Where she got that letter from the Juneau newspaper we never knew, but we were damned sure not going to Alaska to find out." Instead, Godshall reassigned her to the professional division, whereupon Mrs. Liederman filed suit against Godshall and the director-general of the Pageant for $50,000 each.

The fact that Mrs. Liederman had no newspaper backing was what bothered the Pageant. That she was a married contender for Miss America was of no moment because to this point nobody had bothered to write a rule saying Miss America couldn't be married. In those days, *Miss America* was always coming up short on rules, and then writing them after the fact. The next year, 1924, Mrs. Mildred M. Prendergast, the wife of an attorney and mother of a seven-month-old baby, turned up as Miss Boston. The Pageant had not yet gotten around to writing a marriage rule, so when they barred her arbitrarily, she sued for $5000. This time they also remembered to write the rule.

The cruelest blow came the following year, though, when Bernarr Macfadden's New York *Graphic* came out with a series of articles in November claiming that the fix had been in for

Fay Lanphier. According to the *Graphic*—which sold syndication of the scoop to eighty-six other papers—Miss Lanphier had been selected in advance to appear as the star in *The American Venus,* a Paramount film about a beauty contest winner. The *Graphic* wrote of a shadowy "Beauty Trust" and even claimed that Miss America, Jr., a baby parade that had been held that year for the first time, was also a tank job.

And there were more implications. Broadway impresario Earl Carroll was revealed as having been a judge in the Miss Coney Island Pageant, where one of his showgirls was selected to go on to Atlantic City. When Carroll heard that, he protested that he was an innocent victim. He fired the girl, Kathryn Ray, he fired her PR man, and then he sued the *Graphic* for $1,000,000.

In fact, there surely was some hanky-panky at the lower level that year. The presence at Atlantic City of Miss Ray and Dorothy Knapp, another New York showgirl who suddenly materialized as Miss Manhattan after the original winner took "sick," had been the reason that Ruth Malcolmson refused to return to defend her crown. She had wise counsel.

Miss Knapp arrived in town with both ankles in bandages. She was carried, with much fanfare, from the train by two huge behemoths, who said that she had been in a serious accident. However, following the predictable publication of numerous pictures of Miss Knapp in this estate, she appeared shortly thereafter in the Rolling Chair Parade without any bandages. Indeed, it is reported that she Charlestoned much of the length of the Boardwalk.

Then, on Thursday, when Miss Ray showed up for the evening gown competition "wearing a Nile green gown incrusted with brilliants," a PR man named Milton D. Crandall began screaming in protest from a proscenium box. Fulton Lewis, Jr., the commentator, who was there, recalled that at this, many in attendance starting jamming the doors, and "somebody turned in a riot alarm, which wasn't necessary because the police reserves were swarming the joint."

Crandall was merely trying to call attention to the fact that his clients, Miss Pittsburgh and Miss Erie, were herewith retiring from the contest because of the continued disputed presence of a professional in the Pageant. When Lewis went to phone this bulletin in, he came back to find an enraged Earl Carroll demanding his arrest. Two cops then grabbed Lewis and knocked him to the Boardwalk, tearing his pants at both knees.

Nevertheless, in the face of all this hullabaloo, there is no evidence that anybody has ever fixed a *Miss America.* The only thing people were really guilty of was using the Pageant to extract publicity. Most particularly this includes the *Graphic,* which built its scandal on the word of an unidentified passenger on the *SS Manchuria* (out of San Francisco and bound for New York, through the Panama Canal). This confidant reported that he had overheard Fay Lanphier's representative boast that she had been assured victory, and the paper bolstered this contention by claiming that an official from Paramount had signed Fay to a contract before she was declared Miss America.

This was true, so far as it went. The Paramount man, Glendon Allvine, later revealed that he had been dispatched to Atlantic City to sign all the top contenders in advance, so that the studio could be assured of getting Miss America cheap for *The American Venus.*

Insupportable as they were, the *Graphic* accusations did cast an incriminating shadow over the whole show. As had Earl Carroll, the Pageant promptly sued—for $3,000,000—and while neither ever collected, *Miss America* had the satisfaction of at last drawing an abject retraction out of Macfadden. He wrote in his paper that "the information upon which we relied proved unreliable." Unfortunately, this about-face did not come until September 22, 1928, when the Pageant was dormant.

The Pageant was not revived until 1933, and even then most of the city greeted it coolly, even suspiciously. The Hotel Men's Association refused to support it, and in these circumstances holding a pageant is like trying to work Lourdes without the water. The Mayor and the City Council did endorse the new Pageant, though, and Armand Nichols, who had previously served as the Mayor's secretary, took charge. *Miss America* was quickly up to its old tricks, though it was difficult to separate the controversy from the chaos. Soon, the overriding concern was whether or not a queen could be selected before the whole shaky enterprise went broke. A queen was crowned but the effort was so hastily discredited that for years afterward the Pageant refused to acknowledge the existence of a Miss America 1933.

Thirty girls from twenty-eight states showed up, many near a state of exhaustion; they had been selected at amusement parks and then dispatched on a seven-week vaudeville tour in an effort by the parks to recoup expenses. Misses Maine and New Hampshire neglected to bring bathing suits. Miss Oklahoma suffered appendicitis shortly after her arrival. As she started to greet the judges, Miss New York State fainted from a bad tooth. Miss West Virginia later succumbed to a stomach-ache, presumably brought on from eating lobster with ice cream. There were many shady characters about. Miss Connecticut's mother, her chaperone, was advised by a friendly observer never to leave her daughter's side. Miss Arkansas was revealed to be married, and Misses Iowa, Illinois, and Idaho were eliminated when it was disclosed that they were all ringers from other states. Miss New York City took this opportunity to quit, claiming the competition was "not on the up and up." Neither, it seemed, was her action, for RKO, which had promised a screen contract to the winner, promptly announced at this point that it was awarding the contract to Miss New York City and billing her as "the girl who turned down the title of Miss America." By coincidence, RKO had originally helped sponsor the Madison Square Garden preliminary where Miss New York City was chosen.

The girls who were left were all quartered at the Ritz-Carlton Hotel. At least one contestant had to be warned twice to exhibit a more decorous public behavior at the hotel. Miss Connecticut, Marian Bergeron, who was just fifteen years old at the time, says, "If I would have been a little bit older I think I would have had a ball." She had originally entered the contest only because her father, a policeman, had friends who operated some theaters in New England. They were putting on a Miss New Haven contest at the Rivoli Theatre in West Haven that summer, when they discovered that they needed an extra contestant to fill out the line. It was just a bathing suit show. The manager remembered Officer Bergeron's cute little daughter, and he called him up. "Hey Elmer," he said, "how about sending Marian over?"

She picked up her bathing suit and dropped around to the

theater. "I was pretty well developed even if I was just fifteen," Marian says. "I was pretty well developed at twelve even." It was all a lark; she wasn't paying much attention until they pulled her out of the line and handed her a bunch of roses. A little while later, at Noroton, she won again and became Miss Connecticut. "It was only then that reality began to set in," Marian says, "because I realized I was going to be late for school." Luckily, she had one formal dress to take to the Pageant.

The judges that year included Peter Arno, the *New Yorker* cartoonist, and Russell Patterson, the artist. They drove down to the shore in Arno's Dusenberg, hitting up to 110 miles per hour. After that, nothing much during the week fazed Patterson. Neither he nor Arno was particularly frightened then, when they were halted at the door by a couple of shady types as they showed up for the final judging on Saturday night.

Arno tried to shoulder his way past. Patterson, who had a greater working knowledge of Atlantic City politics, appreciated that the brutes carried some *de facto* authority, so he was not quite so forward. One thug, patting his chest to indicate where a man might find it comfortable to carry a pistol, were he so inclined, addressed Arno. "Tonight it's Miss New York," he growled. "O.K.? Do it our way."

Arno, a big man, was unflinching. He just looked the guy in the eye and snarled back: "Or else?" and then brushed past him into the hall. Patterson followed, and then pulled his cohort aside.

"Hey," he said to Arno, "let's cross them up altogether and pick a girl from out of left field. How about the little blonde from Connecticut?"

Marian, of course, knew none of this. Obviously, someone in the Pageant had given way to desperation and figured that the only hope for survival lay in the extra publicity that would surely accrue from having a Miss New York win. Miss New York City had quit; Miss New York State was the next best. When Patterson and Arno and the other judges went for Marian, though, the Pageant promoters accepted the mandate.

In the confusion that transpired after the tabulation, though, everyone neglected to inform Marian of her good fortune. Instead, the producer, Noel Sherman, merely confronted her backstage and in an effort to hurry her along, snapped: "You'll have to take your bathing suit off." Marian drew back in fright. Although she had never so much as been out on a date before, her mother had discreetly warned her about things like this. Sherman, nervous and impulsive, then just reached out and began to pull one strap down. Marian, looking about in a panic, slapped up at his hand as she backed into the folds of the curtain.

Luckily, at that point, others who were backstage arrived on the scene and interceded. Someone brought Marian her high-school gown, and she struggled into it, pulling it on top of her bathing suit. She still did not know quite what was going on. Her runners-up, Miss New York State and Miss California, were also backstage changing. "Nobody told me I was Miss America until they put the banner on me," Marian says. Then at last she walked out into the lights, with two little pages holding her robe (which she still has). Armand T. Nichols crowned her, placing the diadem at a rakish tilt.

Marian was also awarded a Ford, a Bulova watch, a fur coat, and some property down the coast in Absecon. It is a small plot, and while Marian is not sure exactly where it is located, she says that somebody in the family still holds the deed. She could not accept a trip to Bermuda, since she assumed that she still had to get back to school. Like Tiny, Li'l Abner's brother, she was, after all, still only fifteen and a half years old. As it turned out, though, her school was not keen about all her publicity, so she decided to be tutored for two years, while making singing appearances for the indomitable Earl Carroll and George White. Ironically, while *Miss America* did not yet feature any talent competition, Marian Bergeron was actually one of the most talented of all the Miss Americas. She had been singing blues on a New Haven radio station since she was twelve years old.

She later went on to sing with Frankie Carle and Guy Lombardo. She was signed to a contract by CBS, and served as a replacement for Alice Faye for a while. She even came back to Atlantic City once, working the Steel Pier with Rudy Vallee. He decided that Bergeron was too unwieldy a name, so he went out with her one day, looking for a new name. He gave her Leeds, which he found on a street sign—Leeds Avenue, off Illinois.

Ironically, it was an old Atlantic City family name; Samuel P. Leeds had been one of the prime movers of the 1920s Pageants.

But no one recognized Marian as Miss America by any name, and she soon dropped any references to the fact. Her husband-to-be, Donald Ruhlman, a Dayton, Ohio, research representative, had no inkling of his fiancée's distinction until the couple went back to Connecticut to meet Marian's family, and he picked up some old scrapbooks. When the Pageant started up again in 1935, under the leadership of the Variety Club of Philadelphia, it immediately denied any association with the disreputable 1933 interloper, and refused to recognize Miss Bergeron. It was years before the Pageant decided to acknowledge her existence. "I was hurt when I didn't hear from them for so long," she says, "but it was understandable. What did I do for them?" Since a newspaper reporter, whose daughter was in Mrs. Ruhlman's Girl Scout troop, uncovered her true identity in 1954, Marian has gone on to become an active public speaker and a most energetic supporter of *Miss America.* She is still petite and pretty, and very popular as well, so she is often used to illustrate the theory that a certain divine judgment is invested in judges at the moment they must pick the queen.

Even before the Pageant was revived again, in 1935, controversy returned. In August of that year, at the San Diego Fair, Florence Cubbitt was named "Miss America." Stacked at 5 foot 9 inches, blue-eyed and blond, the daughter of an unemployed Chicago plumber, Miss Cubbitt was awarded the title by two gentlemen—who also ran midget and nudist concessions at fairs.

Since *Miss America* was, as usual, a little slow to act, there was not much it could do about the San Diego claimant. It wasn't until the 1950s that the Pageant at last got around to copyrighting the name of *Miss America,* although it was so exercised when Sally Rand danced as "Miss America" at the Golden Gate Exposition in San Francisco in 1939 that she dropped the title rather than make a legal issue of it. In 1935, though, *Miss America* just suffered the embarrassment of Miss Cubbitt's existence. What made it even more discomfiting was a coincidental association with nudity.

To begin with, it was announced that Miss Cubbitt's prize for becoming the San Diego Miss America was the "right" to pose in the buff for two years. The guys who ran the dwarf and nudie spots guaranteed that. Then Atlantic City picked Henrietta Leaver, a high-school dropout, who worked as a salesgirl in a dime store, as its Miss America. Henrietta said, "Please don't say anything about finding a million-dollar baby in a five-and-ten-cent store. All I want is a job. I never had a full-time job. Honestly, that's all I expect to get out of this beauty business."

Sadly, she got only notoriety instead. Hardly was she named Miss America when Pittsburgh sculptor Frank Vittor unveiled a statue he had made of her a few months before, when she had just been named Miss Pittsburgh. The statue showed Henrietta as nude as Florence Cubbitt had a "right" to be. She protested, emotionally, that she had always posed in a bathing suit, and that her grandmother had been present at all times, but the damage was done. Within a few months, Henrietta, still mortified, at last gave up and eloped with her high-school sweetheart, Johnny Mustacchio, to Oklahoma, where he was the only person in the Depression to go looking for a job. She did not even bother to come back to Atlantic City to crown her successor.

That turned out to be Rose Coyle, Miss Philadelphia. As soon as she won, the New York *Mirror* responded with the accusation that the fix had been arranged for Philly. These charges were leveled periodically whenever a Miss Philadelphia won—they popped up again, with the usual authority, four years later when Frances Burke, Miss Philadelphia 1940, won—but no one has ever produced any substantive evidence to support the claims. However, there is no question but that there were some legitimate grievances at issue in 1936. Even in this Depression year, the girls were worked so hard that they threatened to go on strike. One day the formal schedule began at 10 a.m., and, without respite, ran through an evening ball that *began* at 11:30 that night.

Girls were provided with bicycles to ride down the Steel Pier. In their fatigue, Miss Illinois and Miss Wilmington fell off, and Miss Kentucky dismounted, rested her face on her bicycle seat, and began to cry. A group of photographers came by. "Smile," they told her.

"Oh, I can't," poor Miss Kentucky sobbed. "I'm so tired. I'm so tired of smiling."

A former contestant, speaking like some grizzled old frontline veteran, came by and consoled her: "I know you're worn out, honey. I know it's hard, but you've got to learn to take it. It's part of the contest." Miss Kentucky only burst into tears again, whereupon Pageant officials moved in and whisked her away from the press. The executive director of the Pageant, George Tyson, denied that the girls were overworked, and at last a strike was avoided.

The height of fancy and confusion was to come in the next two years, when, in succession, *Miss America* ended up first with no queen and then with two claimants to the title. In fact, there has never really been anything in the beauty-pageant world to compete with Miss America 1937, not even Miss Universe's intrepid Leona Gage.

The Pageant was then in its third year of revival, and gaining some stability under Lenora Slaughter, who had first come to Atlantic City on loan from the Saint Petersburg Chamber of Commerce in 1935. By 1937, the ceremonies were sufficiently cloaked in dignity to attract the presence of Mrs. Nellie Ross of Wyoming, who had been the nation's first woman governor. Rudy Vallee served as toastmaster at one luncheon, and the Boardwalk parade drew a crowd touted at upward of 150,000, which was the largest attendance since 1925, Fay Lanphier's spectacular year. Although the prizes offered for Miss America were somewhat less than what met the eye, they at least seemed impressive. They were topped by what was supposed to be a $1000 fur coat. "Oh, it was a pip," Miss Slaughter says, shrieking at the memory. The winner was also guaranteed $400 for working a five-day engagement at the Steel Pier, and the chance to pick up a little more, modeling hats in Wanamaker's basement in Philadelphia. There was also the inevitable Hollywood screen test, and though this seems incredible, this year, for the first time, there was actually a promise of a television test.

"We really had no money," Lenora says. "We had to bargain for everything, live on a shoestring. So, one thing we did, we got some of the young men in town to help out as chauffeurs for the girls." Naturally, the Pageant sought to enlist the scions of Atlantic City's best families, and Lou Off, twenty-one, was one of the young men recruited. His father, Frank Off, was finance commissioner of the city. He also owned the Hotel Brighton, where young Lou kept a room, and Brighton Orchid Farms, Inc. Lou did not go to college, but had entered his father's nursery business early. He still runs a large orchid-raising operation outside of Atlantic City. Lou Off is a commanding figure—hard, lean, with an angular, direct face. He has a local reputation of always having been independent, reliable, and without airs. Miss Slaughter remembers him well from 1937. "Oh, he was so handsome," she says. "He was so handsome, young, and arrogant."

A couple days before the Pageant began, Lou dropped by to be assigned the contestant he would chauffeur. There were only two girls left who had not been allotted escorts—Miss New Orleans, Gertrude Miller, and Miss Bertrand Island, Bette Cooper. Off shrugged and told a friend, with whom he had come to the offices, to take his pick. Not surprisingly, the friend selected the lady from faraway, exotic New Orleans. When Off went to meet Miss Bertrand Island, he was very pleasantly surprised at the short straw he had drawn. "I remember there were all sorts of types," he says. "A lot of them were just sort of cute bathing-suit girls, but there was even one stripper in the contest." Miss California was a member of a traveling dance team, with an annulled marriage to her credit. "In this crowd," Off says, "Bette stood out like a beacon light in the middle of the ocean."

She was a cute, dimpled blonde, measuring a modest 32–26–36. She stood 5 feet 6 inches and had languid blue eyes that bespoke her innocence. "She was just as pretty as a picture," Miss Slaughter says simply—and in many ways she did resemble Marian Bergeron of 1933. Most important, like Marian, Bette was in Atlantic City strictly on a lark. Earlier in the summer, Bette and some friends had gone to an amusement park at Lake Hopatcong, near her home in Hackettstown, New Jersey. The park, located on a Bertrand Island, was a modest establishment with a roller coaster, a hot dog stand, and a few other attractions. The night Bette and her pals showed up, though, there were also advertisements posted about a beauty contest and, upon the coaxing and dares of her friends, she entered it.

Bette was stunned when she won, and also surprised to learn that Miss Bertrand Island was franchised by Atlantic City (this one and only year) and was expected to contend for Miss America. The Coopers had a family council at home in Hackettstown. There was some question as to whether Bette, the baby of the family, should pursue such a beauty course. She was only seventeen, going into her senior year at Junior College of Centenary Collegiate Institute, actually a private day school. She was in the top quarter of her class and was captain of the track team. She attended the First Presbyterian Church regularly. She had never been in love, although she did express a strong preference for basketball.

Though Hackettstown is only about sixty miles from Manhattan, it is tucked into the green northwestern section of New Jersey and even today has no real urban identity. The Coopers were strictly small town. Bette's father, LeBrun, was an engineer with the state highway department. "Her parents always felt that I was sophisticated," Lou Off says, "and even though I was just a kid of twenty-one, I suppose that compared to them I was. They were impressed about things like I could figure out how to get around New York." The Coopers at last decided to let Bette enter *Miss America* only because they felt that a week in Atlantic City for them all would be a nice family vacation to close out the summer. These happy plans were marred somewhat by the fact that when they arrived at the beach on Sunday, September 6, Bette disclosed that she had caught a cold.

She had no comprehension of these things, but Atlantic City was also suffering. Authorities had picked this time to swoop down on the town and close up all of the many brothels. Atlantic City was a front-page sintown all over the country. Lou Off says today that in many ways Bette Cooper was the best thing that ever happened to the resort, since she diverted all the whorehouse publicity.

Off and Miss Cooper liked each other from the first. She, and her parents as well, found him to be a steady source of calm amid all the activity, and although Lou felt that Bette was still quite young and immature, he was impressed with her character. "Even then, as a young girl, Bette was a very dignified person," he says. "She couldn't stand cheapness. Even the little bit of leg that the Pageant demanded at the time was not for her."

If he did not view her romantically, it seems apparent that she at least was developing a fast crush on him. Lou sent her orchids every day, and Mr. Cooper declared outright that Lou became "Bette's first fancy." She was also growing sicker with her summer cold, though, and took to subsisting nearly on orange juice. She lost weight, and, her father said, she became increasingly nervous as the excitement and her cold wore on.

Bette Cooper herself still refuses to talk about that week. She is, apparently, the only Miss America who is embarrassed by the distinction—although many other Miss Americas do look back at themselves with bemusement or chagrin, and even a certain amount of wonder. Years after her reign, Mary Katherine Campbell once said: "I've stood and looked up at pictures of that creature that was Miss America, and I think, 'She can't ever have had anything to do with me.' " This is, it seems, a fairly typical view, but Bette Cooper alone of all the Miss Americas is upset that it ever could have happened, even to a little girl of seventeen with dimples.

Her rejection of the fact has been consistent. Lenora Slaughter, traveling with the incumbent Miss America in 1943, crossed paths with Miss Cooper in Louisville. By then, she had finished college and was working as a PR representative. Lenora urged her to re-establish ties with Atlantic City. Bette said simply, "I want no part of it." About a decade or so later, she happened to visit Atlantic City once, and she called up Lou Off to suggest that she and her husband ought to meet him and his wife. He agreed enthusiastically, but Bette hastened to add that there was one stipulation: there could be no mention of "the incident." Today, still living in the greater New York area, recently widowed (though it will serve no good purpose to disclose her name now, or where she lives), Bette is as adamant as ever when it comes to discussing the 1937 Pageant. She is polite, almost apologetic, in declining to talk about it—but she is altogether firm in that stance.

Miss Slaughter, always the romanticist, is convinced that Bette is still responding to the pain of a broken teen-age heart. She holds the vision of Bette running up and down the beach, hand in hand with Lou, a couple of years after the Pageant. The false mythology about the event encourages this image. The tale is usually told now, with snickers, of how Bette ran off with her "driver"; either that, or, in the drippiest of love-conquers-all tones, it is related how she threw over the crown for him. The fact that Edward VIII had abdicated only a few months previously obviously buttressed this romantic view. The day following her selection, Walter Winchell had a hot scoop on his program that Bette and Lou were already married.

Off rejects all this, even somewhat indignantly. He categorically denies that there was anything between the two during the week, and he keeps emphasizing the point about how young and immature Bette appeared to him at this time. He stresses the fact that romance between the two blossomed only a couple of years later, after he felt that Bette had grown up.

Nevertheless, she was obviously taken from the first with her handsome, older escort, and it is impossible to escape the conclusion that he influenced her eventual decision, if unconsciously. Lenora thinks that what he applied was more of an intentional pressure. "The Pageant was young," she says, "and some old families, like the Offs, still had some reservations about it. Lou decided that it was not good for Bette to be in the Pageant—and he told her so."

For most of the week, this was strictly a moot point anyway, since Bette gave herself no chance of winning. She did not fare poorly in the optional talent competition, making the musical promise, "When the Poppies Bloom Again," and she became a genuine contender when she was named the winner in the evening gown competition. Saturday afternoon, before the final night's judging, was an open period for the contestants, and Off picked Bette up at the Lafayette Hotel, where she was staying, to take her out to lunch. "We took a long drive first," he says. "She still had a real lousy cold, and didn't feel well at all. She had even been to see a doctor. I remember, at last we stopped for lunch at Harry Streyer's Restaurant in Somers Point, and when we were sitting there, that was when I asked her, 'Bette, have you really thought what you are going to do if you win this thing tonight?' "

Bette shifted uncomfortably in her seat. "She just laughed and said the thought was ridiculous. 'Well,' I told her, 'I just want to let you know now that if you do win, you can forget about me, because I just don't want to have anything to do with it. The last thing in the world that I want is publicity.' " Bette nodded, and Lou changed the subject to more pleasant things.

She won that night on the third ballot. It was close; at last the judges called the finalists over and interviewed them again. Bette's quiet sweetness probably won the day. She beat out Alice Emerick, Miss Texas, who won a scholarship to dancing school as second prize, and Ruth Covington, Miss North Carolina, who had sung and tap-danced her way into the hearts of the crowd with her version of "Goona Goo." Miss Miami came in fourth, and then Miss California, the ex-bride and professional hoofer. Then, almost as always, the judges were beguiled by virtue.

Rose Coyle, the retiring Miss America, placed the crown on Bette's head, and asked the one question that just about everybody wanted to know. "Where is Bertrand Island?" Rose inquired.

"In a lake somewhere up around Lake Hopatcong," Bette replied, setting that matter straight.

She is also supposed to have gushed next, "I don't know what to say. I'm so happy." If so, it was a brief joy. Perhaps Lou Off's words of warning that afternoon took on more significance a bit later, when it first occurred to her that he had indeed left the dance that followed her coronation. True to his threat, he would have nothing to do with her if she won. She had, and he was gone. Did that influence her? Did she get scared? Or was it all simply the one thing she does say now about it: "It was all my father's decision. He thought I should go back to school." Probably, it was some of all three. Anyway, the phone rang in Lou Off's room at the Hotel Brighton at two o'clock in the morning. It was Bette, and she was in tears.

She was supposed to make her first official appearance as Miss America the next morning, posing for pictures with other contestants and officials on the Steel Pier. Then she would begin her reign with the week's engagement on the Pier. Already, there was a big electric sign glowing: "COME SEE MISS AMERICA 1937." Through her sobs, Off finally understood that neither Bette nor her parents were happy with their victory. He said he would be right over to discuss the situation. The Coopers were coming to depend heavily upon him.

He arrived at their rooms in the Lafayette shortly after two-thirty a.m. By then, Bette had been joined in tears by both her mother and father. None of them knew what to do. "Her parents were really flabbergasted," Off says. "They just did not want her on the Pier in the morning, but they didn't know what to do."

Finally, Off said, "You don't want her to go through with any of this, do you? Isn't that the way you feel? Isn't that it?"

They all sobbed assent.

"Well, all right. You don't have to. You don't have to do anything. Bette won't go to the Pier." By now, the young man was in full control. He told the Coopers to sit tight and relax, and then he left and picked up a couple of his friends, the Pennington brothers, George and Bob. With them, he returned to the Lafayette around five-thirty, just as dawn was breaking over the Atlantic, the Sunday morning of September 12. The three young men went to the Coopers' rooms, and took Bette. They led her down the hall to a fire escape, and pirated Miss America out of the hotel that way. Off had plotted very carefully where they would take her and hide her.

Within a few hours, the first newsreel cameras began setting up on the Steel Pier under the sign advertising the first appearance of the new Miss America. One by one, all the dignitaries, runners-up, and the press arrived until only Miss America herself was missing. Finally, someone called her room, and the awful news was out: the queen was gone. Nobody even knew where she was. Pageant officials wondered if they should promote Alice Emerick to the title, but it was agreed that it would not be wise to make such a move, and, anyway, there was no provision to permit such a settlement. As usual, the Pageant had come up short on rules. Next year, of course, it made a whole bunch of new rules to cover this situation. Then, there were none. Lloyd Butler, who identified himself as a representative of Miss Miami, snarled, "Contracts are no good no more. You can't make nobody do nothin'." The press scurried off to find Miss America. A local police official vowed that if the whole Garden State of New Jersey had to be turned upside down, Bette would be found by nightfall. During the day, she was in fact rumored at different times to be in several different places throughout the East.

Actually, she was the purloined letter. At first, Off had taken her down the coast a few miles to the town of Margate, where he had a fishing cruiser docked. He and the Pennington brothers guided the boat out into the ocean and north, up the beach, as the sun rose in the sky. They cast anchor, of all places, about two hundred feet off the Steel Pier. Off assumed, correctly, that no one would ever think to look for Bette there. He and the Penningtons watched some of the early commotion on the Pier, but Miss America slept for most of the day. She was still sick, and exhausted now from the long, trying night before.

That afternoon, they brought the boat in, and then Off and George Pennington put Bette in the car and drove her to her home in Hackettstown. They left her there, and then, on the way back, they pulled off the road and stopped for supper in a diner. The radio was turned on in the place, and the dial was set to Walter Winchell's weekly report. He said he had a scoop that Miss America and Lou Off had had "a secret marriage."

So ended the fascinating saga of 1937. It would have been difficult for any succeeding Pageant to top those events, but the very next year, a valiant effort in that direction was made. Of course, it required the diligent support of Earl Carroll, who kept popping up regularly at *Miss America*, throwing a monkey wrench into things. This time he invented a new Miss America.

The genuine article that year was Marilyn Meseke, from Marion, Ohio. She was a dancing-school teacher and was the first girl ever to win the title who had, essentially, prepped for it. Now a shy, quiet lady, who teaches piano in suburban Miami, Marilyn had been raised by a grandmother who had heady ambitions for her. She was required to begin studying dancing at the age of four, and thereafter was also tutored in piano, voice, violin, and baton. As a child, she also won many contests, and one year, around 1930, during the interim when *Miss America* was not in operation, Marilyn won the crown of Miss Ohio. At that time she was only fourteen.

At Atlantic City in 1938 she was one of a handful of the top contenders to receive a letter from Carroll—who was annoyed that he had not been invited as a judge—offering a contract. Marilyn, following some outside advice, declined to reply to the offer. The only contestant who did sign a Carroll contract was Claire James, Miss California. She was a beauty, with little talent—and this year, for the first time, talent counted a solid one-third. Claire did a high-kick dance, but could not, unfortunately, kick very high. Claire did win the evening-gown competition, but Marilyn matched that as "best model," and surely also impressed the judges more with her talent and her soft, sincere personality.

As soon as they named Marilyn Miss America, Claire made her move. She declared, "I can't stand it. I've had one insult after another heaped upon me since I came here." She left for New York with Carroll on Sunday morning. He announced that the judges were "incompetent" and should be replaced "with some young jitterbugs who know how to judge beauty." A California henchman of Carroll's added that the judges were "Philadelphia butchers" with an unholy prejudice against the West. Claire, showing a more concerned side, suggested that she did not mind losing so much herself, but that what distressed her so was that various employees at her Atlantic City hotel had lost money wagering on her chances.

With all this fuss stirred up, Carroll then declared that Miss James was the people's choice, and thereupon he crowned her in New York as the real Miss America before a people's crowd of twelve reporters and sixteen photographers. This was a harmless enough publicity stunt, but Miss James took it more seriously, and often, in the years that followed, she would identify herself as Miss America. Once she even used the title in a commercial that she made. Marilyn's first husband, an airline pilot named Stanley Hume (when he died, she married another pilot, Donald Rogers), sued to make Claire cease and desist.

Another time, Miss James showed up to interview for a part in a TV show, and she identified herself to the producer as a former Miss America. Usually, she could get away with the claim, since very few TV producers know the names of all the Miss Americas. This time, though, she had met her match. The producer was Harry Koplan, who is married to Rosemary LaPlanche, Miss America 1941. Claire did not get the part.

Up from Cheesecakery

Bess Myerson once said of Lenora Slaughter, "She picked the Pageant up by its bathing suit straps and put it in an evening gown." In the thirty-three years that she was associated with *Miss America,* usually as a benevolent despot, Miss Slaughter gave an earnest substance to the enterprise, and a direction. She salvaged an expensive gimmick that was altogether frivolous and usually discredited and turned it into a responsible institution that came to possess respectability and a wide base of popularity. Lenora's accomplishment is muted by only two major failings. First, whatever improvements she effected were usually lost on the general public, for she and the whole Pageant have always been blind to public relations. Second, Miss Slaughter saw her advances tarnished in the last decade of her rule, when the Pageant suffered her indisposition to change.

Yet, to judge Miss Slaughter by her whole reign, she was a significant success. The best signal of her merit is that virtually every person who crossed swords with her, disputed her, suffered her whims and autocracy, even those who personally could not abide her, invariably qualifies any criticism of her with an acknowledgment that she must be credited for first sustaining and then upgrading the Pageant. Her greatest accomplishments were to introduce college scholarships into the prize schedule, and to attract civic groups as local sponsors. These twin landmarks of respectability not only revamped the image of *Miss America,* but eventually changed the whole complexion of beauty pageantry.

As a result, almost any pageant that fancies itself as a notable attraction first cuts in some service organization and then hands out scholarship money. A special prize in this category must go to Our Little Miss competition, which awards a $500 college scholarship to the winner in its division for three-to-six-year-olds. Surely the whole public does not accept pageants on their own terms, but at least Miss Slaughter is responsible for the pageants themselves changing their outlook from cheesecakery to do-goodism. That is her legacy.

She was called to Atlantic City in 1935 on a temporary basis, when the Pageant started up again under the aegis of the Variety Club of Philadelphia. She was, at that time, employed by the Saint Petersburg (Florida) Chamber of Commerce, when Eddie Corcoran—a newspaperman and public relations man, who had just been put in charge of the revived Pageant—chanced upon an Associated Press squib that noted that Miss Slaughter was the only woman pageant director in the United States. He prevailed upon Saint Petersburg to let Atlantic City borrow her for six weeks to help organize the Pageant that had been renamed "The Showman's Variety Jubilee." Cleverly resisting the obvious, the Pageant took two decades before it gave up fighting and took *Miss America* as its official name.

Miss Slaughter says that she immediately recognized the potential in the Pageant, and while she is given to dramatizing issues, this is surely an accurate accounting of her thoughts at the time, because when Corcoran later asked her to return to the Pageant on a full-time basis she promptly accepted the offer, even though it meant taking a substantial cut in salary. She was making $5000 in Saint Petersburg and Atlantic City would go no higher than $3000. "But I had to take it," she says with fervor. "I knew it could be done. I knew *I could be on my way.*" She arrived back in Atlantic City in January 1936, and when Corcoran died suddenly a few months later she was left, effectively, in charge. For the next few years a theater official from Pittsburgh, George Tyson, would come in for the summer months to supervise, but Lenora was on hand and in charge for most of the year. She was formally appointed to the post of executive secretary in November 1941, and held that title until her retirement, after the 1967 Pageant, at which time the Pageant awarded her an annual pension of $10,000.

She married a handsome, jut-jawed businessman named Bradford Frapart and appointed him business manager to *Miss America* in the late 1940s, but she is still, professionally, best known by her maiden name. Except for suffering some eyesight difficulties with glare, Miss Slaughter remains as vigorous and as outspoken as ever. She is proud to say that she has been called, among other things, "a combination of Texas Guinan and Aimee Semple McPherson"; anyway, to make a point she has always had the ability to be alternately strident and lachrymose. Lenora still retains a Southern accent from her Virginia childhood, but when aggravated, she used sharp Jersey chords to cut through the honey.

While she has always felt almost a crusader's impulse to drag *Miss America* into respectability, Miss Slaughter's initial chore was simply to keep the Pageant afloat. In many ways this may have been her greatest feat, seeing as how she was originally threatened by financial disaster on one side and ennui on the other. For that matter, far from killing the Pageant, the Depression may have revived it.

Miss America had a large debt outstanding leftover from the 1920s, and while many of the town's most solid citizens had their names on the note, the banks were not disposed to put pressure on them. Under the circumstances, it seemed more agreeable to see if the Pageant could not be re-established and work itself out of the hole. The scheme became more attractive because Corcoran, a popular local figure, was out of work. One man who was privy to all these proceedings even says, "Don't believe anything else. The only reason the Pageant was started up again—the only reason we have a *Miss America* here today—is because a bunch of his friends were trying to help Eddie Corcoran get a job."

While it took only a couple of Pageants for *Miss America* to pay off the old debt, it remained a catch-as-catch-can operation. Harry Godshall, who had begged out of the show in 1925 after the politicians started to move in, agreed to come back on the board. But he recalls with horror that he discovered that Pageant officials were still patrolling the Boardwalk in those days, soliciting shopkeepers for $20, or whatever they could get. A car raffle was another prime element in the budget. Still, when the city offered to help the Pageant along with a $50,000 grant, Godshall helped convince the board that they had to turn the money down. "I was convinced," he says, "that this was the biggest publicity stunt that Atlantic City had, or ever would have, and if it was any good, it had to stand on its own two feet."

By 1938 it was estimated that 112,000,000 American moviegoers saw Miss America, Marilyn Meseke, being crowned in the newsreels. Considering that there were only about 130,000,000 Americans at this time, this was not a bad batting average. In actual figures perhaps up to half the nation saw *Miss America* that year, and enough of them actually went to Atlantic City so that the Pageant was able to balance a budget of $27,000, and exude the faint odor of stability.

Certainly, it was more national in character. In 1935, when the show returned, only three of the fifty-two contestants came from west of the Mississippi, while twenty-four of them represented various crossroads in New Jersey and Pennsylvania. By 1939, steady progress resulted in seven Western states, and Sun Valley, Idaho, being represented, as the unfortunate experience with the little kid from Bertrand Island in 1937 had occasioned some entrance limitations. Up to that point, virtually any hustler or amusement park could set a franchise and enter a queen. In 1937, girls from Augusta and Savannah Beach, Georgia, and Jacksonville, Florida, showed up unexpectedly. They each had been sweet-talked out of several hundred dollars by a flim-flam man who said he represented Atlantic City and needed the money as an entrance fee.

The next year, only states, recognized cities, and a few certified regions could send entrants in their names. The age minimum, which nobody ever appears to have enforced, was, nonetheless, raised from seventeen to eighteen, and contestants were required to swear that they had never been married even if now divorced, annulled, or widowed. This knocked out Miss Western Pennsylvania, who was touted as "the dancing divorcee." There was also little room left for anyone from the small towns and resorts. No more Miss Conshohocken, good-by forever Miss

Leominster and Miss Tamaqua, Miss Roton Point, and Miss Sunnybrook. No more room either for Miss Blue Grass, Miss Anthracite, Miss Buckeye Lake, Miss Eastern Shore. They sounded taps for Miss Long Island Sound in 1938, and Miss Coney Island and Miss Eastern Arkansas had to bid a fond farewell to the World's Playground in 1939. That year was the first time in history that a majority of the girls bore state titles. Of the forty-three contestants, twenty-four represented whole states. It was not for another two decades, until 1959, that every state in the union was represented, but the progress was real. When Lenora had first arrived, only five years before, a mere ten of the fifty-two girls represented states.

The Pageant appeared even more authentic in 1940, when, at last, it moved off the piers and into the huge and prestigious Convention Hall. Miss Slaughter later wrote rhapsodically of that moment in a Pageant remembrance: "Promptly at eight-thirty, the huge curtains rose on the great stage and a veritable fairyland of beautiful flowers and lovely girls came into view." The next year, she was at last given full title to go with her responsibility, and, coincidentally, for the first time the enterprise officially titled itself *Miss America* Pageant. The future had never looked brighter, except for the fact that by now it was November 1941, and just as in all the movies, the Japanese picked the next month to bomb Pearl Harbor.

Shortly thereafter, the Army took over Convention Hall, and in all likelihood the Pageant would have been suspended for the duration of the war, had not Madison Square Garden smelled a distress sale. The Garden, which would book the Amazon River if it could figure a way to pirate it out of Brazil, offered Lenora $10,000 to bring the Pageant to 49th Street. Faced with this challenge, the board decided it was best to slog along, rather than risk loss of the whole show. The Pageant was moved over to the Warner Theatre, where it limped by on a total annual budget of $17,500 in 1942. The show was an intimate one, perhaps the one time when crowd reaction may have influenced the judges. Miss Texas, Jo-Carroll Dennison (who was later married for a while to comedian Phil Silvers), made her talent appearance in a cowgirl outfit, and then broke into "Deep in the Heart of Texas."

The servicemen packed in the galleries picked up the clap-clap-clap for her, and brought the place down. She was a tremendously popular winner.

With the Pageant itself shriveled up, Miss Slaughter was freed, by circumstance, from the usual mundane demands of the effort, and she was able to ponder the whole concept. It may be only a coincidence, but the only really meaningful advancements at Miss America—aside from those dictated by the revelation of its own error—occurred during the war, when the business of attracting tourists was a necessarily reduced factor. *Miss America* had always suffered a resort mentality, with a tendency to rate the Pageant as strictly a publicity dodge. Anyway, it was during the war that Lenora picked *Miss America* up by the straps.

To that point the local contests were still run by newspapers, radio stations, theaters, or amusement parks. They were strictly commercial; no matter how pure the national show might become, the girls had reached it by original sin. Lenora chose the Jaycees—then the Junior Chamber of Commerce—as her ally. "What better," she offers grandly, "than to have the ideal men of America run a pageant for the ideal women?" This particular analogy had escaped others to this point, but there were certainly valid reasons for the Jaycees being perfect partners for Lenora. Both traditionally were conservative and vigorous by nature. The Jaycees had been formed in St. Louis in 1920, a year before *Miss America*, as a club dedicated to the preservation of the more genteel dances, such as the two-step. In 1940, it was the first young men's association to endorse the principle of the draft, and, for that matter, it has remained well to the right. As late as 1968, the Jaycees national convention took a thoroughly hawkish stand on Vietnam, and in 1970 President Nixon received the single most enthusiastic and affectionate reception of his presidency to date when he addressed the convention. Only three per cent of the Jaycee membership is black.

In 1944, Lenora convinced the North Carolina Jaycees to sponsor the State Pageant. She went down herself to show the young men how to put on a Pageant. It made $63, and from there she lined up Jaycee sponsorship in Texas and Georgia. Today, the only profit-making organization left with a state franchise is the Birmingham *News,* but Miss Alabama is run strictly as a community service. In almost all other states, either the Jaycees are in control themselves or former Jaycees, required to leave the organization at age thirty-five, have incorporated a State Pageant firm and continue to run things. In these cases, incumbent Jaycees supply most of the manpower. At the lowest level the locals are invariably sponsored by the community Jaycee group.

For *Miss America* this close affiliation remains ideal. Better than two-thirds of the Jaycee units in the country are located in the suburbs or rural areas, which is exactly where the *Miss America* candidates are found. Maybe, in fact, it is *why* they are found there. Moreover, the Jaycees are respected for taking everything, including even themselves and their good times, very seriously. As stewards of the *Miss America* dream, they are the perfect eunuchs.

At the same time that Miss Slaughter sought out more respectable local sponsorship, she stumbled on another concept that was perhaps to prove even more important to the Pageant in the long run. This happened in 1943, when the event was down to a shell of itself. There were only thirty-one contestants, and just three of the girls came from west of the Mississippi—Misses St. Louis, Oklahoma, and California. Fortunately, there was a deception in the small number. The girl chosen Miss America was the most distant entrant, Miss California. Her name was Jean Bartel, and though today she may be among the more forgotten of the species, she must be, in any ranking of Miss Americas,* unquestionably declared the most important one. Everything changed because of her example. "Every succeeding Miss America owes her the greatest debt," Lenora says.

Jean was a Christian Scientist, a first-generation American whose real name was Bartelmeh. Her parents, born in Alsace-Lorraine, had come to the United States via England, and when Jean won, the government ran a heavy check on her to make sure that the Nazis had not run in a ringer. Jean has always remained the most international of the Miss Americas, and in the late 1940s she did espionage work for the CIA in Lebanon.

* See Appendix 5, p. 303.

She devotes herself now mostly to the international travel business, although she still makes a few TV and movie appearances, and has produced television shows in scores of countries on five continents. Miss Bartel even once produced and narrated a special in South Vietnam on "The Five Faces of Mme. Ky." Earlier, she enjoyed perhaps the best stage success of all the Miss Americas, when she sang the female lead on Broadway in *Of Thee I Sing* and in the revival there of *The Desert Song.*

Miss Bartel was not married until 1970, when she was wed in Japan to an American, William J. Hogue. Since she retained her name until then, she was particularly sensitive to being anchored to a year—Miss America 1943—and always referred to herself only as "a former Miss America." Until her mother died a few months before Jean's marriage, they lived together in a small, precisely decorated house in the Westwood section of Los Angeles. Almost all Miss Americas have their trophies on view in their houses, but displayed quietly, a bit out of the way. Jean's melted into a corner of the living room, almost in keeping, it seemed, with the basic Oriental décor.

Growing up in Los Angeles, Jean had precociously developed a Broadway ambition. At fourteen, lying about her age, she made the Civic Light Opera chorus, singing with Jerome Hines and John Raitt. She was an active student leader in school, and then moved on to UCLA, where a friend convinced her that *Miss America* was no longer just a leg show. To that point she had never even seen a beauty contest, but she won Miss California, and came East with her mother, who paid her own way. Jean was only eighteen although she listed her age as nineteen, a deceit among contestants that was up until then nearly routine.

She won all around, exhibiting a top figure, singing "Night and Day," and positively enthralling the judges, Lenora Slaughter, and the Pageant board. She was not only the first coed to win, but she was the right girl for the right moment. After years of trying, Lenora had finally talked a blue-chip commercial firm into associating itself with the Pageant. Lever Brothers had been lured into signing on, and agreed to pay Miss America $100 a week to tour for them. When she won, the Roxy Theatre in New York offered her $1500 for a week. Jean turned them down and stayed with Lever. "It was the opportunity to travel," she says, "but it was also that I realized how glad the Pageant was to have me, because they had gotten someone they wanted."

No matter how many times it happens, the press finds itself surprised every time a beauty pageant winner is something other than a classic dumb blonde. They wrote about and interviewed Jean endlessly. "Oh God," she says, "they would just all always call me *wholesome*." She was a hit everywhere she went, with everyone.

The tour was sponsored by, along with Lever Brothers, Tussy Cosmetics, Vimms Vitamins, and Butterick Pattern company, and it was endorsed by the War Finance Committee. Everybody got his money's worth. Accompanied by Miss Slaughter, Jean played 34 cities in 24 states and the District of Columbia, working nonstop from September 14 until December 28. She made a total of 469 appearances. She appeared 93 times at service clubs, sang 47 times before the troops, visited 16 soldiers' hospitals and 8 war industries. She played 17 theaters, where the only price of admission was the purchase of a war bond. She appeared on 75 radio shows, met 7 governors, and even appeared at a few colleges, including Harvard. She autographed 50,000 pictures, and everywhere she went she enjoyed major publicity, always including the key phrase "selected at Atlantic City." All told, she sold $2,500,000 worth of bonds, mostly in $50s and $25s, although one man in Louisville purchased a total of $50,000 from her, and a fellow in Hot Springs, Arkansas, bought $5000 in bonds in exchange for a pair of her stockings. She was presented with a certificate for selling more Series E bonds than anyone else in the United States.

It was practically all that she received for her whole year of sacrifice. She made only $3000, much the least of any winner since the Pageant was revived, and in September, when no help was forthcoming from Atlantic City, she took it upon herself to finance a trip across the continent and back just to crown her successor. Some years later, *Miss America* did recognize her with a special $1000 scholarship, but the debt owed to Jean Bartel has never really been fairly acknowledged.

It was not just that she sacrificed her own gain to push war bonds. She brought to *Miss America* a whole new constituency.

Jean made 80 per cent of her bond sales to women. Somehow, for the first time, a Miss America was able to get large numbers of her own sex to respond favorably toward the institution. Heretofore, women tended to be suspicious of beauty queens. Even collegians liked Jean. "The fact that I approached them as their contemporary helped," she says. "I never kidded myself either. They were not listening to Jean Bartel, herself, or Jean Bartel, spokeswoman. They were listening to Miss America."

Lenora realized that she had struck gold. In her report to the board on the trip, she unabashedly referred to Jean as "America's most beautiful, healthy, and talented girl. . . . She was loyal to Atlantic City and the ideals of the Pageant at all times, and she inspired American girls to wear the coveted crown of Miss America." And Lenora also recognized that Jean could be the start of a whole trend. Exhibiting foresight to match her wishful thinking, Miss Slaughter wrote at the time, "She has paved the way for future Miss Americas [to emulate her] and to benefit from her pioneering." Only one thing besides Jean herself seemed to impress Lenora about the trip; because of the Pageant's invariable impecunious state, she was moved to stress the good news that only nine of the thirty-two hotels where they had stayed had billed them.

Of itself, the Bartel tour turned everything around, but a by-product from the trip proved to be equally vital to the future of the Pageant; that is, the scholarship program. Conversationally, without making an issue of the point, Jean says that she originally suggested to Miss Slaughter that Miss America be awarded a college scholarship. Lenora disputes that on a technicality. She says that while Jean was in attendance when the idea originally was broached, while Jean was, in fact, the inspiration for the idea, it was a group of students who originally proposed it.

The landmark day occurred when the bond tour reached Minneapolis. The itinerary places her there on Saturday, November 13, 1943, when she visited the University of Minnesota campus. She was planning to attend a sorority party late in the afternoon, and on her way to the party, she agreed to stop by and meet with the university student council. It was at that meeting, Lenora says, that the subject of Miss America's role and responsibility, and remuneration, was advanced. In the course of the conversation, one of the students mentioned the scholarship idea, and everyone there was soon supporting it. "Yes," Lenora says, "I must say that the idea for the scholarship was not mine and it was not Jean's. The scholarship idea actually came from those kids, from the student council of the University of Minnesota in 1943. I don't know any of the names, but I remember that an ugly little girl with spectacles was the head of it."

That winter, Lenora presented her report on the trip to the board, and since it was all good news, and she was coming off a hot streak, she took the opportunity at this time also to make her proposal that the Pageant move into the scholarship area. In Lenora's behalf, it should be emphasized that, at the time, this was a most progressive step. The higher-education boom, which nobody envisioned at the time, was still a few years off; and the idea of sending women to college was still far from commonplace. In the last year before the war, only 76,000 women had graduated from U.S. colleges, and while returning servicemen filled up colleges on the GI Bill immediately after the war, there was no dramatic rise in higher education for women until late in the 1950s. Today, almost 1,000,000 women a year enter college in the United States.

To that point, then, Miss Slaughter was thinking ahead of her time. The board members do not seem to have grasped the potential in the program. They appear to have approved the idea mostly as a means of humoring Lenora, since she was so keen on it. They stressed that she could go ahead with the scheme if she desired to, but that she must agree not to solicit any local companies for scholarship funds. The Pageant was squeezing them hard enough for donations just to help meet everyday expenses. Lenora agreed to the stipulation, and sat down and wrote 267 letters to out-of-town firms. She was looking for $5000 for the 1945 Miss America; she needed five angels at a thousand a pop.

In the return mail, she received a check from Joseph Bancroft & Sons, and in the months that followed, she also got $1000 each from Catalina, Fitch, and the Harvel Watch Company, but it was almost the last hour before the last $1000 check came, from something called the Sandy Valley Grocery Co. Lenora was ready to put in $1000 of her own savings, which was "about all I had."

As soon as the 1945 Pageant was over, Lenora came right back at the companies and upped the ante to $5000 apiece—for $25,000. That was too rich for the blood of Harvel and Sandy Valley, but the other three went along and were joined by Launderell Washing Machines. Bancroft also went for an additional $5000, when no other company would take the bait. From there, the Pageant has gone on to become, easily, the most benevolent office in the world for the distribution of college scholarships to women. In the 26 pageants since the program was instituted in 1945, *Miss America* has awarded $995,375 in scholarship funds.* The million-dollar mark will be passed at the 1971 Pageant at the moment the announcement is made of the fourth award for an especially talented nonfinalist.

Atlantic City has provided only a small portion of the total *Miss America* largesse, though. Since 1946, the local and state pageants have handed out more than $6,000,000 to the lower-echelon queens, so that the complete total surpasses $7,000,000. The runner-up in this field of female scholarship dispersal may be still another beauty pageant. Junior Miss has presented more than $2,000,000 in scholarship funds since it began to emulate *Miss America* with its competition for high-school senior girls in 1958.

The Pageant was fortunate that, just as Jean Bartel materialized at a propitious moment, so did the first scholarship winner pop up two years later, with all the right credentials. Bess Myerson, Miss America 1945, perfectly personified the new scholarship program; also, she reaped what Miss Bartel had sowed.

At the time of her selection, Bess was the most talented Miss America ever—except, perhaps, for Jean. She played "Summertime" on the flute and Grieg's *Piano Concerto in A Minor* on the piano, and she was talented enough so that a few months later she appeared as a soloist for an all-girl band at Carnegie Hall, where even *The New York Times* acknowledged that Miss Myerson "appeared in the role of a serious pianist."

While Bess's ability, as well as her intelligence and bearing,

* See Appendix 6, p. 304.

were vital to supporting the new Miss America image, it is possible that she was not so much a right accident of history as she was of geography. From the Bronx, well-known as the only Jewish Miss America, Bess competed as Miss New York City, and she was, and remains, the only girl from any part of New York ever to win the title. The national press, located in New York, has always looked down smugly on *Miss America,* and treated it, automatically, with contempt. Nevertheless, the New York/national press has taken pains to separate its own Miss America from these indignities. Bess has always been dealt with seriously. Her case, of course, is only one example of the New York bias that runs through every element of the New York/national press. The Pageant has been rather unlucky that no New York girl has won in the last quarter of a century, for it is nearly predictable that if one ever did, Miss America's image—which is weak in metropolitan areas, especially the more titled East—would be instantly repaired.

This is, after all, approximately what happened twenty-five years ago. Generally immune to the criticisms that have beset the other queens, Miss Myerson has been permitted to rise to a point where she now holds an important political position—Commissioner of Consumer Affairs for New York City. Certified as a substantial American female, she is forever being solicited for her opinion on a variety of subjects. Apparently, she will respond to all queries except those dealing with Miss America. Since she began scaling lofty political heights, the beauty title may have become, in her view, an embarrassment to her new dignity.

Without question Bess remains the most famous of all Miss Americas—although Lee Meriwether, 1955, has been making a late run on the outside as a movie and TV actress. Not only was she from New York, talented, bright, and the first postwar Miss America, but Bess had always had sage powers of adjustment. Says Jean Bartel, "Part of Bess's success has been that she is the only one of us who has been well managed. She was more professionally handled. She had no great talent, but she did possess a strong personality, and when she found out she could not depend on her piano or her flute and was too tall for acting, she was smart enough to shift into other things."

Miss Myerson has possessed that great facility for taking advantage of any situation. When she was crowned, the Pageant and the press were celebrating her wildly as the first college-graduate Miss America, an intellectual giant who would spurn show biz for a Master's in music. Yet this did not stop her from picking up a quick booking at the Loew's State Theatre in Manhattan, where she appeared with an Eddie Bracken movie and on a live bill that featured acrobatics, "ventriloqual antics," the Marimba Co-Eds, and a vocalist singing "a medley of romantic melodies." Then, while still talking about her Master's, she set out to capitalize on her new fame with a vaudeville tour.

Though these memories have grown conveniently dim since she became a dignified political commissioner, Bess first was quoted telling this story in 1950, when it all was very fresh in her mind, and she repeated the tale nine years later for another newspaper.

"After I won the title, I toured vaudeville. I came out in a high-neck gown and played *The Fire Dance* and *Malaguena* on the piano and flute. I could hear the boys up front complaining and muttering, 'Where's the bathing suit?' so in the finale I came out in a white bathing suit, and the boys would cheer. Toward the end of the tour, I realized they didn't want to hear my music, so I just came out in a bathing suit. Finally, I was losing weight and not filling out the bathing suit, so I quit."

When her musical career sloughed off, Miss Myerson made an easy transition to mistress of ceremonies, where she was most famous as the "lady in mink" on "The Big Payoff." She also specialized as a parade float-by-float announcer, working the Mardi Gras, Thanksgiving Day, and Rose Bowl parades. She was best known, though, as the anchor girl on the *Miss America* broadcast, an association that seems to have been profitable for both parties. It focused on Bess a special identity, and in return, Atlantic City was able to display her as just the kind of sharp, lovely, and talented woman that a Miss America is, and always will be.

The honeymoon ended after the 1968 telecast, when Albert Marks at last decided that the Pageant needed some updating, and decided to replace Bess with a fresher Miss America (Debbie

Bryant, 1966, was the eventual choice). He was wrestling with the matter of determining how to give her the pink slip, most politely, when she took the political job and was thus forced to retire from commercial appearances.

Bess remains, however, the most famous of the breed. Generally, in the quarter of a century before her, girls entered *Miss America* as a way to get to Hollywood. In the quarter of a century past, they have entered as a way to get a scholarship. And, unquestionably, the girls have fared better in college than in the movies. In this respect, anyway, scholarships have certainly occasioned an improvement in the Pageant, and Bess, as Exhibit A, provided a rare visibility for a Miss America that surely heightened the advance.

Nevertheless, while the value of the Pageant as a scholarship dispenser is undisputed, this educational patina also serves to gloss the Pageant over with legitimacy, charity, and civics. Also, tedium. The subject of scholarships, and the value of education, is trotted out of headquarters and beaten like a drum at every opportunity. Miss America is awarded a $10,000 scholarship, which is really peanuts compared to the appearance money she earns in her reigning year ($55,000 and up), plus smaller residual amounts that most of the queens continue to make in the next few years. Yet virtually no reference is ever volunteered to the effect that a girl can make this good, big money far and above her scholarship.

The Pageant has pushed the scholarship line for so long and so diligently that it is virtually impossible ever to encounter any participant who has not swallowed the whole bit, and will regurgitate it upon reflex. As a result, while the college-aid program was established to help carry the Pageant to a higher plateau, the growing emphasis on the scholarship has consumed almost all of the theatrical and competitive values of the Pageant and reduced it to a mere crass adventure. In some states, the contests are now even known as "scholarship pageants," which succeeds in making them sound as acquisitive as they really have become. The rare girl who does admit to motives other than scholarship cash for wanting to enter a pageant is looked upon as a queer duck indeed.

Most Miss Americas have taken their $10,000 scholarships* and gone tripping back to college after their reigns, the way they're supposed to. BeBe Shopp, 1948, and Neva Jane Langley, 1953, went to formal music institutions; Yolande Betbeze, 1951, took private voice lessons in New York, the only winner to eschew organized education. However, two queens originally utterly stunned Lenora with the horrifying news that they really might not want to fool with any higher education.

First, in 1946, the judges drifted back to another era and selected Marilyn Buferd, Miss California, as the winner. "She was the last of the movie-crazy girls," Miss Slaughter says. She certainly was; she had no interest in education. She went to Hollywood, had little success, then went on to Europe. In Paris, she met Roberto Rossellini and he put her in a movie entitled *The Machine That Kills Evil-Doers*. He dated her too for a brief period, in the short time after he broke up with Anna Magnani and before he took up with Ingrid Bergman. For this reason, it was called "the hors-d'oeuvres romance." Around the middle of 1948, Rossellini used Marilyn as his translator, when he was conducting a business correspondence with Bergman, trying to set up arrangements for *Stromboli*. In a real sense, then, Marilyn served as a go-between for her own rival. And, incidentally, this linguistic ability derived from the fact that Lenora pleaded with her and finally convinced her that if she didn't want to go to a real college, at least she should take the money and go to Berlitz.

In 1961, Miss North Carolina, Maria Beale Fletcher, was named Miss America. A former A-student in high school, Maria was also the daughter of professional dancers, and had been a Rockette herself. After winning the title she expressed an interest in opening up a dancing school rather than going to college. The possibility so appalled the Pageant that four Miss Americas, who had returned for the ceremonies, were sicked on Miss Fletcher to give her some of that old-time Pageant religion. Eventually, Maria gave in and subsequently she used the scholarship at Vanderbilt University, where she enjoyed an outstanding academic career.

The point is not primarily what she finally elected to do; it is

* See Appendix 7, p. 305.

in the reaction of the Pageant to the idea that anyone might wish to deviate from academic schedule. But anyway, for proof of the fact that Maria certainly did make the right decision, it is cited that she found and married an outstanding young doctor at Vanderbilt. As the Pageant will explain, over and over, a formal education is a most valuable American commodity.

10

The Golden-Age Miss Americas Head into Middle Age

Increasingly respectable and responsible, the Pageant flowered after the war. Lenora was at her most animated and innovative. The girls were bigger, older, bustier, and smarter. By the 1948 Pageant, college girls were in the majority. All but one of the fifty-five girls in the competition that year specifically cited the scholarship as their reason for participating. These were the best of times. The Pageant basked in publicity, and while controversy clung to it like bush burrs, there was no real criticism of the enterprise.

As it should, the attention fell naturally to the queens. Each was different from the other, and capable of projecting a distinct public image without the help of television—though many were also assisted in this regard by the ridiculously simple device of having curious names, BeBe, Jacque, Yolande, Neva, Evelyn Ay. They came from all sections of the land, in contrasting sizes and shapes, distinctly varying interests and temperaments. And, they have all gone on to marriage and are heading into middle age in the same characteristic ways.

This golden age of *Miss America* is defined roughly by the end of the war and the advent of the scholarship on one end and the coming of television on the other. It was a decade or so, the heart of which centered around the three queens of 1948–1951. (There was no Miss America 1950, the title being postdated at that time.) The girls are disparate in the extreme. Two are usually cited as the typical queen and the typical anti-queen; they fairly despise one another and make regular insinuations about the other's mental stability. The youngest of the three is just about to round forty, but the imprint that each left on the Pageant is still clear.

The postwar era was inaugurated by Bess Myerson, but neither of her two successors could take advantage of her lead, even if they did establish the period pattern in dichotomy. Willowy Marilyn Buferd, 1946, was interested only in movies; sweet Barbara Jo Walker, 1947, only in a man. She came to Atlantic City with an engagement ring on, and was back home within a couple of weeks after her coronation. Betty Jo, as she preferred to be called, was Miss Memphis, and the last girl ever to represent a city. She was also the last Miss America to be crowned in a bathing suit.

Still, she was valuable as an image-maker, salt-of-the-earth department. She had taken off twenty pounds to get down to beauty trim, she taught Sunday School, was opposed to smoking, and was of the opinion that no one was physically capable of drinking moderately. She wanted only to be a wife and mother, and have a college degree. She said things like: "I'm only interested in one contract—the marriage contract." She married her intern in June of her reign, an event of such proportions in Memphis that there were traffic jams about the church.

So it was that an erstwhile Miss America crowned the new queen in 1948. The accident of her marriage only heightened the symbolism in this changing of the guard. The two girls shared only a common wholesomeness; the scene was so salubrious that it made up in health for what it lacked, for once, in all-around virginity. BeBe Shopp, the new Miss America, was a big strapping farm girl who stood 5 feet 9 inches and weighed 140, the most to that time. She was 27 inches around at the waist, 37 inches at the bust, but more svelte in the hips with 36 inches, which may be accounted for by her industry. "I am only a farm girl," she said. "I drive a tractor. I clean the chicken coops. I mix cement."

She was barely eighteen, youngest in the field (still the youngest postwar queen), with a full, round baby face, and long brown hair that fell down in waves over her shoulders. Her informal portrait at the time shows her wearing a sweater, with beads. She played glockenspiel in her high-school band in Hopkins, Minnesota. If it is possible, she was even more naïve than the sum of these parts.

But Beatrice Bella Shopp was primarily a very determined and organized young lady. "I remember that I had my own horse as a girl," she says, "but I decided to give it up after a while because it conflicted so with my music, and you can't do your best for both." She was a B student in high school, and planned to attend a small Minnesota college after she graduated in 1948.

The summer before, 1947, when she was still only sixteen and under age, she was prevailed upon to enter Miss Minnesota at an amusement park to help fill out the field. She proceeded through the contest on a lark, but took everything in, with the intention of coming back in a couple of years to try it again. In one of the few times in her life that she was overruled, though, BeBe was pushed back into the competition at Excelsior Amusement Park the next summer, when she was still a few weeks short of her eighteenth birthday, August 17. Her evening dress was her high-school prom gown; her swimsuit was what she swam in; she was inexperienced, if not unawed, at appearing on a stage. She still says firmly, "I was not prepared the way I wanted to be." Playing *Clair de Lune* on the vibraharp, she cut through the field and came to Atlantic City as the youngest girl there. "I don't care how young she was," Lenora says. "She was in command. She had that crown on her head when she arrived, and in many ways, she has never taken it off either."

BeBe's father, a feisty little man, who had fainted dead away when she looked at him as she walked down the runway, recovered and took over. Though strong-willed, he was obviously capable, and useful, so Lenora worked with him and learned. Mr. Shopp was director of the health and education department at Cream of Wheat. Since it is impossible for a Miss America to have either Theodore Roosevelt or Johnny Appleseed as her father, it is only proper that the honor go to the health man at Cream of Wheat. Obvious product association was not lost on the cereal either; it permitted him to use part of his time, and his secretary, in booking BeBe. Mrs. Shopp, a beautiful woman, chaperoned her daughter. By themselves, the Shopps handled

Miss America more efficiently than Atlantic City ever had. She made myriad appearances, capping her reign with a trip to Europe that her father and the Minneapolis newspapers had arranged. BeBe—and always just that, two capital Bs, everywhere but on the *Miss America* trophy—was the first Miss America to go abroad during her year in office; it was like Wilson off to Versailles.

The press ambushed her on both sides of the Atlantic, for she was ideal for these purposes, being innocent and vulnerable. "You have no perspective as Miss America," BeBe says. She is an instinctively friendly woman, and outspoken in a disarming way, since even the most revealing comments she makes may be camouflaged by associate comments about the everyday lives of her four daughters that appear regularly in any conversation about herself. "As Miss America you only have time to do your job, travel, be nice, and represent the Pageant. I was so naïve. My daughter at fourteen knows more than I did as Miss America. I literally didn't know that homosexuals existed until I got to New York after my year. My daughter was reading an article about it the other day."

Going for her jugular, the press asked BeBe almost exclusively about sex, with questions about liquor as a change of pace. What started out as a pleasure trip was soon billed as "Miss America's Moral Crusade." The opinions BeBe first expressed at Idlewild and in London, which were distorted from the outset, she says, were soon blown up even more and sent on before her like an advance guard. Printed fake interviews greeted her as she reached new towns on the Continent.

Mostly, her nemeses were bikinis and falsies. "As far as I can remember," BeBe says, "all I ever said was that if the French wanted to wear bikinis, fine, but speaking as an American girl, they weren't for me. I gave the same sort of reply to falsies: no, I don't wear them, but it's fine with me if other women want to." The papers offered much stronger quotes. They said that she had declared that bikinis were "not decent," and that she planned to "crusade" against false bosoms. In London, the papers quoted her: "A bikini is a dab here, and a bit right down here and back there. It's a matter of morals. So much unrestrained nudity has a bad moral effect on men." And: "I don't wear falsies and I never will. A girl must be her very own self. Falsies aren't honest. Of course, if a girl feels that she must wear a pair, that's her affair. But for me, give me plenty of milk and loads of nourishing food."

The reporters asked her if she had ever been out with a "man of the world" (she hadn't), and what she planned to do with "that fat." There were reports that she was frequenting bars. It was all so upsetting to BeBe that for many years thereafter she could not stand to read her scrapbooks of this period. And all hell was breaking loose back home.

Earl Wilson, the columnist, who had been one of the judges, rushed to defend his own professional opinion, as well as BeBe, protesting that it was ill-bred for anyone to label the queen as fat. On the other hand, he went on to acknowledge that she was "a little too meaty." Lenora declared unequivocally that it was impossible for BeBe to have had anything to drink, since, "she often told me, 'I just don't like the taste of liquor.' " Nevertheless, BeBe's father shot off a wire to her: "Keep out of all wineshops and cocktail lounges," which arrived just before she and her newspaper chaperone, Virginia Safford, were about to go off to the Folies-Bergère. On the telephone, she assured Mr. Shopp, "This girl's not doing anything wrong." BeBe cried.

Reassured, Mr. Shopp began to search out the real villains. "Some Reds or Socialists over there must be writing all these terrible things about my daughter," he at last let on. "Those things might have been made up by a Communist writer who is attempting to undermine the character of my daughter and, through her, the American girl for whom she has set an example." And other big guns moved on line. In a whole long incredible editorial entitled "THANKS MISS AMERICA—Unfair to Men," the New York *Daily News* lionized BeBe, calling her "remarkable" and "as brainy as she is curvy." While the *News* was unable to sniff out Mr. Shopp's Commie specter, it identified an even more invidious conspiracy. The lengthy editorial concluded:

> Who knows how many girls today are passing up their nourishing gravy and vegetables and not worrying about it, because they

know they can regain those alluring contours just by dropping by the beauty counter or hardware department or wherever they do sell those things?

And how about the men, for whom all these feats in personal, female engineering presumably are performed? We bet there's hardly a male animal roaming around who hasn't suspected that he's been deceived, bilked, hornswoggled, or at least made nervous by this falsie fad. The average man, being modest and timid by nature, feels resentful but seldom gets up his courage to protest against such a hoax. . . .

But now Miss America has come right out and backed up the notions that we meek gents have had about those danged things all along. Miss Shopp has gone and said it; and we're glad, glad, glad.

"I'm not on a crusade," BeBe protested, but no one believed her, and at the 1949 Pageant her reign ended in a symbolic standstill. After playing an exhibition on the vibraharp, she curtsied in her heavy, bouffant dress. The hoops formed a suction effect and she was unable to rise until the emcee came over and nearly lifted BeBe to her feet, so that she could welcome her successor. Even that was a comic scene. Miss America turned out to be the lightest queen ever, the shortest one since Margaret Gorman. She was six inches shorter than BeBe, thirty-five pounds lighter. She also had the tongue of a carnival bally and the moves of a second-story man. BeBe Shopp had been resolute and efficient, but Jacque Mercer, the new queen, was bold and calculating—and while no one knew it, there was an even tougher cookie coming along next.

Jacque, who was named for her mother's favorite doll, was a descendant of Daniel Boone and James Polk. She was the last Miss America not to be born in a hospital. She was born in a house in Thatcher, Arizona, in the southeastern corner of the state. Like BeBe, who is four months older, Jacque was a farm girl, though her family did move near Phoenix, to Litchfield, where she grew up. Her father was a farmer and an elementary school principal, and since Jacque was never renowned as a beauty until she decided that she was one, she concentrated her early efforts in the fields of her father—soil and scholarship. She won a ribbon in the 4-H for her radishes and was eighth-grade valedictorian. Then, at the age of fifteen, Jacque Mercer decided that she would also like to be Miss America.

To that point, nobody had prepared for that eventuality. Becoming Miss America was something totally unexpected that happened to you, like appendicitis or winning a raffle. Jacque was the first person to sit down and start from scratch in constructing a Miss America—that it was herself, was nearly incidental. Jacque refined the process of becoming Miss America, just as BeBe straightened out the business of being one.

"It was about three years before I won that I first started collecting information on the subject," Jacque says. She speaks easily, expressing assuredness on most subjects and treating inflection as a craft, so that it always seems, somehow, that whatever she is saying is important or in confidence, or both. It is easy to understand how Jacque impressed the judges so; many years later Helen Gurley Brown worked the same bunko with less art.

"From the first, I didn't know where to turn, so most of my early research just involved clippings from relatives from other parts of the country. The Jaycees got me an Atlantic City press kit. That helped. Before the contest I was going to Stanford, but then I decided to really try for this, so we put the money into it. O.K., my parents said, what do you need? I moved into an apartment downtown for a month to avoid distractions, and I paid for four coaches—let's see now, dramatics, fashion, my presentation, and sort of a head coach, I guess. They came at me in shifts. I would have had more money to work with but the Jaycees were rained out for Miss Arizona, which killed their gate, so they couldn't afford to give me any help when I won. I got one pair of sunglasses from them.

"But what the hell—nobody ever figured I could do anything anyway. Seven people saw me off. When I came back, a squadron of planes met mine at the Arizona line and escorted me to Phoenix, but when I left seven people saw me off to Atlantic City. It was just dependable old Jackie. I had done some modeling, but I had never even been nominated for homecoming queen or anything. But I just figured, if you could learn to be a brain, you could learn to be a woman. It was all just a matter of: let's give old plain Jane some sex appeal."

Even sex, however, is easier to come by than size. Despite all her careful plotting, even Jacque could not know how strong is the prejudice against short girls. It was as if, on top of everything else, nobody would listen to Demosthenes because he had bad breath. Jacque was the runt of the litter at Atlantic City, even after she added an inch to her true height and listed herself as 5 feet 4 inches. She also wore platform shoes and clothes that are supposed to foment the illusion of height. Luckily, she did happen to come from an alphabetically benign state—Arizona was first in line in one of the three contestants' groups, so that Jacque was always on the end and could not get trapped in derision between two tall girls. She received a lot of fan mail from the Philippines after she won.

Before she reached Atlantic City, as soon as she learned their identity, Jacque began to scrutinize the judges. She decided on a talent presentation of the potion scene from *Romeo and Juliet*, because she felt that both its classical and lugubrious aspects were likely to impress them. Similarly, Jacque felt that the Elizabethan clothes would strike the special fancy of the judges, and call positive attention to herself. For balance and more affable display, she practiced smiling "at lamp posts, mailboxes, anything."

On her entry sheet, Jacque maintained the fiction that she was still going on to Stanford; certainly it sounded better than Phoenix JC. For a hobby, she noted that she "raised Maltese dogs," which was aimed at proving her best instincts of patience, discipline, and motherhood. She purposely flashed a distinctive brooch that all but demanded queries about it, which was exactly what she wanted—I'mgladyouaskedmethatquestion. The pin contained an Arizona stone that her grandfather had chanced upon, and gave Jacque the opening to go off on a long spiel about family, state, and heritage which, on a good day, could even carry clear back to Daniel Boone.

Judges were still being met over meals. Jacque always ate in advance, so she did not have to concern herself with appetite on these occasions. She made it a point to stay clear of tall girls, and to spend as much time as possible in the company of the shortest, homeliest contestants that she could find. She tried to discern in advance what color dresses girls planned to wear for some function, and then Jacque would come in the best contrasting outfit: black, with short sleeves when others at her table came in white, with full sleeves. She took Miss Arkansas along as a confederate in another ruse. Because of the alphabet, Arizona and Arkansas often were required to stand side by side. On those occasions, Jacque would turn to Miss Arkansas and say: "ABC." Arkansas would reply, "DEF" Jacque would counter "GHI," and so on for as long as they felt the judges were watching them from some distance. It made them appear bright and animated, never tired or at a loss for good conversation. Each night, the Arizona chaperone and two of her cronies whose girls had no chance would sit with Jacque and give her a detailed critique of her performance of the day. Mr. and Mrs. Mercer were expressly forbidden to try to make any contact with their daughter for as long as the Pageant was on.

"I had all this doped out," Jacque says. "I'm a very scientific nature. The whole key is to make yourself stand out, but not appear freaky—and that's a very fine line. It was a matter of building up to a mood; it was a lot like creating an advertising presentation." She swept to an easy victory. When her name was announced, behind her she could hear other girls cursing and saying, "Oh no, not her."

The seeds of her own comeuppance were, indeed, already sown. The cunning Miss Machiavelli was nearly destroyed by her own intense design. Someone who knew her well then says, "I don't think Jackie herself knows how close she came at times to a complete nervous breakdown. She wasn't just a high-strung kid. She looked like she was ready to jump off a tall building."

Each year as she grew up her father had given Jacque a battery of standard personality tests. The development of her character was charted consistently, and in the year before she became Miss America, her indices of drive, ambition, and self-confidence had risen so high that they appeared to have soared off the curve. She took the same tests following her year as Miss America, and found that those three characteristics were shattered. Her best had been broken. Finally, five years later, she took the same tests one more time. Married by this time, a mother, far removed from that year and the title, she says that the tests showed that her drive, ambition, and self-confidence had come back to reality—not to the mad pre-queen peak—but to a sensible level just above the norm. All other personality factors always measured practically the same, before, after, and long after she was Miss America.

"That year is so drastically superficial, that jelling takes five years afterward," Jacque says. "You learn things that work, you practice them, but eventually you start to go stale, but you can't compensate any longer—or soon, you don't even realize that you must compensate. You just know that things are not working any more, and you don't know why. You don't know why, but *you* are not working anymore."

Jacque's pace was grueling but lucrative. "I was a very lucky Miss America," she says. "BeBe came in the trial year. I really hit it in the first peak year." Then, just before New Year's Day 1950, as the world prepared to celebrate its half-century, the Pageant received the stupefying word from Arizona that its clever little queen had climbed into her prize Nash sedan and run off somewhere in the desert to marry her high-school sweetheart.

There was no rule prohibiting marriage, of course. Betty Jo Walker, 1947, had married in mid-reign only two years before. The rule in effect today, that "at their discretion" the Pageant Board can forfeit Miss America's title and scholarship if she marries, was established at Miss Mercer's insistence after her own teen-age nuptial folly ended, which was soon. Since that time, no Miss America has married during her year. However, waiting to marry until just after the reign is concluded appears to offer no more in the way of long-term marital bliss.

With the exception of Miss Walker and Evelyn Ay, 1954, who were engaged before they were crowned, the first seven Miss Americas, who either married during their reigns or within a few months after, all saw their marriages end in divorce. (Debra Barnes, 1968, who married four months after she passed on the crown, is presently the only Miss America with a marriage outstanding that has a chance to break that dismal record.)*

Says Jacque, "The pressure on you subtly forces you into mar-

* See Appendix 8, p. 305.

rying the old boy friend, to prove that you have not changed, that the title has not gone to your head. Obviously, you are a stuck-up if the romance is broken off for any reason. Marriage is not the easiest thing for Miss A's, anyway. We tend to marry twc distinct types, either strong men who can accept the competition, or retiring sorts who are content to relax in their wife's reflected glory. I think athletes are such a good match because they had a lot of acclaim themselves, but it must fade as they grow older, which is a lot like what happens to a Miss A." Jacque always refers to Miss America as Miss A.

BeBe Shopp adds, "That's fine as far as it goes. That only takes in the types that work out. The third kind of husband is the one that can never accept the Miss America. I almost married one, and it would have been hell. I only dated a couple of men who were totally unimpressed by the title. I married one of them."

A change in the prevailing type of Miss America occurs about every decade or so, and nothing reveals that a change in type has been made so much as the queens' taste in husbands. In the early days, which, coincidentally, were times of prosperity, all Miss Americas, every one of them, married businessmen. Later, when a few show-business husbands appear in the ranks, they first turn out to be producers and managers in the arts who are somewhat older than their Miss America wives. Not until the late 1940s and 1950s do the celebrities—the actors and athletes—start appearing. Then suddenly, in the 1960s, and for the first and only time, doctors and lawyers appear in force.

The classic Miss America marriage must be attributed to Colleen Hutchins, 1952, another of the distinct queens who were produced in the golden age of the Pageant in the years before TV. The sister of an all-American basketball player, Colleen married another, Ernie Vandeweghe, who played respectably for several seasons with the New York Knickerbockers of the National Basketball Association. But Vandeweghe was not just an athlete; while playing in the pros he was also an intern. Thus, Colleen was able to stay in vogue with one husband: she had Ernie the athlete in the 1950s, when jocks were fashionable, and Dr. Vandeweghe, when physicians became stylish.

Colleen was not at all a Pageant type; she had to be implored to go on to Atlantic City after she won a campus contest at

Brigham Young University. Finally she went when she decided she could also go to New York and see a lot of musicals. She was the oldest queen of all (twenty-five), the tallest (5 feet 10 inches, but well over 6 feet tall in heels), and the heaviest (143 pounds). Yet, like so many other queens, she craved a Broadway career and migrated to New York after her reign, where she subsisted on large amounts of asparagus and chocolate pudding and finally got a small part in one musical. Then she married her athlete-doctor, and returned to Southern California, where the cycle had begun when she went to BYU and became Miss Utah. A Mormon, disciplined and considerate, she appears today to be easily the healthiest and most physically active of all Miss Americas. Her children are all especially sports-oriented, to a point where not long ago an article in *Sports Illustrated* implied harshly that Colleen and her husband were trying to construct their own super race. "We may be square," she says, "but, good grief, that doesn't make us evil, does it?"

At almost the same time, a piece appeared in *The New York Times* which focused on Macon, Georgia, and Colleen's successor, Neva Jane Langley, who is now the wife of a wealthy real-estate broker, William Fickling. The article infuriated Neva, as it packaged her in the easily recognizable stereotype of the rich, smug, plantation gentry. Former Miss Americas are looked upon as fair game for the national press, for most of them live in the sticks, have kept their looks, and have grown older, rich, and conservative.

The one exception, besides New York's Bess Myerson, of course, is the girl who, even in this postwar period of original, piquant women, was the most beautiful, intriguing, and spectacular of them all: Yolande Betbeze, Miss America 1951. In a navy blue suit, with a white satin blouse, she stepped off the train in Atlantic City that September day in 1950, and Miss Slaughter, there to meet her, was reduced to superlatives. "She was the sexiest, most glamorous thing I had ever laid my eyes on," she says.

Standing there with Lenora, Brad Frapart said, "She can't lose unless the women judges run away from her." As it was, Yolande is supposed to have been a unanimous choice. She was deluged by movie offers, which she refused out of hand. Naturally, it was then presumed that she was only being coy, and, to her disgust, the antes kept rising. "Howard Hughes wanted me to take one of those personal contracts, like the one I think Jane Russell still gets paid under," Yolande says. "He had a weird little fellow follow me around for two years. He assumed I would come right with him. Instead, I said, 'Who is Mr. Hughes?' So then he thought I was crazy, which indeed I was." David Selznick told friends that at last he had found his Scarlett O'Hara for a musical *Gone with the Wind.*

All those who knew Yolande, whatever their personal regard for her, assume—do not speculate, but assume matter-of-factly—that she would have been a star and celebrity of the first rank had she been at all inclined to devote herself to that end. She was not. She almost signed with Twentieth Century-Fox once, but a fat, oily executive there patted her on the rear and said, "We'll have to take some of that off." Yolande said thank you, excused herself, and departed, without leaving a forwarding address. She joined a rodeo on its way to Cuba. Yolande Betbeze has done a lot of things and been credited with many more.

Yolande (the final e in both first and last name is not pronounced: Yo-lond Bet-bees) came from a fairly prominent Mobile, Alabama, family, whose name was its most substantial resource. Sissie, as she was known then, was raised by her mother. Her father, a maverick rascal, came in from his woodland cabin occasionally to visit, and he impressed his daughter as being a dead ringer for Cary Grant. Indeed, on perhaps the one occasion in her life when Yolande was struck dumb, Cary Grant suddenly loomed before her on an airplane and said, "I understand I look like your father."

Sissie became BeBe, like Miss America 1948, and for twelve years attended Visitation Academy, a girls' Roman Catholic convent school. She was afraid to smile behind braces, seldom went out with boys, and instead devoted herself to books, music, and the world beyond Mobile. Yolande possessed all the background elements of a classical Tennessee Williams heroine, except the mentality. And she did have real talent. By the age of sixteen she was singing leading roles with the Mobile Opera Guild, and dreaming of ways to escape the South. At eighteen, she hit on *Miss America* as "my *via aperta.*"

Needing a sponsor to enter the State Pageant run-throughs in Birmingham, she walked into the office of the Mayor and solicited his support. She received no other backing from her home town—"not even a handkerchief"—an oversight that was to prove expensive to mercantile Mobile some months ahead. Yolande recalls that she had to visit Birmingham three times for interviews, where she suspects that the judges credited her with a great command of operatic German because of her lisp. In fact, it was only that she still talked strangely in her braces. "I finally prevailed upon this dentist to stay away from his fishing one Sunday and remove them just before I went to Atlantic City," she explains. "I was so glad to be rid of the damn things that I smiled like a fool the whole time, which is probably what won for me." She also doctored up her biography sheet, answering truthfully only to her name and the color of her eyes. The experience with eighteen-year-old Jacque Mercer and her mother, who wanted to sign all the contracts and get involved in all the decisions for her underage daughter, had soured the Pageant on minors, so Yolande dutifully added three years to her age and made herself almost twenty-two—an addition that has been somewhat painful to her recently.

Realizing immediately that she was the girl to beat, the other contestants at Atlantic City viewed her with envy. For her part, Yolande showered the others with intellectual contempt and they responded next with suspicion, then malice. As so many other Miss Americas, as both BeBe and Jacque before her had, she won her swimsuit division, but Yolande did not, ironically, triumph in talent. When she sang "Sempre Libera" from *La Traviata*, she and the *Miss America* orchestra, basically a jazz band, began playing against each other. After a trumpet player cut in on a high trill, Yolande froze the man with a stare, stopped singing, and snapped, "I'll finish alone," which she did. For the finals, she located a piano accompanist in Philadelphia and switched to "Caro Nome" from *Rigoletto*, and even more difficult selection. "You're not supposed to switch talent," Yolande says, "but at that point, rules were the last thing I was interested in." She and the accompanist practiced no more than twenty minutes. "She was very good," Yolande says, "but I did the hell out of that number." As she finished, Deems Taylor, one of the judges, slapped his loose-leaf book shut, and in the silent moment before the applause began, could be heard plainly to say, "Ladies and gentlemen, that's it." For perhaps the only time in the history of the Pageant, a performer was called back for two curtain calls.

Shortly thereafter, Yolande and the other finalists were ushered to five chairs just offstage. It was customary then, before TV, for the new Miss America to be informed somewhat in advance of her appearance onstage so that she could compose herself—especially since so many dissolved into tears or a near faint. When Yolande was told she was the choice, she nodded dispassionately and reached for an eyelash curler, which she then carried at all times as a sort of functional talisman. Without a word, she curled one set of eyelashes, then the other, put the curler back, rose, said, "Let's go," and strode serenely onstage.

Following this coronation she returned to the dressing room. On her mirror, in lipstick, was written: "HAIRY SITS HERE." "You know," Yolande explains, "I'm a Mediterranean type; I have to pluck my eyebrows. So, that's what the bitches wrote. I suppose they thought it would destroy me. Well, I was standing there, still with my crown and scepter and all the other trappings, and suddenly I noticed that a matron had also seen the writing. She started to rush over to rub it off, to spare our queen this indignity, and I just turned to her, and I said, 'Don't you dare. Don't anyone dare rub that off my mirror.' And then I just said 'thank you' so sweetly to all those dear ladies, and explained to them that I must excuse myself because the press was waiting impatiently outside to talk to their new Miss America."

"She was always ornery, but underneath a very nice girl," Lenora says in assessment. She got her surprise the next morning when Yolande declared that she had no intentions of spending any more time posing in bathing suits. She was a singer, she explained, not a pin-up. Jean Bartel had said approximately the same thing seven years before, but there was a difference. When Jean Bartel was Miss America, Catalina was not a sponsor.

Though stunned by this revelation, Lenora was secretly pleased, and supported Yolande in this battle against cheesecake. Nevertheless, while Yolande removed Catalina, the enemy within, she was directly responsible for the establishment of Miss Universe, the Pageant's main competitor. Jacque also played a supporting role in this affair. It began the same day that Yolande announced that she would not pose in Catalinas. For fun, Jacque, who had just been retired as queen, went up the Jersey shore to Asbury Park with E.B. Stewart, the president of Catalina, to watch the Mrs. America finals. Lenora got so mad at Jacque when she learned of this that she vowed never to speak to her again—and literally did not say another word to her for the next four years.

This pettiness did not endear the Pageant to Jacque, and the upshot was that, a few months later, when she was making an appearance for Catalina in Des Moines, E.B. Stewart found a very receptive ear when he began cataloguing some of his complaints against *Miss America.* "Well, if that's the way it is," Jacque said, "why aggravate yourself? Why don't you start your own Pageant?" She suggested Miss United Nations, which Stewart thought was a magnificent idea, and which remained the working title of the new show until Universal-International joined the venture and made Miss Universe the more politic choice.

Thus it was that one Miss America inspired Miss Universe and another suggested it. A third, Rosemary LaPlanche, 1941, crowned the first winner in Long Beach in July 1952. Stewart also lured the emcee and some judges from *Miss America,* spent $350,000 in promotion, and ran things his way. Pointedly, it was declared that beauty was the girls' "only talent," and each U.S. entrant—33,000 in 42 states—was required to purchase a Catalina suit.*

The loss of the Catalina revenue was no blow to either *Miss America* or Yolande. It only required them both to uncover new compensatory sources of income, and no one ever played that game better than Yolande. By her own measure, she believes that the Catalina publicity "tripled my other fees," and she was, in general, easily the most acquisitive Miss America of them all. Mobile first learned the cut of her jib when she informed her home town that, while she found it dear that the city wanted her to return for municipal honors, she had a price tag on such marketable sentiment. "Checks preferred," she declared for openers,

* See Appendix 9, p. 306.

but when negotiations were concluded, she agreed to accept no less than a gift from each participating merchant, a diamond and sapphire bracelet, a full wardrobe, complete with mink coat, and a large cash bonus that the city itself had to pay. And the proud home-folks filled the ballpark to salute their sweet little Southern gal. Before she left town Yolande gave away some of the surplus watches that had been presented to her, and, Miss Slaughter says, she also laid some of the tackier clothing gifts about the back yard and moved between these pieces of apparel, auctioning them off to neighbors with the style of a rug merchant.

"I was the only one who ever looked at it strictly from a business sense. The Pageant uses its Miss Americas, and most of them don't even know they're being taken. They come into Toledo or Pocatello and see their picture in the paper and think how wonderful it is. Five miles outside of Toledo, nobody knows Miss America is alive. So you work the sticks, and you receive no recognition. You might as well try to get some money out of it. Look, every day it's another alligator farm. You bet, it was no more than a job with me," Yolande says. She has long since lost her accent, but she retains a natural drawl that marks her wit, not her origin. She affects a comic's pace, drifting along in languid narrative to set up the whip of a punch line. She dots any conversation with idle observations, most of them irreverent, but otherwise she speaks with the authority of a double-your-money-back-if-not-satisfied guarantee.

In 1966 she toyed with the idea of returning to Mobile and running for Congress. The fact that she was a flaming liberal assaulting an entrenched Whig constituency was of no concern to Yolande. She blithely maintained that she could have smiled magnolias and "y'alled" her way out of any tight spots. Yolande has lived in Washington for several years now, and although talk is cheap there and Yolande likes to talk, she will not relax and trade in the endemic blarney. She is always forthright, and a cynic.

"At some point I remember Atlantic City telling me that I had the honor of going to Paris and wearing our American cotton dresses into the very heart of *haute couture*," she says. "I was a good-will ambassadress, you see, so someone came up with one of these incredible ideas, that I was to take a vial of water from the Hudson and deposit it in the Seine in the name of Franco-American amity. I think the Pageant earnestly believed that I was America's answer to Lafayette at last. If I remember, too, all the damn water ran out of the vial on the plane over, and I had to refill it with water from the faucet in my hotel.

"But anyway, when all this first came up, and they were outlining the trip for me, I said something terribly subtle like, 'How much do I get?' 'But Yolande, dear,' they cried, 'you don't understand, this is a chance to go to Paris.' I told them rather sweetly that I would rather be in Cairo, Illinois, and get the money. They never knew what to make of me."

James Hatcher, the director of the Miss Alabama Pageant, an old friend and a valuable Yolandophile, recalls one especially illustrative occasion when she was queen. She was sick and weak, and her *Miss America* representative wanted her to go into a hospital. A lady from Miss Alabama, who was also traveling along, felt that it would be best for Yolande merely to rest up at some rustic clinic. The two women began arguing in the living room of their hotel suite. Yolande, who was always more concerned with the money, called Hatcher into the adjoining bedroom and shut the door.

Hatcher says, "She was so tired. She just said, 'Honey,' and I said, 'Yes, BeBe?' and she said, 'Will you just help me pack, because I'm sick?' We packed her clothes, and she brushed her hair, and when she came out into the living room the two women were still arguing where she should be sent. Yolande just stood there until they noticed her and stopped talking. Then she said, 'Ladies, Miss America is leaving for New York. You have ten minutes if you wish to accompany her.'

"She really was like a queen, yet she was such a refreshing personality for a Miss America because she refused to stand in awe of the title. She had one delightful device that could absolutely backfire on anyone else who tried it. Most anyone, when they say good-by, will say, 'I'm so glad to have met you,' or something to that effect. Yolande would always turn that around and say, 'I'm so glad you got the chance to meet me.' And they all loved it, from her."

At the end of her reign, Yolande said, "I have gotten so that I sometimes think of Miss America as another person and I frequently find myself wondering what she will say or do next."

At that time, as BeBe Shopp had done, Yolande went to New York. She enrolled in the New School for Social Research. She also continued to pick up a lot of Miss America bookings, and, with her voice out of shape from the lengthy layoff, she made no effort to continue her musical training. She did toy casually with the theater, and one of her fantasies is to produce a *Macbeth,* casting three Miss Americas as the witches. It was Yolande's social interests, however, that began to dominate her character and her time. She worked nights for the NAACP, and also involved herself with CORE and SANE. In the first wave of protest picketing around 1960, Yolande was on line when Woolworth's was the initial target. Atlantic City was shocked. Lenora still says huffily, "That was against her dignity." Though she had at first maintained ties with Atlantic City and had twice even come back to judge, within a decade after her reign Yolande and *Miss America* were in different worlds, and flying apart further every year.

A full ten years before they received wide acceptance, Yolande was wearing pants suits. The reigning Miss America of that time, Nancy Fleming, not only refused to make a choice between John Kennedy and Richard Nixon, but soberly informed reporters that she was even unable to decide for herself which was the better-looking. About the time Yolande moved to Washington, Miss America 1964, Donna Axum, declared that Doris Day was her favorite actress and that rock-'n'-roll was surely no more than a passing fad. She would not even discuss such a woman as Elizabeth Taylor. A couple of years later, as Yolande grew more outspoken, Lenora ushered the new Miss America from a room when the subject of race was introduced at an interview. By 1967, going backward faster all the time, *Miss America* got on the Vietnam bandwagon just as everyone else was scurrying off. Miss World refused to go, but Miss America and other state queens traveled to the war zone with a revue entitled "What's Happening Back Home." By this time Yolande had fallen so far from middle-American grace that it had been disclosed, completely erroneously, but with a smug finality, in the New York *Daily News* that that brazen hussy wore no underwear.

Long the prodigal daughter, by now Yolande had become the scourge of *Miss America,* surfacing regularly to put the Pageant down as racist, anti-feminist, outdated, vapid, or whatever else might occur to her on the spur of the moment. Her complaints began to be registered more frequently, as a sad circumstance made her more visible again. In 1954, appropriately on July 4, with Colleen Hutchins as her maid of honor, Yolande had been married to Matthew Fox, a multimillionaire, who was best known for his film ventures, although Drew Pearson also credited him with helping to finance Sukarno's drive for power in Indonesia. A stocky man, charming, and a genius, Matty Fox was forty-three, almost double Yolande's age, when he married her. They lived on Park Avenue, spent weekends in California, and the best of times abroad. Yolande was entirely removed from *Miss America.* Then, in 1964, a month short of their tenth anniversary, Fox died suddenly, leaving Yolande with an infant daughter, also named Yolande. "My name has always been the prettiest thing I have," she says.

Yolande moved to Georgetown, where she returned to some prominence as a close friend of Barbara Howar, the leading Washington hostess of the LBJ years. Yolande attracted more attention, however, for her sparkling, braided romance with Cherif Guellal, then the brilliant and charismatic Algerian ambassador, who is two years her junior. Unsupported accounts—all untrue, Yolande says—began appearing, saying that the handsome ambassador's domestic political future was threatened by his love for the beautiful Widow Fox. Where these things are tabulated, Yolande was stamped as the widow of a Jew and the mother of a half-Jewish daughter. The star-crossed romance, twisted even more when Algeria severed diplomatic relations with the U.S., was even considered as prime material for a modern musical, with the working title "Love in the Six-Day War" considered. Yolande and Guellal have outlasted the doomsday gossips, however. The romance is as solid as ever, and Yolande, falling back on her best schoolgirl vernacular, describes it simply, happily, as "neatsy."

Coincidentally, she was in Algeria when the Fiftieth Anniversary *Miss America* Pageant was celebrated in 1970, but she would not have been welcomed in Atlantic City had she been available. The Pageant has become so rabbit-eared that it did not invite her, which would be the equivalent of the Academy Awards asking every Oscar winner back except Katharine Hepburn. Even George Wallace invited Yolande to his inauguration when he returned to office, so it might be said, as a political note, that Yolande has succeeded in proving that *Miss America* is to the right of George Wallace.

By contrast with Yolande, by any gauge, BeBe Shopp has had an adult life so commonplace—and also so filled, active, and happy—that she might more accurately be described as a representative Mrs. America. She honest-to-God met her husband under the Biltmore clock. He was a Harvard man, a lacrosse star, and then an Air Force officer. Today, Bayard Waring is an executive with Restaurant Associates in New York. As his background suggests, he is solid and reliable, and friendly, too, but with a reserve that is foreign to BeBe. "People always find out who you are," she says. "Until about seven or eight years ago, sometimes I wished that I could just run and hide, but Bayard helped a lot at those times, and now I don't care much about it."

The Warings are instinctively suburban. Like so many of their generation, they never lived in the city. There is nothing diversionary to them about the suburbs, it is their native habitat. When the Warings left Boston for New York, they scouted to find a new suburb that contained the properties of the town they were departing. They selected Weston, Connecticut, and live there in a large, modern New England frame house that is set far back from the main road, beyond a man-made pond, rising high over a sylvan knoll and other new houses spread about it. The vibraharp is downstairs, in the family room, with the republican posters.

BeBe's husband spends at least three and a half hours a day commuting back and forth from New York. Her life, at a fast pace, revolves around the town and her four daughters, ages ten to fifteen. She says, "I've got to be someone who goes. I'm a doer." Almost compulsively, she is involved in numerous community activities: PTA, Scouts, church, Republicans, drug education, and scattered other *pro tempore* projects. She has also served as an alumnae leader at the Manhattan School of Music, which she attended with her Miss America scholarship, and for a while, in the years immediately following her reign, she was the first Miss America to get involved judging and emceeing regularly. At one point, she even managed to get herself entangled in local pageant politics back in Minnesota.

Simply by her nature, BeBe is incapable of any casual participation. At the Fiftieth Anniversary Pageant, she was the Miss America who took it upon herself to become sort of the captain of the line. The other queens called her "The Cruise Director." "Nag, nag, nag," Jacque cried from the other end of the line, as BeBe would snap things like, "All right, all right, let's go, let's *go*. If we're going to do it, let's do it right!"

BeBe is slimmer now than when she won the crown, more fetching and more refined. Most Miss Americas, when they win, are neither especially beautiful nor sexy. They become more beautiful with age. "Basically, I think the Pageant is good," BeBe says. "I wanted to give up music one time when I was in school, then I realized that this ability made me just a little bit different, so I kept on. That is why I believe in the Pageant, because it does have the effect of making girls just a little bit different. You must have something to look up to, particularly nowadays. There is not a young boy in the land with a bat in his hands who does not see himself growing up to become a major leaguer. Girls can do the same with Miss America. This country has been built on dreams. Take them away and what have you got?"

Although Jacque was the only one of the three queens from these pivotal years who returned home to live, hers was not a direct route back. She was briefly a studio starlet in Hollywood until one day she peeked at her folder and discovered that the consensus verdict was written out: "No Sex Appeal." Hardly was she divorced from her youthful first husband than, in Mexico City, she stumbled into a second marriage to a playboy and it lasted two weeks. At last, safely enrolled in Arizona State University, she discovered that all the professors assumed she was a dimwit. Moreover, all the students avoided her, sure that any Miss America must be as stuck-up as she is stupid.

Jacque was in school for six weeks before anyone approached

her with a civil conversation and an invitation for a date—and he was only doing it to win a bet from other members of the football team. His name was Dick Curran, and he married her a couple of years later. She bore him the first of their two children over a Christmas vacation when she was teaching; she did not miss a class. Curran, solid and enthusiastic, played for one season with the Green Bay Packers before he made his real mark as an advertising executive. Now he plays arena polo for recreation. The Currans live in a rambling ranch house at the very base of Camelback Mountain, in Scottsdale, next to Phoenix. Curran has a phone in his car, which Jacque and the kids gave him for his fortieth birthday. She has just turned forty herself. Yolande, the youngest of the three, will cross that bar soon.

"I guess I'm lucky that I could work for my husband," Jacque says. "He could hide me. I won advertising copy-writing awards, but nobody ever knew it. Can you see any advertising director telling the company president that a Miss America was writing his copy? He'd fire the guy on the spot. In school, I really did have to work like the devil for grades after I won, because no one could believe that a Miss A could get good marks. The story of my life, I could never put it all together. I spent the first part being a brain that nobody would recognize for her beauty, and the second part the other way around.

"When Dick and I first moved here, everybody knew right away who I was because one neighbor found out and got drunk and started singing 'There She Is' loud enough to hear on the other side of the mountain. They always know who you are. Women stand off from you. You really have to prove yourself, because everyone has decided not to like you. I started a debutante ball and a girls' club, and after that a few older women did acknowledge me, and that helped.

"I guess they didn't feel threatened by me. At parties, I will never talk to a man for more than five minutes, because, in his wife's eyes, I have a gleam in my eye that I really don't. On the other hand, I notice that women flirt excessively with my husband. Now I am really not giving Dick's charm its proper due when I say this, but the truth is that they want to show old Miss A that she hasn't got it all. Husbands make out much better out of this than we do. It's dirty pool."

Jacque and BeBe will criticize the Pageant, if perhaps more empirically and with less vehemence than Yolande manages at her best. BeBe agonizes over the backward techniques that hold it all back. "How can you possibly explain or excuse these bouffant hair styles," she asks, "when everywhere, every girl in America is wearing long hair that is fresh and today? Kids, the good girls, see that, and they know the Pageant is out of touch, so they don't get involved. Pageant people will argue that three-inch spiked heels are good for the appearance of the legs, and that may be, but so what? It is not good for the appearance of anything else. It dates the whole show."

Jacque agrees with such complaints, but it is her belief that a whole institutional overhaul is required to save *Miss America* from collapse. She sees the decay already eating rapidly at the bulwarks. "What burns me up," she says, "is that it's me they're playing with. If *Miss America* loses prestige, I lose prestige. It's like the Rose Bowl. They were *the* bowl, and then they got hung up on a lot of little rules and refused to keep up, and all of a sudden they're just one of a lot of bowls.

"The main trouble with *Miss America* is that it's still so provincial. It's gotten bigger than Atlantic City. Look, I don't want to take it away from Atlantic City. It developed the Pageant and it deserves it, but the trouble is the perspective. *Miss America* is still just an Atlantic City show that is permitted to go out over a national network, whereas it should be a national show that just happens to come from Atlantic City."

For her part, Yolande seems to have grown weary of the whole business. For so long, after all, she was the house critic, on twenty-four-hour call anytime anybody wanted to get a derogatory remark made about *Miss America*. Yolande would punch out a quip on request or meet a pro-Miss America for a debate. Since Women's Liberation began to pick up the cudgel for her, though, and especially since a black girl made the Pageant, Yolande has lost her edge for the old battle. Now, she starts to go off on an old-fashioned barrage, but then pulls herself up. "Aw," she says, "I just don't feel like getting in trouble any more."

★ 11 ★

Live, from NBC

The changes that television has forced on *Miss America* are incalculable, although the medium has become so pervasive throughout every facet of our life that it is difficult to perceive exactly how drastically it has transformed the event. The Pageant itself is nearly paranoid about the fact that it has not sold its soul to television. This is the only stand that any popular institution can take nowadays to resist being consumed by TV, so it is a wise posture. It has saved *Miss America* from extinction, or, at the least, from a dire transfiguration.

If the Pageant had ever sold out to television, by now it surely would have been moved to Burbank, videotaped in a studio, included a lot of male dancers in the opening number, and have slick routines by a comedian named Joey interspersed throughout. All the judges would be Nanette Fabray and Jan Murray, and their vote totals would be lit up on big electronic boards. Second-rate male celebrities would be employed to escort contestants, "There She Is" would be sung by this year's hot new male lead that the network is pushing, George Jessel would be presented with a special award by Dinah Shore while the judges debated their final choice, and Miss America would be crowned by a leering Joe Namath. If you think that is farfetched, you have never seen what many other beauty pageants are coming to on TV.

America's Junior Miss, a Pageant for high-school seniors that is closely patterned after *Miss America,* is generally respected for striving to invest itself with taste and forbearance. In the 1970 TV finals, though, the ten quarter-finalists ended up taking multiple-choice tests in a setting that was altogether patterned after any daytime quiz program. Where was George Bernard Shaw born? What is the name of the angle that is greater than 90°, less than 180°? The 23rd Amendment gave the vote to? Miss Teen-Age America has offered DJ Dick Clark as the master of ceremonies, with Bobby Van dancing to "Give My Regards to Broadway"—direct from Dallas. Finalists were given a set of social circumstances and asked to improvise—situation comedy rather than game show.

For TV, Our Little Miss starred Shari Lewis, the puppeteer, and Frankie Avalon, the thirty-year-old that teen-age passed by. Our Little Miss is for "beautiful, talented, and poised" little angels from ages seven to twelve, but in the event a restless mother wants to get her infant on the Pageant road at an earlier age, the contest also provides the La Petite division, which is for youngsters from three to six. For TV, complete with spotlights thrown about the hall, Shari babbled on with her puppet, Frankie recited the gooey "What Is a Little Girl?" and constant reminders were provided to the effect that the parents of the contestants were not pushy. The show was sponsored by a paper diaper company and a toy firm which produced an Our Little Miss doll, complete with cape.

La Petites were judged in party dress and sportswear, although, presumably, in the event of a tie, the one with the earliest postmark would win. The retiring La Petite champion was interviewed for TV and said, in one breath, "I met Paul Harvey and the Governor of Louisiana and Miss America and I singed with Conway Twitty and I met a lot of nice little girls." Then she crowned her successor, but, sadly, moved the wrong way at the crucial moment and upstaged a distressed Shari Lewis. Her voice dripping with ire, the mistress of ceremonies steered the child aside and said, "And will you get out of our camera shot?"

Miss America has been spared a decline to these depths almost surely because of the diligence of one man. Albert A. Marks, Jr., the president of a local stock firm, is chairman of the Pageant's executive committee; it is symbolic of the times that he first came to power because of his television acumen. Though he devotes perhaps a third of his time to the Pageant, Marks is merely a volunteer civic worker. Were it not for the coincidence that he lives in Atlantic City, he would be running the local Red Cross, or chairing the Chamber of Commerce. In fact, once he did that too. In Atlantic City, *Miss America* is a civic item.

Since Lenora Slaughter was retired as executive secretary in 1967, much of the real power in the organization has fallen to Marks, which is, at the same time, a profit and a loss. On one hand, it is risky for any organization to depend on part-time leadership. It also encourages a fragmentation of powers within the office. Ruth McCandliss, Lenora's secretary and then assistant, has succeeded her in title. She heads the office and maintains contact with the states. George Cavalier, Lenora's protégé from California, devotes himself almost exclusively to the production of the show itself—and the state shows. Mrs. Doris Kelly handles the bookings for the reigning Miss America. Everybody runs his own fiefdom, turning to Marks at the brokerage for ultimate decisions and guidance.

This would be an intolerable situation but for the counterbalancing fact that Marks is such a highly capable administrator. He is extremely articulate, quick, perceptive, and candid. He has not always exhibited the keen anticipative senses needed to keep the Pageant up with the times, but then, long-range policy is a luxury he has little time for. It is enough for him just to keep what he calls "this strange beast" together with his left hand.

Moreover, his motives appear to be pure. There is no suspicion that Al Marks bothers with *Miss America* for any reason other than that he feels it is his duty. He does enjoy running things, and since he is sharp and entertaining and quick on his feet, he does not shy from the spotlight, but these are natural, harmless vanities that sit well with him. He acts altruistically, but, one suspects, also because he realizes there is no one else. The television people hold him in the highest regard, a status Marks has earned as an antagonist, as he has been in the front line of TV negotiations almost since they began in 1953.

Miss America has bounced around to all three networks, and the threat of another shift encourages everyone, even the network that presently owns the rights, to court Marks regularly and assiduously. Yet he walks a tightrope too. For all his stanch declarations that *Miss America* controls her own destiny, that the Pageant is merely an event that television covers, TV has effected great changes in *Miss America,* and TV is very evident. And TV revenue accounts for two-thirds of the annual budget of Miss America. Every year for Marks is like a new Doris Day movie. He plays the professional virgin, seductive but firm, although in the end, he and everyone else knows that he must give in, even if stylishly and for all the right reasons.

Marks came in on the discussions in 1954 that led to the first telecast because he was the immediate past president of the Chamber of Commerce. ABC had begun snooping around the year before, making inquiries about a telecast, but it backed away when a blackout of Philadelphia was stipulated. Lenora was terrified that television might hurt the house gate. "We weren't knocking them loose in those days," she says. Also, she had just doubled ticket prices. The next summer, though, Pops Whiteman, who was doing a summer show with his orchestra out of the Riptide Room of the Penn-Atlantic Hotel, brought the subject up again before Pageant President Hugh Wathen. When Whiteman produced Philco as a sponsor and the assurance of $10,000 rights fees from ABC, *Miss America* accepted. That was the most front money the Pageant had ever seen. In earlier years it virtually gave its name away to Bulova Watch and Warner Brothers (though a film with "Miss America" in the title has never been shot).

The first TV Pageant, in September 1954, drew 27,000,000 home viewers, a 39 per cent share of the audience.* During that period, the five finalists were kept offstage, coming out before the crowd as their final placing was announced. ABC placed a camera backstage, in order that it could capture the expressions of the finalists as their names were read off. At last, only two girls were left, Ann Daniel, Miss Florida, and Lee Meriwether, Miss California, who was a drama student at the City College of San Francisco and the holder of a sharpshooter medal in the National Rifle Association.

Miss Meriwether's father had died only a few weeks before.

* See Appendix 10, p. 308.

When the first year's television emcee, Bob Russell, called off Miss Florida's name as the first runner-up, Lee was left behind as Miss America. Before she walked out to accept her crown, she cast her eyes to heaven and very clearly said: "You know I know how happy you are." Lee had no idea she was on camera. Thereafter, she proved to be the champion crier of all time, and kept bawling for happiness until at last her mother barked at her, "Stop sniffling." It was knock-out show biz in TV-land. Not only that, but the $10,000 brought the Pageant a slim profit on the year, and ticket sales did not appear to be affected.

When negotiations for the 1955 rights began, Philco came in pleading poormouth. Marks was not conned; he played the heavy for the Pageant. "My, I didn't realize how impressive that young man could be till then," Lenora remembers. Marks understood how valuable the rights were. For some prime evidence, Nash—which had been a scholarship sponsor for years—had quit in a huff as soon as it found out that Philco had been awarded the TV commercial rights without Nash being permitted to bid. Obviously, if Philco was not prepared to pay the price, some other sponsor would. Philco paid what Marks wanted—$25,000. The show drew 41 per cent of the national TV audience.

Two years later, Marks switched the show to CBS, and, for the first time, it attracted better than half the available audience. The next year, 1958, CBS expanded the show from ninety minutes to two hours, and almost two-thirds of the sets turned on in America were tuned in. That formed an audience of 60,000,000, more than doubling the original TV figures in only five years. When some technical difficulties kept *Miss America* off the air in Milwaukee, those who missed the station apology deluged it with so many phone calls that the entire UPtown 3 exchange was almost put out of order.

The ratings have held pretty firm since then, taking about two-thirds of the audience every year. *Miss America* is such a powerful draw that the program that immediately precedes it on the network is sucked along to success. In 1970, the special in that spot, a circus show, outrated every show on TV in that two-week rating period—except *Miss America,* of course. "Laugh-In" was first previewed in the slot before the Pageant in 1967.

In 1966, *Miss America* moved to NBC and first went on in color. To counter the transfer, CBS scheduled the opening game of the National Football League directly opposite the Pageant. It was a dream match between the defending champion Green Bay Packers and the recognized top contenders, the Baltimore Colts —then the undisputed best and most glamorous teams in the country's favorite TV sport. There was betting among TV people that *Miss America* had at last met its match, or, at the least, would see its usual ratings lead diminished severely. That was a sucker bet.

A few days before the Saturday night television confrontation, a convention of about 400 chemical engineers meeting in Atlantic City was addressed by Marks. He asked for a show of hands of preference between the football game and the beauty pageant, and about 95 per cent of the hands shot up for football. Then Marks asked the men what program would in fact be turned on at their house. About 95 per cent of the hands sheepishly rose for *Miss America.* In the final ratings, the Pageant swamped the best that football could offer by almost 3 to 1, with a 38.2 rating to 14.7 for the Packers and Colts. The audience for *Miss America* seems to comprise one solid bloc: females, ages twelve to seventy-five. And, apparently, the hand that rocks the cradle also turns the TV dial.

The popularity of the show continues apace. When *Miss America* fell out of touch with the times as the 1960s wore on there was some erosion in its high ratings figures, but the Pageant's slight subsequent concessions to reality appear to have been enough to have reversed that trend. In 1970, the show drew its largest audience ever, again taking a two-thirds share. By usual rating standards, this translates into 22,360,000 homes every minute of the two hours, which is further computed by Nielsen to mean that a total of 80,000,000 persons watched the show. It is probable, however, that the true figure stretches close to, or even beyond, the 100,000,000 mark, since so many middle Americans assemble in groups on *Miss America* night to have a party around the television set.

However, even without making any sophisticated correction to account for group viewing, the 1970 version was the fifth most popular special in television history. *Miss America* 1970 even drew more viewers than "The Fugitive" did on that magic night when at last he caught up with his quarry. Now, in all time, the only shows that have ever topped *Miss America* are two Academy Awards, a Bob Hope Christmas Special, and a Super Bowl. Five times in the 1960s *Miss America* was the highest-rated show of the year; on three more occasions it was second. Year in and year out there are only two things in all of the United States that have evidenced the sustained popularity to compete with *Miss America.* One is the Academy Awards; the other is Bob Hope. Since Bob Hope is the perennial star of the Academy Awards, it becomes all the more obvious why politicians try to stay close to him. Were Bob Hope to crown Miss America at halftime of the Super Bowl, the nation would crunch to a complete halt, since the figures prove conclusively that every man, woman, and child in the United States of America would be watching television at that moment.

Moreover, the success of *Miss America* in the medium has spawned a plethora of pageants, many of which have been created only as TV vehicles. Recently, there have been as many as ten beauty pageants on network TV in a single year, and that figure is swelled even more by the pageants picked up by independent networks, and by state pageants, which are televised only regionally. About one-third of the *Miss America* state shows are telecast every year.

A pageant is tried and true and easy to produce. It is a license to get some old-fashioned cheesecake on the home screen and the talent is free. Miss Universe and its domestic preliminary, Miss USA, are the next best-rated TV pageants after *Miss America.* The girls are better built, but, aside from that, have no discernible talent. Reporters covering it have dubbed it "The Idiot Derby." On the other hand, Miss Teen-Age America has brought in as much as a 42 per cent share of the audience, without any skin, but *Miss America* has the best mix of sex and entertainment. One television executive says, "The teen-age shows, Junior Miss and Teen-Age America, they're kids, they're too young. Even if you are a dirty old man, you don't even get a peek at them in bathing suits. Making obscene phone calls is more fun than that. But Miss Universe is too much the other way. It's strictly a girl-watching thing. After a while, the women viewers get mad at the broads parading around with their big boobs all the time, and even the men get bored. If anything, all this nudity stuff in the movies has got to hurt Universe more than *America.* You want to see boobs nowadays, you can see 'em all in a theater. You don't have to be teased seeing 'em tucked into a bathing suit on TV. *Miss America* is the soft sell. You don't expect much. You see just a little cleavage, you figure you're ahead of the game."

Miss America's tremendous sustained success on the air has, nevertheless, been made at a great expense in other areas. As a whole, television has had a sedative effect on the Pageant. It takes in no more money today from ticket sales, program ads, and the Boardwalk parade than it did before the Angel TV arrived in 1954. No new sources of revenue have been uncovered in that time either. The only major changes in the Pageant have been those specifically required by TV.

Charges that Miss America is a dull, backward woman were never made until television entered the picture. Before then, the queens had to scuffle for recognition, to establish themselves as distinct personalities. TV traps them all into the same cookie mold. Each new Miss America is seen first in a stock setting. She is seen again, as a lame duck, one year later in the identical setting. These are her two formative appearances that establish her image, and the sum and substance of her action includes walking, smiling, being crowned, crying, thanking, and crowning. No wonder all the girls seem the same. If other public women were similarly restricted, Zsa Zsa Gabor and Golda Meir would soon be indistinguishable in the public mind.

The Pageant itself has proved utterly incapable of coping with the damning circumstances that rob the queen of her individuality. Because Miss America is contracted to stay out in the sticks all year, hustling shampoo and working car circuses, she has no chance to make the additional TV appearances that could restore the identity that TV stole from her in the first place. Aside from the Pageants themselves, most Miss Americas make only one regular national TV appearance a year, when they wave from a float at the Rose Bowl Parade. Of course, that serves only to heighten the stereotype, since the queen flashes by with all the distinction of a sputnik circling overhead.

The irony is that Miss Americas can, in fact, differ substantially from each other. A perfect comparison would be the two blondes who won in succession. Judi Ford, 1969, a trampolinist, was an exuberant girl—vivacious, expressive, even somewhat uninhibited. Atlantic City lived in mortal fear that the word would leak out that Judi actually smoked cigarettes. In the course of her reign, she made one national TV appearance outside the usual; on that occasion she was wrapped up in a Betsy Ross outfit and paraded out on a daytime game show on July 4. By contrast, Judi's successor, Pam Eldred, was a quiet little doll, with a face left over from Valentine's Day, and a body made out of Steuben glass. There is no evidence that she has ever found it necessary to sweat. Nevertheless, the public was totally incapable of separating Judi from Pam. They were just two blond Miss Americas. They just came and went the second Saturday of September, in a blur.

Miss America has come off an assembly line at a time when youth is otherwise searching for individuality and originality. This conflict is greatest in those sections of the country that have been most tolerant to the new attitudes of youth. Those sections happen, coincidentally, also to wield the greatest power of opinion. In the years of TV, almost everything new that youth has inspired has been initiated on either the West Coast or in the Megalopolis that is the Northeastern corridor. Everything, good or bad, fad or philosophy—clothes, music, political involvement, social awareness, surfing, drugs, throwing Frisbees, not wearing bras—has seen its genesis with the young people of these two regions, the Coast and the Northeast.

It cannot be merely a coincidence that, since the TV age of *Miss America* began with Lee Meriwether's coronation, no girl from these two huge pilot areas—which together account for nearly 40 per cent of the total population in the United States—has ever been selected Miss America. At a time when the youthful leaders of these sections have been visible and out in front in nearly every aspect of our lives, they are absent from the *Miss America* competition. The figures are so one-sided (16–0) that they support only one conclusion: that whereas TV *Miss America* obviously appeals to the best girls in the traditional heartland of the country, she does not attract the best girls from the influential coastal sections. As a matter of fact, the last sixteen straight Miss Americas have come from precisely those states which political theorist Kevin Phillips includes as part of the "emerging majority" of conservative thought. Specifically, six TV Miss Americas have come from the states of the Confederacy, six from the plains-mountains, and four from the Midwest.

It is academic to argue whether television or the people who watch television are guilty of the change—or lack of it—the Pageant has suffered during this era. The point is that *Miss America* has lost much of its indigenous charm and spontaneity. *Miss America* has become more formal and official, which is not necessarily bad; it has become stereotyped and imitative, which is surely unfortunate. To understand the vast change in climate it is most instructive to examine the inverse, the example of Evelyn Ay, Miss America 1954. She was the last pre-TV queen, crowned September 1953. She was the way they used to be.

By most accounts she could be called the best Miss America of all. Among her peers, those Miss Americas anywhere near her year who know her, she is universally liked and respected. She would be the alumnae Miss Congeniality. Yet she is exactly the kind of girl who would not even get to Atlantic City today, much less win. So when it is asked sometimes if TV has really harmed the Pageant in any way, it is sufficient to say only that because of television, there are no more Evelyn Ays who become Miss America.

She did not approach the competition seriously enough. She was just engaged; no self-respecting trainer would handle a girl diverted by love. She made up a talent presentation practically as she walked on stage. She was not beautiful. She had only one dress for each event, and bought none especially for the contest. She was loose and flip.

Evelyn came from Ephrata, Pennsylvania, a small town about fifty miles northwest of Philadelphia. Both of her parents were born in Germany—the family name is pronounced exactly like the first letter of the alphabet—and though she was a farm girl, who was to impress Secretary of Agriculture Ezra Taft Benson with her ability to milk five cows before breakfast one morning, Evelyn was multifaceted. "My problem at school," she says, "was that I was running everything."

Ephrata then had the largest street fair left in the country. Route 322 was closed for a whole week. Evelyn was induced to enter the fair's beauty contest, and, suffering a moment of inspiration, she decided to do a vocal presentation and selected "Come to the Fair." It happened that she promptly forgot the lyrics dead in the middle of the song, but, as will be seen, Evelyn's greatest talent was to vamp talent. She won the street fair and was adorned with a banner that actually said all of this: MISS EPHRATA FAIR TOBACCO QUEEN OF LANCASTER COUNTY. It was good that Evelyn is tall; she was then 5 feet 8 inches, 132.

She later also became the Pennsylvania Amvet Queen, and, against token opposition, also was named the National Amvet Queen on a trip to Grand Rapids, Michigan, with her parents. She had no lasting interest in the beauty world, however, and soon, with thoughts of some career in medicine, she had proceeded on to the University of Pennsylvania—she is not only the last Eastern girl to win but also the only Ivy Leaguer—where she was, before long, in the process of falling in love with a Penn football player named Carl Sempier.

At this point, an old family dentist from nearby Lancaster got it in his head that Evelyn could be Miss America, and should enter the Pageant. To humor him, she even agreed to go to Atlantic City in 1952, where she saw Neva Jane Langley crowned. Then she went back to Penn and forgot about the whole thing. The dentist was persistent, however, and convinced the local Jaycees to hold a Pageant the next summer. Evelyn, feeling obligated, entered and, of course, won. She had long flowing blond hair that fell down over her shoulders; she tanned well and had a white swimming suit that set everything off perfectly. She measured 37–24–36, which is, statistically, the best that any Miss America has ever measured, and many who saw her at the time said that she had the best build by any standard.

For her local Pageant and for the subsequent Miss Pennsylvania competition at West Chester, Evelyn had devised a new talent, since, after all, she could not remember the words to "Come to the Fair." What she did was go through a bunch of her poetry books and came upon that woebegone old standby by Mary Howitt, "The Spider and the Fly" (" 'Will you walk into my parlor?' " said the spider to the fly"; and downhill from there). For appropriate dramatic effect, Evelyn put a long black glove with sequins onto one hand. This represented the spider. Her other hand pantomimed the fly.

Unfortunately, after she won at West Chester, some of the Jaycees allowed as how they really did not think that her act was sophisticated enough to go over real big at Atlantic City. Evelyn agreed, she guessed. Sophistication was not really uppermost in her mind. She had absolutely no hopes of winning anything at *Miss America.* She assumed that the highlight of the experience had already occurred, when she had returned to Ephrata for her Miss Pennsylvania home-coming parade. All the home-folks, hardly impressed, called out, "Hey, Evvy, how's Zinn's Diner?" She had worked there as a waitress. Much more important to her mind was Carl Sempier, who finally gave her the ring a couple of days before she left for the Pageant.

The Jaycees had forgotten her; she heard no more from them in a way of talent suggestion, and so, just a few days before she left for the Pageant, "it was back to my books." She happened upon a poem she liked entitled "Leaves from Grass House" by Don Blanding. Unfortunately, it took somewhat more than three minutes to read the poem, which is the allotted time limit. To get around that, Evelyn edited it. "God, can you imagine how that would be now, with TV and copyrights? I just left the lines in that I liked, mixed up some stanzas to make it clearer, and cut it here and there to work it all into three minutes."

It was just three days before the Pageant when she finished rewriting, and on the day she arrived in Atlantic City, her new ring on her finger, she had still not memorized one word of the bowdlerized version of the poem. But then Evelyn came up lucky, when she drew the perfect grouping, for her purpose. Contestants at the Pageant are placed into three divisions and Evelyn was, by chance, assigned to the group that had swimsuit first, on Wednesday night, and talent last, Friday. Had it been the reverse, she would have been dead from the start.

She walked out in that white bathing suit Wednesday night, though, and stood the place on its ear. "That changed it all," she says. "Now they noticed me. With the swimsuit and that ridiculous last name of mine, there was at least no way I could get lost in the crowd." The judges interviewed contestants at breakfast meetings then. Evelyn, still not taking it seriously, was loosey-goosey. Her first concern, she recalls, was what there was to eat.

Nights, she would go back to the hotel and try to memorize the poem. She is a little curious in this respect in that she memorizes entirely in her mind. She even achieves inflection silently. What worried her most at Atlantic City was not having to recite the poem Friday night for real, but having to say it out loud in practice that afternoon. For Miss Pennsylvania, she had refused to do "The Spider and the Fly" in rehearsal. "Don't worry," she said. "I have it timed to three minutes. Just have the band play 'Temptation.' " And she went on cold.

Thursday night at Atlantic City, after the evening-gown competition for her division, she went back to her room and started memorizing silently again. By now, she was driving her mother batty. Finally, Evelyn had it down pat and turned over to go to sleep.

"Do you know it?" Mrs. Ay asked.

"Yes," Evelyn said.

"Well, say it out loud," her mother said.

Evelyn would not. "Don't worry," she assured her mother. "I have it all in my mind."

As luck would have it again, at practice the next afternoon, some of the other girls' careful arrangements dragged on, and Evelyn hastily suggested that as long as the orchestra could play *La Mer* for the background, she needed no rehearsal. The director agreed to let her go. "They couldn't follow the script anyway," she says. "I had the only copy. Even Don Blanding couldn't know how I was going to do his poem." So it was that Evelyn Ay got to be Miss America without once, at any level of the competition, saying her talent out loud until she stood on stage to be judged. Nowadays almost every contestant spends a short lifetime deciding what and how she will perform.

When Evelyn performed Friday night she did well enough that she assumes she even got a few fourth- or fifth-place votes. "You know how it is," she says. "You can't lose a girl you've already wasted a lot of points on. If my talent had come first, I wouldn't have gotten any votes, and then they wouldn't have bothered to waste any swimsuit votes on me either. But here they had invested swimsuit points in me, so some of them probably convinced themselves that I had talent too."

Suddenly, at a loss to explain it, she stood in the finals the next night against Miss New York City and three Southern girls. It was a very close race. Any one of the five could win if she fielded the questions particularly well. Luckily, for Evelyn, she gained an edge at this point. Her mind blacked out completely. It won her the title.

The first question asked her was, "What is your definition of true civilization, and why?" Evelyn says, "I heard a tape of all this later. I couldn't believe that it was me. You never heard such schmaltz. I was spouting all this incredible foolishness about fences of roses and never of stone. It was unbelievable." Naturally, it wowed the judges.

Then she was asked, "Where would you like to go to further your chosen profession?" Says Evelyn, "Now, I don't remember any of this at all. At all. Talk about your strange quirks of the mind. As I started to answer, my mother, out in the audience, got chills. She didn't know what had happened to me. When I was about ten years old, I had read an article in the *National Geographic* that had impressed me tremendously. It concerned India, and the need there for medical personnel. I carried that article around for a week and read it over and over. But I completely forgot about it after that brief fascination, and this was ten years later. I know that I had never had a mature thought on the subject of India until I was asked that question. Somehow, it jumped into my mind, and I began to play back that article in the most incredible detail. I spoke about the problems there of starvation and malnutrition and how a medical technician could be of service. I spoke of India with such clarity and emotion that anyone had to think that the subject was on my mind every day. I don't know. It was eerie."

The speech had such impact that not long after Evelyn was crowned, Madame Pandit was on the phone from the Indian UN mission in New York, requesting that she get on the next plane to Bombay. She had to settle for a donation to the milk fund; Lenora kept insisting, "No, no. She's ours for a year. She's ours for a year."

Bright and dedicated, Evelyn was a huge success, if generally unrecognized. "I was serious about the obligation once I found I had it," she says, "but I had trouble periodically. Oh, not trouble, but I don't suppose I was what was expected. I wasn't flamboyant or showy. I always felt that I would rather meet people as Evelyn Ay, who is Miss America, than as Miss America who is someone named Evelyn Ay. I've always believed that if you give me enough time, I can win people over. I play straight."

Mary Korey, who chaperoned Evelyn that year, recalls that she left a bright new image of Miss America behind her wherever they went. "We were in Detroit one time," Miss Korey says, "and we had to go to a luncheon. Evvy had no idea what she was getting into. We thought it was a simple little thing for the United Fund, where she had to say a few words and smile, but we got in there, and it was a huge place, and all men. We must have been the only two women there, and, good God, Billy Graham spoke right before Evvy. Then she just got up and spoke off the cuff for a long time. Oh, she was magnificent. The place was stunned. When she was finished, in the same instant every man in that place was on his feet, applauding her. It drove me crazy. For weeks after that, Billy Graham's secretary kept calling me trying to get her to come and speak, anywhere."

Upon the conclusion of her reign, when Evelyn returned to Atlantic City, she was informed that the Pageant would be televised, so there was no time for her to speak. She was told to crown her successor and get quickly out of the way. That was the new role for TV Miss America.

From the first, then, television forced substantive changes on the Pageant. Even so, Marks's claim that Atlantic City has retained "artistic control" is fair enough, relative to the way television has devoured so many other previously independent activities. At least *Miss America* has gotten a fair price for services and sacrifices rendered, and TV is hamstrung in this case, because it cannot just buy its way in. *Miss America* wants to take only enough out of a network to balance the budget. It has no choice but to remain a nonprofit organization, for the structure that supports it at the state and local levels is founded entirely on volunteer labor. Thus, Marks makes TV (and, too, the sponsors that he selects) pay in other ways, with various types of peripheral support—and an understanding that everyone must live by the rules that Atlantic City decrees.

Though the figure rises almost every year, even today NBC pays a mere $375,000 for the rights to telecast the 1971 *Miss America* Pageant, while, in comparison, it dishes out $2,500,000 for the Super Bowl. "Sure," Marks says, "if it were only top dollar we were looking for, $375,000 wouldn't even be in the ball game. That's cheap for any show, never mind the highest-rated one in the country. But I am a great deal more concerned with maintaining our national image than with ratings *per se,* or money. If you take the top dollar, you pay the top price. There are other ways to gain support. We have one sponsor who pours in $2,000,000 a year out of his advertising budget for scholarships and promotion for the Pageant. And he's done it for twelve years—that's $25,000,000 in equity. We've got blue-chip sponsors standing in the wings."

When *Miss America* decides to tap a new sponsor, first it bestows an associate status on the lucky product. It is permitted to give money for scholarships, but not to advertise. The four sponsors who are full-fledged are the only ones who can run commercials on the show. In 1970 they included Toni, which took six and a half of the thirteen commercial minutes, Oldsmobile, Frigidaire, and Kellogg's. The latter says that it joined forces with *Miss America* because "she's as all-American as the World Series or a Moonshot." Toni takes comfort in a survey which disclosed that respondents looked upon *Miss America* as a civic, rather than a mercantile venture, and Marks declares paternally, "Our relationship with our sponsors is *not* commercial."

As far back as 1949, one of the very first scholarship sponsors, the Lane Co., manufacturers of cedar chests, got bumped out of the family because, Lenora said: "We disapproved of Miss America appearing in furniture stores at the point of sale." Eight years later, in a similar situation, Procter and Gamble severed its connection with the Pageant because it would not let her hawk cosmetics at store counters. This paved the way for Pepsi-Cola to come in, and it was delighted at the new association, for its new slogan was, "Now it's Pepsi for those who think young." However, as the world began to pass *Miss America* by, Pepsi decided that *Miss America* was an old tin can tied to the tail of its swinging generation.

At last, in 1968, the alliance came to a bitter end, with Pepsi claiming that it was pulling out because *Miss America* was out of touch with kids and with the cities. "It's a waste of time even to try to do anything with it in New York," Pepsi announced. "*Miss America* as run today does not represent the changing values of our society." In support of, rather than conflict with, this charge, Pepsi bottlers and distributors in the hinterlands often continue to help sponsor local pageants. Though no one in Atlantic City will acknowledge the fact, it is apparent that the Pepsi attack burned *Miss America.* It may be only circumstantial evidence, but the efforts at updating the Pageant began soon after Pepsi pulled out. Marks, quite out of character, gets a little testy when the subject is broached, and snaps that Pepsi did not defect, but was ejected. "Pepsi was kicked out," he says. "They were kicked out because we didn't like the way they wanted to use *Miss America* in a hard sell. Look, we can be very tough. Don't be deceived. We're very tough when we have to be. Nobody influences us, commercially or otherwise."

For television, the Pageant even uses its own free-lance team to produce and direct the show. Many of these principals are normally salaried by NBC, but this particular week they take vacation time and sign on with the free-lance team. NBC provides the scenic designer, lighting and sound personnel, and its best camera crew. The network also kicks in with extra promotion money, and it tapes come-on interviews with all the contestants, that are sent to the local NBC stations back home. Like the sponsors, the network knows it must stay in line to hang on to *Miss America.*

NBC also takes it upon itself to hover protectively over the whole production, supersensitive to the most remote possibility of a fix—or even anything that might somehow convey that thought. For instance, it used to be that as soon as the voting for the final five girls was tabulated, a Pageant official would notify the cameramen of the choices. It was only a matter of another thirty seconds before Bert Parks read out the five names, but those few moments gave the cameramen time to pinpoint the winners and get right on them for reaction shots. An NBC watchdog discovered the practice and vetoed it.

An NBC lawyer is the only outsider permitted to sit in on judges' deliberations, and at the front of Convention Hall, the ballots literally pass through his hands on the way to the CPAs. These procedures may satisfy the network that nothing is rotten, but they only encourage a surprisingly large number of Pageant people to sneer that *Miss America* and NBC are in cahoots, trying to arrange the selection of the finalists so that a good cross-section of talent is presented on TV. In fact, the finals seldom offer much variety, but, apparently, until *Miss America* ends up with ten lyric sopranos all singing opera, the cynics will continue to whisper that hanky-panky is afoot.

NBC also duels with Marks himself over his obsession about having *Miss America* billed as an all-live show. "This is a large part of the fascination," he says. "I regard our TV as no more than a pickup of a news event. It varies from everything else on TV." Everything is done with this goal in mind, and as a consequence large parts of the final night competition are repeated. The Convention Hall audience, wonderfully tolerant, sits by as first the judges really study the ten semifinalists at length. Then, when the cameras start grinding, the whole procedure is repeated. Since nothing is said to suggest otherwise, home viewers are led to believe that the announcement of the semifinalists is all a surprise. Actually, the girls and the live audience have known for more than an hour, and the contestants are well into the competition before the cameras turn on.

It is a harmless enough little deception, which technically supports the assertion that the show is all live. (That the show is not all real or spontaneous is not at issue any more.) The most curious part of all this convoluted logic concerns the additional fact that the songs in the show have been pre-recorded, and Bert Parks and the other cast members must lip-sync the words on-stage. For reasons that only a man who also understands the oil depletion allowance can fathom, NBC feels that this is sufficiently un-live that it must be owned up to. Thus, to Marks's chagrin, a slight disclaimer acknowledging that songs have been pre-recorded appears beneath the words "LIVE FROM ATLANTIC CITY" when they are shown on the screen at the conclusion of the program.

The television people tend to think that Marks is a little peculiar in his singular devotion to the all-live show. "It's the one nutty thing about the guy," one of them says. "So far as I know, if Al Marks sees 'LIVE FROM ATLANTIC CITY' on the screen, he's happy with NBC. If they ever take that away from him, he'll pick up his options and be at CBS the next morning."

Certainly, the value of the all-live concept is open to question. This is, after all, a country which now accepts the notion that a program may be "live, on tape." The fact that the Pageant is the last respectable all-live show left surely does not even occur to most viewers, nor is it likely to impress many of the others who appreciate the fact. Worse than that, though, by restricting all the cameras to the stage at the moment, by not taping interviews or other features which would show the girls in depth, Miss America is portrayed only as a glorified showgirl. Her whole unfortunate image is cast in distortion at this point.

Still, even if Marks has saved his Pageant from being swamped by TV, the medium is so overbearing and so pervasive that even if it is held at arm's length, it will eventually move in and become the event, and then, at last, the prize itself. "All I ever wanted was to get in the top ten, so I could get on TV," Pam Eldred, Miss America 1970, says. "I never thought about being Miss America. That never occurred to me. I just wanted the people at home to see me on TV."

It is not difficult to see where the battle was lost. It has been, really, only a tidying over ever since the day in 1954 when Evelyn Ay, the girl who had outtalked Billy Graham, was informed that the Pageant would be televised, and that TV had decided that there was no time for her to speak at the Pageant. At that moment, the breath of life went out of *Miss America,* and the Miss America Television Program rose, live, in her place.

★★ 12 ★★

You Have Won First Prize in a Beauty Contest, Advance Token to Tennessee at Boardwalk

As one drives to the southern New Jersey coast—or "shore," as it is always called in these precincts—Atlantic City looms suddenly ahead like a Nineveh from across the mephitic inland Garden State marshes. The flaws are more visible only close on. From a distance, it is the grand old hotels that form the skyline, silhouetted across a sky that offers 11 per cent more sunshine than the average in the United States. However, Atlantic City is a doddering resort, with aging attractions for an aging clientele. Bert Parks stays at the Holiday Inn, and most of the Pageant festivities initiated by those who don't reside in the area take place at Howard Johnson's Motor Lodge.

Once, Atlantic City was celebrated as Philadelphia's summer home and New York's winter retreat. Sadly, then airplanes and Florida were invented, and the World's Playground began a decline. It has suffered boss control for decades, with no comprehension of its blacks, 40 per cent of the population, who were attracted in the days when domestics were in demand. Despite its difficulties, Atlantic City has a good location, excellent convention facilities, and a benign climate—cooler in summer, warmer in winter than surrounding areas—so that 15,000,000 tourists visit every year. The thirty-third general convention of the Sheet Metal Workers International Union was already checking in even before the farewell brunch began at the 1970 *Miss America* Pageant. Yet the area struggles, hoping for the legalization of gambling, and with rumors that Howard Hughes will move there and restore the old grandeur.

The kids have turned to other resorts along the beach. Atlantic City did not cater to them when it was thriving and has nothing to attract them now that it is not. What children there are on the Boardwalk appear to be in the company of their grandparents, the old people who haunt the place. At least Saint Petersburg has a stock in geriatrics; there will be more retirees coming down from the North to replace those who die off in the shade of the funeral parlor billboards. The question in Atlantic City, though, is: who will replace this generation when it has died out here?

The Boardwalk, so vital to the essence of the city, was first constructed in 1870 as a device for keeping the beach from drifting into hotel lobbies. The whole thing was folded up and placed in storage, $17 for the winter, but as each major hurricane succeeded in ravaging it—the latest in 1944—a more formidable promenade rose in its place. The present Boardwalk is eight miles long, with five amusement piers jutting out from it. The famous Rolling Chairs, now powered by motors and guided by students with long hair, are available at $3 a half-hour. The monstrous Convention Hall and all the best hotels open onto the Boardwalk, but the tawdry auction side shows are the cynosure. At the time of the 1970 Pageant, the Boardwalk waxworks featured Liberace, Mickey Mantle, Neil Armstrong, and Martin Luther King as the prize attractions.

Atlantic City boasts twenty-five thousand "first-class" hotel rooms within an area along the Boardwalk that is a mile long and a block wide, so the convention business thrives almost the year around. Nevertheless, whatever Atlantic City profited in 1964 when President Johnson determined that the Democratic convention would be held there was lost in the vivid accounts that journalists supplied about their hoary accommodations. Much of Atlantic City is still gracious; all of it, however, is dated. In beach-front hotels, visitors are advised that they must follow strict rules of apparel. The lobbies are huge, fascinating relics extending as far as the eye can see, with potted palms and easy chairs, where a man can sit and wonder when the big-name bands will come back. Nothing emphasizes the fact that Atlantic City is deficient as a modern resort more than this: for the past several years, out-of-town Pageant officials have felt obliged to rent a ballroom each evening so they all could gather there together rather than have to confront the Atlantic City night spots, which feature small glasses and cheap and chubby bump-and-grinders.

Yet almost all new visitors to the resort are bound to feel a warm, sentimental sensation upon arrival in town, because the street plan of Atlantic City was borrowed for the *Monopoly* game board, and everything is strangely familiar from the first. Along Atlantic Avenue (yellow on the board), as one goes north toward Tennessee, the red-colored avenues come by, one by one—Indiana, Illinois, Kentucky. When New York Avenue looms next, anyone can instantly realize that he is in the oranges, going backward around the board. St. James Place and Tennessee must be next, and indeed they are.

The *Miss America* headquarters are located in a large, heavy building at Tennessee, where it dead-ends at the Boardwalk. Upon entering the downstairs hallway, one is lost in a dark, cavernous place where Jean Valjean surely lurks. A glimmer reflects from the *Miss America* storefront, where crowns, scepters, and trophies are displayed. Inside, the offices are homey, vintage American Legion Hall, featuring furniture that was purchased from Lenora Slaughter when she retired to Arizona.

The walls of her old office are still adorned with huge glossy autographed photographs of her queens, each of whom inscribed a tribute to their friendship and Miss Slaughter's service. The Pageant has long since ceased to be such a personal enterprise, however, and Miss Slaughter's successor, Miss Ruth McCandliss, enjoys little personal contact with her Miss Americas. The paid Pageant staff—which, including secretaries, totals nine full-time employees—is taxed so thoroughly around *Miss America* time that in 1970 Miss McCandliss found it impossible to attend the Saturday night finals. Instead, she was required to stay home and finish up some work, watching the show on television.

Financially, *Miss America* is locked in. It could not require its subsidiary state and local pageants to scratch by on volunteer services while it banked profits. It must strive to take in no more than it pays out, otherwise the IRS would swoop down and remove its tax-exempt status. *Miss America* makes about $100,000 each year in ticket sales; $20,000 from the parade; $35,000 from program ad sales; and the bulk, $35,000 from TV. Yet the *Pageant* is not just nonprofit; it is impecunious as well. The penny-pinching that prevailed for so long, when a balanced budget was dependent on successfully cadging free hotel rooms and train rides, is still in evidence. The queens invited back for the Fiftieth Anniversary Pageant, who were used as the front for the whole "going back" theme, and who had to practice for several days, were also required to pay their own fares. As a result, only a few Miss Americas came from any distance. "It was incredible," one said. "They'd call me up and tell me that Frannie Burke and Ruth Malcolmson were coming, and I don't even think it ever occurred to them that they were both from Philadelphia. They talked like they were asking me to come down the street for a cup of coffee. Every time you think the Pageant is moving ahead, something like this happens, and then I realize again that their America still ends just west of Philadelphia."

Yet, while the Pageant staff can be guilty of such oversights, they have become so conditioned to tight accounting that they are really no more than guileless victims of the prevailing Pageant indigence. The office is characterized as well by a warm, enthusiastic air and a certain amount of cheerful disorder. It most resembles an alumnae office, and when an old queen calls or writes about a new child or a husband's promotion, the news is carried tenderly from office to office. Miss McCandliss, who came to the Pageant in 1947 as Miss Slaughter's only assistant, says, "We are an operation based on love." At all levels, the organization is always referred to as "the Pageant family."

While several key members of the *Miss America* staff come from points distant from Atlantic City, the governing Board of Directors is peopled, as it always has been, strictly by natives. *Miss America* is zealous in defending Atlantic City's proprietorship of the Pageant, a fact which irks State Pageant officials, who feel they should receive a representative voice in affairs. It is estimated that the Pageant produces $2,000,000 for the resort every year, but most Atlantic City folk are blasé and not even interested in it. Where once *Miss America* was saluted as a direct tourist draw, now its value is recognized as a more subtle thing.

The actual number of people who show up to see it, and the money they spend, is not considered as important as the fact that the name Atlantic City appears thousands of times a year, all over the land, drilling the place into the subconscious of every American citizen. Eventually, it is believed, this is translated into real revenues for the town.

Albert Marks says bluntly, "It's something very strange. The *Miss America* Pageant is infinitely more important ten miles away from this island." Local citizens have never paid any more heed to the queen than their countrymen at large. Margaret Gorman, the first Miss America, can remember returning to see a Pageant only a couple of years after she had last participated in one, and going entirely unnoticed as she sat by the Boardwalk and watched some of the proceedings. Mall Dodson, who works for the city's convention bureau and helps out as the Pageant's publicity director, says, "About 123,000 out of the 125,000 people in the immediate vicinity don't care about it at all. I walked down the Boardwalk with Pam Eldred eight days after she was crowned and nobody knew her from a rabbit." Dodson even believes that the city's identification with salt-water taffy is more valuable to it than *Miss America*. Adrian Phillips, a past president of the Pageant, who has been in on the event virtually since its inception adds, "It has almost never been supported by the local people the way it should have been. Atlantic City has always been a pass town. We've always supported the free parade better than the Pageant itself." The 1970 Pageant, which was fairly typical, drew a reputed 200,000 to the parade on Tuesday night, and then attracted crowds averaging about 7900, hardly more than one-third Convention Hall capacity, on the three preliminary evenings.

The contestants are unlikely even to see the Pageant offices, and precious little of Atlantic City. They are whisked about everywhere in Oldsmobiles, driven by local volunteers, and seldom have time to set foot in anything but their own assigned hotels, a couple of others where special functions are held, and the forbidding Convention Hall. It is located 12 blocks south of the Pageant offices, fronting on the Boardwalk, a mammoth arena with a ceiling 137 feet high that boasts that no thrown or batted baseball has ever violated it. As another curiosity, Convention Hall features an organ that is the largest ever built, with enough wiring to circle the earth twice.

The girls are first introduced to the Hall on Tuesday of Pageant week. Monday is devoted to a reception, official introductions—more people are introduced at Pageants than even at tennis tournaments—and the traditional group swimsuit picture. Many of the girls find themselves somewhat uncomfortable from the first, because although the temperature is usually in the 70s, custom dictates that "fashion fall" has begun on Labor Day, and thus the girls must cover themselves with heavy autumn clothes. Why, if Atlantic City is anxious to extend its summer season past Labor Day, it always supports the contention that summer ends on Labor Day . . . that is just another of the smaller mysteries not worth delving into any further. Anyway, overheated and overdressed, a certain percentage of the girls invariably come down with colds. In those years when the parade is held at night, many wily chaperones—particularly those in charge of singers—have been known to keep their girls back at the hotel on the pretext that they are sick, lest the night ocean breezes make them sick indeed. Phyllis George became Miss America 1971 on a strict Vitamin C diet. Luckily, she was a piano player; had she been a singer, her chances of performing successfully would have been sharply reduced.

The fifty girls are placed alphabetically in hotels about town—Alabama, Alaska, and Arizona in one; Arkansas, California, and Colorado in another; and so on—and they approach each other's acquaintance somewhat warily. Everybody is a home girl at State; everybody is a stranger at Atlantic City. Generally, the girls from more sophisticated areas of the country expect many of the others to be gum-chewing hayseeds, while the Southerners and some Western girls believe that the more metropolitan contestants will be snooty high-brows. They are almost all pleasantly surprised.

In 1970 the hostesses made a large map of the United States that the girls were asked to sign, in the appropriate state, when they checked in. It would go, as a token, to the eventual winner. A few of the girls embellished the map with Chamber of Commerce flourishes: a sun in California, a geyser in Wyoming, mountains in Colorado and North Carolina, and so on. Miss New York, Katherine Karlsrud, from Westchester County, was a tall girl, with long straight-falling hair, and a natural New York diffidence and candor. When she signed the map she also drew in a smog cloud over New York City, and some of the girls viewed this expression of sacrilege toward one's state with alarm. Despite incurring such dark suspicions, Miss New York soon found herself delighted with the new company. "At each level, the girls get better," she said. "They're not at all the stereotypes we make them out to be in New York. They're so much nicer than I imagined. Anyone here could be my best friend."

In comparison, Donna Connelly, perhaps the prettiest girl of the fifty, came from Hope, Arkansas (pop. 8400), and had never before been outside her state, except to go to bordering Louisiana or Texas. "I expected to come up here and find the biggest bunch of snobs," Miss Arkansas said, "but they're stereotyped all wrong. All these girls are really wholesome and sweet. They're all so much fun. We laugh and call each other names, and we just all like each other so much."

The girls are separated by hotel and by their performing groups, so they seldom have the opportunity to get to know a great many of their competitors well. As a consequence, Miss Congeniality is often won by someone "with a gimmick" to set her apart, as Jeanne Swanner describes it. Jeanne was the biggest contestant ever, which was her gimmick when she won that election. In other years, the smallest girl has won, the only Canadian, the first Indian, the only redhead, and the girl who fell offstage on her horse. When Hawaii first came into the Pageant after the war, Miss Hawaii would win almost every year. Miss Puerto Rico won a couple of times too. The vote totals are never released, but at *Miss America* and many state pageants as well, Miss Congeniality can win with ridiculously small pluralities. It is said that Miss Congenialities have been elected with only three or four votes out of fifty. The voting is not quite so dispersed now, since in recent years girls have been required to cast their votes on ballots with their own names printed on them. Previously, with a nice scholarship going to the winner, most girls voted for themselves as Miss Congeniality.*

* See Appendix 11, p. 309.

The conspicuous excesses that are first visible in large measure at the state level, are even more in evidence at Atlantic City, where the girls have whole state organizations bankrolling them. Many of them arrive with nine or ten pieces of luggage. Some girls bring up to two dozen pairs of shoes, and as many as fifty changes of clothes to choose from for the five or six days. Estimates of the cost of average wardrobe now range upward toward $4000 per girl, and the major madness is that much of the money goes toward the purchase of outfits that the girls wear only to impress each other and the chaperones, not the judges. One of the top favorites in 1970 went out of the running when she performed her talent far below expectations. Her state representatives second-guessed themselves afterward. "We put all the money on her back," one of them said. "If we'd taken that money and put it into talent lessons, she would have made ten. What good is it now that everybody was always telling us how lovely she looked at rehearsal?"

Along with the clothes war, the flower battle is also escalating out of hand. Some states seem to think that if a girl is not sent so many flowers to her room that every time she wakes up she thinks she must be dead, she will feel that no one really cares. In some cases, so one could walk about the room, flowers have had to be moved outside and lined up in the corridor.

At least the girls cannot be spoiled all the time they are in town, for despite efforts to spruce up the Convention Hall dressing room, it remains spare and nearly cheerless. At one of three long wooden dressing tables, each girl has her own designated seat and mirror, but all clothes are kept at some distance away, in a common corner of the room. There is only one bathroom, and it is located upstairs next to an extra room that is known as Sleepy Hollow, as four cots are provided there. Just prior to the Pageant, Sleepy Hollow had been the home of a roller-skating chimpanzee, although a prolonged airing had succeeded in removing his special odors.

In the main dressing room below, Giggle Corner and Prayer Corner have also been designated in past years. A refrigerator remains in evidence, well stocked with Diet Pepsi, milk, and juices, with sandwiches and fruits also in good supply. An ironing board and sewing machines are available on the premises, with volunteers to man them. On the day of her talent presentation, when she goes over her arrangement with the band, and again on Saturday, for the full-scale TV rehearsal, a girl may well be forced to spend most of the day at Convention Hall.

The press, parents, and state officials are permitted to roam about the arena, but access to the girls and backstage areas is expressly denied. Pageant security is, indeed, so professionally effective that a few years ago, Governor Richard J. Hughes of New Jersey was firmly, if politely, refused permission to advance a few steps into a side-stage area where he sought only to obtain a soft drink. In 1962, the late Stanley Berman, the famous gate-crasher, suffered one of his few failures in his specialty. Berman had succeeded, on the occasion of John F. Kennedy's inaugural ball, in filtering through the Secret Service and into the new President's private box. On another occasion, he waltzed right on stage and national TV to make a presentation to Bob Hope at the Academy Awards ceremonies. Naturally, he figured *Miss America* as a breezy caper. He did make it backstage with a television badge, but as he prepared to move out to present the new *Miss America,* Jacquelyn Mayer, 1963, with an orchid, he was accosted by a sturdy member of the board who happened to be an ex-ice-hockey star, and was escorted promptly from the premises. Berman was shocked as much as he was chagrined.

By contrast, press arrangements are so relaxed as to be downright quaint. More than four hundred journalists are advertised to have covered the 1970 Pageant, but the number of those who are bona fide reporters and photographers is far less than the total figure. Press row is set along the runway—most writers on one side, photographers on the other—but it is more like a family picnic. The seats are filled with Pageant officials and hangers-on from the states, who are there in the guise of reporters. They show up with letters of authorization from the editor and publisher of the East Cupcake *Dispatch-Gazette* and *Farm News* and from a friendly disk jockey at radio station KKKK, and are immediately assigned credentials and pre-empt all the best press seats. It is a great gimmick to get a free seat, and a very good seat, too.

There are husband-and-wife teams sitting together along the runway, one carrying a BIC pen, the other a Kodak. There are, evidently, whole families. On the night of the finals, as the reporters cluster about in Mall Dodson's offices for their special Saturday night badges, he deals patiently with some teen-ager. "Now," says Dodson, always unflappable, handing out various desirable credentials, "you've got yours and your mother gets that one. Now what about your father?" The boy replies, somewhat indignantly, that his father certainly requires his usual press pass too. Dodson hands it over.

The ersatz small-town journalists are in Atlantic City from the first of the week, since they are there to enjoy all the attendant festivities. There seem to be no assigned seats, although some old-timers appear to have a lien on the same location that they have enjoyed since Margaret Gorman was a girl. Members of the Pageant press simply drift down to the press tables and exert squatters' rights, Scotch-taping a piece of paper to the table declaring that this is their property for the duration of the week. It works too; at least there are no territorial fights. Then, late in the week certified reporters from large metropolitan dailies and other influential news sources show up for the finals, and they are required to scuffle for chairs. If they should find them, they then must commandeer an empty aisle location, and from that vantage try to cover the proceedings by peering between the various correspondents from the prairie papers. On Saturday, many of the Pageant press also have their wives come down and join them, sitting them behind them, like squaws, so that the area is even more jammed. The circumstances required a reporter from one of the nation's most prestigious magazines to move from seat to seat, resting briefly whenever a favored occupant departed for a visit to the bathroom. Otherwise, he kneeled. Then the Pageant speculates on the injustices that it suffers, getting such good press in East Cupcake, and such bad reviews in New York.

Of course, hardly anybody even pretends to cover the Pageant objectively. All of the parajournalists are devoted to Miss America. Whenever a queen walks the runway, Tom Hensley, the Tennessee executive director, is always first to honor her by rising, but members of the press are second to exercise this obeisance. In balance to these abject cheerleaders are the cynical metropolitan journalists, there to kick a dead horse. Many arrive firm in the belief that they are much too good for *Miss America,* and permit themselves to suffer the assignment only because they can come down hard on the Pageant with the usual litany of surface complaints. So, nobody writes fairly about *Miss America.* Everybody arrives with mind made up and then just paints his story by the numbers.

Never was the juxtaposition of the sweethearts and the cynics more obvious than at Phyllis George's first postcoronation press conference, the morning after her victory. On the one side, there were all the more fascinating questions about her crab, who had been brought along to be photographed and interviewed as well, and other dreary inquiries about her good-luck charms, her family, her surprise, and her, beg pardon, love life. A little man, embarrassed at being so forward, coughed and dropped his eyes and said, "Is there anyone special?" Phyllis said there was, but she preferred not to reveal his name. "Can you tell us his initials?" the nice man asked, giggling hopefully. This was the way all *Miss America* press conferences used to be: What kind of a man will you marry? How many children would you like? Can you cook? Favorite dishes? Hobbies? Preference for music? For movie stars? Etcetera.

Now, though, there are always some rogues in the press contingent, determined to ask a serious question. Lenora would counter that by saying, "She's not the President," and whisk her queen away. Phyllis, though, was flanked only by Adrian Phillips and Mrs. Brick, and while they looked apprehensive it was obvious they were not going to protect her. They both cast a wary eye on the pipe-smoking announcer from WCBS–TV, New York, who got a gleam in his eye the minute the cameras started to roll. This was the enemy. She was a Southern WASP (very few of whom are tuned in to WCBS–TV) and she was NBC, the little lady who had busted up CBS in the ratings the night before. He bore in, giving long speeches designed first to establish his own liberal, with-it credentials, that would be flicked into a question for Phyllis at the end. Her answers so neatly avoided matching his questions in most cases that it was impossible to tell whether she was being cleverly evasive or was just bewildered in the face of compound sentences that did not deal with her crab. She was already falling back on such jabberwocky as, "I am, after all, the American youth's representative."

The announcer seemed pleased that he had shown his viewers how shallow Miss America must be. Ten minutes before the interview had begun, his camera crew drove up before the hotel and parked in a spot clearly designated "No Parking." The cameraman, a burly fellow, got out and started unloading equipment, when a pleasant young employee from the hotel parking lot called over, "Hey, you can't park there." This young man also happened to wear blue jeans, sandals, and his hair down to his shoulders.

The cameraman sneered and shouted, "Hey yourself, you ———. Don't you call me hey. Hey, you get a ——— haircut and take a ——— bath, then maybe I'll listen to you, hey." The announcer, climbing out of the car, laughed so hard at his colleague's clever repartee and incisive viewpoint that his professional bleeding heart almost fell off his sleeve before he could interview Miss America.

Atlantic City is south of the Mason-Dixon Line, and every day of the Pageant it drifts farther into Dixie. The modern Southern belle has, of course, long been the Pageant ideal, so that—even in those years when a Southerner does not win—the likely winner is still probably patterned after that type. Among the contestants, the character and effect of the Southern queen is a lasting topic of discussion. "Those Northerners are more serious than us, but they're catching on," Phyllis explained a few days after they all had arrived in Atlantic City. "They're learning to get rude right back like Southern girls. And they're all starting to say 'y'all.' "

The Southern influence is even more in evidence among the Pageant grown-ups. The Southerners seem to be everywhere, talking the most at the state meetings, asking the most questions, suggesting the most changes, and doing the most kissing and hugging. Pageant people are seldom out of each other's embrace, and if it moves, they kiss it. The Southerners positively control Pageant society, with the Tennessee contingent out front.

The leading Tennesseeans include the Smith twins, perfectly identical brothers, and Tom Hensley, who is even more visible although there is only one of him. Still only 29, Hensley, who works for the state liquor lobby back home, is known to all as The Colonel. Glib and smooth, a regular kissing fool, Hensley bids fair to be a venerable figure, Mr. Pageant, by the time he is thirty. As it is, he and the Smith twins were primarily responsible for initiating the semiprivate affairs that are held every night after the Pageant at Howard Johnson's. Technically, the parties are given by all the states; practically, they are Southern-style get-togethers. They last each night for as long as the traffic will bear, with a scattering of free hors d'oeuvres and drinks, at $1 each, that are measured carefully to the very drop—a practice which seems to keynote Atlantic City hospitality. The parties also feature a dance band, for Pageant people dearly love to dance, almost as much as they love to dress up. They are all very chi-chi chic, even the women who come from areas of the country where chemises are still all the rage; there is as much clothes competition among the officials at Tom Hensley's nightly soiree as among the girls down at Convention Hall.

The climax comes Saturday, when evening dress can be broken out, for the finals and for the Toni Ball that follows. Moreover, before the Pageant that evening there is the official Southern cocktail party, with free drinks and a more subdued atmosphere. Nevertheless, admiring each other's "costumes" (as the Southerners say) requires more hugging and kissing. That never stops. It is also during the Saturday afternoon Southern party that the identity of the top ten is revealed in advance to the press, and at that moment, six o'clock, the news rapidly traverses the four blocks up Pacific from Mall Dodson's office to Howard Johnson's. The reaction is predictable, with more anger and surprise than delight, and bewilderment and bitterness emanating from two or three states whose girls had been favorites to this point.

The girls are guarded from the news, so that they do not know the top ten themselves until they are standing on stage and Bert Parks is reading out the names. Long before Saturday, however, many have given up any real hope, and when they filed off stage after the announcement of the semifinalists, not one of the forty losers was crying, nor did any appear even to be struggling to hold back tears. Connie Lerner of North Carolina had apparently understood her fate on Friday, when Phyllis—who was in her preliminary group—won swimsuit. Connie and Phyllis were both tall, dark, Southern piano players competing for the same points. There were not enough for both of them, and the swimsuit vote indicated for sure to which of the two the judges were inclined. When at last her defeat was revealed, Connie remained placid and stately, as she had been in victory at Raleigh. Phyllis was the favorite all week, and by Saturday's all-day TV rehearsal, it was clear that the other girls were inspecting her every move, and even deferring to her some already. That night, just before the curtain opened on the TV portion of the show, two also-rans willingly left their places and ran across stage to get some water for Phyllis, rather than make her exert herself.

Before the final show begins, the girls stand backstage in their places, and then begin to move about, to hug and kiss the girls standing nearest to them. They all must be somewhat restrained, watching that they don't ruffle hair or clothes, but the scene is in many ways more emotional than the one at the end, when, as soon as the curtains fall, the girls dash up the steps to the throne and mob their new queen. Before the show everyone is still equal, technically anyway; afterward, a pecking order has been decreed, and the relationships may be slightly altered by this recognition.

But there is little bitterness at the judges' choice. Long after the curtain has closed, as the photographers clamor for their prey, the other girls surround Phyllis, and kiss her and cry for her. Debbie May, Miss Congeniality, has sought out the first runner-up, Claudia Turner, Miss South Carolina, and now they stand alone, somewhat apart from the mob around Phyllis. Soothingly, Debbie says, "Oh, I'm so sorry for you. To come so close."

Claudia just looks over at Phyllis and says, "Isn't she lovely? Isn't she so lovely?"

Debbie tries at consolation again. "I hope you don't feel too badly."

Claudia lights up, and takes Debbie's arm and cries, "No, no, she won, *she* won." And she looks over adoringly toward Phyllis again. "It's so wonderful. Just think, I'm first runner-up to Miss America. First runner-up. Of all the girls in the country, I am first runner-up to Miss America herself. That is such an honor."

It is claimed, by someone who has made a study of the moment, that when there are two girls left in the running, and they clasp hands to await Bert Parks' declaration of their fate, the girl whose hand is on top will always win. This phenomenon was first realized when Miss America 1966 won, and was repeated for five years in a row. Unconsciously, it seems, the winner realized who she was, and the loser too, so the new queen was permitted to take, symbolically, a position of authority even in advance of her crowning. Phyllis and Claudia, however, kept fidgeting, so that no one hand ever stayed on top long enough to establish position. They looked at each other a lot, too. Claudia said, "The Lord's with us, and the one that's right will win."

Debbie May, Miss Indiana, had noticed that that sort of attitude was widespread. "The thing that has surprised me most here is the expression of religious faith," she said. "The depth of it is amazing. It has even helped restore my own, and, you know, you can get a little discouraged about faith and religion on a college campus. I was put off at first when I encountered all that sort of talk here. I was ill at ease. One girl told me, 'I know that I have a purpose in life, and I'm just waiting for God to tell me what it is,' and I just didn't know how to react to that. There's so much of it. A lot of the girls try to steer the conversations to God and their faith. Perhaps it has something to do with the size of the towns so many of us come from, with the kind of families we have. I don't know."

At the awards brunch, on Sunday, the last official *Miss America* function, Debbie was called up to accept her Miss Congeniality award. She was not required to say anything, but when she reached the front of the head table, she took the scholarship and paused to thank everyone for that, and for the week's experience in Atlantic City. And then she said, "I read once the expression, 'For that inner peace, try that upward look.' May I recommend it to you all. I hope that God will bless you all"—and here she turned toward Phyllis—"and especially you, for you will need His help the most." Then Debbie leaned across the table and kissed the new Miss America 1971.

An hour or so later, Phyllis was introduced to Mrs. Dorothy Schwager, who would be her traveling companion for the first month of her reign, and they left later in the afternoon for Miss America's first commercial appearance, at a shopping center, in King of Prussia, Pennsylvania.

★ 13 ★

There He Is, and Miss America Too

In the long history of *Miss America*, only two elements of it have become a traditional part of the show—besides the girls themselves, who only seem to be the same. Year in and year out, there is Bert Parks, the master of ceremonies, and "There She Is, Miss America," the song. Everything else is transitory.

By coincidence, both arrived in the same year, 1955, and both have remained ever since, although, incredibly, once, in a pique, the Pageant tried to ditch the song. Other products and institutions spend millions, scheming, hoping, that they might come upon some kind of theme that is instantly recognizable in the public mind. Only *Miss America* could be blessed with such an ideal gift, yet then try to rid itself of the cachet. Luckily for the Pageant, the force of public opinion rescued it from its own worst devices.

Before "There She Is," Miss Americas were usually serenaded at their coronation to either "Pomp and Circumstance" or "A Pretty Girl Is Like a Melody," affording a choice between high-school graduation or burlesque. Then, one magic day in 1954, a songwriter named Bernie Wayne saw a note in the newspaper that *Miss America* would be on TV that year. Wayne, who was once married coast-to-coast on "Bride and Groom," had never before seen a beauty pageant in his life. Nevertheless, the idea was sufficient to inspire him.

"Sometimes you have to be obvious," Wayne says. "I just sat

down in my little office on Broadway, and started writing. I wrote the whole song in the space of an hour, sixty little minutes. Writing is sometimes like self-hypnosis. I just tried to put myself in the place of the lucky girl—walking down the runway—an ideal, walking on air, and so on." He wrote:

> There she is, Miss America,
> There she is, your ideal.
> The dreams of a million girls who are more than pretty
> May come true in Atlantic City,
> Or, they may turn out to be,
> The queen of femininity.
>
> There she is, Miss America,
> There she is, your ideal.
> With so many beauties, she took the town by storm,
> With her all-American face and form,
> And there she is,
> Walking on air she is,
> Fairest of the fair she is,
> Miss America.

At that time, Bob Russell was the emcee of the show. Handsome and stubborn, Russell was so popular a figure in Atlantic City that although he had associated himself with Miss Universe after a decade's tenure with *Miss America,* he was welcomed back in 1954. He brought along a couple of songs that he thought were just right: "This Is Miss America" and "The Spirit of Miss America." Some time in advance of the Pageant, meanwhile, Wayne called up Max Meth, the Pageant musical director, and Vinton Freedley, the producer of the telecast, and invited them over to hear his new song. "I sang it with all my off-key fervor," Wayne says, "and they loved it." Although there were no financial discussions, Wayne left for Atlantic City with the understanding that his song would be the theme. He called his mother, so sure was he, and advised her to watch the Pageant on TV, and to listen for his song.

Friday, at the final rehearsals at Convention Hall, Freedley called Wayne over and told him that his song would not be going on. Russell, Freedley explained, "really ran the show" and had "demanded that his music be used."

"I was brokenhearted," Wayne says. "If ever I felt a song was right for the occasion, it was "There She Is." Well, I called my mother again, told her the bad news, and then I just walked the Boardwalk. The next night I was too disappointed to go see the show in person. I watched it on TV from some broken-down bar."

Wayne went back to New York, put the song away in his piano bench, and went on to other projects. He has since established varied music credentials, as artists' and repertoire head of 20th Century-Fox Records, for instance, and has written such hits as "Blue Velvet" and "Laughing on the Outside—Crying on the Inside," and he believes that only a wild coincidence saved "There She Is" for posterity. Wayne was playing a medley of his songs on the piano at a party on Park Avenue a few months later, when, on a whim, he broke into his unknown *Miss America* song. "It was a noisy room," he recalls, "but as I sang, the place quieted down like magic. When I'd finished, there was such a hush I thought I'd laid an egg. But then, suddenly, everyone broke into applause, and a distinguished gray-haired gentleman standing next to the piano asked me, 'Why haven't I ever heard this song?' 'Why should you have?' I replied. 'Because I'm the sponsor,' the man said."

The stranger was one Pierson Mapes, who was in charge of the Philco advertising account, and "There She Is" was premiered shortly thereafter on a Philco Playhouse television show in a drama about what happens to a Miss America after her reign. The song was rendered in this first public instance by Johnny Desmond, who sang it to Lee Meriwether, the reigning queen, who also starred in the show. Bert Parks sang it for the first time a few weeks later at his initial Pageant in September 1955, when Sharon Kay Ritchie was named queen. Not long after, on tour, she met her first husband, the golfing vocalist, Don Cherry, when he sang the song for her on her visit to his home town of Wichita Falls, Texas. It was also played at their wedding, where she wore her tiara and robe. She was otherwise attired when, subsequently, she took a second husband, Kyle Rote, the erstwhile football star.

Both Parks and Desmond have recorded the song, but neither has sold many copies of it. A Bobby Vinton rock version in 1966 sold several hundred thousand copies, but only because everybody was buying the big hit on the flip side. Parks cannot understand why the Pageant does not hawk records of "There She Is" at Convention Hall or push it in stores during *Miss America* week, and Wayne is also vexed. "Here is a standard that occupies a position unique in modern musical history," he says. "It is the popular equivalent of 'Take Me Out to the Ball Game,' 'White Christmas,' and 'God Bless America,' and yet it has sold relatively few records, and, compared to the others, gets only one national play a year. I would venture to say that 'Blue Velvet' has made fifty thousand times as much money for me as 'There She Is.' But I guess money can't be the common denominator, because everybody knows the song."

The latter is true, with qualifications. Everybody almost knows the song. It is variously referred to as "Here She Is," "There She Goes," and "Here She Comes." Many people are also under the impression that Parks sings the song while crowning the new queen, dancing with her or escorting her down the runway, none of which he does.

Wayne became more closely involved with the show after the theme song caught on. In 1960 he wrote another original song, "Miss America Sisters," and, he says, inspired the more sophisticated musical-comedy Pageant productions that followed, beginning with his first full show score for 1961. Wayne's contentions are refuted by the show's present producer, George Cavalier, who credits Al Cantwell, the producer from 1961 to 1965, with making the substantive innovations. Wayne, who authored the scores through the 1967 Pageant, says that he also traveled, without compensation, to virtually every state in the union during his Pageant tenure, serving as a state judge and musical adviser. Nevertheless, he fell from Marks's favor and was a quick casualty as soon as Miss Slaughter was retired. He was succeeded by Glenn (Abe) Osser, who has also conducted the Pageant orchestra since 1955, and his wife, Edna, who prefers to write her Pageant lyrics in the bathtub.

On May 24, 1968, less than a month after Wayne's contract with *Miss America* officially expired, the New York *Daily News* was leaked the story that "There She Is" would never be sung again at the Pageant. The report was picked up by 367 other newspapers, most of whom accompanied the item with expressions of shock. The mail then began to pour in, to Bernie Wayne, to the papers, and, of course, to the Pageant. Marks even got a mournful letter of protest from the front lines of Vietnam, while nowhere was there any support visible for the Pageant decision to abandon its song.

Although *Miss America* was stunned by the intensity of the protest, it knew what it was doing. Backed by its sponsors, it was determined to rid itself of every vestige of Wayne. The conflict was essentially one only of personality, but it ran deep, and *Miss America* was maddened by the fact that Wayne would continue to make money off the Pageant—and for a very long time indeed. Wayne's copyright on "There She Is" does not run out until 1982, and then he can have it renewed until 2010.

The decision to jettison "There She Is" easily made for Albert Marks's worst hour, but the response was so completely one-sided that, even with sponsor support, he was compelled to sue for peace. "I have a replacement for the song—a good one—and I had one then," he says, still missing the point. The woods are filled with people who wrote magnificent alternatives to "Here Comes the Bride" that nobody ever wanted to hear. It was only forty-eight hours before air time in 1968 when Marks at last made the deal with Wayne to buy Pageant rights to the theme for the next fifteen years for $17,500. "I could have, and probably should have, asked for more," Wayne explains. "Keep in mind that the Pageant had been using the song for absolutely nothing since 1955. At no time in all those years did anyone connected with the Pageant ever mention paying me dollar one for 'There She Is.' Obviously, I'm a terrible businessman. But frankly, when I made the deal right before air time, I felt it was more important for the public to have the song. They loved it and it was their song. The Pageant was—and, for that matter, still is—my love, and if I can't be there in person, well, at least my song is still there to kindle their hearts and dreams."

Yet grudgingly as the Pageant accepted being saddled with Wayne's sixty-minute inspiration, more grudgingly still does it fight to restrict its own best-beloved symbol. At the 1970 Pageant, the Fiftieth Anniversary show, the returning queens practically had to threaten to go on strike before it was agreed that they could walk the runway to "There She Is." "Just because they're mad at Bernie Wayne, they can't take my song, our song away from us," one of them said. Moreover, there is no encouragement offered state or local pageants to use the theme, either as a signature or to salute the reigning Miss America if she should be contracted to appear. Wayne says that he agreed to lease annual rights to the preliminaries for the "startling ridiculous" fee of $100 per state. That means for $5000—less than $1.60 per pageant—every state and local show in the country could have the privilege to play the one song everyone wants to hear. As it is, when Miss America herself appears at many functions, she is greeted with unfamiliar house songs that the Pageant pushes as alternatives. Beautiful as any of them may be—and "Look at Her, She's a Miss America" is quite lovely—the spectators are as disappointed as they would be if "Pop Goes the Weasel" was foisted upon them.

Bert Parks has surely reached the same level of invulnerability as the song he is identified with so completely. By now, he is woven into the fibers of the event, and in recognition his contract has been renewed every December right on schedule, even though some of the recent sponsors have not preferred him. Parks makes something like $20,000 for the appearance, and while he was once so popular that he was doing twelve TV shows a week, *Miss America* is now his only regular television shot. (His last network series was in 1963, when he emceed "Yours for a Song," a show which was created by, of all people, Bob Russell, the man he replaced on *Miss America.*) When Parks succeeded Robert Preston as *The Music Man* on Broadway, it was written into his contract that he could leave the show in September to appear at Atlantic City. In another three or four years he will sing "There She Is" for a new Miss America who was not even born when he first assumed the role.

A big-time announcer for more than three decades, Parks is still young and healthy of appearance, tanned, and animated. In his heyday, when he was doing "Stop the Music" and nearly everything else on the air, it was noted that "he had a smile you can read by," but offstage his teeth are not quite so evident and recede into his mouth, just as other people's do. Still, his gums may be characterized as outwardly mobile, in pursuit of either smile or grimace. At Atlantic City, he does not participate in any of the Pageant-week social activities. Instead, he and Mrs. Parks keep mostly to the company of the Ossers and other members of the show's staff. He is never aloof with the contestants, but does not really initiate much contact with them. When he is with the girls, he never fails to put them at ease, which is, after all, his forte. Never does he let on with them that he understands that most of them hold him in some awe. He is, after all, the only celebrity on the show, the only continuing identity, and in many ways he epitomizes the Pageant more than the individual Miss Americas who just come and go. Women's Lib certainly missed a bet in not protesting the ultimate irony that the public's real Miss America, on reflection, is a man. Parks's paradoxical image somehow recalls Harry Golden's comment when Barry Goldwater was nominated for the Presidency, "At last we get a Jew running for President, and he turns out to be an Episcopalian."

Marks is used to Parks's critics inquiring why he is not replaced. Marks simply replies with a question: "All right, whom would you suggest? And why?" Stuck with a hypothetical situation where Parks is unavailable because of illness, Marks says he would make no effort to fill in with a legitimate substitute, but would instead have two former queens serve as dual hostesses. So, although there are, predictably, rumors every year that the Pageant is out to unload Parks, as it tried with its institutional song, the fact is that he is very secure indeed. Besides, unlike Bernie Wayne, Parks is well liked in Atlantic City, where everybody calls him "Bertie." He is easy to work with and blows up only when real incompetence is evidenced. Once, on the air, when he was given a wrong list of girls' names, he snarled, "Somebody screwed this up." Another year, he was handed the card with the list of the winners' names written in a confusing order. Parks nearly read off the finalists' positions incorrectly, a gaffe that would have gone down in history alongside Clem McCarthy's wrong call of the winner in the Kentucky Derby in 1949. Coolly, though, Parks paused and sought a clarification. After that, he designed his own cards.

"It's fantastic that more doesn't go wrong," he says. "You're playing Russian roulette out there with fifty amateurs. But then, it's exciting in its immediacy, because there is a chance for mistakes. It's live, it's refreshing." Never was it more so, either, than in 1967, when Debra Dene Barnes of Kansas was named Miss America. As she took the traditional stroll down the runway, Parks reached for the mike to sing "There She Is." He forgot that it was affixed to a stand and was not devised to be used as a hand mike. When he jerked at it, it not only came free of the stand, but it also disconnected, and went dead. The climactic litany went out pantomime all over America. Predictably, many critics rushed to acknowledge that it was easily his best rendition of the song.

"Ah, none of the criticism bothers me any more," he says. "Criticism is a bloody bore to me now. I've been criticized by the best. Besides, in the case of *Miss America*, I know that I'm generally seen in a very sympathetic light. It is, after all, one of the highest prestige positions as emcee; it's damned good exposure. It may be too good. I'm identified with it so closely that I think it may even have hurt my career otherwise on television. But look, I like it, and if I can speak for myself, I do a damned good job at what I'm supposed to do. I'm a catalyst, and I never forget that it is not my show. It is the girls' show. I work for them."

The performance itself on the three preliminary nights is good entertainment, being sharp and fast-paced, and, since 1969, fairly contemporary. "I think the one before that finally cleared the air," Parks says. "It had gotten just too cutesy-poo. That was the Cinderella thing, and it was like swatting flies out there. You can't afford a strong story line, because regularly you must get back to the competition. I have high regard for George Cavalier, and I think he understands those problems now. You couldn't believe that one. I mean, if I had to climb out from underneath one more toadstool—You see, the thing is, I wonder whether it really makes any difference how much slicker we become. You can climb mountains out there, do a water ballet, anything, but the thing you must always fall back on are the basic ingredients."

There is another minority view among Pageant officials that television has exaggerated the theatrics of the Pageant to the detriment of the whole project. "At every level now," says Ken Gaughran, who heads the Miss Westchester County, New York, Pageant, "there is so much concern about putting on a good show that no one has time to educate the public in what a pageant is really all about." Speaking strictly in terms of the performance, James Hatcher, producer of the 1960 Pageant, points to the real problem that has no solution. "What you are faced with," he says, "is an ideological conflict between what's good for the audience in the hall and what's good for TV. The year I ran the Pageant, I felt my responsibility was to my audience that had come to Atlantic City. But then TV was still strange enough to only be confusing. By now, of course, that conflict has long since been resolved in favor of television."

The regrettable fact is that the show is never able to put its best together. The preliminary shows are fine entertainment without suspense; the finals are a jerry-built TV program with all the suspense. Since the preliminaries seldom draw more than a third of the huge house—though the best seats are only $3.25—while the finals pack the Hall (25,000 is announced, although 21,013 is the actual capacity figure), it is obvious that the competitive element draws better than the vaudeville.

Miss America maintains that it has tried big-name guest stars and every other conceivable gimmick to hypo the early evening performances, but, significantly, the one thing it has failed to try is the very thing that fills the house for the Saturday night finals. That is, revelation. Obviously, a Miss America cannot be announced every night of the week, but more secrets could be disclosed earlier on to attract greater crowds. As it is, preliminary winners in talent and swimsuit are announced at the conclusion of each evening, but these girls are guaranteed no advancement by their victory—indeed, that fact is emphasized, even if it is usually misleading—so that the drama is empty. Worse, the announcement of the semifinalists at the start of Saturday's show is a giveaway. The house is packed to see the new Miss America crowned at the end of the program. If the semifinalists were revealed at the conclusion of Friday's show, they would have no effect on the size of Saturday's sellout, but they would surely greatly enlarge Friday's gate.*

There is a hard core of 1600 fans on the Pageant mailing list. Most of these rabid beauty buffs come back every year, asking

* See Appendix 12, p. 310.

for the same seats, none of which is very good. Unfortunately, all of the seats within hailing distance of the stage face not the stage, but the runway, where only a small portion of the activity takes place. Still, the crowds are most enthusiastic, and willing to accept the talent for what it is, amateurish but game.

At least today everyone is spared any duplication of talent, since contestants' talent number requests are honored on a first come, first served basis. It used to be that a girl could do whatever she pleased, even if that meant, as it did one year, that three of them elected to sing "Tequila." *Sorry, Wrong Number* skits were legion at almost every Pageant. Joan of Arc has not been fired at the Convention Hall stake since 1967, but for a time there were so many of them that Parks came to refer privately to them all as "chain draggers."

George Cavalier tries to divide the talent up in advance, so there are balance and quality alike on the three preliminary bills. When a girl wins a State Pageant, she is required to send in a tape of her performance, or at least the background music if she is something like a dancer or baton-twirler. From that, Cavalier establishes what amounts to a seeding system, dividing the girls into A, B, and C classifications, and then spreading them around equally. Obviously, he expects to make some large errors in judgment, but in the long run he feels that he will split up the best talent so that all these top girls do not kill each other off in one preliminary.

Many of the girls eschew live accompaniment and work off a recording, but most hand their arrangements over to Glenn Osser and his orchestra and work with them. In 1966, Jane Jayroe conducted the orchestra as part of her musical number, and it is thought that that stunt clinched her the 1967 title, even though the band kept on following Osser's lead. There were sharp words in the Pageant offices afterward that the judges had been conned. Miss America 1958, Marilyn Van Derbur, won the title by playing "Tenderly" and "Tea for Two" on the organ. Those were the only pieces she could play. It works both ways, though. Marilyn Buferd muffed her lines badly, and the judges still made her Miss America 1946.

The conclusion is inescapable that, even though talent officially counts double evening gown and swimsuit, it has no real bearing on the determination of a winner. All it really does is confuse things to that point. Miss Americas almost never win the talent preliminaries, but they frequently win in swimsuit, where the judges' libido is presumably a force.

The judges' confusion is most revealed in the talent where singers are concerned. Every year, there are so many vocalists, that they cancel each other out. The classic case came in the battle for the 1966 crown. Of the fifty contestants, twenty-eight were singers. Of the ten semifinalists, seven were singers. Of the five finalists, four were singers. Beautiful Debbie Bryant, whose act was charitably described as "an imitation of old-time hoofers," was, of course, the winner. Since the scholarship program made talent a serious enterprise in 1945, only two girls have won with straight singing—Yolande Betbeze, 1951, and Donna Axum, 1964. Mary Ann Mobley, 1959, pepped her number up with a bogus strip-tease and Miss Jayroe, 1967, carried the day with her conducting gimmick, but even counting them as singers, fewer than one per cent of the singing contestants have won. To put it another way, any girl who shows up to sing on the Atlantic City stage is a hundred-to-one at becoming Miss America. Since Donna was the last singing Miss America, the winners have included two popular pianists, two dancers, a trampolinist, a ventriloquist, and the orchestra leader.

In these recent years no winning talent pattern has revealed itself. The judges are liable to pick anyone but a singer. In the 1950s, however, when television drama was respectable, when the Pageant itself went on TV, and when Grace Kelly suddenly loomed as ideal and competition alike for Miss America, there was a rash of winners whose talent was drama. Originally, the number of drama contestants in any Pageant was insignificant. In the first years after the war, about one-fifth of the contestants would recite or emote for talent; the figure increased a bit more as the 1950s began, and then suddenly soared. At the same time there was a corresponding drop in the number of singers.

By 1954—when, coincidentally, Miss Kelly happened to be a judge—three of the last five Miss Americas had won with drama (not with music) and the Pageant itself was to be telecast. Perhaps most important of all, a movie named *The Country Girl* was then playing. Every two-bit trainer in the country could see the handwriting on the wall: in the 1930s you got to Hollywood in tap shoes; then in a tight sweater; now, in the 1950s, in grease-paint, streaked with real tears. It was more rewarding to display emotion than cleavage.

The very year *Miss America* went on TV there were, suddenly, more actresses than singers, and in keeping with the obvious demand, Lee Meriwether, who read from Synge's *Riders to the Sea*, was the weepy winner. She was also, by her own admission, flat-chested, and at 5 feet 8½ inches tall, with a 34½-inch bust, is still the thinnest queen of them all. Had she been selected at some other point in time those facts would be merely incidental, but because it was 1954, the shape and size of Miss Meriwether and her breasts became denotative of larger truths. Herewith began *Miss America*'s search for its own reasonable facsimile of Grace Kelly.

At this moment the pinnacle in Miss Kelly's film career was approaching, and she was rapidly being accepted as the only real queen that the United States had ever had. She was beautiful; talented, elegant, gracious, altogether poised, well educated, and from a good family. Not only that, she was even from Philadelphia. Were there any justice in the world, Grace Kelly would have been deposited on the Pageant doorstep as an infant. Her singular influence had grown mighty. She made both actresses and flat-chestedness respectable, and had she been given just a bit more time before she went off to become a real princess, there is no telling but that she might even have done something for Philadelphia, too.

Within another year, by the time of the Pageant in 1955, Miss Kelly had not only won the Academy Award, but was affianced to a certified monarch. At Atlantic City, a record nineteen of the forty-nine girls gave dramatic presentations. Once, in rehearsals during this period, Bert Parks rushed backstage in anguish and cried, "No, no more, I can't stand any more Bobby-sox Bernhardts!" In 1955 there was an Ophelia and a Lady Macbeth both, and the winner was a Sunday-School teacher, Sharon Kay Ritchie, Miss Colorado, who recited "The Murder of Lidice" by Edna St. Vincent Millay. Though a trifle better rounded than Lee or Grace, Sharon perfectly represented the hard road to royalty, the kiss-a-toad queen. She was an example for all peasants, for it was disclosed that she had been chubby and bespectacled as a devout child, who recited the Lord's Prayer in the bathtub.

In these years the winners possessed most of the presumed Kelly attributes, and it was not until the 1960s that the number of drama contestants dropped back to the normal 20 per cent levels. In 1957 blond Marilyn Van Derbur was chosen, and she was promptly celebrated in Atlantic City as a "debutante." Her Denver family was Kelly-like enough for Edward R. Murrow to visit them on his "Person to Person" TV program, and Marilyn, who went on to be the first Miss America Phi Beta Kappa, proved to be a strong, respected Miss America. She is still referred to in Atlantic City as "a very determined young woman." Brad Frapart says that when she was at last faced with the fact that her year as queen was up she became nearly hysterical backstage at Convention Hall moments before she had to go out and crown her successor. He says he had to slap her face crisply to restore her composure.

Marilyn was among an unprecedented concentration of queens who trooped off at the same time to Hollywood and the movies or New York and TV. So many Miss Americas were hustling for the big time at once that it is nearly the law of averages that made two of them end up living together, when Marilyn, 1958, and Lynda Lee Mead, 1960, shared rooms in Manhattan. Lynda taught Marilyn how to twist. Lynda is the roommate Miss America. Had she not succeeded Mary Ann Mobley as Miss America—the two Miss Mississippis, back-to-back—Lynda would have returned to the University of Mississippi and spent the year in Mary Ann's old room at their sorority house. Lynda is also the last of the drama-oriented Kelly queens.

The girls in this era were inclined to celebrity in a number of ways. Blond Marian McKnight, who became Miss America 1957 with an imitation of Marilyn Monroe, was nearly shattered afterward when she discovered that Joe DiMaggio had been in the audience, but, like Lee Meriwether, she later dated DiMaggio. For marriage, however, Marian chose the actor who had played the monster in the movie *I Was a Teen-Age Frankenstein.* Lee and Mary Ann also married actors, Sharon a singer, and then a professional athlete, like Jacque and Colleen just before her. Neva

Jane, Evelyn, and Marilyn all married college football heroes. Nevertheless, champion in the star marriage category must be Vera Ralston, third runner-up as Miss Kansas in 1948, who declared at the Pageant, "I have no talent except to marry and raise children," whereupon she went on to become the movie actress Vera Miles and to prove herself out in both departments, marrying three times and having four children.

Nowadays, since the trainers and judges at the lower levels tend to inhibit originality, bizarre talent presentations are rare. A few surprises slip through, however, and not long ago a girl won a preliminary talent award by driving a tractor onstage and handling it with dexterity. Sadly, the doves in the magic act of Miss Idaho 1968 got loose in the middle and soared all over Convention Hall. There have been sign-language songs, for the deaf and for Indians. Twice, portable ice rinks have been set up on stage. An archer shot balloons out of her father's hand. One girl's whole talent was a speech on how to pack a suitcase for a weekend trip. Miss Idaho 1952, now a district judge, gave a speech on voting, and the number of patriotic and inspirational melodies selected appears to rise in election years. Of course, there was one girl who supplied an impersonation of Ed Sullivan; another, in 1959, showed her colors with a portrayal of a slovenly beatnik. Once, "Ah! Sweet Mystery of Life" was performed on a marimba. Bert Parks swears a girl playing a large drum was so nervous she missed it completely on one swing. In 1949, Miss Montana rode a palomino on stage in an exhibition of her horsemanship. The poor animal lost his footing and dove right into the orchestra. Beasts are no longer permitted to be used as talent associates, although Miss Montana did steady her steed and was voted Miss Congeniality.

Talent, such as it was, was introduced to the Pageant in the year it was revived, 1935. Eddie Corcoran, who died unexpectedly a few months later, was in charge this one year, and it was he who conceived the talent idea—either on an impulse, or reluctantly. In any event, Edna Smith, Miss Missouri, the first runner-up, recalls that it was only the day before the show began that contestants were encouraged to whip up an act. Most sang or tap-danced, or, better yet, did both. For a long time it was considered prudent to dazzle the judges by doing a lot of things poorly, rather than just by displaying a single wretched ability. The first Miss America *cum* talent, Henrietta Leaver, went the multifaceted route, tapping and singing to "Living in a Great Big Way."

About two-thirds of the contestants agreed to perform that year, some with exceptional vigor. Miss Baltimore, who had originally decided that she was a singer, was not pleased with her vocal effort, so she hied to a local night club, where she picked up a dancer and came back with him in a ballroom dancing exhibition. Local papers tried hard not to be hypercritical: "Beatrice Rose Pheiffer, 17, Miss Cincinnati, proved to be another singer."

When George Tyson took over the Pageant the next year, he declared that the girls would continue to enjoy offering up their talents. Presumably, anyway, that is what he meant by, "A young woman with 130 pounds of pulchritude to her credit is just as ambitious today as one less favored by Aphrodite." Rose Coyle, Miss Philadelphia, singing and dancing—in size 4B shoes—to the unforgettable "I Can't Escape from You" for eight full minutes, was the next winner and was immediately billed as "The Most Talented Miss America Ever Selected." Though damned by this faint praise, Miss Coyle struck out on tour anyway, vowing to be in the movies by Christmas. She came out of it even better, marrying the national general manager of the Warner Brothers Theatres.

Through this point, and then including Bette Cooper's victory the next year, the talent was merely a diversion, but in 1938 it became a regular category for the judges to vote on. The records, nearly complete, show that they had to choose between eleven dancers, eight singers, two pianists, four speakers, and fifteen contestants who combined two or more of the above talents in one act. Marilyn Meseke won, tapping to "The World Is Waiting for the Sunrise," but she beat a field that was thin on quality or imagination. In these early days, it seems that almost all Southern girls either sang "Pardon My Southern Accent" or recited a ditty entitled "A Real Southern Gal." Those few who overlooked the opportunity to perform these selections for the Yankee audience sang "A-Tisket A-Tasket," and one night in 1938 a record of sorts was set when Miss Montgomery and Miss Delray Beach rendered this classic back-to-back. The Atlantic City *Press* critic noted deadpan that the next performer "did not sing 'A-Tisket A-Tasket.'" Nonetheless, somewhat later in the evening Miss Kentucky did.

The Pageant, living dangerously, was beginning to take the talent seriously. Professionals, once the bane of *Miss America*, were now encouraged to enter, and contestants were required to note their "professional experience" on their background forms. Miss District of Columbia 1942 replied, "I roller skated and whistled in the fall show at school." Pat Donnelly, Miss Michigan, became Miss America 1939 and was good enough thereafter to sing at the Stork Club and in two Broadway shows, but she has no illusions about the quality of competition at Atlantic City then.

"I got in the thing on a dare myself," she says. "I was going to the University of Michigan till I got all involved. I sang with a band, and the male singer in the band also played the bass fiddle, so when he would sing, I would just sort of pick up his fiddle." At Atlantic City she really wowed the crowd—which was suffering through a record September heat wave—by shifting from a ballad to "Ol' Man Mose," where she sang and played the fiddle. "I didn't play it. I slapped it," Pat declares firmly. Her successor, Frances Burke, Miss Philadelphia, had no pretense of talent. She had just taken a ten-day crash course in dancing and had learned to sing one song.

The judges were least sanguine of all. Mostly they were still artists, there to look at pretty girls, sketch them idly, and speculate endlessly for the sake of press agents and Sunday supplements on what formed The Perfect Girl. Measurements and coloring to fill The Perfect Girl were released periodically all during these years; it was nearly a theological question in the trade. Certainly, none of the judges had interest in enduring a surfeit of broken notes and frantic acrobatic tapping. "We got so sick of it all," says Russell Patterson, who was a perennial arbiter. "Believe me, it was all bad, perfectly awful."

One year, one of Patterson's colleagues, the late Martin Branner, creator of *Winnie Winkle*, saved the day. He found a small door near the judges' box, which, upon inspection, he discovered led to a passageway which itself went nearly directly to a saloon adjoining Convention Hall. Judges would take respites from their chores in shifts. Patterson avers that a man who had good hands and a fierce determination to dim his comprehension of the talent acts on stage, could duck through the door at the start of a song, scramble to the bar, order, and toss down three quick belts, and return to his seat just as the girl concluded her brave effort.

Despite the inferior talent, *Miss America* was finding some substance. The acts pumped a little air into the program, transforming it from a glorified parade into a show. Performing on a public stage was also a very practical vocational exercise for the girls, since the vast majority of them were no doubt entered with the thought of a movie career in mind.

Since the Pageant had been re-established and talent introduced in 1935, however, *Miss America* had not found itself again, or its representative American girl. (An equivalent situation is in force today. The old style 1960s queens are no longer quite right, but the Pageant cannot settle on exactly what the prototype new model should look like.) What *Miss America* was struggling to find in the late 1930s, and is again now, is the girl who fits the faddish demands of the time, yet who retains the good old-fashioned values. In the case of the late 1930s that would be a Margaret Gorman or a Ruth Malcolmson who also had screen potential.

Miss America never really knows the type it is searching for until the right girl is thrust on Atlantic City by the real world about it. After the war, for instance, after the movie-star craze, when a woman was leaving home to work, even to put a husband through college, the Pageant was searching for independent, strong-willed queens—with the good, old-fashioned *Miss America* values—and found them every year. Then, under the impact of TV and Grace Kelly, the Pageant needed actress-types—with the good, old-fashioned *Miss America* values—and they came in abundance. The drift then was to suburbia and academia, to programed, secure coeds—with the good, old-fashioned *Miss America* values—who represented the affluence, might, right of the good times. There was no dearth of them; as the boom of the decade roared on, there were more of them to choose among every year, like Holiday Inns.

Then the country moved on, and this time the Pageant could not keep up with it. It still struggles to find the representative queen of the new restless, troubled America. The Pageant will find her—it always does—and she will be aware, involved, outspoken—and with all the good, old-fashioned *Miss America* values. She will be along shortly, just as Rosemary LaPlanche, the Pageant's ideal movie-type, was suddenly welcomed to the scene that sought her in 1940.

Rosemary was made-to-order. She was from Southern California, home of the movies; perhaps even more appropriate, she was only fifteen and lied about her age. She tapped and did well in school, but her fortune was in her face, which had the map of California etched on it—blond, rosy-cheeked, young, bursting, hopeful. Rosemary much resembled Marian Bergeron and Bette Cooper in their innocent beauty, but whereas they stumbled into beauty contests, she was native to that world. Symbolically, Rosemary was the first Miss America to be born during the reign of another Miss America. She was the first of the era, the first true beauty-pageant type.

She was also, unquestionably, born to the movies, having made her debut on the screen in 1928 at the age of three in a Fatty Arbuckle epic. Even before that, she had triumphed in the Los Angeles *Herald-Express*' Better Baby Contest. Yet, that was not her public inaugural. Earlier, in yet another venture, she had won as Baby with Straightest Back. By the age of fourteen a precocious Miss LaPlanche—"I was eighteen for ten years"—had advanced to Best Business Girl. "We had to lift our dresses a little for that one," she says, belying the fact that beauty contests with the LaPlanches were never more than chaste family hobbies. The older sister, Louise, was also a perennial candidate, and the two girls would always be accompanied by Mother and Father. Sundays, at their home in the Atwater section of Los Angeles, the LaPlanches would scan the newspapers for contests; then, after church, they would all board a streetcar and roll off to one that most interested them.

In 1940, when she made Atlantic City at fifteen, Rosemary estimates that she entered and won at least thirty straight contests, including several *Miss America* preliminaries. Louise, who at various times was Miss Catalina and Miss North America, was one of Rosemary's rivals—under the name of Lola Perry—in the Miss California State Pageant at San Bernardino, but it was the younger girl who won and left a few weeks later with her mother for Atlantic City. Whenever the train would stop at a station during the day, Rosemary would get off and practice tap-dancing on the station platform. She did this, even at all the whistle-stops, to help gain confidence.

On the night of the finals Rosemary was such an overwhelming favorite that one local paper came out with an advance headline declaring her as the winner. It was not till three in the morning that the judges at last concluded their session with the announcement that Frances Burke, Miss Philadelphia, was the new queen. Naturally, this occasioned more heated complaints that the deck had been stacked for Philly. The Pageant, though maintaining innocence, was embarrassed that another Miss California was suffering. Rosemary was invited to stay over and play the Steel Pier, and there remained such a fuss that she says Frances Burke told her once, "Oh, I just wish so you had won it." Then Rosemary went on to New York to model with the John Powers Agency, but before she left, the Pageant informed her that if she could make Miss California again, she would be welcomed back into the competition.

Atlantic City was, of course, still under the delusion that Rosemary was eighteen, and assumed that she would accept the publicity and strike out into show biz, never to be heard again on the Jersey shore. Instead, all Rosemary did was go back to John Marshall High in Atwater, where she was student-body secretary. During the school year, she laid plans for her return the next September. So that she would not appear stale to the judges, she decided to redo her image. She put her hair down and began assembling an all-blue wardrobe. Because she had performed on the Convention Hall stage, she realized how big it was, and added a lot of leaps and jumps to her ballet-tap number to help her fill the stage up. She was really the first Miss America ever to create a plan of attack. She won Miss California at the Coliseum in Los Angeles, and was such a ridiculously easy winner in Atlantic City that there were protests that she enjoyed an unfair edge as a returning veteran. The Pageant, acting after the fact as usual, promptly decreed that no girl could play Atlantic City more than once, a rule still in force today.

Rosemary moved on to become the first of several Miss Americas to skirt the edge of movie big-time. She more or less set the pattern. Jo-Carroll Dennison, 1942, and Marilyn Buferd, 1946, left no marks on the silver screen either. Lee Meriwether, 1955, has had an uneven career that appears to offer more promise as she qualifies for mature parts—the mother, the wife, the frustrated maiden aunt, that type of thing. Mary Ann Mobley, 1959, has been a perennial wide-eyed ingenue, who has never quite escaped being tagged as an Elvis Presley leading lady.

Rosemary, though, had the most extensive film career. She began as an RKO contract starlet after her reign, and eventually appeared in eighty-four pictures, which, it may be said, ran the gamut from grade B to D. Among the latter there were leads in such sagas as *Strangler of the Swamp* and *Devil Bat's Daughter*. Rosemary laughs about it now. "Being Miss America opened some doors," she says, "but then, everybody you meet has an image of Miss America, and whatever that might be, it includes the thought that she cannot act. As a former Miss America, I also had a certain value to the studio that did not help me. They would send me out on the road to publicize RKO pictures, and somebody else would get the good roles back in Hollywood."

Yet the inherent peaches-and-cream in Miss Americas seems to surface periodically. Surely, only a Miss America like Rosemary could have been cast as both Betty Co-ed and Jack Armstrong's all-American girl friend, a double-header that might be matched only by Anita Bryant, who finished as second runner-up to Mary Ann Mobley. In the summer of 1968, Anita sang "God Bless America" at the Republican convention and "Happy Birthday, Dear Lyndon" at the Democratic. Meanwhile, Rosemary went on to actually meet her husband, TV Producer Harry Koplan, at a program of his that was entitled, "Meet the Missus." Rosemary still makes some appearances in commercials, where she has performed in behalf of such products as cosmetics, vitamins, and a savings and loan association. "I think I look like the sort of person you would trust your money with," she says, without complication.

That may be, perhaps, the best description of the species Miss America. They appear quite dependable at any age, as if they could be trusted with money, and husbands as well. These are obviously not attributes that any budding movie *femme fatale* wishes to exhibit. Miss Americas are often mocked for being able to go only so far in movies. In fact, a more reasonable analysis would be that they get further along having been Miss America than they would have otherwise. Invariably, Miss America's most substantial talent is the talent to be Miss America.

14

Female Chauvinist Pigs

From its inception *Miss America* has been attacked as immoral, tawdry, minacious, and a baleful influence upon the land. For a long time, churchmen—generally Bible Readers at first, Roman Catholics later on—as well as free-lance moralists and agitators, were those most often in protest against the Pageant's immodesty. Puritan instincts were so ingrained in the American conscience that assaults on the beauty contest were regularly dredged up from the most unexpected sources. "The young woman who deliberately exhibits her charm of person to a gaping crowd descends into the sphere of the vulgar, if she is not already there. . . . The contests for the 'Miss America' crown have never truly represented young American girlhood or womanhood." The source of this Comstockian outburst was the New York *Herald,* Paris edition, of all things, and at a time when the Roaring Twenties raged on in wickedness—while the reigning Miss America, a Bible expert, finished up high school.

In more recent times, as breasts flopped and bared all around, the Pageant has seemed nearly prudish. Since it has now become impossible to attack it with the old indecency charges, critics have found more up-to-date indictments to lodge with *Miss America.* It is accused of being racist, commercial, establishment, and male chauvinist. Everything striking out against *Miss America* today is captured in one raw moment in the movie *Putney Swope,* when a beauty contestant is crowned—obviously

Miss America—and she takes a convenient pie and slams it into the emcee's face, saying very plainly, "Go —— yourself, Bert." The vignette is very wish-fulfilling, too, for all along, those leading the protest against *Miss America* have been other women.

Indeed, whereas the details may have changed, the base issues seem the same, and the arguments are presented in the same emotional, strident tones as they were back in the 1920s, when Victorian fuddy-duddies led the crusade against *Miss America*. "There's nothing new any more," says Adrian Phillips, a past president of the Pageant. "We heard all this same stuff forty years ago." It appears that so long as some women enter beauty pageants, other women are going to be convinced that their sisters are being exploited.

There is, unfortunately, always a tendency, on both sides, to make a beauty queen more important than she is, and to assume that the issue has great bearing on the whole female race. Obviously, this heightens the emotional and irrational content of the arguments; beauty pageant battles always seem to be fought out of context. The prime recent illustration would be the 1968 and 1969 Women's Liberationist forays onto the Boardwalk and into network television.

These little hassles produced an incommensurate amount of publicity for Women's Lib, which succeeded in giving the movement visibility for the first time. Much of what has followed has been more significant, but in the context of that time, the decision to attack *Miss America* was as vital as any. Women's Lib made it all the more momentous a confrontation with the old trick of elevating the issues to ideology: *Who speaks for the woman?* It is a game both sides have played for long. For instance, Fay Lanphier, Miss America 1925, actually seemed to operate under the delusion that she served as the personification of the whole female race. She never made a serious public statement, it seems, without considering the implications for "womanhood." On one occasion she even concluded that "the ideals of California womanhood" (this was before her ascension to Miss America) would not permit her to pose for a picture with Jack Dempsey. Everything was womanhood in those days. The Pageant was never conceded to be just a frivolous bunch of silly young things parading around at the beach. Always, it was womanhood, on the march, on the defense, on the run, on the downgrade, on the make.

In 1922, a women's social organization known as the Florence Crittendon League got in first licks. Speaking not just for itself, but for "womanhood," it was insulted by the Pageant. Moreover, also serving as a mouthpiece for "our young people," the Circle reported that "modesty, which is one of the greatest safeguards of the Morals of the Nation" was, alas, being "thrown to the winds" by the pernicious *Miss America* scoundrels. The next year, the chairman of the judges almost quit because the girls did not seem to him to properly represent "American womanhood." The year after that, the time Ruth Malcolmson, the choir singer, won, the YWCA protested that the harsh competition, as well as rampant immodesty, was going to be the ruin of "pure womanhood." Not to be outdone, the Methodists joined the fray in 1926. They had already written off the women participants, and only feared that pictures of the Jezebels would produce a "demoralizing effect on young men." At last, in 1927, the Federation of Women's Clubs demanded an abandonment of the entire Pageant, pleading that "American women are sleeping while American girlhood is being degraded."

(For the record, the Pageant did graduate one girl hood. Her name was Janice Hansen, a tap dancer, Miss New Jersey 1944, and later Mrs. Allen Drake, the wife of a comedian. Suspected of being a Mafia narcotics courier, Janice was twice questioned by police for her part in underworld slayings, and she also had the distinction of having dinner with Albert Anastasia on the night before he was gunned down. She was killed herself on September 25, 1959, along with her frequent companion, Anthony [Little Augie] Pisano, on a well-lighted street in the East Elmhurst section of Queens, New York. Miss Hansen and Mr. Pisano made the mistake of sitting in the front seat of an automobile, while some unknown friends, carrying loaded firearms, sat in the back.)

Now, any time the Pageant is attacked, it promptly trots out its scholarship program and the Jaycees, but in the early days, it was sometimes reluctant to offer even a timid defense. The trouble was, *Miss America* really was a girly show, even if it offered only a pale version of that genre. As is surely obvious, most of the girls were guilty of nothing more than a recent bout with puberty, but Atlantic City was always sensitive about a few of the more mature babes that were attracted, especially in the first few years, when the "professional" division existed. Old-timers recall, dimly, that some of the more worldly contestants appeared to hang around town after the Pageant, but nobody can really pin on them any specific misbehavior.

For the most part, the girls in the 1920s had their reputations darkened long after the fact. Quite a bit later, as Miss America became more collegiate, this alleged improvement in character was made to appear all the more substantial by painting the earlier Pageants and their girls as seedier than they had been. The bleaker the past looked, the brighter the present by comparison. "I never saw any of those so-called rough girls who were supposed to have been here," Miss America 1924, Ruth Malcolmson, says. "I never met any dese and dose types." From the first year of the Pageant girls were chaperoned.

Sam Myers, a retired photographer, who has the distinction of being among the handful of people who have seen every Pageant, declares, "All the talk you hear. The Pageant was always run clean. Always. Look, I never smoked or drank, so I could watch these guys. And it was clean all the way. The girls—they wasn't as well shaped as they are now, but these weren't bad girls ever. Now, they may have gotten bad later. I don't know about that. But all along, from the first, there were no bad girls at the Pageant."

Nonetheless, the Pageant was always sensitive to such charges, and to counteract them, it began early on to lean upon family credentials as proof of the high quality of American femininity that it was offering for inspection. The resulting line was an offensive mixture of old-fashioned WASP racism, clean-cut jingoism, and snobbery. In 1923 Mary Katherine Campbell's credentials for Miss America were outlined by Joseph Cummings Chase, one of the judges who selected her. "She is typically American, an altogether ideal type. Her forebears for ten generations have been American born." Two years later Fay Lanphier's victory was attributed blandly to "the difference that comes with generations of American-born ancestry behind a girl."

Contestants were often introduced with detailed accounts of their genealogy, rather like dogs or horses. *The Boardwalk Illustrated News* hastened to explain, for instance, that in the case of Miss Chicago, Margarita Gonzales, "Her breeding is inherited and she descends from two noble families, the Villa Senoras of Spain and the Gathrights of England." As late as 1945, all of the contestants were required to list, on the formal data sheet, how far back they could trace their ancestry. One girl could go back ten generations, another traced back to John Quincy Adams, another to "First Families of Virginia," and one right to the *Mayflower*. Bess Myerson, the winner that year, said she could trace back four generations. She was a first-generation American (every Miss America has been born in the U.S., just like every President) and remains the first and only Jewish girl to win. Lenora says somewhat euphorically that Bess's victory "was one of the things that welded together the Gentile religion with the Jewish religion."

Not surprisingly, running concurrent with this American-first strain was a complementary normal segregationist attitude. In this regard, *Miss America* seems to have mirrored the country during the years; it was never far out of step with the prevailing racial views. It did fall behind in this department rather recently, but that is not attributable to any vigorous new racial attitudes but to the fact that *Miss America* fell behind in everything during this period. It is approximately back to the line now—no more or less overtly racist than any white institution, which is to say, of course, that it is not quite so much the equal-opportunity institution that it fancies itself.

Blacks first appeared in the Pageant in 1922, cast sadly but clearly as "slaves" in His Oceanic Majesty's Court. There is no evidence that another black appeared on stage at any time in any capacity in the Pageant until 1970, when Cheryl Brown, a black girl from New York City, attending Luther College in Iowa, qualified for the Pageant as Miss Iowa. A ballet dancer, she missed making the top ten, but was awarded a $1000 scholarship as an especially talented nonfinalist.

In between these two extremes, there were some stabs at tokenism, with the first real barriers falling in 1959 when the winners at Miss Sacramento and Miss Indiana University both turned out to be black. Before that, as early as 1926, and off and on until 1957, the Pageant would welcome an American Indian queen. First known as Princess America, then later as Miss Indian America, these girls were never permitted to compete, but only to be on hand "representing the first American beauty." Curiously, in 1941 a full-blooded Indian named Mifaunwy Shunatona was elected Miss Oklahoma and came to Atlantic City and participated. She even won Miss Congeniality. After the war, though, the Pageant returned to welcoming Indians apart from the white American queens.

In a fairly similar case, Miss Puerto Rico first appeared as an "official guest" at the Pageant in 1937, was welcomed to the regular competitive lists after the war, and competed through the 1961 Pageant, about the same time that Miss Canada was eliminated from the competition and it was made strictly a state affair. In 1948 Miss Hawaii was Yun Tau, an Oriental, who was listed as "the first young lady of her race" in the Pageant.

It is not known precisely when the first black entered a local *Miss America* contest. Although somewhat vague, but completely open on the subject, Lenora says that no black girl could have possibly entered until "sometime in the middle of the 1950s, whenever it was about then that we took Rule Seven off the books." Miss Slaughter then explains that obscure reference, "Oh, Rule Seven was the one that specified that 'only members of the white race' could enter Miss America. I'm pretty sure it was sometime in the middle 1950s when it went out. I'm sure there's a copy of it around somewhere in the office in Atlantic City."

Baffled at the notion, Marks states that it is inconceivable that there could have been a Rule Seven on the books, at least from 1936 on, that escaped his knowledge. Had there been such statutory racial exclusion, he maintains, the IRS would have denied *Miss America* its tax-exempt, nonprofit status. Of course, whether or not there ever was a Rule Seven becomes academic, however, because it was Miss Slaughter's firm understanding that there was a Rule Seven, and Miss Slaughter ran the *Miss America* Pageant.

Since the first two black winners in 1959, others have also won at that first local level, but not until Cheryl Brown in 1970 did a black girl succeed at State. Black girls found earlier recognition in other pageants. The first black state queen in any recognized previously all-white pageant was Corrine Huff, Miss Ohio 1960, in the Miss USA Pageant of Miss Universe. She was the same young lady who achieved more lasting fame for being frequently seen with Congressman Adam Clayton Powell. Miss Teen-Age America had a black finalist in 1967, and again in 1970, and in 1968 on an NBC presentation that was called National College Queen Pageant, Valerie Dickinson, from San José State, became the first black girl ever to win a predominantly white pageant. She was the only one of the fifty girls who was black.

By then, still no black girl had even made it to Atlantic City, and pressure was growing on the Pageant. There was a threat in 1967 that the local blacks would use the show as a vehicle with which to demonstrate in complaint about the policies of the town's police. Shortly thereafter, Roy Wilkins of the NAACP called *Miss America*, simply, "lily white." At a judicious interval following, the Pageant announced that a local black Episcopalian clergyman had been appointed to the board of directors, and the first two black hostessess were also named. The next year, 1969, Dr. Zelma George, a sociologist, became the first black judge. At that time Marks declared, "We are now integrated in every aspect of the Pageant except that we've never had a contestant here. Look, I would love to have a colored girl here to take the heat off this thing, but we won't fix anything, so we just have to wait."

While the national headquarters protests that it is maligned unfairly, and Atlantic City may indeed be pretty clean, there remain gaping abuses of omission at the lower levels. *Miss America* is separated from its locals by the State Pageants, which it franchises. There is a clause in the contracts that the State Pageants must sign which specifies that there must be no discrimination—except against men; that had to be stipulated after a male in Texas tried to enter Miss Universe. The clause is without teeth, though, so long as tacit discrimination is practiced at the local level, while neither the states nor Atlantic City have either the apparatus or the inclination to police the locals.

The issue is complicated by the fact that racial discrimination *per se* is not a large factor. In few places, if any, are Jaycees or other local Pageant officials sitting around plotting how to "keep the niggers out"; for one thing, they don't have to. The local pageants are segregated most by geographical and class patterns, which, while they happen to exclude blacks, also tend to bar almost all non-middle-class WASPS. Miss America merely deals in the same processes that also keep blacks, and other minorities in some instances, from the best schools, houses, jobs, and suburbs. In that way it reflects the land.

Miss America follows the path of the middle class. As it retreats from the center cities, the Pageant moves with it, removing itself in the process from the cores of black population. In smaller towns, where the blacks remain as technically a part of the local Pageant constituency, there is too often a laxness in recruiting them. The Jaycees, standard-bearers of the middle-class ethic, seldom are inspired to move outside their own neat communities and schools in search of *Miss America* candidates. It is coordinate too that almost everywhere pageants are run on an invitational basis, and then a girl is invited only to apply, not to enter. Gratuitously, local Pageant officials are quick to protest, "Why, we'd love to have some colored girls in our Pageant, but none ever applies," a response that is insensitive.

The provincial small-town and suburban demography is so hardened that it would be difficult for Atlantic City to break down the system. The Pageant does have two full-time field directors, who travel extensively at the middle level, working with state associations, but there is no one fulfilling a troubleshooter role at the local level, and *Miss America*, which lost $19,000 in 1970, must plead poverty to any new extension of its services. Probably, the best hope for broader racial representation in the precincts lies with the national Jaycee organization. If it seriously encouraged its member chapters to work for more integration in pageants, progress would surely be achieved.

Getting *Miss America* back into the cities looms as a much taller order, since the subject of women tends to bring out the more sensitive, explosive sides of race. Nobody ever says, Would you want your brother to marry one? It seems that Americans will cross racial lines to vote for politicians, root for athletes, laugh at comedians, even pay for prostitutes faster than they will vote for beauty queens. Miss Subways in New York fools no one by tiptoeing around this panoramic prejudice by always having black and white candidates—and two winners. This is perhaps one of the more graphic admissions that the Kerner Commission was right in perceiving two separate societies in the one country.

Certainly this is true in the beauty bailiwick. Although no one at the brewery will admit it publicly, there is no real dispute that Miss Rheingold had to be jettisoned because her pretty WASP face was driving all ethnics to other brands. At the time the Miss Rheingold election was dropped in 1964,* it was still easily the second largest vote in America, and brought the beer untold amounts of free publicity, but at a prohibitive ethnic cost. Very few products identify themselves any longer with a symbolic pretty girl, except in those cases where she is obviously a stereotyped foreigner—Chiquita Banana, the Scandanavian take-it-off Noxzema girl, and a variety of kilted Scottish lassies who stand for thrift, not sex. The Dodge Girl was a major exception to the rule, but then she was succeeded by the Southern Sheriff, a transparent white buffoon, so equal time was achieved. Unless a product is being directed at a nearly all-male audience, using a beauty queen can be dynamite. Long before Rheingold became aware of any racial implications, it selected the candidates for their wholesome qualities more than their sensual ones. Women will not buy beer or anything else from sex pots.

Nevertheless, while the urban beauty climate is a sticky one, *Miss America*'s claims of tolerance are challenged by the fact that the only place in the United States not represented in the Pageant happens also to be the only place with a black majority. This, of course, is the capital city of Washington, which gave the Pageant its first winner, another in 1944, and a succession of topflight contenders until it was knocked out of *Miss America* after 1963. Indeed, the last Miss Washington finished as first runner-up that year.

Of course, this girl and the eight Miss Washingtons preceding her all came from outside the city limits, from either the Virginia or Maryland suburbs. The last native Miss Washington served in 1954. Seizing on this fact, *Miss America* approached

* See Appendix 13, p. 311.

the District Pageant sponsor, radio station WWDC, and informed it that it must henceforth draw its contestants only from within the city limits. WWDC had a much better record with Miss Washington than did either Miss Maryland or Miss Virginia at Atlantic City, and the station also had much of its listening audience in the suburbs, so when the edict was issued it dropped the District Pageant. Since that time, well over half the State Pageant sponsors have dropped off and been replaced by new control organizations, while only Washington remains disenfranchised. The fact hardly attests to the best of *Miss America*'s avowed racial intentions.

The best chance for more substantial black participation in the Pageant lies apart from both the suburbs—where there are no blacks—and the cities—where there are no pageants—but on college campuses, where *de facto* patterns of segregation and tradition are not ingrained. Marks has striven to enfranchise predominantly black colleges as one way of virtually assuring black representation at the state level. The selection of a black Miss Iowa was something of a fluke. In the future, black queens will almost surely come from those more urban states with a higher percentage of black population. Moreover, it should be no surprise if sometime in the 1970s—very possibly in the next two or three years—Miss America turns out to be black.

Miss America's tardiness in courting black contestants has meant that the Pageant will continue to lose a number of potential contenders to the welter of Miss Black America pageants that have sprung up, in Atlantic City, in Madison Square Garden, and elsewhere. There was a national Miss Sepia contest run in Chicago as early as 1944, but the new wave of segregated black pageants has been produced strictly out of protest against *Miss America*. The sardonic turnabout, though, is that the black pageants imitate, exactly as they oppose. This is especially surprising at a time when black people are striving to find their own indigenous variations of expression, and leads—more than anything else—to the conclusion that though beauty pageants in their present form may be mocked, scorned, ridiculed, derided, and dismissed as cornball and antique, they are resilient and institutional, and nobody seems to be able to improve on them.

Writing before Miss Black America in the *Manhattan Tribune,* Clayton Riley wrestles with this conflict:

> A Pageant? Yeah baby, just that. One of those echoes of the dying ethic, a ghost voice—Bert Parks crying from some technicolor cemetery, bathing-suit competition, gowns, talent exploration. All that same Atlantic City bullshit revisited in the company of Afro princesses. . . .

The racist charge was tied in with a host of others by the Women's Liberationists when they began to attack *Miss America* in earnest in 1968. Robin Morgan, a former child actress, now a radical poet who was instrumental in the Atlantic City guerrilla campaigns, has best summarized the Women's Lib views on the Pageant. "It has always been a lily-white racist contest. The winner tours Vietnam entertaining the troops as a murder mascot. The whole gimmick is one commercial shell game to sell the sponsors' products. Where else could one find such a perfect combination of American values? Racism, militarism, and capitalism—all packaged in one 'ideal' symbol: *a woman.*"

Various other elements of the movement have, at different times, also charged that Miss America is a sex object standing for what men want their women to be, "wholesome, inoffensive, bland, and apolitical." Also, besides finding her a "wind-up commercial" and war cheerleader, they charge her with standing for age discrimination as well as racial prejudice, and she "perpetuates the American myth of competitive spirit, of having to get ahead in order to have any worth." Women's Liberationists claim, as well, that Miss America, as a symbol of "virginal prettiness," buttresses the sexual double standard and undercuts the female goal of equal orgasm for all. Women's Lib protesters regret that the contestants are "enslaved" and always make the point that they are in sympathy with these girls themselves and are acting only in opposition to the pageants and the males that run them.

The Liberationists have laid so many evils at the Pageant's door, that it becomes perfectly obvious that they are only flailing, hoping to land a lucky punch. While the Pageant makes no real effort to try to understand its antagonists, the feminists fail even more in comprehending their foe. "So far as I can see," Marks says, "the feminists are saying we are economically exploiting female flesh. They never say that we are exploiting it *vis-à-vis* anything—just that we are exploiting it. They make good copy, I know, and I firmly believe that by creating so much attention they have done us some good by comparison." Surely this is true. The innocence, grace, fluff—in fact, all that is best about the Pageant—must glimmer all the more in the face of such strident malarkey. Women's Liberationists, and other critics, too often forget that much of the content of *Miss America is* escapism. That quality appears even larger in times such as these, which are depressing and hateful. To point a finger at *Miss America* and accuse it of being escapist or frivolous is to support it, not to sabotage it. It is like bringing Tinker Bell back to life by acknowledging the existence of the species.

By the same token, Women's Lib was more concerned with the coverage of its attacks than with the substance of them, and it profited handsomely. The feminists produced the only original news to emanate from Atlantic City during Pageant week since the bland TV era began. The first, and major, confrontation came in 1968, the year Judi Ford was named Miss America. Approximately one hundred women picketed Convention Hall. Beyond that, there is no consensus as to what happened, since both sides were so emotional that a kind of Boardwalk *Rashomon* was played out. The opinions are much more revealing than the truth, anyway, because what actually happened is inconsequential. The only real concern was attention, and the Libs slaughtered the Pageant at this game. Not only did they also make network TV, but in a paper like *The New York Times*, the protesters received a story that was a full ten times as long as the one on Judi Ford's victory. To the Women's Liberation Movement, the skirmish at Convention Hall is roughly analogous to the Boston Tea Party.

The disputed points involve even the most basic issues. The Libs claim that they knew they would be carefully scrutinized by critics who would be quick to characterize them as jealous harpies, envious of the attention paid the pretty beauties. Therefore, the protesters say they made the point of dressing up nicely in skirts. Says one, "I'm speaking objectively now. I've been in a lot of demonstrations and seen a lot of other gatherings, and I honestly believe that that time we had the best-looking large group of women that I've ever seen." In contrast, Pageant people use these words to describe the girls, "ugly, hideous, the worst-looking women you ever saw in your life, witches, dirty, vulgar, ratty, vile, they actually smelled they were so dirty, you can't believe women anywhere could dress like that, sad, frightful creatures" and so on.

Pageant defenders always refer to these women as "bra burners" and speak increasingly of 1968 as a conflagration along the lines of the Great Fire of London. The feminists say that they only wanted to make a symbolic pyre of one brassiere, and that instead all they did was toss various undergarments, magazines, and articles of make-up into a "freedom trashcan" on the Boardwalk. *Miss America* advocates aver that they were rocked by the dirty and abusive language that the pickets shouted, and it is documented that the girls displayed placards with such sentiments as "MISS AMERICA SELLS IT" and "THE LIVING BRA—THE DEAD SOLDIER." The Women's Liberationists maintain that they shouted no obscenities, and that even if they had, bystanders could have not heard them because they were set too far away behind police barricades. One picket says that the barricades kept her so distant from the Boardwalk crowds that she was trying to reach that at last she gave up the task as futile and ducked away into a women's public rest room, where she handed out leaflets.

The protesters claim that it was the crowds that cursed them, that the police were obviously in total sympathy with the Pageant, and that they made no effort to apprehend "a wild Texan" who tried to run an elderly protester down in his mechanized rolling chair. A newspaper reporter sympathetic to *Miss America* declares that he was stoned by the Women's Liberationists and felt "seriously in danger."

Such ballyhooed controversy was sufficient to encourage the protesters to return the next year, 1969, but by then Atlantic City was prepared for the assault. The police, for instance, called up the Women's Lib center in New York, and, on the pretext of issuing parking permits, inquired as to the name of the charter-bus company that would transport the pickets. By a wild coincidence, the bus company called up the girls two hours later and informed them that all of a sudden all its buses had broken down at once. This cut into the number of pickets going to Atlantic City, and those who reached the Boardwalk found that Marks, wisecracking and cagey, had obtained an injunction that left the intruders nearly powerless. Other details Police Chief Mario Floriani handled in his own fashion. According to Lindsy Van Gelder, a Women's Liberationist and a reporter on the New York *Post,* the girls were threatened with arrest for carrying placards that featured *Playboy* nippled fold-outs that had been purchased at Atlantic City newsstands. Mrs. Van Gelder says Chief Floriani told reporters, "I don't give a damn about First Amendment rights. In Atlantic City, a poster that I think is obscene is obscene, and I'll bust the person carrying it."

Atlantic City would have won it all with a quick TKO, but the feminists were worthy scufflers and had one more trick up their sleeves. They permitted the word to leak out that one of their persuasion had infiltrated the Pageant, and would, at the proper moment, reveal herself (by holding a flaming bra aloft?), commandeer the microphone from Bert Parks ("I'll grab her by the throat and keep singing," he said with a smile), and then denounce *Miss America* and all it stood for from that nationwide platform. In every hotel in Atlantic City disbelieving chaperones and hostesses eyed their charges carefully. Could it be? Was their girl the Judas among the fifty?

Was there, in fact, really a spy in the crowd?

Possibly, although not likely. Surely such a girl would have revealed herself by now, long after the event had passed, and she had used up her scholarship and was beyond any recrimination. When the girl did not come forward at the time, Women's Lib released the story that the girl had gotten cold feet when she learned that she might be charged with conspiracy. The protesters declared that the unfrocked spy had been "harassed" by Pageant officials until she agreed to hold her tongue.

Marks swears that part of the tale is ridiculous, which it surely is, but neither he nor anyone else can be absolutely sure that there never was an infiltrator. Even at the time the Pageant had to hedge its bets a little, just as it might do in the event of a bomb threat, and so the rumors were fanned some more. Some

State Pageant officials are still mad that Marks did not squash the story altogether. Since that time, the story that a Woman's Liberationist infiltrated the Pageant has been picked up and appeared in print as a matter-of-fact truth.

Ironically, the credibility of the tale was strengthened by another Pageant fiction. It has long been part of the lore that if any contestant is caught breaking a rule of conduct, she is disqualified without being informed of the fact. She just proceeds on her way, while only high Pageant officials and the judges know that, in fact, she simply does not exist any longer. The truth is that this is a patent falsehood, but the story retains a wide currency because it is indeed true that since 1935 no contestant has been publicly disqualified. What is also true is that since that time no contestant (out of a total of 1784) has ever been guilty enough of misconduct to be expelled. Indeed, there have been only a handful of indiscretions that merited so much as a warning. Nonetheless, the lie that girls were rubbed out in secret encouraged the easy belief in another, more complicated, lie—that there was an infiltrator from Women's Lib, that she was smoked out and threatened with conspiracy charges, which scared her, so she agreed to be quietly eliminated from the competition but to participate till the bitter end.

Another scenario produced even more intrigue: the girl was a double agent. According to this account, she had first entered a local Pageant with the idea in mind to write an exposé of the inside pageant world, *à la* Gloria Steinem in the Bunny Club. The pretty muckraker triumphed at the local level, though, and, still collecting notes, moved on to the State Pageant. At about this point, though, she began to get religion, and to discover what an uplifting experience a Pageant really was. Also, she was suddenly just one step away from being Miss America and putting $40,000 after taxes in the bank. She confessed to Atlantic City and admitted that by now she had also hatched a plot with Women's Lib to charge the microphone. The Pageant told her to continue to lead the movement into thinking that she remained game for the scheme, so that it would be diverted from any other mischief.

Having been dragged into a war of escalating fantasies, the Women's Liberation Movement decided to disengage itself from the conflict before the 1970 Pageant. The women had received so much serious attention that, practically speaking, they did not need *Miss America* any more. For one thing, the Lib was beginning to get the uncomfortable feeling that it was becoming part of the show, halfway between the parade and the evening-gown competition. For another, the presence of a black girl in the Pageant removed one major plank from its platform. Also, the times were suddenly not quite so ripe for conspicuous protest. In 1968, the Pageant fell only two weeks after the Democratic Convention in Chicago; in 1969, it took place when momentum was just beginning to be rolled up for the October 15 Moratorium.

Suddenly, for the 1970 proceedings, it was as if none of this had ever happened. Only a lonely young couple drove over from Philadelphia to picket. Passers-by viewed them idly till at last they just got in the car and went back home. Miss Slaughter had returned from retirement on a visit to Atlantic City, and was called on to greet the contestants. She talked at length about the values of the Pageant, how important it could be to a girl, how lucky she was to win a scholarship, and on in that homely vein, concluding, "But remember, all of you, that the most important thing in your lives will be your marriage, and the main test, as a woman, will be how much of a success you make of yourself with your husband and your family." There was no visible demur on the part of the contestants to this dated sentiment.

The majority of them now do profess agreement with most of the concrete goals of Women's Lib—though generally rejecting many of the more studied demands and the methods advocated to achieve them. Pam Eldred, the quiet little Miss America 1970, always maintained that whenever she had the opportunity to sit down and talk, woman-to-woman, with her tormentors, she was invariably able at least to provide some new degree of understanding of the Pageant. And, she admitted, such discussions helped make her understand better the reasons why other women could feel so strongly opposed to *Miss America.*

The main point is, rather, that *Miss America* is forever undeserving of most of the agitation that surrounds it. It is not nearly so grave or meaningful as advocates on either side make it out to be. The essence is diversion; it has nothing much at all to do with womanhood, with morality, with big business, with modesty, with Vietnam, or most of the other things that it has been associated with, come hell or high water. Nor is there any real evidence that a substantial number of the participants become markedly changed by the experience, one way or the other. Even excessive amounts of poise will not help you find happiness, strength, or God.

Miss America is a harmless exercise that keeps a lot of people busy and out of trouble. It is a bunch of pretty girls parading around. If the banners were taken from them or too many clothes forced on them, it probably would not work. It is that fine a line. Indeed, if *Miss America* were not so basic, if any of the controversies that it is obliged to suffer were genuine, it would have succumbed long ago.

The extremes, when expressed with consideration and reason by even the most involved advocates, do not appear to range so far. Lindsy Van Gelder, the reporter from the New York *Post,* is a young wife and mother, a Women's Liberationist who picketed the Pageant. She is from the Midwest and graduated from a Big Ten school. Blond, sharp, and pretty, she won a fraternity beauty contest once. Debbie May, a few years younger than Lindsy, is also from the Midwest and a Big Ten school. She too is blond, sharp, and pretty, and of course she has won a lot of beauty contests. She was also voted as Miss Congeniality at Atlantic City in 1970.

Says Mrs. Van Gelder, "The gist of it is, that so long as you have beauty pageants, the opinion is reinforced that women are judged, not on the basis of how valuable they might be to society, but by how well their looks please men. A beauty pageant supports the assumption that men have a right to check out women—and whether there are women judges or not is incidental. Can you imagine what it feels like to walk down any street, where men, any men, think they have the right to look you over, to comment, to whistle, even to say something obscene? Well, a beauty pageant is only that, on a larger scale. It supports that attitude of women. Don't you see, it dignifies, it legitimizes that kind of behavior? That is why, although I have nothing against the girls who enter, and I am sure a lot of them get a lot out of it, I must be against beauty pageants."

Miss May says, "What is the madness that drives a woman to

participate in this? A beauty pageant, it's just a different world, but who's to say what's real? I believe that this week is the antithesis of all that Women's Lib stands for, and I think that their effort is futile. For as long as a woman is the center of the home, there will be no substantial changes in the ways that men and women treat each other, and in the roles they must play. I wouldn't want it any other way. If I'm brainwashed, well, all right, I'm brainwashed, and I like it. I enjoy being flattered and looked at, and, perhaps, told that I am pretty. And that's what this week is, and that is what I am. Not all of me, of course, not all. But I enjoy being a woman."

★ 15 ★

Hostesses, Chaperones, and Traveling Companions

Nothing seems to bemuse the general public so much about *Miss America* as the lengths to which the Pageant goes to protect its contestants in Atlantic City from everything and everybody—most particularly, it seems, from the girls themselves. There are occasions when the contestants are not permitted to venture alone to the ladies' room. Unless the conversation is completely monitored, a girl cannot speak to any man for the whole week, even her father. She must wear rigorously modest attire, is forbidden to smoke or drink, and even to frequent places where others may obtain alcohol. She must sleep in the same room with a chaperone from her own state, and, during waking hours, must always be shadowed by a local matron who is known as a hostess. Under these circumstances, it is hard enough for the most determined girl even to chance upon indiscreet thoughts, much less try to *do* anything errant.

Consider this conversation from the 1969 Pageant:

CONTESTANT (to reporter): I'm sorry I'm sweating so much. I just finished practicing my dance.
HOSTESS: Sweat is not a proper word.
CONTESTANT: I'm sorry I'm perspiring.
HOSTESS: Miss Americas do not perspire.

To be fair, however, the system lends itself to a mocking criticism, which is often trite and overdone. Since an efficient and intelligent woman, Mrs. Mildred Brick, head of the Hostess Committee, invested the proceedings with some common sense a couple of years ago, the whole matter of custody at Atlantic City has become smooth and nearly reasonable. Mrs. Brick has introduced the revolutionary assumption that the girls deserve the Pageant's trust and confidence.

Theretofore, the Pageant code was based on the conclusion that *Miss America* contestants were incapable by themselves of good taste, good behavior, and good judgment. Inherent in this philosophy (and some of it still clings) is the Pageant's paranoia that everyone is conspiring to do it in. Applying this to the girls produced the conviction that if they were left to their own devices they would immediately do their damnedest to bring shame on the Pageant. Hence all the defensive absurdities: cover-up bathing suits, which were nearly impossible to buy; skirt-length dictums which, as late as 1969, required that all reach to within two inches of the knee; the censored interviews with the press; prohibitions on seeing men or attending the ball after the Saturday night coronation.

Making concessions only to the girls' maturity and to everyday life, most of these punctilios have been modified, or burned to a crisp in their own unctuousness. Only a few vestiges of the preachy past remain to reveal that the Pageant still possesses some delusions that the world goes on plotting against it. It is worth speculating, for instance, on why a contestant cannot talk alone, even in the middle of the Convention Hall stage at high noon, with her father.

The reason for this edict is explained in the *Contestant's Guide* under the section entitled "We Love Your Parents—But!" To wit: "They [fathers] are generally too young and too handsome to be considered by the general public as anything but a 'gentleman friend.' " Q.E.D., the public firmly believes that gentlemen friends are a malignancy; at least, their existence is not to be acknowledged. In fact, of course, the general public has nothing at all against gentlemen friends or fathers-looking-like-gentlemen-friends or even gentlemen-friends-looking-like-fathers. Only the Pageant is in opposition to gentlemen friends. In 1952,

Neva Jane Langley's young beau burst on stage in a natural display of affection and exuberance following her victory. He even managed to reach her and give her a kiss, whereupon he was led away by a convoy of moral defenders, and no one has dared try that again.

Sadly, the Pageant is still so insecure that it looks over its shoulder and erects all its major moral defenses against innuendo. Mrs. Brick has relaxed the censorship rules on press interviews—"If we say that we have intelligent young women, then we should let them express opinions," she says—but hostesses are still required to audit these conversations. The regulation is not meant to muzzle journalists, but the presence of the eavesdropper—even if most of them are innocuous and good sports—inhibits a conversation and destroys rapport. Thus, it is one more way that the Pageant manages to make its contestants and Miss America herself stale and dull.

A reporter sits with Miss California 1970, Karin Kascher, a lovely blond violinist. She is fresh, frank, and fun, totally at ease because she has just graduated from high school and understands that therefore she really has no chance to win. The hostess sitting with her has nothing to fear from Karin. She is so devoted to her violin that she has not had the time for the last two years to go out with boys. She carries no giddy teen-age tokens with her; instead, in her purse she keeps William Faulkner's Nobel Prize acceptance speech, with his "universal truths . . .—love and honor and pity and pride and compassion and sacrifice." Karin is also 37–21–36, which, by the by, is as good a subject as any to begin the interview with. It goes from there, yet is always restrained. No reporter can work at depth in his craft so long as the silent woman is also there to inhibit the discussion. He always gets two responses, the one from Miss California, and the other, which it is almost possible to hear, the hostess thinking to herself.

KARIN: Yes, that's funny about the measurements.
REPORTER: Funny?
HOSTESS (thinking): *Why did he bring that up? And first. Why not the violin? Or her high-school grades? Is this a writer or some kind of sex maniac?*

KARIN: I never knew what they were until they took them. There's really no need to know them. You have to know your clothes' sizes, of course, but what good are measurements?

HOSTESS (thinking): *You better not read any double-entendre into that, buddy. Don't take that literally.*

KARIN: I'm not even sure exactly quite how they measure.

HOSTESS (thinking): *Oh my God, he's not going to volunteer to show her. He better not.*

KARIN: I've changed a little anyway. I've lost an inch off the top and gained one around the middle.

REPORTER: Well, no one will know.

KARIN: I've got a funny figure anyway.

REPORTER: It looks just fine to me.

HOSTESS (thinking): *The way you're looking, I'll say.*

KARIN: No, from playing the violin so much, my right arm is larger than my left.

REPORTER: That's like a baseball pitcher. He'll develop the same sort of lopsided muscles.

KARIN: That's what it is. I'm really too muscular in my right arm. Anyone can tell.

REPORTER: Really?

KARIN: Sure, want to see?

HOSTESS (thinking): *Wha-?* (out loud) Wha-?

KARIN (starting to take off the jacket to her suit): It's hot in here anyway.

HOSTESS (thinking): *My God, what does this look like? Is anybody looking? She's taking off her clothes, I mean her coat, but it will look like she's taking off her clothes, what will people say?*

REPORTER: Here, let me help you.

HOSTESS (thinking): *Is there a rule to cover this?*

KARIN: Thank you.

HOSTESS (thinking): *Don't worry, I'm watching, buster. Don't you touch anything but that jacket. No funny stuff.*

KARIN (turning): See? Can you see the difference?

HOSTESS (thinking): *No, no, don't do that. From any distance, who's going to think that this madman is looking at your arms? I'll tell Mrs. Brick, she took off her coat to let him look at her arms. Her arms, Mrs. Brick, her arms. I swear, he was only looking at her arms where she plays the violin. Of course no one will believe that. They'll laugh me right out of the hostesses.*

KARIN (flexing, with decorum): See, look at that muscle.

HOSTESS (thinking): *Put that arm down. Miss America does not flex her muscles.*

KARIN: That's the worst thing about the violin.

HOSTESS (thinking): *I'm glad we're back to the violin.*

KARIN: But I don't care, really. I'm a performer. I'm just in this because of the scholarship and because I was fortunate to have the physical attributes.

HOSTESS (out loud): I think it's time we went back to the table and joined the other ladies.

KARIN: Good. I want to show you something else.

HOSTESS (thinking): *Wha-?* (out loud) Wha-?

KARIN: I really want you to see that speech of Faulkner's. It's a magnificent thing.

The system is so constructed that, even when it is modified, the hostesses must come off as boogeymen. And it makes villains, too, out of otherwise honorable reporters. The trouble is, as long as a hostess stands by, even as a massive deterrent that is most unlikely to be unleashed, she is a very real symbol of censorship. Most journalists will take it, at least, as a challenge. The presence of the hostess slants the interview, encouraging hard-line questions, as the reporter strives to take the girl and the censor to the limits. It is a game. Members of the press always boast about "what I got out of" Miss So-and-So. *Miss America* requires hostesses to be present at interviews for the protection of the girls because it is sure that writers are disposed to be mean to beauty contestants. In fact, the Pageant, in supplying the monitors, throws down the gauntlet, makes the press mad, and brings down on itself the very thing it wants to avoid.

The system so encourages the pursuit of controversy that it distorts all coverage. Soon, the reporters lose perspective. A wire-service man, writing for national distribution, confronts some of his colleagues. "What do you think I just got Miss New York to say?" he asks. He is breathless with excitement. "Something really controversial." What can it be: genocide for New Jerseyans? Free love during Pageant week?

The wire-service man, in his most confidential tones, at last lets on: "I got Miss New York to say that she is in favor of the birth-control pill." The other reporters nod, roll their eyes, and congratulate the man on uncovering this impressive news flash. Were the wire-service man to reflect for just a few seconds he would be the first to admit that he could walk out onto the Boardwalk, and the first twenty-five women he stopped would express support of the pill. He could get the first twenty-five students he approached at Chelsea Junior High to back birth-control pills. Probably, he could get the first twenty-five parishioners coming out of Our Lady Star of the Sea Church to favor use of the pill. Yet, because the reporter got one beauty contestant to make this declaration despite the looming presence of her hostess, he immediately deceives himself into thinking that he has stop-press news.

The night shift belongs to the chaperones, who are required to sleep in the same room as their charges. The Pageant splits the hopefuls into seventeen hotels, but each girl and her chaperone have a comparable-size double. There are no suites, and parents must be sequestered on a separate floor. Chaperones are of various types. Some are the officious self-styled trainers who intrude everywhere. "Those are the only ones who have ever bothered me," Bert Parks says. "And we have a way of diplomatically handling them; they're out of there before their feet hit the ground again." Others, from small, distant states, come to Atlantic City not only as chaperones, but as the State Pageant directors and newspaper-radio correspondents. Many of the chaperones return year after year. Others are Jaycee State Pageant directors' wives; a few are former contestants themselves. Most are close to their queens.

Mrs. Brick's hostesses endure a more formal responsibility. They are more accurately described as marshals than as hostesses. There are twenty-five senior hostesses, each of whom escorts two state contestants. Twenty-five assistant hostesses serve as back-up accompanists and in other supportive capacities. The hostesses, who have tended to be younger in recent years, have made more of an effort to be friendly to the girls. On Sunday night, they throw what is known as a Mix-'n'-Mingle party for the contestants, and another on Saturday for the forty losers upstairs in Convention Hall. Originally, the hostesses conceived the idea for Miss Congeniality, but now the girls vote for that title among themselves. The assistant hostesses who are assigned to the dressing room now vote a "Neat as a Pin" honor for their Miss Tidy, and the opinions of the hostesses are taken into consideration later in the year when the Pageant selects the Vietnam troupe. That has become a sort of high-level consolation prize. Pageant regulars say things like, "I don't think she'll make ten, but I can see her in Vietnam." Or, in code, just "Vietnam," which means the same thing.

Hostesses often exceed their minimum limits of responsibility, ministering to buttons, zippers, hair, and other important features at crucial moments. There was a time when artificial improvements were considered unfair, and hostesses were on their marks to find and confiscate falsies. Desperate contestants who had come to depend on such novelties were not above stuffing their fronts with Kleenex. Now, since padding is as acceptable as lipstick, the marshals do not have to police the dressing room any more, and can even assist the girls in their small deceits. Hostesses have been known, literally, to clap a hand on a contestant's mouth if she started to say something that the lady considered out of sorts. The award for exceptional assistance, on the other hand, must be presented to the hostess assigned to Miss Florida 1968. When she made the finals, Miss Florida discovered that she would not have enough time between her evening gown presentation and her talent performance to improve sufficiently a wad of Dubbl-Bubble gum, which she employed in her flapper routine. Her marshal agreed to provide the necessary mastication to "get it into bubble condition for me." Miss Florida popped the well-chewed blob into her mouth just before she went on stage. Such an exemplary performance is the kind that wins for hostesses the designation of "HONORARY MASCOT" from a para-official group that calls itself "The Confederate Press Association."

The care, support, and, above all, the protection of Miss America candidates have always been part of the Pageant. In 1921, the very first year of the operation, contestants and their chaperones were welcomed with a very spiffy, formal party at the Almac Hotel by Harry Latz, the head of the bathers' revue. The mayor, his wife, and many prominent social and political figures were in attendance—another fact which gives lie to the widespread notion that early Pageants were tawdry Bacchanalias. Chaperones were absolutely required from the first, although there was some laxity in the rules, and occasionally chaperones turned out to be contemporary companions more than steely-eyed guardians. Most, though, were distinguished doyennes who took the responsibility seriously. Margaret Gorman, for instance, was chaperoned by Mrs. Basil Manley, who was no less than the president of the Arts Club of Washington. Moreover, within the next two years a Court of Honor of local matrons was formed, which served the same broad purposes as the modern hostess committee, which was itself another of Miss Slaughter's innovations.

She moved to establish it in 1937 when the Federated Women's Clubs of New Jersey were on the warpath again, charging, with more ardor than usual, that *Miss America* was a prime agent of the devil. Lenora figured she had to fight fire and brimstone with fire and brimstone, so she went out to get some all-star moralists on her own first team.

Atlantic City was then run by Quakers, including Mayor Charles D. White, who had only recently convened a town meeting for the express purpose of discussing the future of *Miss America* in Atlantic City, which is to say whether it had any future. Essentially, Lenora got a hung jury, and she also got, not long after, her first Quaker board member—J. Haines Lippincott of the Chalfonte-Haddon Hall Hotels. This was a step up in class and Lenora pressed her advantage. "My training had always been working with civic leaders and proper people," she says, "and I realized that the best way to protect the Pageant was to protect the girls from scandal, and the best way to do that was to get the best people in town on my side."

She told Lippincott that she wanted Mrs. Charles D. White, the Mayor's wife herself, to head up her proposed new hostess committee. "She was the Quakerest of Quakers," Lenora says. "Why, one time I went to see her, I was so scared I took off all my nail polish and lipstick." Lippincott agreed to approach Mrs. White on behalf of the Pageant. He called her up and said, "Margaret, I would like to have a word with thee about *Miss America.*"

She accepted the position immediately, with the stipulation that she must have full, independent control of the committee. Lenora granted that readily; in fact, it was a bounty for the Pageant. That September, when it appeared that Bette Cooper had run away with Lou Off, the Pageant escaped a lot of heat in town because nobody wanted to take on Mrs. White in the bargain. After all, it was her new escort rules that had put Bette and Lou together all the time in the first place. That was corrected the next year; never again were male escorts permitted off stage. Girls were also banned from night clubs in 1938 and placed under a one a.m. curfew. From there, all the other modern strictures evolved. "My Quaker lady laid down the rules that still exist," Lenora says proudly. "Oh, there've been changes, of course, but only like the Constitution of the United States, where changes are not just changes, but very careful amendments."

Unfortunately, until Mrs. Brick came to power in 1969, the hostess-committee personnel turned over even more tortuously than the rules. "To serve on that committee was *the* social attainment in Atlantic City," Miss Slaughter says, and while this quality originally scented the Pageant with a respectability it desired, the committee eventually became top-heavy with age and family. To join, a newcomer had to be tapped by the chairwoman.

Today, membership is applied for. When there is a vacancy, the applicant's references are checked, and even her husband's character is examined. A stern, hour-long interview follows, and even then only one-third of those who applied are accepted.

Hostesses meet several afternoons each summer for special training sessions, and each receives a loose-leaf book that is two hundred pages long. The contestants and other official Pageant visitors are issued a sixty-page hostess guide that is nearly as thorough. It deals with everything from the ten "Precepts of Conduct" to "Good health is great—but not always with us!" which covers every possible contingency except how to adjust the Atlantic City hotel air conditioners, which are the main cause of afflictions. The Guide is separated into seven sections, each one on different-colored paper. In explanation, Mrs. Brick gives a meticulous accounting.

> Pink reminds me of pink carnations and mothers and so was selected for the Hostess Committee and State Chaperones. Green signifies stop-and-go lights and represents Rules and Press Rules and Regulations. Canary could only be chosen for our Contestant's Guide for it immediately reminded me of their talent. Arrival and Transportation are blue tones representing the open sky of travel. Housing is colored orange to remind us of food. State Pageant Executive Directors are certainly as sturdy and valuable as ivory. Salmon are noted for returning to the rivers of their origin and so salmon color was chosen for the End of a Wonderful Week and your going home.

For whatever reasons the Pageant always attended much more to its contestants in Atlantic City than to its Miss Americas on the road. To suggest that there was more temptation to fear in Atlantic City than abroad in the land would surely be an overstatement of the World's Playground's enticements. Nonetheless, long after Mrs. C. D. White's moral minions were deployed, on ruthless surveillance, during Pageant week, Miss Americas were left to roam the country and fend off turpitude on their own. For instance, on one of the rare occasions that Bette Cooper appeared as Miss America, she rode in the American Legion parade in New York, and that night, Lou Off chaperoned her by sleeping, like a watchdog, on the floor of the corridor outside her Manhattan hotel room.

Most girls who traveled in the earlier years were accompanied, at least occasionally, by their mothers. Marilyn Meseke, 1938, employed her grandmother as a chaperone. Lenora was the Pageant's first official traveling companion—the term preferred by the Pageant—when she attended Jean Bartel in 1943. However, that was no lasting arrangement. Mothers often handled the chore, and, in 1951, because *Miss America* accepted Yolande Betbeze as twenty-one, she was permitted to travel by herself. Occasionally, she took along teen-age friends younger than herself as chaperones.

Moreover, as late as 1953, Neva Jane Langley, nineteen years old, traveled for months by herself. One of the more beautiful Miss Americas, Neva believes, not surprisingly, that the queens today are "over-chaperoned." She had a ball on her own. She was an active queen too, with the rare distinction of representing one state, but being native to another. Neva was from Florida, but became Miss Georgia as a student at Wesleyan Conservatory of Music in Macon. Neva was proudly claimed by both states. "She may have made the most of all my girls," Lenora says. "She socked it to them all."

Bright and a sovereign spirit like the other girls of the pre-TV era, Neva was quite capable of handling herself. At one point, unescorted, she says she came across the U.S. on a train, being joined as she went along by the members of the Grantland Rice *Look* magazine all-America football team, as they headed to New York for photographic sessions. Neva says she scheduled appearances around Ann Arbor, Michigan, once so she could spend a week near her beau there, and on another occasion she lengthened her stay in the Washington area since she had become "quite serious" about a colonel that she had met there. Near the end of her reign, Atlantic City rushed a new chaperone out on the road to meet Neva. The idea was not that Miss Langley needed any assistance, but the reverse—that she could break in the chaperone.

Miss America has thereafter been guarded by an older women every step of the way. One Miss America is alleged to have gone briefly AWOL in Corpus Christi, Texas, but the modern queens have usually been too exhausted to try to escape their sentries. As late as 1958, the Miss America at that time, Marilyn Van Derbur, says she had as many as twenty-two appearances in a single day, and while the modern regulations strictly forbid such endurance contests, the constant movement is punishing enough.

Miss America can never appear for more than four hours in the course of a day, and she can make no more than four separate appearances. At least one major segment of any day—morning, afternoon, or evening—must be left free. The queen may have a press conference upon her arrival in a new town, but no spontaneous TV appearances are permitted. Lest such a show embarrass a sponsor, details of the program first must be approved by Atlantic City before permission is granted to let Miss

America appear. The sponsors and state and local pageants may book Miss America at the special rate of $250. Civic sponsors are charged $500, anyone else—and there are precious few takers—$1000.

There are no exceptions permitted to the rule that Miss America cannot attend any function where alcoholic beverages are consumed. The Pageant maintains that it is not concerned with placing temptation in the way of its queen. Rather, it is afraid only that where liquor is served there is a greater chance of drunks, and drunks have a tendency to annoy Miss Americas, if they possibly can. Peggy O'Neill Lloyd, who chaperoned eight straight Miss Americas nearly full time and then three more part time, was so intimidated by this canon that she never dared take a drink in the company of the queen.

In August, a month before the new queen is elected, the Pageant starts blocking out her schedule when the four sponsors are queried as to their requests. They get first crack at her. Maria Fletcher, Miss America 1962, lays it on the line. "The sooner you realize you're a product, the better." But Miss America is a well-paid product. She has no transportation or other expenses on the road, nor is she required to pay an agent's or booking fee to Atlantic City. The bonanza is neatly spread over two tax years, too. Besides a free wardrobe and the $10,000 scholarship, any Miss America makes upward of $50,000 in her year. The queen who recently took home the most was Vonda Kay Van Dyke, 1965, who cast her bread upon the waters. "She did so many Youth for Christ appearances," explains Doris Kelly, Miss America's schedule coordinator.

Vonda Kay took home about $65,000. In real terms, Evelyn Ay, 1954, was probably the biggest winner. She estimates that she earned about $60,000, but virtually all of that went into a little growth stock named IBM. The year after her reign she and her husband lived off $80 Navy paychecks and refused to touch any of her capital. By her own account, Rosemary LaPlanche, 1941, grossed far more than any other queen. She maintains that she earned $150,000 in the course of her year, but she had to pay her own expenses out of that, as well as additional large fees to Atlantic City and other agents. "Everybody was cutting in on it," she says. "I probably never even saw a third of it."

43. Mrs. Lenora Slaughter Frapart re-formed and ruled the Pageant, reigning from 1935 to 1967.

44. Albert A. Marks, Jr., a stockbroker, really runs the Pageant today—in his spare time. *Fabian Bachrach*

45. The Fair Daughter of Venus is unknown, but the gentleman is Harry L. Godshall, Sr., the last surviving member of the committee that created *Miss America* in 1921. This picture was probably taken the next year. Note the policeman in the background in bathing garb. In those days, everybody connected with the Pageant dressed in beach attire.

46, 47, 48. For many years, the accompanying Boardwalk parades drew more attention than the beauty pageant itself. These pictures certainly show why.

49. King Neptune's barge approaches the World's Playground, carrying His Oceanic Majesty and court.

50. The Mighty Monarch of the Sea crowns Miss America 1926, Norma Smallwood. The lady in the foreground is Princess America II, a token Indian who was often brought on as window dressing.

51. In its first year, 1921, the Beauty Maids walked right down the beach. This is Thelma Matthews who, as Miss Pittsburgh, had come furthest of the Civic Beauties.

52. Fifteen-year-old Miss Connecticut won the 1933 Pageant, a financial disaster that was disowned by Atlantic City that year. Still, the show attracted some celebrity judges, including cartoonist Peter Arno (upper right) and the married columnists Mark Hellinger and Gladys Glad (on the far right). The man at the microphone was, of course, Norman Brokenshire.

53. Contestants used to represent exotic regions and favor provocative or bizarre poses. Miss Eastern New York of 1940 shows how.

54. The host state's most famous queen was tap-dancing Janice Hansen, Miss New Jersey 1944. She and an old friend, Anthony (Little Augie) Pisano, were found shot full of too many holes one day in 1958.

55. Bess Myerson 1945 is the best-known Miss America, but she is a politician now and plays down the old association. She is also the only Jewish Miss America, the first scholarship winner, and the last and only New York queen.

56. The pageant moves to Convention Hall at last, in 1940. This opening scene struck observers as "a veritable fairyland."

57. Grace Kelly (with glasses) had a great influence on the Pageant in the 1950s, and in 1954 she served as a judge. Another judge was Pops Whiteman (seen back of Miss Kelly), who had played a larger role earlier that year in bringing *Miss America* to national TV.

58. Bert Parks with Pam Eldred 1970, his fifteenth Miss America. In just a few more years, Parks will announce a Miss America who wasn't even born when he first performed that task in 1955.

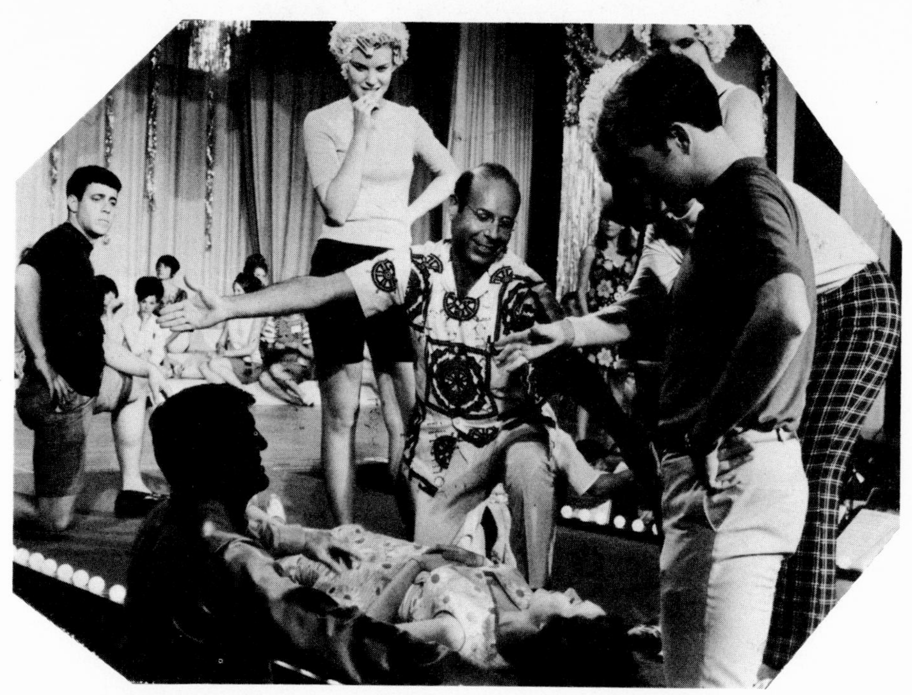

59. Bernie Wayne wrote "There She Is" and became a *Miss America* fixture for as long as Lenora stayed in power. Here, at a state pageant in the mid-1960s, he provides an Al Jolson imitation. The supine lady is Maria Fletcher, Miss America 1962. *Bernie Wayne*

60. The Miss America Trophy.

61. There He Is.

62. The five finalists in 1940, in their panel bathing suits. Frances Burke, Miss Philadelphia, was the winner but fifteen-year-old Rosemary LaPlanche, Miss California (to Miss Burke's right), finished second and came back next year and became Miss America 1941. After that, they changed the rules and prohibited return challenges; it was another thirty years, however, before they changed the panel bathing suits.

63. The final ten, in the traditional pose, in 1958. Mary Ann Mobley, fifth from right, proceeded to become an easy winner as Miss Mississippi, but Miss Oklahoma, the second runner-up (third from right), has gone on to more fame. She is Anita Bryant.

64. Marian McKnight 1957 is now Mrs. Gary Conway. He is an actor, famous for playing the title role in the movie *I Was a Teen-Age Frankenstein.*

65. Lee Meriwether, Miss America 1955, married Actor-Producer Frank Aletter, who is shown here with her and their two daughters. Miss Meriwether has enjoyed a modest success in Hollywood and has replaced Bess Myerson as the Pageant's grand mistress of ceremonies.

66. Rosemary LaPlanche, Miss America 1941, had the most extensive film career of any Miss America, playing everything from horror pictures to Betty Coed. Her husband is Harry Koplan, a TV producer. The Koplan's two children are more impressed with their mother's painting than her old beauty exploits.

67. Donna Axum 1964 is the only Miss America ever to have a husband who held elective office. Gus Mutscher is the Speaker of the House of Representatives of Texas, and the Mutschers live right in the State House in Austin.

68. Miss Elkin Valley, Nan Holt, made ten at the North Carolina State Pageant on the strength of her ballet. Whenever a pageant is televised—local, state, or national—TV takes over at the expense of the paying customers, but pageant fans never complain. *Fred Burgess photo*

69. The 1970 North Carolina contestants rehearse for the opening number, a tribute to communications. *Fred Burgess photo*

70. The classic moment of the beauty pageant: the smiling loser, the weeping winner. Andrea Gilliam, Miss Lexington, has just been announced as first runner-up, leaving Connie Lerner, Miss Asheville, as the new Miss North Carolina. *Fred Burgess photo*

71. Miss Wilson, North Carolina, 1970 and her court.

72. Miss Wilson 1946, Trudy Riley, went on to become Miss North Carolina.

73. Thirteen Miss Americas assembled at the Fiftieth Anniversary Pageant in 1970. Reading down the bannister: Mary Ann Mobley 1959, Jacque Mercer 1949, Marilyn Meseke 1938, Debbie Bryant 1966, Donna Axum 1964, and Pam Eldred 1970. In the middle at the top is Marian Bergeron 1933, and to her left is Lee Meriwether 1955. Then, reading down, is BeBe Shopp 1948, Vonda Kay Van Dyke 1965, Evelyn Ay 1954, Judi Ford 1969, and Ruth Malcolmson 1924.

She made $750 a week dancing, and also endorsed shoes, hats, and cigarettes, which was quite proper at the time.

There is so much to be made that the girls can accept the grueling pace. Lynda Lee Mead, 1960, had only nine days off in her entire year, aside from the traditional Christmas holiday of two weeks, and also, one cold morning in January in Chicago she received a phone call that her mother had died unexpectedly back in Mississippi. Lee Meriwether had to return quietly to Atlantic City for an eye operation. Donna Axum lost so much weight that she had to carry candy bars around and nibble on them. She and her traveling companion, Lucille Previti, were nearly trapped in a fire in the Roosevelt Hotel in Jacksonville on December 29, 1963, that took twenty-one lives. Miss Previti, overcome, was carried unconscious from the room after Donna had tried unsuccessfully to lug her still body to a window for air. When at last help came for Miss Previti, Donna followed, carrying their purses and the crown. Then they were ushered down ten flights of stairs to safety.

When Yolande Betbeze first came to New York, she complained about her accommodations—not to the Pageant, but to one of the sponsors at that time, American Motors—and ended up with the presidential suite at the Waldorf-Astoria. Lee Meriwether once asked the Shah of Iran to dance at a party, and he accepted, with evident delight. Evelyn Ay received a red rose at every hotel she visited, from her fiancé. Colleen Hutchins, thriving on four hours' sleep a night, never missed an appearance, but she was excluded from some profitable work, because Nash didn't want the public watching such a big girl struggling to get in and out of its little compact cars. Peggy O'Neill, traveling companion for twelve years, never had her queen miss a flight. Jane Jayroe had never ridden in an airplane before she went to Atlantic City, and then logged around 100,000 air miles, which is about the average tour.

In 1943, Jean Bartel, who scraped by on a Hershey bar diet, fell seriously ill of pneumonia in Nashville. A Christian Scientist, she would have no medication, and Lenora, her chaperone, grew frantic. Finally, she left the room and called a doctor, and prevailed on him to pose as a newspaperman. Jean, who is unbelievably conscientious, agreed to see the reporter from her sickbed, and the doctor made a cursory diagnosis as he feigned an interview. He prescribed penicillin, which Lenora gave to Jean in a glass of orange juice. For more than a quarter of a century, till now, she has never dared reveal this ruse to Jean.

Lenora had been faced with an even thornier problem a couple of months earlier, when she first joined Jean on tour. Miss Slaughter had at last managed to obtain a qualified, well-known sponsor, Lever Brothers, to associate with the Pageant, but when she arrived in Chicago to meet Jean she discovered that the Lever Brothers' representative had been trying to put the make on Jean ever since he caught up with her. Lenora placed Jean in a private home with friends in Chicago, and flew back to Atlantic City to discuss the matter with the board. They acted forthrightly, and reported the culprit to Lever Brothers. They responded in kind, firing the scoundrel, and maintaining support of the Pageant.

Then, jouncing their way across the land, sitting up on day coaches, Lenora and Jean headed off on the momentous bond tour. "No one knew anything about management then," Jean says. "When it was over, Lever Brothers just dropped me back in Los Angeles right after Christmas, and I was on my own then. That's when everything just ended. Suddenly it was all gone, just like that."

Venus Ramey, Miss America 1944, a bluegrass redhead who had won as Miss Washington when she went there to work as a wartime secretary, never even had that much of a spin. She had forged her mother's signature to the contract that tied her to Atlantic City and Lever Brothers, and then, as soon as she won, she revealed this fraud and announced that she would make her own deals. "I wanted to get into show business," she said years later, just before she disappeared from public view. "I thought the contest would be a good entree. It is, all right—an entree into oblivion. Forever afterward, you're like a broken-down actress trying to make a comeback."

What followed Venus's coronation was black comedy from the theater of the absurd. By some accounts, even the Lever Brothers Lothario, with the moves of a salmon, found his way back to the scene. Venus was whisked to New York with a press agent and a mysterious figure, identified only as Burt, who said that he represented the various products that the Pageant had contracted for her services. Venus kept protesting that, since she was nineteen and under age, no contract she had signed was valid. Burt soothed her, lodged her in a tiny room at the Waldorf-Astoria with a strange woman, who, for a chaperone, is said to have evidenced strange attentions, and had the hotel divert all of Miss Ramey's calls to his own room. It was years before Venus discovered that he had waylaid calls from such people as the William Morris Agency, which was prepared to offer her $850 a week.

Venus finally perceived that she was a prisoner in the Waldorf, but much of the damage was already done. Jean Bartel got through to her and came over to offer support, but Burt tossed her out unceremoniously. Mrs. Ramey, an astrology savant, was brought in from Kentucky, but she refused to sign the original contract that her daughter had forged. She did add an arcane touch to the restless proceedings, though. Lenora explains, "She wanted me to take this astrology book along if I ever went out on tour with Venus, and before we went out every morning, I was supposed to read the predictions that the book made, and then decide whether it was all right for Venus to go out. Nobody ever believed that Venus was her real name. Let me tell you, if you had met that mother talking astrology, you wouldn't have any doubts. I had some mothers to deal with in those days. First I had the Texas mother. We took Jo-Carroll to Saks to buy her some clothes, and when she picked out a dress for $39.95, her mother pulls out two tens and a five and says, 'I'll give you this for it.' In Saks! Then I had the Christian Scientist mother and that astrology mother and the Jewish mother."

Negotiations continued, with Venus growing more chary all the time, especially after Burt made an offer of $10,000, all payment to come after the tour "if you're a good girl." At last, she said, she took $750 to endorse Lux Flakes, and fled Burt for her own tour, which, by her own admission, was a disaster. She did a tango and rumba by herself, and such demand as there was for these dried up altogether on January 1, when she was suddenly Miss America 1944 trying to play 1945. Venus made only $8500 for the whole year, and soon added this song to her vocal repertoire:

For the benefit of those who never knew
I'm a Miss America! How do you do!
I won a prize in '44 and of course all this is through with;
And I have a great big loving cup! that I don't know what to do with. (Don't tell me.)
I'm a Miss America . . . so what?
They had me posing like I wouldn't
And they photographed me where they shouldn't.
But it's nice to be a Miss America, it makes life *très gai*,
Now if I could only find a way to eat three times a day.

By 1948 Venus had returned home, where she married an automobile dealer in Stanford, Kentucky. Three years later she ran in the Democratic primary for the seat in the Kentucky House of Representatives that both her grandfather and father had held, but she finished a dismal last in the field of four. Somewhat later she took her two redheaded sons and left for Texas, where eventually she dropped from sight. Of all the Miss Americas, Venus suffered the most disappointment and departed the experience the bitterest.

Today, the system has become so well organized and predictable that no Miss America is either deluded by grandiose expectations or impeded by the lack of any marketable talent. Some of the more recent queens never performed their specialty on the road, and since television, only Mary Ann Mobley and Vonda Kay Van Dyke executed their talent extensively. Even the Pageant will acknowledge that the modern queen is, functionally, a display package, and that basically she is required to do nothing more than trigger the right response. Her mere ambulatory presence on a runway automatically obliges any dutiful audience to rise, reverently. It is both a symbolic and critical reflex, for while it is the very dearest moment to Pageant people, epitomizing all the best in their world, it strikes others—particularly younger people—as quite the opposite. They find it a gross display of undeserving respect that is at once trite, uncomfortable, and painfully excessive. From any point of view, the scene is liturgical.

Because being Miss America is an end product in itself, the whole year following the coronation is, in a sense, anticlimactic. She is a perennial lame duck, and her speeches are necessarily regressive. As a general rule, she delivers one all-purpose speech for the first half of her year, which stresses her thanks to the American people for bestowing this quite unexpected honor on her, and, for the second six months, she expresses awe at what a marvelous experience she has been privileged to enjoy. Critics are wrong when they question the sincerity of the girls. Their sincerity is nearly indelible. What is fairly suspect, though, is the purpose of it all: to achieve something primarily for the purpose of expressing gratitude for the achievement. The lesson of Little Black Sambo's tigers is applicable: that no matter how dedicated anyone is to an enterprise, if it involves only going around in circles, you must at last be reduced to sweet melted butter.

"Look," says Marks, "we don't want a trained seal. Of course, she doesn't do that much. It's just who she is. Who can possibly mind a charming, gracious, attractive, beautiful young woman coming to any function?"

Tedium is often the main enemy, as Miss America winds back and forth across the country, moving to wherever there is a market for her smile. At least it is all new to the girl, but Peggy O'Neill, the long-standing chaperone, recalls that as many as 80 per cent of the bookings are repeats. The scrapbooks tell the same tales, year after year: Miss America at Niagara Falls, at Cypress Gardens, at the Thomasville Christmas Festival, at any gray military installation. A disproportionate amount of her time is spent in the South, where she is most popular. Beginning in 1967, each queen has made the trip to Vietnam, and for years before that, when Bancroft was a sponsor, Miss America would make an annual fashion visit to Europe. Lee Meriwether went to South America on a special tour shortly after she was elected. She met with Juan Perón on the fifty-ninth birthday of the dictator, and wowed him. He sent her roses and dispatched his personal helicopter to carry her on a tour of Buenos Aires.

Lee carried fifty gowns in eleven suitcases, but that was an unusual expedition. By contrast, on their normal domestic routes, Miss Americas quickly learn to travel light. In two little pink suitcases, Pam Eldred usually carried two evening gowns, two cocktail dresses, and some comfortable street clothes. The queens do have the advantage of never being in the same place for long, so they can wear the same clothes over and over without apparent duplication. Miss Americas also become expert, if they are not already, in the care and feeding of their hair. Portable driers and curlers and other coiffure paraphernalia take up valuable space in the luggage. Getting wrinkled clothes presentable in a hurry is a constant problem that Miss America and her traveling companion often solve by hanging up the rumpled clothes in one of their suite bathrooms, and then turning on all the hot water, so that the wrinkles will be steamed out.

Perhaps the most difficult adjustment that a Miss America must make is to the older generation; she is transported into their world for her year. She is alone, much of the time, with a woman who is more than twice her age, and only rarely does she find the opportunity to act her own. "Everywhere you go, everyone you meet, they think of Miss America as being extra sweet and about twenty-eight years old," says Judi Ford, 1969. "I was eighteen, that's all, and a kid-around person." To see Pam Eldred suddenly burst out in a wild bougaloo at a fairly private Jaycee party, is to see regeneration on the hoof. The false, extra, woman's years that she has been carrying for weeks peel from her and it is a joy to watch the pretty little blonde from Mercy College once again. But she is there for only a brief moment. The pumpkin is parked outside waiting for Miss America to return.

Two nights later, she sits in a drab hotel restaurant across from her chaperone. Miss Americas like their traveling companions, they genuinely do, but there must be limits to the friendship, for it is, after all, an arranged marriage structured by age. There are times when there is literally nothing for the two women to say, because they enjoy only a joint existence, not a common one. Conversely, they share so much that there is nothing much new to reveal to the other. So they sit, eating lavishly, primly, staring and glancing about, with minutes between words.

Except, perhaps, on the brief trips home (easier to arrange for a queen like Pam, who lived close to the good connections at Detroit's big airport), Miss America seldom gets to enjoy the company of contemporary males. As long as she is on tour, she is under the jurisdiction of the Pageant, and even if she had the time to go out on a date, her traveling companion would have to toddle along with the young couple.

Lenora, the original Pageant duenna, was perhaps the most lenient, but then, she was the boss, so it was easy for her to bend her own rules. Mary Korey, who served in the role for only two years, intentionally patterned her rather flexible policies after Lenora's. "Mary had the rare quality of making a scene warm and informal, and yet maintaining dignity," Evelyn Ay says. With both Evelyn and Lee, Mary would pick out the prize young man at a gathering, sidle up to him, and ask if he would like to take her to the movies later. If the kid had his wits about him, he could figure out who might also be along. Mary arranged one time for Evelyn to obtain some flat shoes so she could go out with Eddie Fisher, whom she towered over. It was all just fun for her, because she was engaged for her whole year to Carl Sempier. Evelyn saw her fiancé on only four occasions, but on one of them a huffy representative from one of the scholarship sponsors was on the scene and, playing strictly by the book, would not let Evelyn go out with her husband-to-be. Mary pleaded. "Are you crazy? These kids are engaged, and they haven't seen each other in months. How can your rules matter here?"

The sponsor held firm. Mary got on the phone and invited Sempier up to her room. Then she extended the same invitation to Miss America, and took a little walk herself. Certainly, studied application of the letter-of-the-law can lead to some ludicrous situations. One day in Vancouver, Canada, at a fashion show, a kindly alderman leaned over to accord Maria Fletcher, 1962, a friendly peck of welcome on the cheek. Fearing, no doubt, that an alderman, no less than a father, might be taken for a gentleman friend, Maria's traveling companion jumped in like a boxing referee and separated the two, leaving the embarrassed official holding a pucker, and both him and Maria swaying in different circles.

Miss America now has two regular traveling companions, who switch on and off every month. Mrs. Irene Bryant, the mother of Miss America 1966, Debbie Bryant, is one of the escorts. Outgoing and bold, she always works Vietnam. Mrs. Dorothy Schwager, quieter and more reserved, is the other chaperone. They serve a function much like the Atlantic City hostesses', hovering around the queen at all times, sentinels for the press, wolves, and inebriates. Travel is relatively calm, since Miss America usually goes unnoticed at terminals and on planes. When she is recognized, observers tend only to assay her curiously, not to besiege her.

Everywhere, there are always an Oldsmobile car and local sponsors to meet and escort the two women. If there is any sustaining problem, it is the lack of established protocol with regard to the traveling companion. No one ever knows quite where to seat her. Even the Pageant is fuzzy on this issue. At a luncheon in Atlantic City, when Pam Eldred was still the queen, she was, naturally, placed at the head table. There was no room for Mrs. Schwager there, nor was any appropriate place found for her at a floor table. She ended up being shunted aside to a long spare table, where she was forced to sit by herself.

Sitting there, smiling perfectly, Mrs. Schwager watched Pam rise and deliver all-purpose speech number two. This was at the end of her reign, so she recalled many of the wonderful things she had done and all the fine people she had met. It rolled on, a computer punchout. Judi Ford gave the same speech the year before and Debra Barnes before her and Jane Jayroe before her; and Phyllis George will give the same speech next year, and Miss America 1972 after that, and so on. It is the same, everywhere: "wonderful . . . marvelous . . . surprise . . . honor . . . opportunity . . . experience . . . unbelievable . . . never forget . . . kind . . . can't thank enough . . . great country . . . schedule . . . busy . . . rewarding . . . wonderful . . . marvelous. . . ."

Jacque Mercer, Miss America 1949, sat in her home in Scottsdale, Arizona, one night with her husband, Dick Curran. "The most ironic thing is the year itself," she said. "Everyone thinks only of the moment, the day that the new Miss America is crowned. It never occurs to anyone, least of all the girl, what must come next, so she heads off to do something for which she is perfectly inadequate, since she has had no training.

"That is the start of her year. By the end of the year, what Miss America is and who she is doesn't matter. You learn certain phrases, actions, and poses that work and practice them to perfection. Given a few months, anyone could manage as a Miss America for all that is required. You could take an orangutan, and with the same training the girl gets, by the end of the year, it would be a perfectly adequate Miss America. . . . Oh, I don't want to say that."

CURRAN: "Well, it's true, isn't it?"
JACQUE: "Of course it's true. That's the whole point."
CURRAN: "Well, then, go ahead and say it."
JACQUE: "Oh, all right. That's the way it is. You could take an orangutan, and with a year's training, it could be Miss America."

★ 16 ★

Miss America Goes Home

On the morning of Sunday, September 13, 1970, Pam Eldred woke up as a former Miss America, and prepared to go back and finish her education at Mercy College of Detroit. She said that she appreciated that if she had ever had a chance to be a successful dancer, she had lost that playing Miss America for a year, and that now she hoped for a career in television. But Pam had no regrets. The night before, she had told the Pageant audience, in her valedictory, that her year had taught her "the true meaning of the words of 'The Star-Spangled Banner.' "

By Sunday night, as Pam went to home and welcome obscurity, Phyllis George had arrived in New York to spend a few days in a holding pattern before she would begin her touring tenure in earnest. She appeared on the "Johnny Carson Show," and, like all Miss Americas, had to spend most of her day dealing with those fashion and hair experts that Evelyn Ay calls "the people-makers."

The real year began a few days later, with the first trip into the heartlands, and first stop, Clovis, New Mexico. As the plane taxied up to the terminal, Phyllis heard a band playing, and saw it out the window. "Look, there's a band, Dorothy," she said to Mrs. Schwager. "There must be someone arriving on our plane."

Mrs. Schwager replied, "Phyll, it's for you. You're Miss America now." And sure enough, there was an Oldsmobile to meet them—everywhere, Oldsmobiles and hotel suites and flowers,

Jaycees and Toni men, reporters and cameras and bright lights and headlines: MISS AMERICA HERE TODAY. Then another airplane, Oldsmobiles, flowers, interviews, and on and on, almost every day for a year. Here is the schedule for November, although it could be any month:

Houston for a dairy convention; Boston for a luncheon and visit to a factory; Anderson and Greenville, South Carolina, for Oldsmobile, and then Atlanta for a big show for Olds; Huntsville, Alabama, to visit a school; Chicago for Toni; Indianapolis for Olds, and back to Boston, for Olds this time. Then Freeport, in the Grand Bahamas, for Frigidaire; Los Angeles for Olds; then Dayton for Frigidaire; and return to Atlantic City for three days for the opening of a new exhibit section of Convention Hall; then on to Charlotte for a parade. Then Detroit for Olds; Philadelphia for the Army-Navy football game; and at last, on the 30th, attend the ball at the University of Tampa. Then December and January and so on, although Miss America's calendar is more distinguished around the middle of the months, when Mrs. Schwager and Mrs. Bryant switch on and off.

The sameness of this landscape is broken up by the Vietnam trip in the summer, and by the real highlight of any Miss America's year, her Homecoming, when she returns in late October or November to receive her own people, and to be honored by them. Whole streets may be renamed for the queen, schools are let out, political schedules are adjusted, and proclamations are issued. Immediately after her victory, Denton set up a Phyllis George Appreciation Committee and notified the high-school band to stand by for big doings. Preparations for a great weekend's reception began, bumper stickers saying MISS AMERICA AND I ARE FROM DENTON, TEXAS, were ordered, and five billboards featuring Phyllis's dimpled smile and the words "I'M FROM DENTON" were scheduled for area roadside locations.

Phyllis has spent all her life in Denton, even going on to attend North Texas State University in town (where her mother works as a secretary), but the pressures of big-time pageantry have pirated her from her home town. Phyllis began as Miss Denton a couple of years ago, but she finished as a runner-up at Miss Texas that time. On her road to Miss America 1971, she did not begin again as Miss Denton, but as Miss Dallas. The large cities can be the rotten boroughs of *Miss America.* They scout out the most promising small-town queens, and then invite them to try again in the big city. Dallas is thirty-eight miles south of Denton on Interstate 35–E, and Phyllis can remember going there as a child to shop for school clothes and Christmas presents. She went to Forth Worth—which is about the same distance away from Denton as Dallas—even less, until she was crowned Miss Texas there and was then required to transfer from North Texas to Texas Christian University in Fort Worth.

Fort Worth has a bitter, envious rivalry with Dallas, its glamorous competitor a few miles to the east. One thing Fort Worth claims that Dallas cannot is the Miss Texas State Pageant, so it is with some mixed emotions that Fort Worth finds itself, at last, with a Miss America—who also happens to be Miss Dallas. Even worse, Fort Worth then discovers that long before Phyllis was chosen Miss America, Dallas had contracted with Atlantic City to have Miss America 1971 appear at the opening of the State Fair in Dallas the second Saturday in October. Suddenly it occurs to Fort Worth that its Miss America is first going to come back to Texas . . . to Dallas. Fort Worth pleads that it must have Phyllis first in Texas. Poor Denton, the only true home-town claimant, is so exasperated that it will have to share its girl with Dallas and Fort Worth that it doesn't want her at all under these circumstances. At last, it is decreed that Fort Worth will get her Thursday and Friday before she opens the State Fair in Dallas, and then Phyllis will officially come back to Denton a couple of weeks later. The trouble, of course, is that too many state queens are not state queens at all, but only franchised organization queens. In this case, poor Phyllis has found out that she has not been Miss Texas after all. She has only really been Miss Texas Pageant Organization.

She arrives at Fort Worth on a cold, blustery morning, to be greeted by civic volunteers scurrying about, young men in blazers who are called the Fort Worth Action Ambassadors. Her parents and best friends are there, and all the State Pageant people, as well as sorority sisters—displaying hand-lettered welcome-back signs—and the band from Texas Christian University. Phyllis was in school at TCU for all of about a week before she won *Miss America*, and while she is gracious and never, never comments on the childish pageant politics that toss her about, she always betrays herself with a vacant smile whenever she is asked where she goes to college or required to endorse the fact that she does attend TCU. She feels all the attachment to the place that she would to a post-office box number. "I couldn't expect a warmer Texas welcome," Phyllis assures everyone at the airport.

Fort Worth planned a private Pageant-people party for her that evening at the house of the state executive director, Bob Horan. The Texans have even invited back the judges that exhibited such wisdom in choosing Phyllis Miss Texas. The pride and joy that oozes from the Fort Worthians is unmistakably genuine. Alternately, they talk of her loudly, in belligerent campaign rhetoric, and then softly, in hushed terms of adoration. "No one person in the world has ever met Phyll for ten minutes and not fallen in love with her," Bob Horan declares to an audience, and the murmurs that sweep the room afterward do not only affirm that point, but dare anyone to debate it.

It has been twenty-eight years since there was a Texas Miss America, and many other states have waited longer or forever in vain. If the faithful who perform the Pageant's dreary dirty work are not permitted to celebrate now, and even to be a little bit selfish when the epitome is achieved, then what is the purpose of any of it? Phyllis is at once the child and parent of their dream. She is their Miss America, but it is she who has given them a Miss America too.

The State Pageant organization—a Jaycee graduate group—does not place great demands upon Phyllis. It even lets her go home to Denton and sleep in her own bed every night—although for some reason she is also accompanied by a security officer, who stays up all night in the Georges' living room, succeeding only, Mrs. George says, "in about scaring the poor dog to death." All the Fort Worth people really want is to be with her and tell her how much they love her and show her off before she goes to Dallas. Besides the party and the airport welcome, there are a press conference, and a magnificent country-club dance in her honor, and a luncheon reception for her downtown at the Fort Worth Club, where the Mayor, local commerce and industry, and other officials, including a representative of the Governor himself, vie to give her yellow roses and tell her how sweet she is. Neither Phyllis, nor her successor as Miss Texas, nor any other of the exquisitely attired ladies in attendance—not a single one of them—wears a hat or gloves. One wants only to cry for all the Wilson, North Carolinas, and for all those young ladies who are learning for a world that does not exist any longer, not even with *Miss America*.

Of course, in many ways the only difference between Denton and Wilson seems to be that Denton is the one with the Miss America. With a population of 39,000 Denton is slightly larger and it revolves around two large universities—North Texas State and Texas Women's—but otherwise it is not significantly different from any of those small, happy towns where *Miss America* still thrives. It is Denton, but it could be Wilson, or Spartansburg, South Carolina (pop. 43,000), or Portland, Maine (64,000), or Columbus, Mississippi (25,000), or York, Pennsylvania (50,000)—which are the four places where Phyllis's top runners-up came from.

Denton is the county seat of Denton County, 911 square miles where it is impossible to buy a drop of liquor legally. Of the 65 churches in Denton, 15 are Baptist, which helps account for this fact. The average Denton household brings home $10,000 a year. Victor Equipment, makers of welding apparatus, and Moore Business Forms, Inc., are the largest commercial employers in town. There are 4 hospitals, 21 dentists, a daily newspaper, radio station KDNT, and at least 121 active organizations, including the Jaycees, who sponsor Miss Denton, the American Legion, Weight Watchers, the Shakespeare Club, and the United Daughters of the Confederacy. If a man must depart, 28 Continental Dixie Motor Line buses are deployed every day "to all points of the compass."

There is still only one high school in town, so that, as a lady who married into Denton says, "everybody's kids know who everybody's kids are, and they know it all their lives." Phyllis George graduated from Denton High in 1967. The center of town is so homespun that the place seems hardly *au courant* enough for Penrod, let alone Miss America. On the steps of the town hall, old men in coveralls lounge, sunning and spitting in the autumn air. The building was constructed in 1896. Denton was incorporated in 1866, four years before Texas was welcomed back into the union, and the statue that stands in the square is a gift from the DAR, in tribute to the Confederate war dead. Across the street there is the Monky Ward store, with pick-up trucks angle-parked all around, resembling nothing less than horses drawn up at the hitching post.

But the tableau is nearly meaningless, because there is another Denton, the real one. The northern fringe of the town, along University Drive, which is being widened, is a displaced downtown. Phyllis used to hang out around there, particularly at a soda joint called The Sonic. On University Drive, for block upon block, there are shopping centers, gas stations, supermarkets, trading-stamp redemption stores, tire bazaars, and every conceivable franchise restaurant that has not gone bankrupt in the great hamburger bust. This is the Denton, and the America, that Phyllis George comes from. To see Phyllis in her Denton is to understand that her whole life has been constructed, unconsciously, so that eventually, some day, she would be available to serve as Miss America.

To begin with, if the offices of the United States Bureau of the Census were turned over to the Pageant for the express purpose of uncovering the one most appropriate house that is also in the one most appropriate neighborhood in the one section of town in the one town in the one state in the one section of the country that Miss America should live in, the census would put computers to work and inspectors on the road for a year, and when all the data were processed, the census would inform the Pageant that there is only one house perfectly located and ideally related to everything else in all the land that fits your specifications, and that one house is at 2509 Rockwood Lane, Denton, Texas, the residence of a Mr. and Mrs. J. Robert George.

And then suppose further that the Pageant decided that it would no longer use judges to select the queen, but would do it scientifically, so it went back to the Bureau of the Census and asked it to get out the computers again and search for Miss America, according to the usual specifications. This girl, first of all, must have poise. She must be tall and nicely built, only nothing over 37 inches. She must be a college student, just capable enough of performing a respectable talent adequately on the

Convention Hall stage. She must look quite pretty on TV, but at the same time, she must be vivacious in the company of various small groups of Toni distributors, a fine, modern Southern-style girl—talkative and sprightly, as coy as she is in command. If this were to happen, the Census Bureau would come back to Atlantic City, and say that, whereas this was difficult to believe, nonetheless, only one such girl in all these United States existed, and, lo and behold, she lived at 2509 Rockwood Lane, Denton, Texas.

But then, when one encounters her surroundings it is impossible not to concede that the land about Phyllis could shape her into a Miss America, and that the judges did no more than endorse this obvious fact. Sure, another kid, just as quick and pretty, from the same environment, will die tomorrow in bed with a strange trick and too many marks from a rusty needle in her arm. Nor is it so pat as Phyllis's father suggests (even if it was indeed this easy for him). "You take them to church, you tell them to believe in the United States Constitution, you lay the right foundation and they will develop right." Still, the substance of Phyllis George is obviously drawn from the town where she has lived all her life, and from the house and the neighborhood where she has lived since she was eight. "I've been very happy," Miss America says. "I have a wonderful family. I've had a lot of friends and a wonderful place to grow up. I'm just Phyllis."

Mr. George, a supervisor in the city's utility department, moved his family from a more modest section of Denton to the better new residential area during the middle of the Eisenhower years. Theirs was the second house built on the block, and the neighborhood has grown up around it, never changing, just getting larger and nicer. The Georges have always had the inclination and just enough of the wherewithal to spoil Phyllis and her younger brother, Robbie, who is fourteen. Phyllis, like any pretty girl, has always been better equipped to make the best of affluent times. "I had to have a new dress for every time something new came up, whether I needed it or not," she says, "and I knew I could always get it from my daddy. Then he gave me a Falcon when I could drive, but the first day, right around here, I had an accident—the very first day I drove it—and it cost $300 or $400.

But I got out of it with the police and everybody. I just cried. That's all, you just cry."

"Phyllis has always been just a real normal American girl," Mrs. George says. "Of course, I've been a very doting mother, and she could do anything with her father, so now she doesn't know how to do anything for herself."

It is no wonder, for the neighborhood is such a reproduction of the American dream that any child growing up in it would naturally assume that she was living in a television world, where there are no nasty little chores nor any future to grow up into. The setting is so precious that, surely, Archie Andrews must live down the block, and the whole well-scrubbed Nelson family, Ozzie and Harriet and David and Ricky, are living their regular week, the one with seven Saturdays, across the street. This much is real. The Georges live on Rockwood, and the streets around them are Glenwood and Greenwood, Redwood, Laurelwood, Mistywood, and many more. And just next to these there is another whole cluster of streets named for Robin Hood and His Merrie Men: Locksley Lane, Nottingham Drive, Robin Circle, Maid Marian Lane, and even smaller thoroughfares recalling Friar Tuck and Allan-A-Dale. Who knows, maybe somewhere a developer is naming his streets after Miss Americas?

The houses in Phyllis's neighborhood, which is just inside the corporate limits of Denton, are not ostentatious. They are neat and trim and well kept, ranch style and split level, set back a good distance from the roads, with plenty of trees. Most, like the Georges', have a basketball backboard attached to the garage. In a driveway here and there, a boat is parked, and in others there are pick-up trucks. There are still telephone poles and high television antennas, to pick up the Dallas and Fort Worth channels. Dogs bark, and children ride bicycles in the street and toss mock oranges at each other.

A half-block from Phyllis's home, there is a lovely neighborhood park, with a brook flowing through it, flowers and benches, and green grass that is tended as well as any lawn in the vicinity. There are swings and other Junglegym equipment, and tennis courts for the older children and grown-ups. The new elementary school is a couple of blocks farther, a short walk away.

In this setting, Phyllis grew up as a "live wire" and somewhat of a tomboy, but she never caused any serious trouble, and she learned quickly how to be a woman when it was time for that. "We were at this party, a Coke and potato-chip party, when I was in the eighth grade," Phyllis says, "and everybody was, you know, kissing for the first time, and they were all saying, go on Phyllis, y'all kiss too, but even though all the others were doing it, I couldn't kiss this boy I was with even when I closed my eyes and counted to three." On the other hand, once she overcame this reluctance, Phyllis, after the fashion of the times, never really played the field, but had one serious boy friend after another.

She has displayed the same loyal approach to her hair. For years she wore it in a long pony-tail that at last reached to the waist. When, after some soul-searching, Phyllis decided to cut it off, it was decided to save the hair, and it is still kept, like an heirloom, in a safe place in the house. Next, Phyllis wore Buster Brown bangs, changing finally to the long hair she now has, with a brush-back pompadour on top and a little flip at the bottom. It is significant that the occasion which caused her parents most distress came when she ran off, as a young child, with friends to go to a beauty parlor, and have her hair done. One sees Dick Whittington with his cat, pausing, as the Bow Bells of London call him to his destiny.

The places of commerce closest to the Georges' are a half-mile away. These are two establishments, a bowling alley and a gas station. They seem particularly appropriate for growing up in these times: leisure and gas. Indeed, to drive the five miles from Phyllis's house on Rockwood to the sorority house on the North Texas campus, where she lived her junior year, is to pass through the very picture America of the 1960s, of the time Miss America 1971 was formed. In order: lovely suburban residential four-bedroom homes; then respectable, self-service, quick-service commercial establishments; then huge rolling farms, with cattle grazing (though still in the city limits); to a shiny new clover-leaf and Interstate highway; to North Texas State, with clean orange modern brick buildings, and students with peace medallions and long straight hair walking hand-in-hand down fraternity row.

North Texas is Phyllis's old school. All she wanted to do, when at last she could escape Fort Worth and come back to her real home, was to rush over to the Zeta Tau Alpha house, where all her old sorority sisters awaited her. They all laughed and reminisced and asked her about her own new life. One of the Zetas, Phyllis's old roommate, Chere Mauldin, had sent her this telegram on the day of her swimsuit competition in Atlantic City:

> We wish we could be there on Friday night,
> Cuz Phyll in her swimsuit will look out-of-sight.
> Her legs are so shapely, her waist is so small,
> The other sixteen won't be noticed at all.
> Her profile's fantastic in a quarter-turn;
> With envy the other girls' eyes will burn.
> Her striking beauty comes from deep within her—
> No doubt about it—we've got a winner!

Phyllis stayed all afternoon at North Texas, so long that a man from Louisiana who was putting together a Billy Graham show, called the George residence at least a dozen times, trying to get Miss America's assurance that she would appear on the bill. Mrs. Louise George answered the phone patiently. Her husband, a kind, shy man with a mournful face, had seen so little of his daughter that he had gone along with her to the sorority house.

Though this was weeks after Atlantic City, on the piano in the living room, the sheet music was yet untouched, as if any change would burst the bubble. Still on top was the music to "Raindrops Keep Falling on My Head" and "Promises, Promises," the two pieces Phyllis had played for her talent. Until she was thirteen, she was recognized as a very promising pianist. Her teacher called her a prodigy, and Phyllis gave recitals. Then one day she gave it up, because she would rather be a junior-high-school cheerleader.

How marvelous that is, how utterly American, that a piano prodigy would give it up to become a cheerleader. And yet, that is it really, probably the key to the whole business. That is what Miss Americas are—pretty girls who give up other things to become cheerleaders. And Miss America is the biggest cheerleader of them all. You cannot be exceptional at something and be Miss America too.

Growing up, Phyllis was into many things besides cheerleading. Her teachers remember her well, as a very active girl, and one who talked too much. She was an A student until she began devoting her attention to other interests—the cheerleading, of course, and acting and class politics and sororities and the Methodist Youth Fellowship, among other things. She entered her first beauty contest at sixteen, but her muscular cheerleading thighs cost her the chance to be sweetheart of the Hi-Noons Lions Club. She was achievement-oriented, however, and soon she learned another achievement, how to win beauty pageants: Miss Denton High, Miss Denton, Campus Beauty, Miss Dallas, Miss Texas, *Miss America.*

Phyllis rushed into the house with her father, laughing and gay, and on an impulse, she just threw herself down onto the floor. Her father, a few steps behind her, fell to the floor himself, and rolled over like a kid. They both just rested there, giggling at their own foolishness, while listening to all the messages from Billy Graham's man in Louisiana and to Mrs. Schwager's reminders that it would not be long before Phyllis had to fix her hair and dress for the country-club dance. At last, Phyllis moved, but only just enough to turn over on her back, propping herself up on her elbows, in a position that was markedly more comfortable and revealing than it was ladylike.

Immediately, Mrs. George started rolling her eyes at Phyllis and making gurgling noises and wigwagging desperate signals to her to change her position quickly, but when Phyllis caught on to what her mother was telling her, she did not move right away. Instead, Miss America just scrunched up her nose and said, "Oh Mother, don't you know that I'm so tired of trying to look pretty all the time?"

Appendixes

Appendix 1

Judges

Since 1960, through the 1970 Pageant, 102 judges have served on the national Miss America panel. (Many judges have participated more than once, but they have been counted separately each year that they have served.) Here is the judges' breakdown by profession or other main identifying factor:

Stage-movie-TV personnel	35
Musicians	22
Journalists	11
Educators	8
National Jaycee Officers	8
Artists/designers	6
Women's Club officers	4
PR men	3
Photographers	3
Former Miss America	1

Approximately 56 per cent of *Miss America* judges come from "show business."

Appendix 2

Winners in Preliminary Competition

(Contestants from the places printed in capital letters went on to become Miss America. Contestants from the places that are followed by an asterisk went on to become first runner-up. Contestants from the places printed in italics were dual winners, taking both talent and swimsuit.)

	SWIMSUIT	TALENT
1935	Baltimore, Connecticut, New York	no results
1936	no results Cook County won "Best Model"	Birmingham, California, PHILADELPHIA
1937	no results BERTRAND ISLAND won "Evening Gown"	California, Massachusetts, New York City
1938	no results OHIO won "Best Model" California* won "Evening Gown"	Asbury Park, Jacksonville, Utah
1939	no results	California, Minnesota, North Carolina

complete results hereafter

1940	California,* Kentucky, PHILADELPHIA	District of Columbia, Michigan, Myrtle Beach
1941	CALIFORNIA, Kentucky, North Carolina/ Westchester (tie)	Birmingham, North Carolina, Western Pennsylvania
1942	Birmingham, Chicago,* *TEXAS*	Cincinnati, New York City, *TEXAS*
1943	*Boston*, *CALIFORNIA*, District of Columbia	*Boston*, *CALIFORNIA*, Cincinnati
1944	*Birmingham*, *DISTRICT OF COLUMBIA*, *Florida*	*Birmingham*, *DISTRICT OF COLUMBIA*, *Florida*
1945	Chicago, Tennessee, NEW YORK CITY	California, Minnesota, Birmingham/NEW YORK CITY (tie)
1946	*Atlanta*, CALIFORNIA, New York City	Atlanta, Louisiana, Pennsylvania
1947	Canada, Kentucky, New York City/Oklahoma (tie)	MEMPHIS, Minnesota,* Miami Beach
1948	Atlanta, Kansas, MINNESOTA	Montana, Utah, (missing)
1949	Colorado, Illinois, *ARIZONA*/California (tie)	*ARIZONA*, Canada, Minnesota

titles postdated hereafter

1951	ALABAMA, Arkansas, California	Connecticut, District of Columbia, South Dakota*
1952	Arkansas, *North Carolina*, South Dakota	Alabama, *North Carolina*, UTAH
1953	Chicago, *GEORGIA*; Alabama/California (tie)	*GEORGIA*, New York City, North Dakota
1954	California, PENNSYLVANIA, Wyoming	Delaware, South Dakota, Virginia
1955	CALIFORNIA, Florida,* South Carolina	District of Columbia, Ohio, Michigan/New York City (tie)
1956	Hawaii, North Carolina, Oklahoma	Alabama, Florida, Massachusetts
1957	California, Chicago, Hawaii	Alabama, Arkansas, Nebraska
1958	Arizona, Georgia,* North Carolina	Missouri, Oregon, Indiana/Pennsylvania (tie)
1959	California, Indiana, North Carolina	Connecticut, MISSISSIPPI, Oklahoma
1960	New York, Washington, Wisconsin*	Illinois, Michigan, Connecticut/District of Columbia/Pennsylvania (three-way tie)
1961	District of Columbia, *MICHIGAN*, South Carolina	Indiana, Utah, Alabama/*MICHIGAN* (tie)
1962	Arkansas,* Minnesota, NORTH CAROLINA	California, Texas, Utah
1963	Illinois, Michigan, Wisconsin*	Hawaii, Mississippi, Maryland/Nebraska (tie)
1964	*Alabama*, ARKANSAS, *District of Columbia**	*Alabama*, *District of Columbia*,* Virginia
1965	California, New Mexico, West Virginia	Alabama, Minnesota, North Dakota
1966	KANSAS, Mississippi,* Nevada	Alabama, Indiana, South Carolina
1967	*California*,* New Hampshire, South Carolina	*California*,* Ohio, OKLAHOMA
1968	Arkansas, Idaho, KANSAS	Florida, Indiana, Rhode Island
1969	Alabama, *ILLINOIS*, Iowa	Florida, *ILLINOIS*, Virginia
1970	Connecticut, MICHIGAN, *Ohio**	Minnesota, New Mexico, *Ohio**
1971	Hawaii, South Carolina,* TEXAS	Alabama, Florida, Oklahoma

In the TV era, beginning with the 1955 queen, 84.5 per cent of outright preliminary winners then went on to the semifinals.

In this TV era, 89 per cent of the talent winners go on to the semifinals, as do 80 per cent of the swimsuit winners. However, talent winners are also-rans. SWIMSUIT WINNERS BECOME MISS AMERICA.

In the TV era, seven swimsuit winners have become Miss America, while only two talent winners have scored. Two other modern queens —Nancy Fleming, 1961, and Judi Ford, 1969—swept their events, although Nancy only got a tie out of her talent.

Seven other swimsuit winners have finished first runner-up in this period, while *no* talent winner has. Three runners-up—Washington, D.C. 1963, California 1966, and Ohio 1969—won both swimsuit and talent.

Since 1940, when talent and swimsuit were first contested on a basis similar to the modern one, the score is: 13 Miss Americas were swimsuit winners, 3 were talent winners, 8 won both, or a share of both. Among runners-up, results are similar. Nine first runners-up won swimsuit, 2 won talent, and 3 won both.

MISS AMERICAS WHO WON THEIR SWIMSUIT PRELIMINARY (since 1940):

Frances Burke, 1940
Rosemary LaPlanche, 1941
Marilyn Buferd, 1946
BeBe Shopp, 1948
Yolande Betbeze, 1951
Evelyn Ay, 1954
Lee Meriwether, 1955
Maria Fletcher, 1962
Donna Axum, 1964
Debbie Bryant, 1966
Debra Barnes, 1968
Pam Eldred, 1970
Phyllis George, 1971

MISS AMERICAS WHO WON THEIR TALENT PRELIMINARY:

Mary Ann Mobley, 1959
Jane Jayroe, 1967

MISS AMERICAS WHO WON BOTH TALENT AND SWIMSUIT:

Jo-Carroll Dennison, 1942
Jean Bartel, 1943
Venus Ramey, 1944
*Bess Myerson, 1945
**Jacque Mercer, 1949
Neva Jane Langley, 1953
*Nancy Fleming, 1961
Judi Ford, 1969

* Tied for victory in talent.
** Tied for victory in swimsuit.

MISS AMERICAS WHO DID NOT WIN A PRELIMINARY:

Sharon Kay Ritchie, 1956	Lynda Lee Mead, 1960
Marian McKnight, 1957	Jacquelyn Mayer, 1963
Marilyn Van Derbur, 1958	Vonda Kay Van Dyke, 1965

Seven girls have won both their preliminaries and failed to be elected Miss America.

Appendix 3

The original 1921 Pageant committee included:

Thomas P. Endicott, dry-cleaner	Pageant Director General
Harry Latz, hotelman	Vice-Director General and Chairman of Bathers' Revue
Willard Eldredge, storage company head	Chairman, Rolling-Chair Parade
Charles Godfrey, music store proprietor	Chairman of Bands
William Fennan, pier manager	Chairman of Night on Steeplechase Pier
Harry L. Godshall, insurance man	Chairman of Inter-City Beauty Contest
Fred Packer, novelty store proprietor	Chairman of Prizes
Louis St. John, advertising man	Chairman of Judges
Linton Arnold, hotelman	
Arthur Purinton, trolley-car company head	

Appendix 4

Depending on the interpretation, it is possible to say that either seven, eight, or nine girls competed in the original *Miss America* competition in 1921. The figure usually settled on is eight, although there is some conflict then as to which girls are included in that total. In any event, there is no argument against the following seven girls being counted among the original contestants:

Margaret Gorman	Miss Washington, D.C.
Kathryn M. Gearon	Miss Camden
Margaret Bates	Miss Newark
Hazel Harris	Miss Ocean City, New Jersey
Nellie Orr	Miss Philadelphia
Emma Pharo	Miss Harrisburg
Thelma Matthews	Miss Pittsburgh

The original eighth contestant was Ethel Charles, Miss Atlantic City, who, although chosen as an authentic competitor, then graciously declined to compete on her home grounds and assumed a position of hostess instead. (Miss Charles' decision began a tradition that was followed until 1960, when the Miss Atlantic City competition was discontinued.)

Thus it appears that Margaret Gorman was named winner of the nonprofessional "civic beauty" division against six opponents. Kathryn M. Gearon, Miss Camden, was runner-up.

Then, in a second level of competition, Miss Gorman was judged head-to-head against a Miss Virginia Lee of New York City, who had won the professional division against an undisclosed number of competitors. There is no evidence that Miss Lee was invited to Atlantic City as "Miss New York" or that she competed under that title or any other. On the other hand, had she won, she would have gone down in history as Miss America, so the matter of geographical accreditation becomes moot.

In any event, for the record, it should be noted that contemporary accounts list eight contenders, including Miss Atlantic City, but *not* mentioning Miss Lee, the professional division winner from New York. Subsequently, however, even the Pageant itself has come to list Virginia Lee in the eight, instead of Miss Atlantic City—and to give her the title of Miss New York City.

Appendix 5

Top Ten

Ranking Miss Americas is, obviously, a most arbitrary procedure. Nonetheless, there is a firm basis for some judgments. Taking into consideration the many and varied contributions of the forty-three Miss Americas, here are the top ten, a listing of the Most Important Miss Americas:

1. Jean Bartel, 1943	Most responsible for the introduction of scholarships and Miss America's wholesome modern image.
2. Yolande Betbeze, 1951	Recognized as the most outspoken and intriguing queen, she delivered the knockout blow to cheesecake.
3. Bess Myerson, 1945	Most famous, only New York winner, and most successful career girl.
4. Jacque Mercer, 1949	She made preparation for the Pageant a diabolical art, and a much bigger business; and made future queens stay single.
5. Fay Lanphier, 1925	Best-known of the early queens, she was the first one from California, the first to make the movies, and the first to make money out of the title.
6. Lee Meriwether, 1955	First TV queen, and best-known show-biz Miss America in modern times.
7. Margaret Gorman, 1921	The original, and still the smallest.
8. Vonda Kay Van Dyke, 1965	Only Miss America also to win Miss Congeniality, she is author of best-selling children's books.

9. BeBe Shopp, 1948	First to be well-marketed all-American girl; her publicized "Moral Crusade" abroad lifted the Pageant to new levels of recognition.
10. Bette Cooper, 1937	Still the most controversial.

Appendix 6

Scholarship Prize Money

The distribution of the scholarship money provides perhaps the best method of determining how the states rank at the Pageant, at least since the war. Total winnings are not, by themselves, an altogether fair gauge since relative amount is not taken into consideration. California, for instance, leads Mississippi at the top of the money-earnings list by a few thousand dollars, but Mississippi has hardly one-tenth as many people as California, and one-tenth as many potential Miss Americas. Unfortunately, simple per capita rankings have, for complicated reasons, no statistical legitimacy at all, so total money earnings must remain the best method of judging the states' performance.

SCHOLARSHIP PRIZE MONEY, BY STATE, 1945–1970

1.	California	$47,300	28.	Oregon	15,700
2.	Mississippi	43,300	29.	Connecticut	15,300
3.	Illinois	36,100	30.	Virginia	13,100
4.	Alabama	36,000	31.	New Mexico	12,450
5.	Colorado	33,200	32.	Nebraska } tie	11,700
6.	Arkansas	32,900		West Virginia } tie	11,700
7.	South Carolina	32,100	34.	South Dakota	11,000
8.	Michigan	31,900	35.	Rhode Island	10,875
9.	Kansas	30,800	36.	Louisiana	10,800
10.	New York	28,900	37.	Idaho	10,600
11.	Arizona	28,700	38.	Nevada	10,400
12.	North Carolina	27,200	39.	Wyoming	10,200
13.	Oklahoma	26,700	40.	Montana	9,900

14. New Jersey	26,200	41. Washington	9,800
15. Texas	25,200	42. Vermont	9,500
16. Utah	24,500	43. New Hampshire	8,900
17. Pennsylvania	23,800	44. Maine	8,800
18. Ohio	23,400	45. North Dakota	8,700
19. Florida	23,100	46. Kentucky	8,200
20. Minnesota	21,100	47. Maryland	8,000
21. Indiana } tie	20,700	48. Missouri	6,900
Tennessee } tie	20,700	49. Delaware	6,300
23. Hawaii	20,250	50. Alaska	5,350
24. Georgia	18,700	*Discontinued*	
25. Massachusetts	18,400	Washington, D.C.	14,700
26. Wisconsin	17,600	Canada	8,650
27. Iowa	16,100	Puerto Rico	3,000

Appendix 7

Although additional extra consolation money may occasionally be awarded by special dispensation, the following is the usual *Miss America* prize schedule, totaling approximately $55,000.

Miss America	$10,000	Seven Nonfinalists Voted Most Talented	1,000 each
First Runner-Up	6,000	All Preliminary Winners Not Included In Above Awards	1,000 each
Second Runner-Up	3,000	All Others	500 each
Third Runner-Up	2,500		
Fourth Runner-Up	2,000		
Five Semifinalists	1,500 each		
Miss Congeniality	1,000		

Appendix 8

Miss America Marriages

The seven Miss Americas who suffered divorces after marrying either during or shortly after their reigns were: Fay Lanphier, Henrietta

Leaver, Bess Myerson, Jacque Mercer, Sharon Kay Ritchie, Marilyn Van Derbur, Donna Axum.

Other Miss Americas with at least one divorce include: Norma Smallwood, Marilyn Buferd, Jo-Carroll Dennison, Venus Ramey. Thus, 11 of the 41 Miss Americas who have married were divorced at one time, although most remarried happily. (The last two Miss Americas, Pam Eldred and Phyllis George, have not yet married.)

Rose Coyle and Marilyn Meseke were widowed once, and have subsequently remarried. Margaret Gorman, Bette Cooper, and Yolande Betbeze are widows who have not remarried.

Those records available indicate that all Miss Americas have been married a total of 55 times, with 13 divorces—meaning 23 per cent of Miss America marriages have ended in divorce, a figure only about 1 per cent above the cumulative U.S. figures since 1925, when Miss Americas started marrying and divorcing.

The queens of the 1950s and 1960s have had only 3 of 22 marriages end in divorce, a very good rate indeed. Like so many other things about Miss America, the "common knowledge" that the queens are forever getting divorced is quite erroneous.

Appendix 9

Miss Universe

Miss Universe remains a thorn in *Miss America*'s side, even though the two pageants seldom compete directly for the same kind of girls or sponsors. If anything, it is mostly a TV battle.

Miss Universe remains essentially a beauty contest, with a cash grant ($10,000), an appearance contract (another $10,000), as well as mink coats and a full wardrobe for the winner. It also has commercial sponsors, but whereas Miss America runs on volunteer labor from the hometown, Universe gets an outright subsidy from Miami Beach. Miss Universe moved there a decade ago, after Long Beach would no longer pay the price.

Universe probably would have cut into *Miss America's* long lead in the 1960s, when *Miss America* went into its tailspin, except that Miss Universe was never able to produce a bombshell movie star for a queen, and also, Universe long suffered the criticism that there were shenanigans in the judging, and that world news, not beauty, determined the winner.

That report was first circulated in the opening year, when Miss Finland just happened to win in that country's Olympic Year. Bud Westmore, the Hollywood make-up artist, says that he bowed out of Universe judging after he was informed that the South Americans were protesting and the Pageant needed a South American winner. Miss Peru was Miss Universe 1958, with other Latins finishing second and fourth. The next year, South Americans finished one-two. In recent years, rumors that the show was fixed have disappeared.

About 65 or 70 girls compete each year in Miss Universe. The proceedings are dragged out for 11 days, but only on Wednesday (when a swimsuit winner is named) and Saturday (final winner) of the second week are the girls on stage. Since there is no talent, "beauty of face and figure" count high. Girls meet at a luncheon with judges, and are always accompanied by a chaperone who is properly bilingual. Miss Universe is held in July, while Miss USA is held in April, also in Miami Beach, to determine the American Universe representative.

Since Catalina and its president, E. B. Stewart, were responsible for helping start Miss Universe, bathing suits at Miss Universe are also always called swimsuits. This is one thing *Miss America* and Miss Universe agree on. The other thing is that Miss Universe has the better bodies in the bathing suits.

COMPLETE LIST OF MISS UNIVERSE WINNERS

1952	Finland	1961	Germany
1953	France	1962	Argentina
1954	United States (South Carolina)	1963	Brazil
		1964	Greece
1955	Sweden	1965	Thailand
1956	United States (Iowa)	1966	Sweden
1957	Peru	1967	United States (Alabama)
1958	Columbia	1968	Brazil
1959	Japan	1969	Philippines
1960	United States (Utah)	1970	Puerto Rico

Repeat winners: US—4 Brazil, Sweden—2

There is also the Miss World Pageant, which is held in London, and which has an American queen who is known as Miss World-USA to distinguish her from Miss Universe's Miss United States.

Also on the foreign front, there is Miss International Beauty, which began in Long Beach when Universe went to Miami Beach, but was later shifted to Tokyo. There is also talk of the super-beauty show of all time, which will be called Miss Venus and will offer $500,000 first prize.

Domestically, the drift in pageants seems headed toward teen-agers. America's Junior Miss, run by the Mobile (Alabama) Jaycees, is recognized as the miniature *Miss America*. It is for high-school seniors and has an annual budget of $200,000. It's competitors are Miss Teen-Age America (Fort Worth) and Miss American Teen-Ager (Palisades Park, New Jersey). Palisades also offers Little Miss America for the five-to-ten crowd, and Texas competes with Our Little Miss.

At the other end of the spectrum, the Mrs. America Pageant appears to be second only to *Miss America* in seniority, having been held originally on August 30, 1938, at, of all places, Palisades Park, New Jersey. Since then it has played a number of towns including San Diego, Minneapolis-St. Paul, at least three different sites in Florida, and others in New Jersey, most notably Asbury Park.

Appendix 10

All-Time *Miss America* National Television Ratings

Year-Network	*Rating*	*Per cent Share of Viewing Audience*
1954—ABC	20.9	39
1955—ABC	22.1	41
1956—ABC	21.9	42
1957—CBS	28.7	52
1958—CBS	38.0	66
1959—CBS	38.0	69
1960—CBS	37.7	72
1961—CBS	41.8	75
1962—CBS	38.3	66
1963—CBS	40.0	72
1964—CBS	40.3	68
1965—CBS	35.6	65
1966—NBC	38.2	64
1967—NBC	37.2	64

1968—NBC	34.8	63
1969—NBC	35.1	62
1970—NBC	37.2	66

Appendix 11

Miss Congeniality Winners

1939 Miss Mississippi*
1940 No winner
1941 Miss Oklahoma
1942 Miss Mississippi
1943 Miss Birmingham
1944 Miss Texas
1945 Miss Northern British Columbia
1946 Miss New York State
1947 Miss Texas
1948 Miss Hawaii
1949 Miss Montana
1950 Miss Hawaii
1951 Misses Hawaii and Puerto Rico
1952 Misses Oklahoma and Washington, D.C.
1953 Miss New Jersey
1954 Miss Illinois
1955 Miss Hawaii
1956 Miss Vermont
1957 Miss New Mexico
1958 Miss Rhode Island
1959 Miss Hawaii
1960 Miss New York State
1961 Misses California and Puerto Rico
1962 Miss New Hampshire
1963 Miss North Carolina
1964 Miss Arizona (Miss America 1965)
1965 Miss Iowa
1966 Miss Virginia
1967 Misses Arkansas, Colorado, and New Hampshire
1968 Miss New Mexico
1969 Miss Nebraska
1970 Miss Indiana

* Her name was Doris Coggins.

Neat-as-a-Pin Award Winners

1969 Miss New Jersey
1970 Miss Alaska

Appendix 12

A Sensible Proposal

The Pageant's traditional policy of jamming everything into Saturday's show appears to be a self-defeating policy. As it is now, and always has been since the present system was evolved late in the 1930s, a talent and swimsuit winner are named each of the three preliminary evenings. It is emphasized that preliminary victory does not assure a path to the semifinals. In fact, this is an old wives' tale, only technically correct. In the past decade, 85 per cent of the preliminary winners have ended up in the semifinals. Thus, to add to the tension and value of preliminary night attendance, it is clearly advantageous to declare that any preliminary victor *automatically* qualifies for the semis. By the end of the Friday night preliminary, this would mean that six semifinal spots would be filled (although the number might be five, or conceivably even three or four, in the event that one girl in a division won both swimsuit and talent).

Not only might this firm disclosure encourage higher preliminary attendance, but it would also encourage a great deal more publicity. The media would be much more responsive to featuring news of a "semifinalist" than of some mere preliminary winner. It is even quite possible that many local NBC-news programs would pick up the announcement of semifinalist nominees if the cameras were turned on and a video tape made of this small portion of the show. Even competitive stations might request use of the tape, if a girl from their state was one of the winners.

By the conclusion of the regular portion of the Friday show, six semifinalists would have been named. At this point, the judges' votes for the rest would be tabulated, in the same way the procedure is presently handled. This offers no logistical problem; in fact now the identification of the top ten is revealed to certain Pageant and NBC officials right after the Friday curtain has been lowered. Then, the remaining semifinalists would be introduced. Indeed, it would be advisable to have the girls line up at the end of the show and be briefly interviewed by Bert Parks. This would: a) be yet another attraction to help build the Friday night crowd; b) relax the girls and prepare them for a similar, more important such exercise—

should they make the finals the next night; and c) provide more good tape for interested TV stations.

The advantages of announcing the semifinalists a day in advance are obvious. The selectees would stir a valuable full day's comment, not only in Atlantic City, but in the national media—especially in the ten lucky states. Saturday is a traditionally slow news day, and *Miss America* would only be stepping into a vacuum. Pictures and biographies of the ten semifinalists would be assured of publication in many of the country's afternoon papers. Commentators could be expected to discuss the candidates and speculate on the victor. The amazing thing about *Miss America*'s ratings is that they are achieved virtually without building any hoopla and suspense. Debate over the merits of Oscar nominees and Super Bowl qualifiers goes on for weeks, for instance, adding interest all along.

There is always the chance that a few disappointed viewers in the states whose queens were eliminated would refuse to tune in that night, but that number would be exceeded by extra viewers in the ten lucky states and others attracted by the swarm of new publicity.

All contestants would welcome the early decision. Those who lose are going to find out anyway, and none would quit or fail to cooperate on pain of loss of scholarship. Saturday rehearsals would be light and painless for them. The rehearsal could be more precise, so the show would run more smoothly. The semifinalists would even have time to rehearse their talents one more time with the orchestra.

Profit would be realized across the board by this elementary change. Even if it seems too drastic to send preliminary winners directly into the semis, the Pageant should certainly adopt the procedure of announcing all ten semifinalists at the close of the Friday show. At the least, it should give the method a test on the state level, where the same problem exists—sellout for the finals, weak gate the rest of the week.

Appendix 13

Miss Rheingold

The most famous Miss Rheingold, Jinx Falkenburg, was also the first one, elected in 1940. She is so well known that she is often believed to have been Miss America. (Anita Bryant, second runner-up at Atlantic City in 1958, is perhaps the only other major personality who suffers that citation regularly.) Perhaps the next best known Miss Rheingold was Madalyn Darrow, 1958, who, like many beauty queens of that era, married an athlete, Pancho Gonzalez, the tennis player. In fact, she married him twice, a divorce intervening. They stand 2–1 in sets, possibly in a best-of-five match.

The Miss Rheingold contest hit its peak in the late fifties, around the time of Miss Darrow's reign. Trivia experts can still recite the memorable ditty that Marge and Gower Champion warbled over the airwaves in an effort to heat up the campaign:

Vote, vote for Miss Rheingold,
Miss Rheingold, nineteen fifty-nine,
Vote, vote for Miss Rheingold,
Send her across the winning line.
Robbin Bain would like the title;
Emily Banks says, "Vic'try's vital!"
Gretchen Foster'd like to win the prize from you.
Audrey Garcia's bubbling over,
Sandra Goss is all in clover,
Penny Peterson'd like to be Miss Rheingold too.

This classic race was so close that the ballots for Robbin and Emily actually had to be counted, and not simply weighed, as was the usual procedure. Robbin won, but Emily returned to run again and become Miss Rheingold 1960.

Appendix 14

Your Miss America Scorecard

Miss Americas, 1921–1970

Several of the facts listed in this compilation differ from the Pageant's own official review of its queens. Changes have been made only where the Miss Americas themselves have attested to the inaccuracy of the facts or where contemporary first-hand sources strongly dispute the Pageant figures.

Year	*Name*	*Residence*	*Height*	*Measurements*	*Weight*	*Age*	*Hair*	*Eyes*
1921	Margaret Gorman,	Miss Washington, D.C.	5–1	30–25–32	108	16	Blond	Blue
1922–23	Mary Campbell,	Miss Columbus, Ohio	5–7	35–26–36	140	15	Auburn	Blue
1924	Ruth Malcolmson,	Miss Philadelphia	5–6	34–25–34	137	18	Brown	Blue
1925	Fay Lanphier,	Miss California (Oakland)	5–6	34–26½–37½	138	19	Blond	Hazel
1926	Norma Smallwood,	Miss Tulsa, Oklahoma	5–4	33–25–34	118	18	Brown	Blue
1927	Lois Delander,	Miss Illinois (Joliet)	5–5½	33–25–34	115	16	Brown	Blue
1928–32	No Pageants							
1933	Marian Bergeron,	Miss Connecticut (West Haven)	5–4½	32–26½–37½	112	15	Blond	Blue
1934	No Pageant							
1935	Henrietta Leaver,	Miss Pittsburgh	5–6½	33–23–35½	120	17	Brown	Blue
1936	Rose Coyle,	Miss Philadelphia	5–6	34–23½–34½	114	22	Black	Brown

Year	Name Residence	Height	Measurements	Weight	Age	Hair	Eyes
1937	Bette Cooper, Miss Bertrand Island, New Jersey	5–6½	32–26–36	120	17	Blond	Blue
1938	Marilyn Meseke, Miss Ohio (Marion)	5–7	34⅜–26–36¼	128	20	Blond	Blue
1939	Patricia Donnelly, Miss Michigan (Detroit)	5–7	36–25–34	126	19	Brown	Brown
1940	Frances Burke, Miss Philadelphia	5–9	34–23–35	120	19	Brown	Green
1941	Rosemary LaPlanche, Miss California (Los Angeles)	5–5½	34–24–36	120	16	Blond	Hazel
1942	Jo–Carroll Dennison, Miss Texas (Tyler)	5–5	34–22–34½	118	18	Brown	Brown
1943	Jean Bartel, Miss California (Los Angeles)	5–8	36–23–35	130	18	Brown	Blue
1944	Venus Ramey, Miss Washington, D.C.	5–7	36½–25–37½	125	19	Red	Blue
1945	Bess Myerson, Miss New York City	5–10	35½–25–35	135	21	Black	Hazel
1946	Marilyn Buferd, Miss California (Detroit, Michigan)*	5–8	35½–25½–36	123	21	Brown	Blue
1947	Barbara Jo Walker, Miss Memphis, Tenn.	5–7	35–25–35	130	21	Black	Hazel
1948	BeBe Shopp, Miss Minnesota (Hopkins)	5–9	37–27–36	140	18	Brown	Hazel
1949	Jacque Mercer, Miss Arizona (Litchfield)	5–3	34–22–34	106	18	Black	Brown
1950	Queen was selected this year, but title was postdated one year, to 1951						
1951	Yolande Betbeze, Miss Alabama (Mobile)	5–5	35–24–35	119	18	Black	Brown
1952	Colleen Hutchins, Miss Utah (Los Angeles, California)*	5–10	36–24–36	143	25	Blond	Blue
1953	Neva Jane Langley, Miss Georgia (Lakeland, Florida)*	5–6¼	35–23–35	118	19	Brown	Green
1954	Evelyn Ay, Miss Pennsylvania (Ephrata)	5–8	37–24–36	132	20	Blond	Green
1955	Lee Meriwether, Miss California (San Francisco)	5–8½	34½–22–35	124	19	Brown	Blue

Year	*Name* *Residence*	*Height*	*Measurements*	*Weight*	*Age*	*Hair*	*Eyes*
1956	Sharon Ritchie, Miss Colorado (Grand Island, Nebraska)*	5–6	35–23–35	116	18	Auburn	Blue
1957	Marian McKnight, Miss South Carolina (Manning)	5–5	35–23–35	120	19	Blond	Blue
1958	Marilyn Van Derbur, Miss Colorado (Denver)	5–8¼	35–25–36	130	20	Blond	Green
1959	Mary Ann Mobley, Miss Mississippi (Brandon)	5–5	34½–22–35	114	21	Brown	Brown
1960	Lynda Lee Mead, Miss Mississippi (Natchez)	5–7	36–24–36	120	20	Brown	Green
1961	Nancy Fleming, Miss Michigan (Montague)	5–6	35–22–35	116	18	Brown	Green
1962	Maria Fletcher, Miss North Carolina (Asheville)	5–5½	35–24–35	118	19	Brown	Hazel
1963	Jacquelyn Mayer, Miss Ohio (Sandusky)	5–5	36–22–36	115	20	Brown	Hazel
1964	Donna Axum, Miss Arkansas (El Dorado)	5–6½	35–23–35	124	21	Brown	Brown
1965	Vonda Kay Van Dyke, Miss Arizona (Phoenix)	5–6	36–24–36	124	21	Brown	Brown
1966	Deborah Bryant, Miss Kansas (Overland Park)	5–7	36–23–36	115	19	Brown	Blue
1967	Jane Jayroe, Miss Oklahoma (Laverne)	5–6	36–24–35	116	19	Brown	Green
1968	Debra Dene Barnes, Miss Kansas (Pittsburg)	5–9	36½–24–36½	135	20	Brown	Blue

* Selected out of home state as queen where attending college.

Year	Name	Residence	Height	Measurements	Weight	Age	Hair	Eyes
1969	Judith Ford,	Miss Illinois (Belvidere)	5–7	36–24½–36	125	18	Blond	Green
1970	Pamela Eldred,	Miss Michigan (Birmingham)	5–5½	34–21½–34	110	21	Blond	Green
1971	Phyllis George,	Miss Texas (Denton)	5–8	36–23–36	121	21	Brown	Brown
Composite, all Miss Americas			5–6½	35–23¾–35½	123	19	Brown	Blue
Composite, early Miss Americas		1921–1944	5–6	34–24½–35¼	123	18	Brown	Blue
Composite, recent Miss Americas		1945–1971	5–7	35½–23–35½	123	20	Brown	Green

COMPLETE LIST OF FINALISTS

	Winner	*Runners-Up (in order)*	*Number of Contestants*
1921	Miss Washington, D.C.	Miss Camden, New Jersey	8
1922	Miss Columbus, Ohio	Miss New York City Miss Seattle, Washington	57
1923	Miss Columbus, Ohio	Miss Brooklyn, New York Miss Coney Island, New York Miss Philadelphia, Pennsylvania Miss St. Louis, Missouri	76
1924	Miss Philadelphia, Pennsylvania	Miss Columbus, Ohio Miss Santa Cruz, California tie { Miss Chicago, Illinois Miss Manhattan, New York	83
1925	Miss California	Miss Los Angeles next 13 honorable mention	64
1926	Miss Tulsa, Oklahoma	Miss Washington, D.C. next 13 honorable mention	73
1927	Miss Illinois	Miss Dallas, Texas tie { Miss Philadelphia, Pennsylvania Miss Tulsa, Oklahoma Miss Hammond, Indiana	69
1933	Miss Connecticut	Miss California Miss New York State Miss Virginia	30
1935	Miss Pittsburgh, Pennsylvania	Miss Missouri Miss Kentucky	52
1936	Miss Philadelphia, Pennsylvania	Miss California Miss Connecticut Miss Cook County, Illinois Miss Birmingham, Alabama	48

1937	Miss Bertrand Island, New Jersey	Miss Texas	46
		Miss North Carolina	
		tie { Miss California Miss Miami, Florida	
1938	Miss Ohio	Miss California	42
		Miss Utah	
		Miss Asbury Park, New Jersey	
		Miss Jacksonville, Florida	
1939	Miss Michigan	Miss Oklahoma	43
		Miss Washington State	
		Miss California	
		Miss Virginia	
1940	Miss Philadelphia, Pennsylvania	Miss California	41
		Miss Michigan	
		Miss Massachusetts	
		Miss Kentucky	
1941	Miss California	Miss Western Pennsylvania	43
		Miss Washington, D.C.	
		Miss Westchester County, New York	
		Miss North Carolina	
1942	Miss Texas	Miss Chicago, Illinois	30
		Miss Michigan	
		Miss New Jersey	
		Miss California	
1943	Miss California	Miss Florida	33
		Miss Boston, Massachusetts	
		Miss New York City	
		Miss Washington, D.C.	
1944	Miss Washington, D.C.	Miss Boston, Massachusetts	33
		Miss Florida	
		Miss Chicago, Illinois	
		Miss Birmingham, Alabama	
1945	Miss New York City	Miss South Dakota	41
		Miss Birmingham, Alabama	
		Miss Florida	
		Miss Minnesota	

1946	Miss California	Miss Arkansas Miss Atlanta, Georgia Miss Louisiana Miss Utah	48
1947	Miss Memphis, Tennessee	Miss Minnesota Miss Canada Miss Alabama Miss California	54
1948	Miss Minnesota	Miss Wyoming Miss Alabama Miss Kansas Miss Oklahoma	55
1949	Miss Arizona	Miss Mississippi Miss Illinois Miss Colorado Miss California	52
1950	titles postdated hereafter		
1951	Miss Alabama	Miss South Dakota Miss Florida Miss Arkansas Miss Oklahoma	54
1952	Miss Utah	Miss Indiana Miss North Carolina Miss Arkansas Miss Florida	52
1953	Miss Georgia	Miss Indiana Miss California Miss Alabama Miss Chicago, Illinois	51
1954	Miss Pennsylvania	Miss New York City Miss Virginia Miss Alabama Miss Mississippi	52
1955	Miss California	Miss Florida Miss South Carolina Miss Pennsylvania Miss Michigan	50

1956	Miss Colorado	Miss Oregon Miss Chicago, Illinois Miss North Carolina Miss Oklahoma	49
1957	Miss South Carolina	Miss Washington, D.C. Miss Alabama tie { Miss Arizona Miss Kansas }	50
1958	Miss Colorado	Miss Georgia Miss Oklahoma Miss California Miss Florida	52
1959	Miss Mississippi	Miss Iowa Miss Oklahoma Miss California Miss North Carolina	52
1960	Miss Mississippi	Miss Wisconsin Miss Washington State Miss California Miss Arizona	54
1961	Miss Michigan	Miss California Miss North Carolina Miss Washington, D.C. Miss Indiana	54
1962	Miss North Carolina	Miss Arkansas Miss Utah Miss Texas Miss Minnesota	55
1963	Miss Ohio	Miss Wisconsin Miss Texas Miss South Carolina Miss Hawaii	54
1964	Miss Arkansas	Miss Washington, D.C. Miss Hawaii Miss Tennessee Miss Arizona	52

1965	Miss Arizona	Miss Arkansas Miss West Virginia Miss Texas Miss Minnesota	50
1966	Miss Kansas	Miss Mississippi Miss Indiana Miss Florida Miss Wisconsin	50
1967	Miss Oklahoma	Miss California Miss Tennessee Miss Ohio Miss New Hampshire	50
1968	Miss Kansas	Miss Mississippi Miss Wisconsin Miss Rhode Island Miss Florida	50
1969	Miss Illinois	Miss Massachusetts Miss Iowa Miss Oregon Miss Indiana	50
1970	Miss Michigan	Miss Ohio tie { Miss California Miss New Jersey } Miss Minnesota	50
1971	Miss Texas	Miss South Carolina Miss Maine Miss Mississippi Miss Pennslyvania	50

In 44 Pageants, a total of 2202 girls have competed, an average of almost exactly 50 per year

STATES WITH MISS AMERICAS

5 times: California
Pennsylvania
4 times: Ohio
3 times: Michigan
2 times: Arizona
Colorado
Illinois
Kansas
Mississippi
Oklahoma
Texas
Washington, D.C.
once each: Alabama, Arkansas, Connecticut, Georgia, Minnesota, New Jersey, New York, North Carolina, South Carolina, Tennessee, Utah

STATES WITH FIRST RUNNERS-UP

7 times: California
3 times: Arkansas
Mississippi
New York
Washington, D.C.
2 times: Florida
Indiana
Ohio
South Dakota
Texas
Massachusetts
Wisconsin
once each: Georgia, Illinois, Iowa, Minnesota, Missouri, New Jersey, Oklahoma, Oregon, Pennsylvania, South Carolina, Wyoming

TOTAL STATE POINTS, 1921–1971

These figures are based on awarding five points for a Miss America, four for a first runner-up, three for a second, two for a third, and one point for a fourth runner-up.

Rank	State	Points	Rank	State	Points
1.	California	74	22.	Colorado	12
2.	Pennsylvania	35		Georgia	12
3.	Ohio	30		Utah	12
4.	New York	28½		Wisconsin	12
5.	Washington, D.C.	28	26.	Tennessee	10
6.	Mississippi	25	27.	Washington State	9
7.	Illinois	24½	28.	Connecticut	8
8.	Oklahoma	23		South Dakota	8
	Texas	23	30.	Iowa	7
10.	Alabama	22	31.	Oregon	6
	Michigan	22	32.	Missouri	5
12.	Florida	21½		Virginia	5
13.	Arkansas	21	34.	Hawaii	4
14.	New Jersey	15½		Kentucky	4
15.	Indiana	15		Wyoming	4
	North Carolina	15	37.	Canada	3
17.	South Carolina	14		Maine	3
18.	Arizona	13½		West Virginia	3
	Kansas	13½	40.	Louisiana	2
20.	Massachusetts	13		Rhode Island	2
	Minnesota	13	42.	New Hampshire	1

The following 10 states have never had a finalist at Atlantic City: Alaska, Delaware, Idaho, Maryland, Montana, Nebraska, Nevada, New Mexico, North Dakota, Vermont.

CLOSE, BUT NO CIGAR

Florida is the only state among the point leaders that has never had a Miss America. Florida girls have reached the finals ten times without victory, twice finishing as first runner-up.

Indiana, Massachusetts, Wisconsin, and South Dakota have all also finished second twice without a victory.

California girls have finished second seven times, but, of course, they have also won five times. California has finished first or second eleven times—25 per cent of the Pageant. Once California finished first and second the same year.

Florida's bad luck is emphasized further by the fact that Miss America 1953, Neva Jane Langley, was still living in Florida at the time she won as Miss Georgia, where she was a college student. Nebraska, which has never even had a girl in the finals, was the resident state of Sharon Kay Ritchie, Miss Colorado and Miss America 1956, when she won as an out-of-state student. Venus Ramey had left Kentucky for Washington, D.C., only briefly before she became Miss America 1944 as Miss Washington, D.C.

BOOBY PRIZE

Awarded to the State of Maryland

A Maryland representative has been in the Pageant in an unbroken line dating back to 1922. Only New Jersey, Pennsylvania, and New York have a better attendance record—a perfect one. Like Maryland, California also has been represented every year but the first one. Alabama is next on the attendance list, having a queen at Atlantic City every year since 1922, with the exception of 1926.

Of these six most loyal *Miss America* states, all but Maryland have been consistent contenders. Maryland has never even placed a finalist, much less a Miss America. Maryland's string of forty-three straight defeats is an unparalleled mark of futility.

THE CONTESTANTS

Information on the following pages concerns, not just the winners, but all the girls who have competed at Atlantic City since the mid-1930s. Extensive vital information about the contestants in the first eight Pageants, through 1933, is too incomplete for any serious attempt to be made at compiling group statistics. All of the information here is nearly complete back to, and including, the 1937 Pageant, and in some instances 1936 and 1935 as well.

The facts have been obtained from the contestants' own biographical sheets, filled out at the time they competed. Nearly all of these 1651 sheets are still on file, and virtually all of them are complete.

Unfortunately, it is impossible to tell how accurate the figures are —especially since the contestants themselves supplied the facts.

Over-all, the girls are probably about three-quarters of an inch to a full inch shorter on the average than they claim, and about three to five pounds heavier. They are also probably about one-quarter inch smaller at the bust than they claim, about one-quarter inch more at the waist, and a quarter inch more at the hips. In the 1930s and 1940s, they also added, we may guess, about a year to the average age.

Accepting their own figures, the composite Atlantic City contestant is:

19.35 years old
5 feet 6 inches
119 pounds
34.9—23.9—35.4
brown hair
blue eyes
fair complexion

With an educated adjustment of the figures, the composite contestant is:

19.0 years old
5 feet 5¼ inches
122 pounds
34½–24¼–35¾

Age

Year	*Average*	*Year*	*Average*
1936	18.9	1955	19.6
1937	18.3 (lowest)	1956	19.5
1938	18.7	1957	19.3
1939	18.9	1958	19.3
1940	19.2	1959	19.4
1941	19.0	1960	19.2
1942	19.2	1961	19.1
1943	19.3	1962	19.3
1944	19.0	1963	19.5
1945	19.3	1964	19.7
1946	19.5	1965	19.4
1947	19.5	1966	19.4
1948	19.5	1967	19.6
1949	19.6	1968	19.7
1950	19.9 (highest)	1969	19.7
1951	19.6	1970	19.5
1952	19.7		
1953	19.4		
1954	19.7		

1936–1970 average: 19.35

The average age of contestants has remained remarkably stable since the scholarship was introduced in 1945. The peak to 19.9 in 1950 is probably accounted for by the fact that many states learned that the Pageant was looking for an older queen that year, and the girls were encouraged to add to their age. The Miss America selected that year (Yolande Betbeze) was an eighteen-year-old who passed herself off as twenty-one.

Weight

Year	*Average*	*Year*	*Average*
1937	116 (lowest)	1959	120
1938	117	1960	119
1939	118	1961	119
1940	118	1962	118
1941	119	1963	118
1942	122 (highest–tie)	1964	119
1943	119	1965	118
1944	118	1966	119
1945	120	1967	118
1946	120	1968	118
1947	119	1969	119
1948	122 (highest–tie)	1970	117
1949	120		
1950	120		
1951	121		
1952	119		
1953	119		
1954	121		
1955	119		
1956	120		
1957	120		
1958	119		

1937–1970 average: 119
The average range in weight is quite small, from 116 to 122.
1970 was the lowest average weight, 117 (by a pound) of any year since 1938.

Height

Year	Average	No. of Short Girls (under 5′5″)
1937	5′5.1″	16
1938	5′5.3″	12
1939	5′4.9″ (lowest)	18 (most)
1940	5′5.8″	14
1941	5′5.9″	12
1942	5′6.2″	4
1943	5′6.2″	6
1944	5′6.0″	7
1945	5′6.2″	7
1946	5′5.8″	11
1947	5′5.9″	11
1948	5′6.5″	7
1949	5′5.8″	12
1950	5′5.8″	11
1951	5′6.4″	8
1952	5′5.8″	14
1953	5′5.8″	11

Average height in pre-TV era (1937–1953): 5′5.8″

23 per cent of the contestants listed themselves at under 5′5″, but only one short girl, Jacque Mercer, 1949, became Miss America

Year	Average	No. of Short Girls (under 5′5″)
1954	5′6.1″	8
1955	5′5.8″	9
1956	5′6.1″	6
1957	5′6.5″	5
1958	5′6.1″	4
1959	5′6.5″	6
1960	5′6.1″	10
1961	5′6.4″	7
1962	5′5.9″	5
1963	5′6.2″	5
1964	5′6.3″	6
1965	5′6.4″	5
1966	5′6.2″	5
1967	5′6.2″	6
1968	5′6.4″	7
1969	5′6.7″ (high)	5
1970	5′6.5″	2 (least)

Average height in TV era (1954–1970): 5′6.2″

14 per cent of the contestants listed themselves at under 5′5″, and none of them became Miss America

The average height for all contestants from 1937 on is just a shade over 5′6″.

In this period 279 girls have listed themselves at under 5′5″, and only one has won the title. Since she won in 1949, 141 short contestants have competed without success at Atlantic City.

Miss Iowa 1956 was the last contestant shorter than 5′. She was 4′11″, and weighed 99 pounds. In the 1960s, the shortest entrant was Miss Vermont 1967, who stood 5′½″ tall.

Since 1937, 21 of the Miss Americas selected have been taller than the average height of the field, 5 have been about the same size as the average, and 8 have been shorter.

The number of tall girls competing—those over 5′8″—has nearly doubled in the TV era. From 1937–1953, 5.3 per cent of the girls were that tall. Since then, 9.8 per cent have been that tall. The most tall girls ever to compete in the Pageant is 8, in 1948 and again in 1969. In 1937 and 1939, no contestant stood higher than 5′8″, and on five occasions—most recently 1962—only one contestant has been that tall.

For reasons that are not altogether clear, Nancy Fleming, Miss America 1961, is always referred to as "Little Nancy" by Pageant officials, even though she was a regulation size, 5′6″. She may have attracted the diminutive for being the last high-school girl to win.

Shape

Year	*Bust*	*Waist*	*Hips*	
1937	34.0	25.0	35.6	
1938	33.7	25.1	35.2	Smallest bust. Largest waist.
1939	33.9	25.0	35.0	Tied for smallest hips.
1940	34.0	24.3	35.1	Waist goes under 25″ first time, bust reaches 34″.
1941	34.0	24.4	35.5	
1942	34.5	24.9	35.7	Tied for largest hips.
1943	34.1	24.2	35.0	Tied for smallest hips.
1944	34.4	24.2	35.4	
1945	34.4	24.1	35.2	
1946	34.4	24.3	35.0	Tied for smallest hips.
1947	34.3	24.0	35.1	
1948	34.8	24.6	35.3	
1949	34.6	24.4	35.1	
1950	34.6	24.2	35.3	
1951	35.0	24.4	35.6	Bust reaches 35″ first time.

Year	*Bust*	*Waist*	*Hips*	
1952	34.9	24.0	35.3	
1953	35.0	23.9	35.1	Waist goes under 24″ first time—and for good.
Pre-TV Average				
	34.4	24.4	35.3	

Average

Year	*Bust*	*Waist*	*Hips*	
1954	35.1	23.9	35.4	
1955	35.1	23.4	35.2	
1956	35.3	23.4	35.4	
1957	35.5	23.4	35.6	
1958	35.4	23.2	35.6	Tied for smallest waist.
1959	35.6	23.4	35.6	Bust catches up with hips for first time.
1960	35.4	23.4	35.4	
1961	35.4	23.2	35.5	Tied for smallest waist.
1962	35.3	23.3	35.4	
1963	35.3	23.2	35.5	Tied for smallest waist.
1964	35.6	23.4	35.7	
1965	35.6	23.3	35.5	Bust greater than hips for first time.
1966	35.7	23.4	35.7	Tied for largest bust and largest hips.
1967	35.6	23.7	35.4	
1968	35.5	23.5	35.5	The perfect Miss America figure: 35½–23½–35½.
1969	35.7	23.8	35.7	Tied for largest bust and largest hips.
1970	35.3	23.7	35.3	
TV era Average				
	35.4	23.4	35.5	
Average, 1937–70				
	34.9	23.9	35.4	

As it should, the shape of Miss America contestants offers much more intriguing material than their other aspects. While they have hardly changed over the years in age, weight, height, and other factors, their figures show marked differences.

BUST

The girls have added about an inch and a half since the late 1930s, although the figure seems to have stabilized around 35½″ for the last

15 years, never dipping below 35.3″ or exceeding 35.7″ in that period.

The small bust at Atlantic City is nearly a collectors' item. In the last 5 years, from 1966–1970, only 3 of 250 girls—1.3 per cent—had busts measured at 33″ (and none less). By contrast, in the first 5 years that statistics are available (1937–1941), 61 of 220 girls—28 per cent—listed their bust measurements at 33″ or less.

At the other extreme, in the first 7 years of statistics (through 1943) only 1 of 278 contestants listed a bust measurement greater than 36″. That is 0.4 per cent, compared to 18 per cent of above-36″ in the last 7. It was not until 1946 that any contestant came in with a bust over 37″, although the Pageant lists Miss America 1944, Venus Ramey, at 37½″ (see Chapter 4). However, her own biography sheet claims only 36½″.

Eighteen Miss Americas have larger busts than the average of their competitors, 15 have smaller, and 1 about the same size. At Atlantic City, it is more important to be tall than to be busty.

WAIST

The variance in the waist is greatest of all, decreasing better than 6 per cent in little more than a generation. The smaller waist is an accompanying factor, too, in making the bust appear larger. In 1938, for instance, the average difference between bust and waist was hardly 8½″. Now it is approximately 12″.

The trend toward a smaller waist has been slightly reversed in the last five or six years. In the early 1960s, the average waist threatened to crash down through the elusive 23″ barrier, but in the last few Pageants, the average has turned toward 24″. In 1970, Miss Hawaii was the first contestant in more than 900 girls—in the whole TV era, even dating back to 1952—to have a 27″ waist, and she won a swimsuit preliminary. Whether this will create a boom in larger waists is, of course, yet to be seen. The last genuine wasp waist in the Pageant—20″—competed in 1963.

HIPS

Unlike the bust and the waist, hip measurements have been fairly stable, the average ranging only from a low of 35.0″ in 1939, to 35.7″, which was last reached in 1969. Not since 1955 have hips dipped below 35.4″.

There are virtually no hip extremes listed at Atlantic City. In the last two decades only 2 girls have registered hips as small as 32″, and only 4 girls, all in the 1960s, listed 38″ hips.

As pointed out in Chapter 4, all hip measurements have grown especially suspect, as it appears that most contestants merely give themselves the same hip figure as the bust. This search for symmetry is increasingly fashionable.

From 1937–1944 only 16 per cent of the contestants listed equal bust and hip measurements. From 1945–1953, the figure nearly doubled to 33 per cent. Since then, in the TV era, the figure has almost doubled again, as 62 per cent of the girls from 1954 on have claimed matching bust and hip measurements.

There is also a slight rise in the number of girls whose bust measure is greater than their hips. In the pre-TV era, only about 7 per cent made that claim. Since then, 13 per cent have listed a bust measurement greater than hips.

HAIR

Since 1936, 55 per cent of the contestants have boasted some shade of brown hair.
32 per cent have listed blond hair.
8 per cent have listed black or brunette hair.
5 per cent have listed red or auburn hair.

Browns have led every year, except in 1945, when an equal number of browns and blonds were on hand, and in the next two years, 1946 and 1947, when blonds outnumbered browns.

Relatively, blondes fare worst in becoming Miss America. While 32 per cent of the girls at Atlantic City have been blond since 1936, only 26 per cent of the Miss Americas have been blond in that period. Of the girls who won, 54 per cent have had brown hair, 14 per cent black hair, 6 per cent red or auburn.

EYES

Since 1936, 39 per cent of the girls have had blue eyes.
32 per cent have had brown eyes.
16 per cent have had green or gray eyes.
13 per cent have had hazel eyes.

Only 9 of nearly 1700 girls have listed their eyes as "black."
Blue was the leading color in the following years:

1936	1944	1952	1958
1937	1946	1953	1959
1940	1947	1954	1960
1941	1948	1955	1962

1942	1949	1956	1966
1943	1950	1957	1967

Brown was the leading color in the following years:

1938	1951	1964
1939	1961	1965
1945	1963	1969

In 1968, brown eyes and blue eyes tied.

In 1970, blue eyes and green eyes tied.

Thus, blue led in 24 of the 35 years and tied in one other;
brown led in 9 years and tied in another; and
green tied in one year.

Green has had an upsurge in popularity in the last decade, passing hazel for third place. Green also has the best winning percentage. While only 16 per cent of the contestants since 1936 have had green eyes, 26 per cent of the Miss Americas have won with them. Also, 31 per cent of Miss Americas have had blue eyes, 26 per cent brown eyes, and 17 per cent hazel eyes.

Green is very hot. Four of the last five queens have had green eyes.

COMPLEXION

Complexion has never attracted much attention among the girls, probably because the word usually has bad connotations—pimples. Through the years, only a very small number of contestants have applied themselves to the subject and credited themselves with interesting complexions such as: peach, cream, or ivory. Since 1936, 59 per cent of the girls have listed themselves as "Fair" and been done with it. Another 13 per cent have selected "Medium," rather as if they were pieces of steak, 5 per cent called themselves "Light," 4 per cent "Dark," and 19 per cent "Olive," which enjoys heady periods of vogue. The decade after the war attracted the most olive-complexioned girls, although a record 16 appeared in Atlantic City in 1960.

Fair has led the lists every year, although Medium made a run at the title in 1970, losing 24–17, in the greatest challenge ever issued Fair.

Miss Iowa 1970, the first Negro in Pageant history, listed her complexion as "Black."

Education

Year	Attended High School	High-School Graduate (or still attending)	Entering College This Month	In College	College Graduate	Year	Attended High School	High-School Graduate (or still attending)	Entering College This Month	In College	College Graduate
1937	1	36	Records Incomplete	8	0	1954	0	12	5	29	4
1938	4	27		9	0	1955	0	11	8	26	4
1939	0	32		10	1	1956	0	11	5	32	2
1940	3	33		10	0	1957	0	5	9	35	1
1941	0	32		11	0	1958	0	5	12	34	1
1942	0	28		2	0	1959	0	3	9	40	2
1943	1	20		11	0	1960	0	3	7	38	6
1944	0	28		5	0	1961	0	5	10	38	2
1945	0	24		14	3	1962	0	1	8	41	4
1946	4	27		16	1	1963	0	0	9	42	1
1947	1	27		26	0	1964	0	0	9	41	0
1948	0	22		30	3	1965	0	1	5	41	3
1949	0	14	9	28	1	1966	0	1	4	41	4
1950	0	11	5	34	4	1967	0	0	6	41	3
1951	0	11	7	29	5	1968	0	0	4	42	4
1952	0	8	9	30	5	1969	0	0	4	45	1
1953	0	9	8	29	6	1970	0	0	6	41	3

Put at its simplest, *Miss America* has gone from a Pageant that was for working girl/high-school graduates to one for incumbent college girls.

Through the 1947 Pageant, the majority of contestants every year had no college education and no plans for one. That has been completely reversed.

For the last decade, the pattern has been virtually the same every year. Better than 80 per cent of the contestants are in college, about 6 per cent have graduated, and about 10 per cent have just graduated from high school and will be reporting as freshmen following the Pageant.

Not since 1947 has a contestant not had a high-school diploma.

Not since 1966 has a noncollege girl entered.

The last high school girl to win the Pageant was Bette Cooper, 1937.

The first coed to win was Jean Bartel, 1943 (although Mary Katherine Campbell, 1922–1923, was the first Miss America to enter college, some time after she wore the crown).

The last working girl to win was Venus Ramey, 1944.

The first college graduate to win was Bess Myerson, 1945.

Nancy Fleming, 1961, was the last Miss America to win after graduating from high school the previous June. Maria Fletcher, 1962, won after being a Rockette for a year. Both Nancy and Maria began college after their reigns. Any girl who goes to Atlantic City after her June high-school graduation but before she has spent time at college is given little chance of becoming Miss America now.

The last girl to come to Atlantic City with no more than an elementary-school education was entered in 1937. She noted that she had gone through "grammer school."

Miss America Goes to War

During the heart of World War II, contestants were required to cite their contributions to the war effort. All managed to note something, although a few were hard-pressed to think of any patriotic response other than buying war bonds. Miss Boston 1943, who finished as second runner-up, was champion in this category, placing "48 per cent of my salary in war bonds."

Other contestants who deserve special attention include the young lady who was a riveter, another who had signed on with the FBI, and a third who noted cryptically only that "I entertain the boys in the service."

Hobbies and Sports

Each year, the contestants are also required to list what activities they enjoy in life. There is no limit in the number of hobbies and sports a girl may note. Some list only one activity that they are devoted to. Others list virtually every amusement they have ever known, including "being wih people," "helping others," etc. Furthermore, many of the responses are too broad and general to provide any real understanding. Every year except one since 1959, for instance, the favorite hobby has been "Music." There is no differentiation between participant or spectator sports, so the response "Basketball," for instance, is meaningless.

Nevertheless, despite all this confusion, some trends can be seen in the entertainment choices, that are interesting, if not particularly startling.

HOBBIES

Every year from 1936 through 1947, the girls' favorite hobby, usually by a large margin, was DANCING. It was also the leader in 1949, 1953, 1955, and 1958, and until 1970 dancing always garnered about a 15–20 per cent mention. Suddenly, in 1970, only 2 of the 50 contestants cited it as a favored activity.

MUSIC has been mentioned by about 30–40 per cent of the girls almost every year since 1954. For what it is worth, since 1936, 393 girls (of nearly 1700) have cited music, 374 dancing.

ART has received 256 mentions, at a steady pace almost from the first. Year after year about 20 per cent of the contestants cite it as a hobby. READING has received 213 mentions, although its popularity describes a more ragged graph. In 1964, for instance, 20 contestants —40 per cent—named it, an even greater number than picked music or any other hobby that year. Yet in 1968, only six girls mentioned it. Perhaps because it might cast aspersions on her intellect, a girl never mentions TV as a source of amusement. The taboo is carried over to movies. Films are never cited as a hobby.

Virtually no Miss America contestant plays CARDS—only 15 in 35 years. TRAVEL has gained only 22 responses all told, but 13 of them have come in the last 5 years. *Miss America* contestants are, however, COLLECTORS. In the early days, movie-star memorabilia was a favorite collectors' item, but recently, the bulk has been made up of records, as well as figurines, china, dolls, and other items of special interest. All told, 169 girls—about 5 a year—have listed themselves as collectors.

WRITING has become more popular in the last decade. In that period, it has been mentioned by 8 per cent of the girls. It was only seldom mentioned in the early years, however, and altogether rates only a 2 per cent mention. Curiously, while PHOTOGRAPHY has become increasingly popular in the land, it holds no attraction for the Pageant girls. Never, in any one year, have more than two girls mentioned it, and in most years none do.

Among household pleasures, SEWING is the big favorite. In fact sewing (including knitting, needlework, etc.) has had 269 mentions over the years, which places it ahead of art and reading and behind only music and dancing. In 1956, it led all hobbies mentioned, as it first had in 1948. In the early years before scholarships were introduced (whatever the connection), sewing was virtually never mentioned. In those years dancing was mentioned 22 times for every time sewing was once. Since 1960, however, it has been cited more often than dancing, by better than one-quarter of all the contestants.

COOKING is next most popular around the house, although, like sewing, it held no charm for the prewar and wartime girls. It has been cited 140 times since 1936, about half as often as sewing, but since 1967 has received a high mention of better than 20 per cent. DESIGN (clothes mostly, but also hair, as well as interior decorating) has shown a marked decline in popularity in the affluent sixties, when girls could afford enough new clothes not to have to worry about making them. Through the first decade of statistics (1936–1945) more girls cited design as a hobby than did cooking and sewing combined. It has run a distant third in the TV era, though, and in an extreme year, 1969, while 16 girls cited sewing as a hobby and 16 cooking, not one out of 50 mentioned design. Only 8 girls in 35 years have been moved to record GARDENING as an amusement.

The definition of VOLUNTEER SOCIAL WORK as a hobby has come into vogue only in the late sixties, but is obviously a comer for the next decade.

SPORTS

SWIMMING has been the most popular sport with each and every Pageant class, dating back to 1936. Until about 15 years ago, it invariably was mentioned by 60 to 75 per cent of the contestants. Since then it has fallen off some and now is referred to by only about half the girls.

The drop in swimming can almost surely be accounted for by the rapid rise in popularity for WATER SKIING. Since 1959, it has been the favored sport next to swimming in 10 of the 12 years, gaining a steady 30–40 per cent mention. Over-all, it has gained 221 responses to rank behind only three other sports, but 219 of those mentions have come since 1950. For the first 15 years that statistics were kept, only two girls water-skied. SNOW SKIING has also risen markedly in the last decade. Whereas as recently as 1958, only one contestant mentioned it, almost 20 per cent of all contestants in the last decade cited skiing as a favorite sport.

TENNIS is preferred to GOLF nearly three-to-one, and in every year but two since 1936. Over-all, about one out of six girls plays tennis, and it has a fairly consistent appeal year after year. BOWLING was fairly popular in the 1940s, went out of favor for the 1950s, but has come back with a steady 5 per cent mention in the last decade. BOATING has never been very popular with the girls, rating 51 mentions in the last 35 years. ICE SKATING has been cited 83 times, ROLLER SKATING only 15.

Although the country may be turning more urban, the girls show a steady, devoted interest to HORSEBACK RIDING. It has attracted 354 mentions over the years, almost 20 per cent, to rank only behind swimming. It has shown a slight decline in the last decade, but not a significant one. Moreover, there has been a sudden small show of strength for HUNTING AND FISHING, which attracted 26 mentions through 1964, twenty-nine years, and then 25 in the last six.

About one girl a year names CYCLING or HIKING, and three in 1970 mentioned JOGGING for the first time. BASKETBALL has had 93 mentions, VOLLEYBALL 32 (almost all in recent years), ARCHERY 20, FENCING 15, GYMNASTICS 15, BADMINTON 12, SURFING or SKIN DIVING 10, TRACK 9, and SHOOTING RIFLES 8.

Talent

The girls' talent presentations at Atlantic City have been divided here into eight categories. Combination refers to an act which includes two or more talents, usually singing and dancing, or singing and playing the piano or another instrument.

Year	*Combination*	*Sing*	*Dance*	*Piano*	*Other Instruments**	*Dramatics/ Monologue*	*Art/ Fashion*	*Other*
1937	18	10	12	2	2	3	0	0
1938	15	8	11	2	0	4	0	0
1939	10	14	8	2	1	5	0	0
1940	16	9	12	2	2	3	0	0
1941	12	14	10	0	0	4	1	0
1942	7	10	8	2	0	3	0	0
1943	6	15	5	2	0	2	0	3
1944	7	15	9	0	1	1	0	0
1945	4	23	4	1	2	6	1	0
1946	6	18	4	2	1	14	2	1
1947	7	24	9	2	1	4	6	1
1948	6	20	5	4	1	12	7	0
1949	3	16	5	3	2	15	3	5
1950	6	23	4	0	3	13	1	2
1951	5	19	4	2	1	13	4	4
1952	5	18	7	5	3	11	1	2
1953	3	20	11	4	0	11	1	2
Pre-TV Average (by per cent)	17	36	17	5	3	16	3	3

	Combination	*Sing*	*Dance*	*Piano*	*Other Instruments**	*Dramatics/ Monologue*	*Art/ Fashion*	*Other*
1954	1	14	8	1	3	17	5	1
1955	3	12	5	3	2	19	3	2
1956	2	15	5	6	3	14	4	1
1957	3	15	7	4	3	13	4	2
1958	6	10	10	6	2	11	2	5
1959	6	12	10	5	0	18	2	1
1960	1	17	12	1	1	16	6	0
1961	9	16	8	6	1	12	0	2
1962	8	13	11	3	2	11	3	3
1963	5	17	12	5	2	9	1	1
1964	10	12	8	4	3	7	0	5
1965	3	28	6	2	1	9	0	1
1966	6	20	8	5	3	8	0	0
1967	6	19	3	6	2	9	2	3
1968	4	20	12	3	1	6	1	3
1969	5	14	6	8	5	11	0	1
1970	5	22	8	8	4	2	0	1
TV Era (by per cent)	9	32	16	9	4	22	4	4
Total number 1937–1970	219	552	267	111	58	316	60	52†
Total (by per cent)	13	34	16	7	4	19	4	3

† Includes 20 baton-twirlers
* Other instruments, showing years played:
11—Organ: 1950, 1952, 1954, 1955, 1956, 1958, 1962, 1967 (2), 1969(2)
10—Accordion: 1940, 1946, 1954, 1957, 1958, 1960, 1964 (2), 1966(2)
8—Violin: 1944, 1949, 1950 (2), 1954, 1964, 1970 (2)
5—Clarinet: 1939, 1940, 1952, 1958, 1968
3—Drum: 1956, 1969 (2)

Leading Names

Here is a list of the names found most often at each Pageant since 1935. Some arbitrary rules have been required in making these lists. Unless it is otherwise absolutely known, first name only. Thus, Mary Alice Smith, must be listed as a Mary, even though she may have been Alice to her friends, or Mary Alice. Also, in a few cases where the difference in spelling is slight and pronunciation is not affected —such as Ann and Anne, Carol and Carole—the names are listed together. The figure in parentheses following the name refers to the total number of contestants so named that year.

1935 Ann (3), Helen (3), Elizabeth (2), Jean (2), Mary (2), Mildred (2)
1936 Evelyn (3), Virginia (2)
1937 Mary (3), Dorothy (2), Evelyn (2), Frances (2), Margaret (2), Ruth (2)
1938 Ruth (4), Blanche (2), Dorothy (2), Evelyn (2), Mary (2), Marjorie (2)
1939 Margaret (3), Louise and Luise (3)
1940 Carolyn (3), Dorothy (3), Gloria (3), Virginia (3)
1941 Catherine and Katherine (2), Gloria (2), Patricia (2)
1942 Charlotte (3), Betty and Bettye (2), Dorothy (2), Patricia (2)
1943 Dorothy (2), Emma (2), Joan (2), Mary (2)
1944 Betty (3)
1945 Virginia (4), Dorothy (3), Lee (3)
1946 Mary (3), Anne (2), Dorothy (2), Marilyn (2), Martha (2), Patricia (2)

4—Flute: 1937, 1945, 1952, 1969
2—Harp: 1965, 1970
Saxophone: 1961, 1962
Vibraharp: 1948, 1956
1—Trumpet: 1937
Miramaphone: 1945
Guitar: 1947 (7 other girls have sung, accompanying themselves on guitar)
Electric Guitar: 1949
Bassoon: 1951
Autoharp: 1955
Dulcimer: 1957
Marimba: 1963
Violoncello: 1963
Oboe: 1966
French Horn: 1970

1947 Ruth (4), Dorothy (3), Margaret (3)

1948 Barbara (3), Betty (3), Donna (2), Dorothy, Lois, Patti, Virginia

1949 Barbara (3), Betty (3), Carol (3), Shirley (3)

1950 Mary (3), Barbara (2), Bette and Betty (2), Carolyn (2), Gloria (2), Irene (2), Joanne (2), Margaret (2)

1951 Carol (3), Patricia (3); Beverly (2), Colleen (2), Jeanne (2), Phyllis (2)

1952 Barbara (5)

1953 Patricia (3), Elaine (2), Geannine (2), Helen (2), Lois (2)

1954 Barbara (4), Carol and Carole (2), Janice (2), Mary (2), Phyllis (2), Regina (2)

1955 Margaret (3), Patricia (3)

1956 Barbara (3), Joan (3), Gail (2), Mary (2), Sandra (2)

1957 Carol (2), Janet (2), Joan (2), Mary (2)

1958 Mary (5), Sandra (4), Anita (3)

1959 Linda and Lynda (5), Sharon (4), Carol and Carole (3), Mary (3)

1960 Ann and Anne (4), Sally (3)

1961 Carolyn (2), Diane (2), Karen (2), Nancy (2), Patricia (2), Sherry (2), Susan (2)

1962 Margaret (3), Patricia (3)

1963 Cheryl and Cheryle (4), Barbara (3), Carolyn (3), Judith (3)

1964 Carol (3), Ellen (2), Jane (2), Judith (2), Karen (2), Kathleen (2), Sandra (2), Sharon (2)

1965 Kathleen (3), Mary (3), Sandra (3)

1966 Mary (5), Nancy (4)

1967 Linda and Lynda (5), Patricia (3), Barbara (2)

1968 Karen (4), Linda (3)

1969 Jeanne (3)

1970 Linda (4), Cynthia (3), Nancy (3)

MOST TIMES WON OR TIED FOR MOST POPULAR NAME:

8—Mary 6—Patricia 5—Barbara 4—Carol and Carole

It's a Grand Old Name

The taste in names changes rapidly. Looking at the most favored ten names in the first five years that good records were kept (1935–1939) and the last five (1966–1970) shows that only one name is on both lists.

1935–1939	1966–1970
1. Mary	1. Linda and Lynda
2. Evelyn	2. Mary
Margaret	3. Karen
Ruth	4. Nancy
5. Dorothy	Jane
6. Frances	6. Sharon
Helen	7. Carol and Carole
8. Ann and Anne	Patricia
Alice	Susan
Claire and Clare	10. Kathleen
Jean	
Virginia	

Name Records

In the 37 Pageants since *Miss America* was revived in 1935, girls with 475 different names have competed at Atlantic City. Of those, 280, well over half, appeared only once, attesting, if nothing else to the ingenuity—and often the bad taste, as well—of Miss America parents.

M is the most popular initial, as 228 girls had names beginning with that letter. J was next with 194, then C—156, B—123, D—120, L—114, and S—113. There was only one U, one Z, and not a single Q or X.

Mary was much the most popular name, with 64 entries. Only in 5 Pageants did a Mary fail to make it to Atlantic City. Altogether 44 names appeared at least 10 times. In order, they are:

Mary	64	Gloria	16
Barbara	42	Helen/Helyne	16
Patricia	42	Susan	16
Carol/Carole/Karol	36	Beverly	14
Betty/Bette/Bettye	32	Catherine/Katherine	14
Dorothy	30	Kathleen	14
Linda/Lynda	28	Lois	14

Margaret	28	Donna	13
Joan/Jone	23	Jean	13
Nancy/Nanci/Nancee	23	Janice/Janis	12
Carolyn	20	Shirley	12
Sandra	20	Alice	11
Virginia	20	June	11
Ann/Anne	19	Marjorie	11
Karen	19	Martha	11
Marilyn	19	Phyllis	11
Ruth	19	Frances	11
Sharon	19	Cheryl/Cheryle/Sheryl	10
Jeanne/Jeane/Jeannie	18	Charlotte	10
Judith	18	Evelyn	10
Jane	17	Marion/Marian	10
Diane/Dianne	16	Sarah/Sara	10

ALL OTHER NAMES
(Complete total in parentheses)

A (75)

5–Anna, Audrey/Audre; 3–Arlene; 2–Anita, Annette, Annie, Alberta; 1–Adelynn, Aubrey, Almeda, Adeline, Avis, Ada, Annyse, Arminta, Antonie, Annalou, Adelyn, Avelina, Anabel, Adrianne, Amanda, Ardyce, Astrid, Alansa, Annice, Angela, Angeline, Adria, Annabelle

B (123)

5–Bonnie; 4–Brenda; 3–Billy/Billi/Billie, Bobby; 2–Beatrice, Blanche, Betsy, Bernice; 1–Beryl, Bess, BeBe, Betha, Barrie, Bee, Britta, Bertha, Beth, Bea, Burma, Brantlee

C (156)

9–Claire/Clare; 8–Connie; 5–Cynthia, Charlene/Charlean; 4–Christine/Kristine; 3–Colleen, Cathy/Kathy, Claudia; 2–Cherie, Constance, Cecelia; 1–Cornelia, Chris, Carene, Carolee, Clara, Charlavan, Celeste, Cleo, Chardelle, Cloris, Carre, Charmayne, Charlat, Carmen, Claudette, Crystale, Cody, Cheryl-Leigh, Candace

D (120)

8–Diana; 7–Dolores/Delores, Doris/Dorris, Deborah; 3–Dawn/Dawne; 2–Dolly, Dixie, Dora, Dana, Debra, Darlene; 1–Daphne, Dell-Fin, Dottye, Dalyce, Deanna, Daly, Danica, Drina, Dusene, Donnalynn, Donna-Marie, Dorcas, D'Ann, Denise, Dellynne, Dulcie, Debbie

E (70)

9–Elaine; 7–Esther, Ellen; 6–Elizabeth; 5–Eileen; 4–Emma, Eleanor/Eleanore, Edna; 3–Ethel; 2–Edith, Emilie/Emily; 1–Elissa, Emmajar, Eula, Evangelina, Edye, Ella, Elisa

F (24)

5–Florence; 2–Frieda, Flora; 1–Florine, Ferol, Fairfax, Francine

G (74)

8–Gail/Gale/Gayle; 6–Geraldine, Georgia; 5–Grace; 3–Geannine/Jeanine; 2–Genevieve, Gertrude, Gerry, Gladys, Georgina, Gwendolyn, Glenda; 1–Glynnelle, Georgiana, Georgietta, Gene, Gordean, Gabriella, Gretchen, Gunnel, Gwen, Ginger, Gussie, Georgine, Georganne, Greta, Glenna

H (31)

2–Hilda, Helena, Holly; 1–Helene, Harriet, Helga, Heather-Jo, Heriya, Heather, Honora, Hela, Henrietta

I (15)

6–Irene; 2–Iris; 1–Isabel, Irmgard, Itha, Irma, Idell, Ina, Ingrid

J (194)

9–Jacqueline/Jacquelyn, Janet; 8–Joyce; 7–Joanne/Jo-Anne/Joann, Judy; 5–Jo; 4–Joy, Jeannette/Jeanette; 3–Juanita; 2–Jewel, Julia, Julie, Jennie/Jenny, Janie/Janey, Juliana/Julianna; 1–Jackie, Jenelle, Jinx, Jerry, Jessie, Janene, Jere, Joanna, Joleen, Jill, Josephine, Jo-Carroll, Joey, Jini, Jacque

K (54)

6–Kathryn/Kathryne; 5–Kay; 2–Kitty, Karlyne/Carlene; 1–Kristina, Kippy, Karlyn, Kari, Kirsten, Kayanne

L (114)

7–Lee; 6–Lillian, Louise, Luise; 5–Lynne/Lynn; 3–Laura, Lorna; 2–Loretta, Lorraine, Lucia, Lorene, Leona, Lenore, Lucille, LaVonne, Leslie; 1–Libby, Loreen, Lu, Lo, La Donna, Lael, Loni, Laverda, Lyndra, Lila, Leinaala, Launa, Lita, Leslyn, Louisa, Lisa, Lola, Luna, Lennie, Lelia, LaFern, LaBruce, LaRue, Lena, LeFrance

M (228)

7–Mildred, Marie/Maree; 7–Marsha/Marcia; 6–Miriam; 4–Margo, Marlene, Margueriete/Margarete; 3–Margie, Maxine, Madalyn/Madeline, Maria, Muriel; 2–Maureen/Maurine, May/Mae; 1–Margretta, Marlinda, Maryann, Mardi, Mabel, Marjean, Maggie, Marlyse, Marjoria, Marylynn, Marvene, Matilda, Mattigene, Monnie,

Mitzi, Mifaunwy, Milena, Mona, Mineola, Myrna, Meta, Meredith, Michaline, Melissa, Merrilee, Molly, Michelle

N (37)
3–Norma; 1–Norine, Nickey, Nellie, Nadine, Neva, Nydia, Nettie, Nona, Nell, Nannette, Noralyn

O (6)
2–Olive; 1–Othelia, Ora, Otilia, Onalee

P (95)
6–Pamela, Peggy; 5–Paula; 4–Patti/Pati, Polly, Penny; 2–Pauline, Pam, Pepper, Patsy, Priscilla, Penelope; 1–Paulina

R (72)
7–Rebecca, Rosemary; 4–Roberta; 3–Rita, Robin; 2–Rhonda, Robbie, Regina, Rosalie, Roseann/Rosanne, Rae/Raye; 1–Rosita, Ronnee, Rejean, Rachel, Rosanna, Rose, Rosa, Rosella, Ruby, Rosemarie, Raven, Roselyn, Ruthellen, Reba, Renee, Rowena, Rankin

S (113)
9–Suzanne; 5–Sally; 4–Sherry/Sherri; 3–Sue; 2–Sandy/Sandi, Sylvia, Sheila; 1–Shir, Sonia, Serena, Sonya, Shelby, Stuart, Sherrylyn, Scarlett, Sydney

T (23)
5–Trudy/Trudie; 3–Teresa; 2–Thelma, Tillie, Terry, Tommy/Tommye; 1–Toula, Tusca, Tamara, Tia, Toni, Timmy, Therese

U (1)
1–Urania

V (46)
5–Vicki/Vicky; 4–Violet; 3–Valerie; 1–Vera, Vanita, Velva, Vivienne, Venus, Vivian, Vonda, Van, Viola, Vernell, Verona, Vendora, Vern, Veronica

W (9)
3–Wanda; 2–Wendy; 1–Wilma, Wilhelmina, Waumeta, Winnie, Wayring

Y (6)
2–Yvonne; 1–Yolanda, Yolande, Ysleta, Yun

Z (1)
1–Zoe

Names come and go. The following have not appeared once at the Pageant in the last three decades, since before the war: Aubrey, Blanche, Gussie, Henrietta, Isabel, Lena, Mitzi, Rachel, Rosa, Rose, Thelma, and Veronica.

Others, including some of the most popular names of today, appeared seldom if at all until the last decade or so. Most particularly, these include: Cheryl, Cynthia, Diane, Diana, Gail, Judith, Karen, Kathleen, Linda, Nancy, Pamela, Sandra, Sharon, and Susan.

The biggest names to fall from fashion are Betty, Dorothy, and Ruth. Marilyn (in 1938, 1946, 1958) is the only name to repeat as Miss America in this era, although since 1921 there have also been two Marys (1922–1923 and 1959) and two Marians (1933 and 1957).

Contestants: Our Own Hall of Fame

Thelma Blossom
Helen Clum
LaRue Wilson
Claire Spirt
Leonna Mucha
Othelia Mitsch
LeFrance Boyette
Gussie Short
Wayring Smathers
Waumeta Bates
Irmgard Dietel
Yolanda Ugarte
Emmajar Newby
Mattigene Palmore
LaFern Mueller
LaBruce Sherrill
Ferol Dumas
Lorene Snoddy
Jenelle Strange
Mineola Graham
Vernell Bush
Itha Duerrhammer
Matilda Agin
LaVonne Bond
Raven Malone

Eula McGehee
Fairfax Mason
Pepper Shore
Pam Camp
Yvonne Fix
Bonnie Jean Bland
Ysleta Leissner
Flora Sleeper
Britta Berg
Joan Teets
Meta Justice
Velva Robbins
Rankin Suber
Dixie Sarchet
Bertha Mae Huebl
Jewel Smerage
Ardyce Gustafson
Alberta Futch
Dusene Vunovich
Rejean Bowar
Joleen Wolf
Roberta Tarbox
Louisa Ann Flook
Dulcie Scripture

Index